Territorial Inequalities

SCIENCES

Geography and Demography, Field Director – Denise Pumain
Geography of Inequality, Subject Head – Clémentine Cottineau

Territorial Inequalities

Coordinated by
Magali Talandier
Josselin Tallec

WILEY

First published 2023 in Great Britain and the United States by ISTE Ltd and John Wiley & Sons, Inc.

Apart from any fair dealing for the purposes of research or private study, or criticism or review, as permitted under the Copyright, Designs and Patents Act 1988, this publication may only be reproduced, stored or transmitted, in any form or by any means, with the prior permission in writing of the publishers, or in the case of reprographic reproduction in accordance with the terms and licenses issued by the CLA. Enquiries concerning reproduction outside these terms should be sent to the publishers at the undermentioned address:

ISTE Ltd
27-37 St George's Road
London SW19 4EU
UK

www.iste.co.uk

John Wiley & Sons, Inc.
111 River Street
Hoboken, NJ 07030
USA

www.wiley.com

© ISTE Ltd 2023

The rights of Magali Talandier and Josselin Tallec to be identified as the authors of this work have been asserted by them in accordance with the Copyright, Designs and Patents Act 1988.

Any opinions, findings, and conclusions or recommendations expressed in this material are those of the author(s), contributor(s) or editor(s) and do not necessarily reflect the views of ISTE Group.

Library of Congress Control Number: 2023934057

British Library Cataloguing-in-Publication Data
A CIP record for this book is available from the British Library
ISBN 978-1-78945-101-6

ERC code:
SH2 Institutions, Values, Environment and Space
  SH2_9 Urban, regional and rural studies
  SH2_11 Human, economic and social geography
SH3 The Social World, Diversity, Population
  SH3_1 Social structure, social mobility
  SH3_2 Inequalities, discrimination, prejudice, aggression and violence, antisocial behaviour

Contents

Foreword. Territorial Capital and Spatial Inequalities xi
Thomas PIKETTY

Introduction xix
Magali TALANDIER and Josselin TALLEC

Chapter 1. Metropolization and Territorial Inequalities 1
Magali TALANDIER

    1.1. Introduction. 1
    1.2. T200 years of territorial inequalities 2
        1.2.1. The development of the French metropolitan area. 3
        1.2.2. Processes of population concentration and deconcentration 5
        1.2.3. The spatiotemporal model and territorial inequalities. 8
    1.3. Metropolization: 30 years of changing territorial inequalities 10
        1.3.1. Methodology and databases 10
        1.3.2. The majority of French household income is concentrated
in suburban rings 11
        1.3.3. Higher incomes in suburban areas than in the city centers 13
        1.3.4. Fewer territorial disparities in areas polarized by small
and medium-sized cities 14
        1.3.5. Typology of territorial inequalities. 17
        1.3.6. Rapid growth in per capita incomes in periurban rings 19
        1.3.7. Geographic inequalities in terms of income per capita 20

1.4. Wealth circulation and the reshaping of territorial inequalities 22
   1.4.1. The economic base theory: an operational conceptual
   framework for the analysis of income flows 22
   1.4.2. Productive residential systems 26
   1.4.3. PRSs and territorial development 29
1.5. Conclusion 30
1.6. Appendices 32
1.7. References 39

Chapter 2. Inequalities in Territorial Development: Enigmas and Threats. 43
Laurent DAVEZIES

2.1. Introduction. 43
2.2. The evolution of development inequalities 44
   2.2.1. How should local or regional development be defined? 45
   2.2.2. The widening of productive inequalities 50
   2.2.3. Reducing inequalities in territorial income 51
   2.2.4. Territorial inequalities do not equate to social inequalities. 52
   2.2.5. Policies for the "neighborhoods" or for the people?. 53
   2.2.6. Inequality and poverty 54
   2.2.7. A reduction in territorial inequalities in terms of income. 57
2.3. Public mechanisms for territorial cohesion 58
   2.3.1. Redistribution mechanisms for public funds 59
   2.3.2. Interterritorial redistribution linked to social
   welfare budgets 59
   2.3.3. The redistributive effects of public budgets
   between regions. 61
   2.3.4. Fragmented European cohesion 63
   2.3.5. Unequal treatment of equals. 65
   2.3.6. The "Catalonia" effect 68
2.4. The risk of rejecting intranational solidarities 71
   2.4.1. The revolt of the rich regions 72
   2.4.2. Questioning the cohesion model 74
   2.4.3. Wealthy regions independent of poor regions 75
2.5. References 76

Chapter 3. Which Geographical Figures Should Be Mobilized Against Particular Territorial Inequalities? 79
Xavier DESJARDINS and Philippe ESTÈBE

    3.1. Introduction. 79
    3.2. The Saint-Malo-Geneva line. 81
        3.2.1. An obscure and enlightened France 81
        3.2.2. From map to policy. 84
        3.2.3. A paradoxical ingratitude?. 85
    3.3. The countryside and the city. 88
        3.3.1. The long persistence of a rural densely populated world. 88
        3.3.2. The marriage of the Republic and the countryside 91
        3.3.3. Solidarity through networks. 93
        3.3.4. Cycles of inequality. 95
    3.4. The Paris–countryside divide 96
        3.4.1. The meeting of Maurras and Stalin 96
        3.4.2. Would France have won against Paris? 99
    3.5. Conclusion 102
    3.6. References 103

Chapter 4. The Periurban Question. 107
Éric CHARMES

    4.1. Introduction. 107
    4.2. Periurbanization in figures and tables 109
    4.3. The revitalization of the countryside 114
    4.4. Villages: from community to club 116
    4.5. Unequal intermunicipal governments 118
    4.6. When the periurbs rebel 121
    4.7. City life in the countryside: an unequal dream 123
    4.8. The *Gilets jaunes* crisis. 125
    4.9. From the right to the city to the right to the village?. 128
    4.10. The moral devaluation of the periurbs 130
    4.11. From urban sprawl to the revitalization of the countryside:
    toward a reversal of the stigma? 132
    4.12. Conclusion: beyond "peripheral France". 134
    4.13. References. 136

Chapter 5. The European Union: Territorial Inequalities and Development Policy 143
Frédéric SANTAMARIA

5.1. Introduction. 143
5.2. Inter-territorial inequalities in the framework of
European construction 147
    5.2.1. The reduction of territorial inequalities as a fundamental
    building block of the European project 147
    5.2.2. An early awareness for a late political consideration 149
    5.2.3. Maintaining the objective of reducing territorial inequalities
    in spite of major change 151
    5.2.4. Substantive policies. 156
    5.2.5. The EU in the world: a relatively homogeneous space 157
5.3. The limits of EU action in the fight against territorial inequalities . . . 161
    5.3.1. Significant wealth inequalities at different levels within
    the EU 161
    5.3.2. The 2008 financial crisis and the challenge to convergence 168
    5.3.3. Beyond the financial and political framework of the
    EU's action to reduce territorial inequalities 171
    5.3.4. Major conflicting objectives. 177
    5.3.5. A territorial approach of imperfect inequalities 179
    5.3.6. A scientific approach lacking clarity. 184
5.4. Conclusion 187
5.5. References 189

Chapter 6. Medium-sized Cities and Territorial Inequalities 193
Josselin TALLEC

6.1. Introduction. 193
6.2. From positions to conditions: a brief history of planning and its
relationship with territorial inequalities 197
    6.2.1. Growth and redistribution: the idea of a certain "golden
    age" of planning (1950–1975) 200
    6.2.2. Repairing and supporting territories "in transition"
    (1975–1995). 202
    6.2.3. Animation and concentration: a shift from competitiveness
    to differentiation (1995 to the present) 204
    6.2.4. Differentiation at the bedside of territorial inequalities? 208

6.3. Medium-sized cities: a long-term figure in the planning and
the treatment of territorial inequalities. 209
    6.3.1. Medium-sized cities: elements of contextualization
    of a stratum of urban systems. 212
    6.3.2. Medium-sized cities and a progressive differentiation
    of demographic dynamics and economic activity 218
    6.3.3. Medium-sized cities and the permanence of a political
    object for treating territorial inequalities 220
6.4. Conclusion 228
6.5. References 230

Chapter 7. Urban Segregation 235
Sylvie FOL and Leïla FROUILLOU

7.1. Introduction. 235
7.2. Emergence and uses of the notion of "segregation" 236
    7.2.1. Segregation and the ghetto in the United States 236
    7.2.2. The concept of "the ghetto" in France. 241
7.3. Analyzing the causes of segregation 248
    7.3.1. Segregation as the result of individual preferences 248
    7.3.2. Segregation as a consequence of structural mechanisms 249
    7.3.3. Segregation resulting from public policies 252
    7.3.4. Segregation as the result of a combination of
    several processes 253
7.4. Methodological debates concerning the measurement of
segregation. 255
7.5. The effects of segregation 259
7.6. Anti-segregation policies. 262
7.7. Conclusion 267
7.8. References 268

List of Authors 279

Index 281

Foreword

Territorial Capital and Spatial Inequalities

Thomas PIKETTY
EHESS, Paris, France

This book will appeal to all those interested in the issue of spatial and territorial inequalities. The subject occupies a central place in public debate; however, it is unfortunately too often simplified and a source of much confusion. Are territorial inequalities steadily increasing or are they decreasing? It all depends on what we are trying to measure and understand. If we are to make any progress on these core questions, we must adopt a patient and rigorous approach, precisely defining sources and methods and bringing together the skills and approaches of researchers from various disciplinary traditions, such as geographers, social scientists, economists, historians, political scientists, and so on. This is precisely what this magnificent work invites us to do.

It is impossible to do justice to the richness of the contributions in a just few pages so we will limit ourselves here and only emphasize a few points.

The first chapters mainly deal with inequalities on a regional level, while the following ones focus more on the municipal and neighborhood levels. In this foreword, we will follow this order, focusing primarily on the former. In terms of regional inequalities, the first source of confusion arises from the fact that we observe contradictory developments depending on whether we are interested in either the distribution of production or income. Indeed, as Laurent Davezies shows, using the available data for the French regions during the period 1960–2020, there has been a significant increase in the dispersion of regional gross domestic product (GDP) per capita in recent decades, particularly since 1990–2000. However, at the same time, the differences in average regional income have rather tended to narrow. This apparent contradiction is explained by the existence of multiple private and public flows, which considerably complicate the link between regional GDP and disposable income at the regional level. For example, the growing concentration of French GDP within the region of Île-de-France partly reflects the growing weight in national production of the headquarters of large French and international companies, particularly in Paris and in the Hauts-de-Seine, and especially in the finance, services and digital sectors. This component of regional GDP includes very high salaries located in Île-de-France: many works, such as those of Olivier Godechot, have shown how the highest salaries in the country were very strongly concentrated in the Ile-de-France region – and in certain municipalities and certain districts within it – since the 1970s. But this component of regional GDP also includes profits belonging to the shareholders of these multinational companies and which are not necessarily found in the income available to the inhabitants of Île-de-France, who, conversely, may find themselves benefiting from the flow of profits and dividends corresponding to investments they have made in other regions and other countries, directly or indirectly through their financial intermediary, sometimes without knowing it.

In addition to private flows, public ones must naturally be taken into account. As Davezies shows from the latest available data, Île-de-France pays 29% of the country's social security contributions (which roughly corresponds to its share in the total wage bill and the national GDP), but its inhabitants receive only 18% of the social benefits paid in France. However, it is imperative that this redistribution is not misinterpreted: this does not mean that high earners in the Île-de-France region pay benefits to low-wage earners in the rest of the country (this is not how French social security works), but rather that retirees are increasingly moving out of Île-de-France to live elsewhere and so their pensions and health insurance benefits are counted in the region where they reside, even if they have worked their entire career in Île-de-France. Other systems, concerning, for example, the financing of national public services or income from means-tested transfers, are more akin to true redistribution. As it stands, the most well-established and the most striking phenomenon is the growing concentration of commodity production in certain territories; the reduction of regional inequalities in disposable income results from multiple phenomena linked to the evolution of residential mobility over the course of a lifetime and deserves an in-depth examination on a case-by-case basis, focusing on the people more than on territories as such.

Regarding regional inequalities at the European level, the data available at present do not allow for much of a historical perspective. If we look at the subregions of the member states of the European Union (EU), on a constant and homogeneous basis, then we observe contradictory developments. As Frédéric Santamaria shows, the differences in GDP per capita seem to have decreased between 2000 and 2009, before again increasing between 2009 and 2018.

In their respective chapters, Davezies and Santamaria insist on small scale regional redistribution mechanisms at the EU level, especially compared to the redistributions between regions carried out at the national level (in particular, via the financing of public services by national taxation). This is due to the well-known fact that the European budget (about 1% of GDP) is extremely small compared to national budgets (between 30% and 50% of GDP depending on the country). As such, it is more advantageous to be a wealthy region in an even wealthier country than a poor region (or even an equally rich one) in a less prosperous country. For example, the former Midi-Pyrénées region, although richer than Catalonia in terms of GDP per capita, is relatively poor inside France, which allows it to benefit overall from a significant additional amount of public expenditure compared to the taxes paid by its inhabitants. Conversely, Catalonia is relatively wealthy inside Spain, thus part of its taxes escapes it. As Davezies shows, this negative system has the consequence that rich regions within their country of origin may have an interest in seceding and aiming for reintegration within the EU as an independent country. It would be different if there were more powerful systems of regional redistribution at the EU level, for example in the form of a federal income tax (as in the United States), with the consequence of the richest Catalan taxpayers continuing to pay the tax in question in all cases, whether or not they leave Spain. In the current EU architecture, it is quite the opposite: systems, such as the 1996 Posted Workers Directive, certainly bring benefits to a certain number of workers from the least prosperous regions and countries, such as Poland and Portugal (while bringing even greater profits to their employers), but this redistribution is essential to the detriment of other relatively modest German or French workers, and not of the wealthiest taxpayers from the different countries. This is not necessarily the best way to ensure the political sustainability of the EU, as the experience of Brexit has shown.

It is imperative to note that the (sometimes substantial) transfers made by European regional funds always must be examined together with the private flows affecting the regions concerned. Take the case of Eastern European countries (see

Figure F.1): the inbound net public flows to the EU are certainly very significant (between 2% and 4% of GDP per year on average between 2010 and 2018), but it turns out that the outbound private flows from these countries in terms of profits and property income are nearly twice as high (between 4% and 8% of GDP).

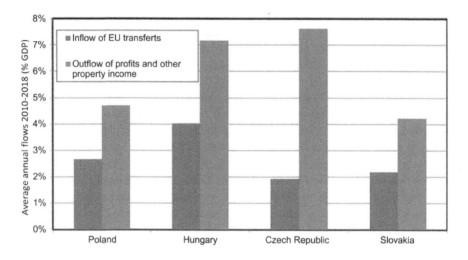

Figure F.1. *Inflows and outflows in Eastern Europe (2010–2018). For a color version of this figure, see http://www.iste.co.uk/talandier/territorial.zip*

COMMENT ON FIGURE F.1.– *Between 2010 and 2018, the annual flow of net transfers from the EU (the difference between total expenditure received and contributions to the EU budget) amounted to an average of 2.7% GDP per year in Poland; over the same period, the outflow of profits and other property income (net of the corresponding outflow) amounted to 4.7% of GDP. For Hungary, the same figures were 4.0% and 7.2% (source: Piketty).*

These private outflows include the profits made by investors from the West, especially from Germany and France, who have profited due to the eastwards expansion of the EU and the manufacturing sites they have established there, often while keeping wages low, or at any rate lower than what the countries in question would have expected. For the continent's dominant economic powers, these private flows should be set aside in favor of public transfers, which are seen as an act of generosity on the part of the market winners. This way of naturalizing market forces is convenient for the dominant actors, but it is hardly convincing: the ways in which wages and profits are set at Eastern European manufacturing sites are not particularly natural. They depend on specific rules and institutions, such as labor law and trade union law, corporate governance of companies, the existence or not of social and fiscal harmonization and tax harmonization, etc. Given the large amounts involved, it is critical that these issues are included in a more general discussion of territorial inequalities and on the overall distributional balance of political and economic integration at the EU level (as well as at the level of Global North-South relations, where we find the same hypocrisies, only worse). More generally, the notion of regional GDP and "regional productivity" must be placed in perspective and approached critically. The fact that a given territory is confined to the role of a reserve of cheap labor, within the framework of highly hierarchical center-periphery relations, is not an objective reality that falls from the sky: it depends on the strategies of public and private actors, which must be analyzed as such, in comparison with other possible strategies, carried out by alternative institutions. The very measurement of regional GDP reflects specific power dynamics. For example, if a large company (such as McDonald's) managed to increase the salaries of its executives in its Paris headquarters, while reducing the salaries of its waiters in its provincial restaurants, then the GDP of the Île-de-France region would increase at the expense of the provincial GDP although it has not suddenly become more "productive" than the provinces. The same would be true if the Société Générale (SocGen) were to increase the salaries of its managers and traders because of the savings made on the backs of its managers, and so on.

It also happens that the GDP statistics, on which some of these analyses are based, were manipulated simply for venal reasons. Santamaria notes that the deduction of outgoing income (in practice, mainly profits and other property income) explains why gross national income (GNI) is about 20% lower than GDP in Ireland and over 25% lower in Switzerland and Luxembourg. In all three cases, it is very likely that a large part of the excess GDP accounted for in these countries does not correspond to any actual economic activity carried out there and represents a pure accounting device: large multinational corporations bill their subsidiaries in areas with the lowest tax rates for valuable services and then show the corresponding amounts as low-taxed profits and dividends. There may come a day when these practices will be subject to legal action and correction by the European public authorities, or failing that, by the injured national public authorities. At this stage, the sacrosanct principles of the absolute free movement of capital and business secrecy have prevailed, with the result that the statistics on which we base our analyses of regional disparities are sometimes somewhat obscured. For example, it is unclear whether the current GDP per capita in Southern Ireland and Eastern Ireland is much higher than that of the Île-de-France, despite what the European statistics say.

Let us turn to the inequalities at the central and municipality levels. Here again, we must unfortunately be brief. In her chapter, Magali Talandier strikingly illustrates the importance of questions concerning method and measurement. By using tax data on the evolution of the distribution of average incomes by communes in France between 1984 and 2018, she shows the complexity of the transformations underway, which the sometimes too systematic opposition between city centers and towns has made clear: towns gentrified and peripheral areas tends to mask. In fact, Talandier shows that in the majority of French metropolises, the suburban municipalities have now become richer than the city centers in terms of average income (although the case of Paris is an exception in this respect). This was not the case in the 1980s and early 1990s, but has become the norm over the course of the 2000s and 2010s.

This is particularly interesting, especially in a country with a long tradition of rigidly opposing large and small municipalities ("urbaphobia" whose long genealogy Philippe Estèbe and Xavier Desjardins trace, at least since Gravier's publication of *Paris et le désert français* in 1947). Éric Charmes insists on the immense diversity of the suburbs, often caricatured as anti-ecological and anti-social in its existence, whereas it can also be the bearer, under certain conditions, of innovative forms of solidarity and promotion of local production. In their chapter, Sylvie Fol and Leïla Frouillou present a thorough and fascinating overview of the literature on urban segregation and its development in France. Moreover, they demonstrate the limits of simplistic oppositions based on the size of an area's distance from the city center. These often prevent us from measuring the complexity of the changes at hand, for example, with segregation increasing according to certain criteria (such as age or non-European origin) and decreasing for others, or even a stronger socioprofessional segregation in Île-de-France as opposed to former industrial areas in the north of the country.

Let us conclude by underscoring the fact that territorial inequalities are on the whole still significant and that there is an urgent need to rethink modes of redistribution and decentralization. The fact that some spatial inequalities have increased while others have decreased should not obscure the fact that territorial inequalities have always been substantial. Growing up and living in a particular department, and even more so in a particular municipality, leads to major inequalities in terms of access to public service and to life and development opportunities. In other words, inequalities in average income between communes may have remained broadly stable since the 1980s and 1990s, but they are nonetheless very high. In concrete terms, if we rank the communes by percentile of average income, we can see that the poorest communes currently have an average tax income per year and per household of barely €15,000–20,000, whereas the richest communes have average incomes exceeding €100,000. These income scales of 1–5 or 1–6 are found for almost all commune sizes. Notably, modest and medium-sized suburban municipalities often have average incomes of €100,000, which is in stark contrast to other slightly larger and equally "suburban" municipalities with average incomes of less than €20,000 per household.

From this perspective, being a country with 36,000 municipalities is perhaps a strength in terms of the richness of democratic life (although this is open to debate), but it is also, and perhaps above all, an objective factor of fragmentation into extremely unequal communities. It should also be pointed out that the differences are even greater if we consider them from a basis of local taxation and not revenues. For example, if we classify the municipalities by percentile according to the property tax base per inhabitant, the differences range from 1–10, not 1–5. Insofar as municipalities finance access to multiple public services public services cultural and extracurricular activities or sports facilities, it is obvious that this leads to considerable structural inequalities for people with disabilities. The existing mechanisms – such as the overall operating grants or the various measures developed under the "urban policy" – only partially compensate for these inequalities. In some cases, the hypocrisy borders on indecency: the starting point is a structural inequality where resources per capita vary by a factor of 1–5 or 1–10, then puts in place a patch that reduces a small fraction of this gap, and at the end of the process, we pretend to be surprised that the social situation has hardly improved, when we do not loudly wonder where all this good money has gone. The solution of pooling resources at a higher level by encouraging groupings of municipalities and communities of agglomerations has well-known limits, if only because it clashes with old communal political sociabilities.

Under these circumstances, it is not impossible to imagine other ways to reconcile decentralization and equity, local freedom and equal opportunity. For example, each municipality could continue to set its own tax rate for municipal taxpayers within certain limits, but with a national equalization mechanism to ensure that the revenue collected by the municipality is equal to the product of this rate and the average base per inhabitant at the national level and not the average base of the municipality (the latter being the result of a long history of territorial inequalities and the absence of a corrective mechanism). Switching to such a system would naturally result in losers on the side of the wealthiest municipalities and would likely only be possible after a gradual transition period of 10 or 20 years, including the approval of a much more progressive tax system compared to what exists at present. For example, this could consist of making greater contributions to large estates, by naturally taking into account financial assets and debts and by favoring small estates, within wealthy municipalities as well as less prosperous ones; that is, by finally replacing our archaic property tax with a progressive and modernized tax on global net worth.

Although there is nothing in the provisions currently being debated which suggests the future adoption of such a system, there are, in fact, many systems in the current fiscal and social landscape that no one could have predicted 50 or 100 years ago and so profound changes are not impossible or hopeless endeavors. This is without a doubt the main strength of this collective work: by contextualizing preconceived certainties and innovative and multidisciplinary approach to transforming territorial inequalities, this book invites everyone to take ownership of these issues and to participate in these reflections and debates.

Introduction

Magali TALANDIER and Josselin TALLEC
Pacte, Université Grenoble Alpes, France

Land use planning is the idea of dealing with territorial inequalities by focusing first on the logic of equipment (transport infrastructure, construction of services and housing, etc.), and then on local economic development. Today, the question of territorial inequalities, understood here as the socioeconomic gaps between multiple geographical units (between regions, municipalities, etc.), is changing the face of the debate. For instance, we are increasingly seeing the emergence of more plastic notions, such as "territorial fractures", "peripheral France", territories with "several lives" or even spaces to "repair". A strong political resonance can thus be observed, in the image of the decoupling between the metropolitan region and the rest of the United Kingdom on the occasion of Brexit or the French *Gilets jaunes* movement. These divergent trajectories of development between territories often give rise to hasty interpretations that are essentially binary, posing oppositions between metropolises and the "peripheries", cities and the countryside, the Global North and the Global South and between the East and the West of the European Union (EU). Ultimately, all of these perspectives concern the aggregate characteristics of social groups present in various territories and their political expressions.

This book offers a detailed analysis of these differences, that is, what distinguishes certain social groups in a territory and what causes them to be discriminated against and sometimes penalized. Here, we can very quickly think of the concepts of disparity, discontinuity, discrimination or egoism, to mention only a few examples of the diversity of forms taken by the spatial imprint of inequalities. To this end, the contributions have been chosen in order to approach the subject of land or regional planning in its economic dimensions at different scales of action and levels of observation, that is, from the local to the global level.

The aim of the book is to describe inequalities and how they are dealt with according to the geographical units in question and in terms of the interdependencies between them. This approach makes it possible to reconsider which scales of analysis pertain to these processes and the much debated "right scale" of action needed to contain them.

When it comes to shedding light on such a vast and ambitious subject, the preferred angle of approach is that of territorial development. Territorial development measures the improvement (or lack thereof) of the living conditions of a specific population and the consequences in terms of public policy, that is, the development of space. Territorial action plays out in many different fields of intervention, including the economy and production, transport and mobility, education and training, etc. The primary objective of these policies is to reduce territorial disparities in order to progress toward spatial equity or to provide access to services, employment and housing anywhere in a given territory in order to equalize development conditions. In this sense, planning constitutes the territorial facet of national or community solidarity mechanisms within the framework of the EU's policy for cohesion, for example. This leads us to the question of how best to apprehend and act on these territorial inequalities vis-à-vis the diverse dynamics and the plurality of the scales of action underlying them?

Measuring the development trajectories of cities and territories involves a variety of indicators, often based on a socioeconomic understanding, for example, drawing on the income growth rate or variations in GDP per capita. This limited perspective, already the subject of much debate and scholarship, struggles to clearly grasp the reality of life in a given territory. A diversity of actions (individual and collective), systems and interventions impact all the components of people's daily lives, for instance, their access to education, health and the infrastructures that support them. The spatial scales of measurement can also be brought into the debate: a "large" scale of analysis (e.g. national or regional) leads to the erasure of local situations which differ profoundly from one context to another.

As such, the multiplicity of factors that contribute to the identification of fragility, disengagement or, on the contrary, "rising" development, covers a whole series of concrete, individual and collective situations as well as the public actions that oversee the territorial regulation of these contexts. The purpose of these territorial regulations by local/public authorities is thus central to understanding the role played by planning and territorial development. Brought together as a

Introduction xxi

cumulative process (development leads to development), these measures make it possible to grasp the much-debated issue of territorial inequalities. We can try to describe and understand its origins, its rejections, its justifications and, of course, its treatments. This last point remains, in part, a task for the collective action that constitutes the development of the space.

In an attempt to shed some light on these issues, the book compares retrospective and multiscalar diagnostic elements with analyses of actions taken in Europe and France to try to curb these disparities. Thus, by taking up factual elements, mobilizing empirical works, but also by bringing together several scientific literatures (geography economics, spatial planning spatial planning and urban planning, urban sociology and political science), the book seeks to update the ultimately "classic" but still lively and fundamental discussion of territorial inequalities at the subnational (local) level. However, we will not deal with international inequalities, that is, between different countries and regions of the world that have been widely documented, particularly in economics. Rather, while 55% of income inequality measured between individuals remains tied to national systems, the remaining 45% is still due to subnational systems. Inequality between territories remains very high, despite the financial resources allocated to social redistribution and territorial rebalancing as part of various development policies.

The dialogue between the authors of the book plays out on several levels. The concepts, measures and elements of objectification intersect with historical analyses of territorial inequalities and public policies. The whole book is apprehended from the European "macro-regional" scale to the sub-municipal scale of the priority neighborhoods of the city policy in France.

On this basis, the book was conceived as a series of four intersecting viewpoints. Thomas Piketty, a leading author, has provided the Foreword. Over the last 10 years, his work on income inequality has had a profound impact on scientific and political circles worldwide. At once personal and laudatory, Piketty offers a synthesis of the questions asked and the knowledge presented throughout this collective work. The authors' thorough and detailed analyses grapple with one of the essential questions for our nations: namely, how are we to reconcile decentralization, equity, local autonomy and equal opportunity? Faced with these challenges, Piketty concludes his chapter by proposing new perspectives in terms of local taxation, calling for new forms of spatial solidarity which are more locally based and more ambitious than those at present.

Chapters 1 and 2, written respectively by Magali Talandier and Laurent Davezies, open this book by proposing a comprehensive account of inequalities at several scales and over time. On the basis of these two intersecting analyses, Talandier investigates the mechanisms of wealth circulation that have reshaped subnational inequalities over the past 30 years, while Davezies details the complexity of inequality indicators, along with impacts (including bias) they can have on so-called integration policies, especially at the EU level.

These inequalities are then discussed in terms of economic specialization, social concentration and territorial interdependencies, with regard to several fracture lines which contribute to the global narrative on inequality. In Chapter 3, Philippe Estèbe and Xavier Desjardins propose a historical rereading of these great French geographical oppositions which accompany the action in the image of Paris and the French desert, or, more recently, the opposition between metropolises and France periurban France. Éric Charmes, in Chapter 4, extends this reflection by taking a more detailed look at peripheral France, the so-called *Gilets jaunes*, suburbs often perceived as being neglected or outright ignored by development and urban planning policies.

Following these chapters on diagnosis and multiscalar analyses of territorial inequalities, Frédéric Santamaria (Chapter 5) and Josselin Tallec (Chapter 6) propose a discussion of public planning policies, the former looking at Europe and the latter focusing on the French case. Santamaria offers a thorough reading of cohesion policies, their main objective being to reduce inequalities between regions. Tallec, introducing the issue of medium-sized cities, presents a comprehensive overview of French policies on the reduction of inequalities since the advent of land and urban planning as a public policy measure following the Second World War.

Lastly, Sylvie Fol and Leïla Frouillou (Chapter 7) build on this to offer us an extremely rich synthesis of international scientific works that deal with the issue of urban segregation. This includes the underlying theoretical frameworks, the causes, the debates on the methods of measurement as well as public policies aimed at these processes of segregation.

It goes without saying that the territorialized approach to inequalities is part of the broader work of the human and social sciences on this difficult issue. It naturally calls for political choices seeking to avert such inequalities. The originality of this approach lies, however, in its identification of the role played by cities and territories in the origins of these inequalities, the processes of their deployment and their treatment. From this perspective, land and urban planning faces several challenges. In particular, it is a matter of examining the possible contribution that this interdisciplinary approach could make to the analysis of the different registers of justification of inequalities (think in particular of the idea of "flow" which is by no means automatic). Another point would be to promote awareness of the interdependencies and affinities existing between cities and territories in order to get out of an exclusively categorical logic of intervention (e.g. the idea of devices exclusively dedicated to small cities). A territorialized public action that takes inequalities seriously as the expression of difficulties inscribed in existing relationships within territorial systems is at the heart of the debate. In the end, it is still the incessant question of the "right scale" (social and spatial) and the interdependencies of action that reappears. At the risk of being hijacked (think of the idea of "peripheral France" and "territorial fractures"), planning cannot free itself from these questions which, like any form of collective action, are resolutely democratic in character.

1

Metropolization and Territorial Inequalities

Magali TALANDIER
Pacte, Université Grenoble Alpes, France

1.1. Introduction

Economic, political, social and environmental crises impact territories – defined here as systems of places, relations and actors – in different ways in terms of space and time. It is possible for these multiple impacts to be experienced, anticipated and overcome differently from one territory to another. The structural and cyclical effects combine with specific and local factors to determine the trajectories of territorial development. Consequently, territories are continually reforming. These processes partly explain the evolution of territorial disparities, which are also being reconfigured over time. For the past 30 years, metropolization has characterized the spatial fact. This process of concentration of population, economic activities and added value in the major urban areas of the world constitutes the spatial facet of the globalization of flows. Paradoxically enough, the excessive growth of trade has led to a growing concentration of certain activities in space. The division of labor between "developed" and "developing" countries has led the former to specialize and support a so-called knowledge economy and the latter to develop a low-cost manufacturing industry. Today, this account is outdated and more complex in practice, as it is possible to observe metropolization on a global scale. Developing countries have been improving their research and engineering sectors and other high value-added services, for the most part in large cities. As for established industrial

For a color version of all figures in this chapter, see http://www.iste.co.uk/talandier/territorial.zip.

countries (like France), they are discovering, perhaps a little too late, the importance of maintaining a certain industrial sovereignty[1].

New economic geography models (Krugman 1991) have made it possible to explain the components of this urban concentration by analyzing the logics of the location of activities, but also those of skilled labor. Concentration factors (economies of scale, network effects, labor market dynamism, etc.) generate a cumulative spiral process in favor of the largest centers. A quick analysis of these mechanisms would suggest that territorial inequalities have regularly increased – that is, cities have developed faster and to the detriment of other areas, including what some call "Peripheral France" (Guilluy 2014). However, the figures are not so definitive. There has been a growth in jobs, population and income in many French territories that have not been "metropolitanized". This discrepancy between rhetoric, theory and observations is due to the fact that the city is both a source of centripetal and centrifugal flows: the city attracts young graduates, students, executives and some of the creative professions, but pushes away other demographics and jobs. Moreover, cities generate flows of wealth that metropolitans spend in other territories. This invisible circulation of wealth (Davezies 2008) contributes to the reduction of territorial inequalities.

In order to trace the long history of these dynamics, this chapter has been organized into three sections. First, we will conduct a historical analysis of the issue of territorial inequalities in France from the industrial revolution to the present day. We will then show how territorial income inequalities have evolved over the last 30 years, namely, in the context of metropolization. Finally, we will conclude by shedding light on the mechanisms behind the spatial circulation of wealth.

1.2. T200 years of territorial inequalities

Metropolization questions the links, but also the possible fractures between centers and their peripheries. Unfortunately, in order to trace the long history of these interterritorial relationships between cities and the countryside, the departmental or regional data on income are not sufficient. On the other hand, we have exhaustive demographic data from national censuses on the scale of the 35,000 municipalities[2].

---

1 Here, we are referring to the industrial recovery policies that France is putting in place, as well as to the feeling of a loss of sovereignty more broadly as a result of the shortages of masks, sanitizer gels, ventilators and vaccines in connection to the Covid-19 pandemic.

2 The database we used for this work was built in two stages. In 2007, we collected, from the regional departments of INSEE, a first series of data for 17 French regions over the period 1871–1999 (Talandier 2007). At the time, this was partly supplemented with the purchase of data

This database offers an exceptional geographical framework for analyzing the links between the settlement, geography and economic changes. Cartographic analysis of demographic dynamics reveals major changes, from the 19th century to the present day, in the ways people live. In the agrarian model, dating back to the beginning of the 19th century, people lived as close as possible to the land, the essential resource. In the current cognitive model, the places of production, life and consumption have become totally disconnected. Thus, economic developments are accompanied by a differentiated spatial distribution of the population and their respective incomes. The evolution of this relationship between population and productive forces over a long period of time informs us about the evolution of territorial inequalities.

1.2.1. *The development of the French metropolitan area*

From 1806 to 2017, the population of France grew from 29.6 to 67 million inhabitants. However, this demographic growth was not regular throughout the period, nor was it homogeneous from one area to another. Thus, the number and type of municipalities that gained or lost inhabitants varied over time. For example, after the revolutionary period, the First French Empire (1805–1814) was a period of low population growth. The numerous wars and defeats, including the French campaign of 1814, meant that the demographic balance was only slightly positive. On the other hand, the following years of the Restoration (1814–1830), the July Monarchy (1830–1848) and the Second Republic (1848–1852) were marked by a demographic growth that was both sustained and spatially diffused. The entire country benefited from this upsurge since nearly three quarters of French municipalities recorded a growth in population. It was only in very small municipalities (with fewer than 250 inhabitants) that the population was on a slight decline. The population remained relatively well distributed spatially in 1851 with nearly two-thirds (61%) of the French population residing in a rural municipality (i.e. a municipality with fewer than 2,000 inhabitants), and only 8% of the population living in a municipality with more than 20,000 inhabitants. This period of equidensity in terms of settlement resulted in low territorial inequalities. The following century was marked by industrialization and its spatial corollary, namely rural exodus. During this period, more than three quarters of the French municipalities experienced a loss of population. A more detailed analysis shows that, overall, it is the municipalities with less than 2,000 inhabitants that experienced a population loss as their inhabitants moved to towns and cities (which benefited in turn). Thus, the threshold of 2,000 agglomerated inhabitants, which makes it

---

from the Historical Data Laboratory. In 2016, because of the development of the Cassini site, we were able to standardize, update and meticulously complete this database for the entire period 1806–1946. For more details on the base standardization method, see Talandier (2016).

possible to distinguish rural municipalities in France from urban units, has a strong influence as to how rural areas are perceived (Talandier 2007)[3]. If this threshold, chosen arbitrarily, had been 5,000 inhabitants, for example, the rural municipalities would never have recorded a population decrease, thus modifying the representations of these areas. If this were the case, it is possible that a good number of public works and public policies would have been different.

The period between 1911 and 1921, marked by the First World War, saw a sharp decline in France's population, affecting nearly 90% of the municipalities. Yet, in this context of demographic decline, medium-sized cities (with populations ranging from 20,000 to 100,000) were gaining inhabitants. Population growth resumed in the years 1920–1930 and the urban concentration of people and wealth continues to this day. The Second World War lead to a new decrease in population, this time in the medium-sized cities, albeit without really disrupting the process of urbanization.

From 1946 onwards, a period of exceptional demographic (and economic) growth began. However, this only benefited one-third of the municipalities – namely, those located in the industrial regions of the north and the east, as well as Île-de-France. In the 1950s, spatial inequalities were at their peak, dividing France in two: industrial and modern France, which was the center for the new productive dynamics of the country, and agrarian France, which had not yet experienced the same kind of development.

This trend was reversed in 1968, the year that officially marked the end of the rural exodus which had been taking place for a century. The population of municipalities with less than 2,000 inhabitants reached its utmost minimum in that year (14.7 million inhabitants). From then onwards, even if the country's rate of population growth slows, it now benefits the majority of rural and urban municipalities. Over the last 30 years, three quarters of the municpalities have recorded an increase in population, marking a return to the trends observed at the beginning of the 19th century.

However, this phenomenon of demographic rebalancing is not without consequences. While it systematically reduces spatial inequalities in income between the municipalities, it has also resulted in rapid periurbanization, a reduction in agricultural land and an increase in motorized vehicle use. Nevertheless, it is this reduction in population that allows some isolated rural areas to also experience

---

3 To clarify, the notion of an "urban unit" is based on the continuity of the built environment and the number of inhabitants. An urban unit is a municipality or a group of municipalities with a continuous built-up area (i.e. there is no space of more than 200 m between two buildings) that has at least 2,000 inhabitants.

demographic and economic renewal after decades of decline. Residential mobility from the city to the countryside contributes to the reduction of territorial inequalities, without diminishing the demographic and economic dynamism of cities.

1.2.2. *Processes of population concentration and deconcentration*

Figure 1.1 shows the spatial movements of population concentration and deconcentration within the French territory since 1806. In both 1806 and 1821 (the red and purple curves in Figure 1.1 that almost merge), nearly a quarter (23%) of the population was distributed over 50% of the surface area of French municipalities; conversely, three quarters of the population was distributed over 50% of the same area. Between these two dates, the concentration rate (Gini coefficient) decreased very slightly, indicating that the population remained very diffuse, or even bordering on deconcentrated. Yet, from 1821 onwards, this rate increased slightly until the middle of the 19th century, then accelerated rapidly after 1851. From this date, migration movements from the countryside to towns and cities continued for more than a century, albeit at different rates depending on the period. The annual rate of spatial concentration remained relatively sustained and more or less stable until 1936. Thus, on the eve of the Second World War, 75% of the population was concentrated in 30% of the French municipalities. From 1936 to 1954, the concentration slowed down considerably, and the geographical distribution even stabilized. In 1954, three quarters of the population lived on 25% of the surface area of the municipalities. The second half of the 20th century marked a new turning point in the spatial distribution of the French population. The effects of extremely rapid urbanization can be observed between 1954 and 1968, wherein the rate of urban concentration increased like never before, at twice the rate of the period of rural exodus. It was in 1968, not today, that spatial concentration reached its peak, with more than three quarters of the population spread over just 15% of the surface area of the municipalities. From then on, the trend has gradually reversed: a slow movement of demographic deconcentration observed at first to the benefit of the peripheries of the cities, then extended to the more remote rural areas. The most recent available findings (for 2017) confirm the trend. Strikingly, there has been an acceleration in the decrease in the Gini coefficient, which measures the spatial concentration of the population. In 2017, the spatial concentration of the population even returned to a level prior to that of 1968! Although these decreases in population size appear to be relatively minimal at the national scale, they have a significant impact on low-density areas. These migration reversals and patterns of minor urban deconcentration contribute to the growth of inter-territorial income flows, which we will return to in the third section of this chapter.

6   Territorial Inequalities

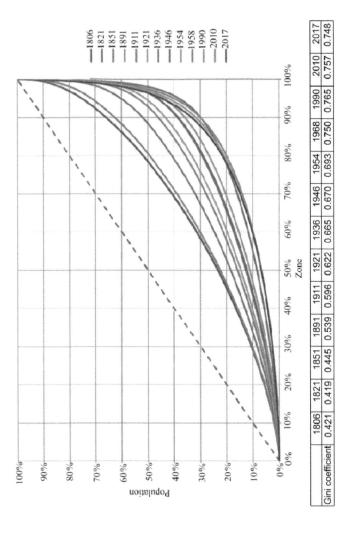

Figure 1.1. *Concentration curves from 1806 to 2017 (source: author's calculations based on population census, INSEE). Note for the reader: in 1921, 75% of the population was concentrated in 30% of the national territory*

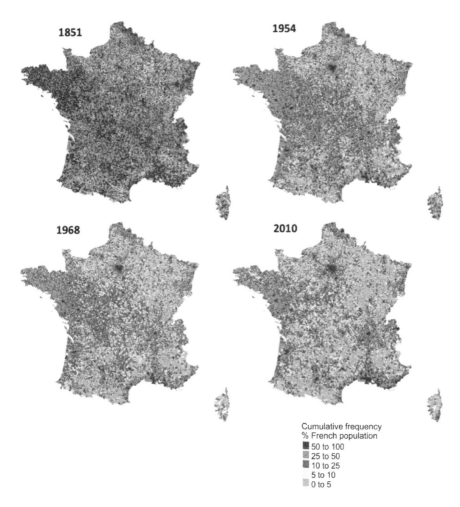

Figure 1.2. *Spatial concentration of the population in French municipalities in 1851, 1954, 1968 and 2010 (source: author's calculations based on population census, INSEE)*

Figure 1.2 utilizes the model proposed by Lévy (2013), but over several years of observation. Note that 50% of the French population resides in the municipalities mapped in dark blue; this rises to 75% if we include the municipalities that are in light blue. Evidently, in 2010, three quarters of the French population resided in less than 15% of the national surface area, divided between the heart of Île-de-France, the Lille-Roubaix-Tourcoing conurbation and the Rhône Valley, as well as all the major cities and their immediate surroundings. If we look at the same spatial construction carried out with the 1851 data, we observe an equipartition of the population over the entire territory. France is predominantly "blue" indicating that 75% of the population is spread over a large part of the territory. Some regions already appear to be less populated, such as the countryside in the north and northeast, or some villages in the extreme southwest or the Provençal countryside. But overall, the demographic model is indeed that of an equidensity of population. A century later, France was transformed. In 1954, the metropolises were clearly identifiable, even if less extensive than today, and the rural areas (especially in the center of France) were populated. The 1968 map represents the period of maximum concentration, whereas the main difference with the 2010 map is the lesser demographic and spatial expansion of the major metropolises toward their immediate periphery.

These demographic trends reflect differentiated socioeconomic realities that impact territorial inequalities. In the following, we will attempt to summarize the major trends.

1.2.3. *The spatiotemporal model and territorial inequalities*

Figure 1.3 presents the different major socioeconomic phases that have shaped the spatial organization of France. For each phase, we have specified the economic model and the dominant cultural form, the associated spatial figure and the state of the territorial inequalities. We identify, in a fairly traditional way, the agrarian model, then the industrial model and a third "cognitive" model in connection with the rise of the knowledge economy and metropolization. The fourth model, called the collaborative model, is more future oriented. Each model is not a cycle in its own right, but rather a layer that adds to and transforms the previous ones. Between each period, we have transition phases. The first is linked to the industrial revolution and the rural exodus that accompanied and resulted from it. The second is due to the rise of tertiary and cognitive activities that condition urban growth. Finally, the ecological and digital transition appears to be the current transition to a new economic, cultural and territorial model.

The agrarian economy is accompanied by a traditional cultural form, a population that is still largely rural and a relative weakness of territorial inequalities. The industrial economy is associated with modern society. In terms of territorial development, the regional figure dominates, in the sense that only the industrial regions have been developed. Territorial inequalities are extremely marked, with a north/south divide through the national territory, as described by Philippe Estèbe and Xavier Desjardins in Chapter 3. On the other hand, we have been operating in the metropolitan model for the past 30 years, which is characterized by centripetal productive forces that favor the large metropolises and centrifugal forces linked to residential mobility and tourist mobility of populations.

These dynamics largely explain the revival of certain rural areas and metropolitan suburbs since the 1990s. The economy of the metropolises is complex, multiple in terms of the skills mobilized, the economic sectors concerned and the spaces occupied. While the knowledge economy is necessary, it is not sufficient to ensure the development of metropolises, and more broadly of metropolitan systems, which include the metropolis itself, but also its *hinterland* (Talandier 2016).

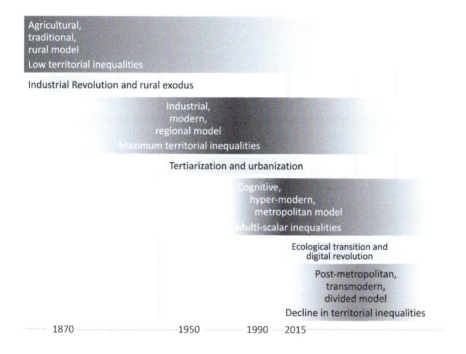

Figure 1.3. *Spatial and economic models and territorial transitions (source: author's own diagram)*

Finally, this metropolization is not just an economic process. It defies urbanists and for some sociologists, it can be considered as a new cultural form – that is, that of hypermodernity[4]. Ascher (1995, 2001) has shown how the-knowledge economy is

---

4 Let us note that the ways of defining the contemporary period (postmodern, hypermodern, modern second, transmodern, etc.) and of analyzing the relations and the differences with the preceding period are numerous and sometimes conflicting between those who think that it is about

linked to a more mobile, interconnected and individualistic society (Ascher 2005). The author evokes the processes of metapolization, in which the increasing flexibility of individuals and their space-time reshapes our various ways of life and generates new inequalities. In this model, it is the relationship between "centers" and peripheries that dominate the question of territorial inequalities. This inequality depends on the scale of analysis. Inequality decreases between sub-national territories, but increases at the sub-metropolitan and sub-municipal levels. The rest of this chapter details these mechanisms in detail.

1.3. Metropolization: 30 years of changing territorial inequalities

1.3.1. *Methodology and databases*

Since the mid-1980s, observation of territorial inequalities has been based on incomes declared to taxes by households. The data indicates the overall amount of income declared by households in their place of residence and at the community level. The income data are standardized in constant-price euros. We have a reconstructed tax base from 1984 to 2018 for all French municipalities[5]. However, we are required, following a change in the tax base in 2006, to distinguish between developments before and after that date.

As far as the scale of analysis is concerned, we prefer the latest INSEE catchment area (see Box 1.1).

In the statistical processing and tables, we will distinguish the five sizes of catchment areas: for example, in Paris, areas with more than 700,000 inhabitants, those with 200,000 to 700,000 inhabitants, those with 50,000 to 200,000 inhabitants, those with less than 50,000 inhabitants and municipalities outside the catchment area. We introduce, for each stratum of catchment areas, the notions of center, suburbs and periurban ring. This allows us to shed light on center-periphery dynamics according to the size of the catchment area. For a better graphic visibility, we have rearranged the centers and their suburbs for the cartographic analysis.

---

an acceleration of modernity and others who see a true rupture there. The debate is certainly fascinating, however, our objective is not to explicitly state and defend our position thereon, but to draw upon this type of sociological analytical framework in order to link the cultural form to territorial forms of development.

5 Excluding statistical confidentiality applied to the smallest municipalities (less than 1% each year).

> The urban area is a group of municipalities (as a single unit and without any enclaves) that consists of a population and employment center and a periurban ring of municipalities, called "periurban" in this text, in which at least 15% of the working population work in the center.
>
> The most populous municipalities with more than 50% of the population of the catchment area are central municipalities. The other municipalities in the catchment area are called the suburbs.
>
> The definition of the largest catchment areas of cities is consistent with the definition of *cities* and "catchment areas" used by Eurostat and the Organization for Economic Co-operation and Development (OECD) to analyze the functioning of cities. The zoning facilitates international comparisons and makes it possible to visualize the influence of large foreign cities in France. Seven of the catchment areas have a foreign city at their center: Basel, Charleroi, Geneva, Lausanne, Luxembourg, Monaco and Saarbrucken.
>
> The areas are then classified according to the total number of inhabitants in the area. We distinguish between the Paris catchment area, and those of:
>
> – more than 700,000 inhabitants;
>
> – between 200,000 and 700,000 inhabitants;
>
> – between 50,000 and 200,000 inhabitants;
>
> – less than 50,000 inhabitants.
>
> Finally, a group of municipalities remains outside the catchment areas.

Box 1.1. *Defining catchment areas of the National Institute of Statistics and Economic Studies (Institut national de la statistique et des études économiques, INSEE. Source: Insee – 2020)*

1.3.2. *The majority of French household income is concentrated in suburban rings*

In 2018, 42.6% of all income reported to taxes was held by outer suburban households (for 43.6% of the population), 28% by households in the municipalities centers, 23.6% by the suburbs and, finally, 5.7% by municipalities outside the catchment area. The Paris catchment area alone accounts for 25% of income for 20% of the population. The city of Paris accounts for 6.6% of French income (for 3.4% of the population). These figures show the extent to which suburban households (and spaces) are absolutely critical in France today, whether from a demographic, economic or political point of view.

It is also interesting to note that medium-sized areas (with 50,000 or more inhabitants) generate almost as much revenue as the large centers of more than 700,000 inhabitants.

Categories of space	Inc2018 (in M€)	Pop2018	%Inc2018	%pop2018	Gap (inc-pop)
50-center	48,839	3,663,362	4.8	5.7	-0.8
50-suburbs	7,724	528,227	0.8	0.8	-0.1
50-periurban ring	51,699	3,750,374	5.1	5.8	-0.7
50-200 center	53,110	3,956,586	5.3	6.1	-0.9
50-200 suburbs	8,872	657,843	0.9	1.0	-0.1
50-200 periurban ring	103,895	7,192,091	10.3	11.1	-0.8
200-700 center	59,588	4,402,988	5.9	6.8	-0.9
200-700 suburbs	32,450	2,128,638	3.2	3.3	-0.1
200-700 periurban ring	120,368	7,770,188	11.9	12.0	-0.1
700-center	54,055	3,628,152	5.4	5.6	-0.3
700-suburbs	45,902	2,978,375	4.5	4.6	-0.1
700-periurban ring	110,053	6,647,012	10.9	10.3	0.6
Paris-center	67,043	2,192,485	6.6	3.4	3.2
Paris-suburbs	143,587	8,065,363	14.2	12.5	1.7
Paris-periurban ring	45,984	2,819,178	4.6	4.4	0.2
Total 'center'	282,635	17,843,573	28.0	27.6	0.4
Total 'suburbs'	238,535	14,358,446	23.6	22.2	1.4
Total 'periurban ring'	431,999	28,178,843	42.8	43.6	-0.8
Outside the catchment area	57,118	4,299,976	5.7	6.6	-1.0
Total	1,010,287	64,680,838	100.0	100.0	0.0

Table 1.1. *Distribution of household income across French territories (source: author's calculations and production based on census and tax department)*

This observation can be made at the level of the municipalities of these two types of catchment areas (each representing about 5% of declared income in France) and their surrounding areas or periurban rings (each accounting for around 11%). On the other hand, the statistical concept of "suburbs" is not relevant to the smallest urban areas.

If metropolization defines the concentration of capital and profitable investments in the largest urban areas, it is clear that in France the socioeconomic power of inhabitants of small and medium-sized cities should not be underestimated.

Thus, more than half of the reported income comes from households residing in a small or medium-sized center and outside the catchment area. This rate rises to 70% if we include the periurban rings of major metropolises.

1.3.3. *Higher incomes in suburban areas than in the city centers*

Income per capita varies by a factor of two between the richest (central Paris) and the poorest areas (municipalities outside the catchment area) (see Table 1.2). Overall, high-income households are concentrated in the large catchment areas. On the other hand, within each area, the farther away from the center, the more household income increases. Thus, the per capita income of the periurban rings is higher than that of the suburban municipalities; this being higher than that of the city centers, in turn. Only Paris is the exception: the incomes of Parisian residents are clearly higher than those of periurban residents.

Categories of space	Inc/cap in 2018	Deviation from average in 2018
50-center	13,332	-14.6
50-suburbs	14,623	-6.4
50-periurban ring	13,785	-11.7
50-200 center	13,423	-14.1
50-200 suburbs	13,486	-13.7
50-200 periurban ring	14,446	-7.5
200-700 center	13,534	-13.4
200-700 suburbs	15,244	-2.4
200-700 periurban ring	15,491	-0.8
700-center	14,899	-4.6
700-suburbs	15,412	-1.3
700-periurban ring	16,557	6.0
Paris-center	30,579	95.8
Paris-suburbs	17,803	14.0
Paris-periurban ring	16,311	4.4
Total 'center'	16,311	4.4
Total 'suburbs'	15,840	1.4
Total 'periurban ring'	16,613	6.4
Outside the catchment area	13,283	-15.0
Total	15,620	0.0

Table 1.2. *Per capita income by place of residence in 2018 (source: author's calculations and table based on population censuses and tax department)*

Outside of Paris, only three large cities (Bordeaux, Nantes and, to a lesser extent, Rennes) follow this pattern, albeit with much more moderate differences in income. Thus, the per capita income in the municipalities centers of the Bordeaux area is 5% higher than that declared in the suburban municipalities. The rate is 4% in Nantes and 2% in Rennes.

Conversely, some catchment areas are characterized by a center-periphery gap, to the benefit of the peripheries, even more marked than the average. This is the case, for example, in Marseille, Strasbourg, Grenoble, Saint-Étienne, Mulhouse, Perpignan and Brest, with gaps of 20–25%, to the benefit of the outer periurban rings. Figure 1.4 confirms these figures. Most large catchment areas have a higher level of per capita income than other areas. Paris stands out for its high-income levels, as do the cross-border worker areas near Geneva and Basel in Switzerland, or in some of the large cities on the Côte d'Azur. Among the medium-sized cities, incomes per capita are higher along the Atlantic seaboard, in the greater Paris Basin and in the southeast quarter. On the other hand, in the central and more rural part of the national metropolitan territory, only Clermont-Ferrand has an above average income level. Finally, some outer periurban rings of small towns in the Massif Central or in the vicinity of the Toulouse area show extremely low-income levels.

As such, these initial findings do not confirm the ideas put forward by some vis-à-vis the impoverishment of a peripheral France. On the contrary, in 70% of the areas, per capita income levels are higher in the periurban rings than in the centers or nearby suburbs. However, these spaces are themselves plural and crossed by social and spatial inequalities that these initial figures tend to erase.

The rest of this chapter focuses on analyzing communal inequalities within each of these categories.

1.3.4. *Fewer territorial disparities in areas polarized by small and medium-sized cities*

Table 1.3 presents the average coefficients of variation in per capita income within each category of space[6]. In 2018, the Paris periurban ring had the greatest inequalities in per capita income. This large Île-de-France territory covers very

---

6 The coefficient of variation measures the inequalities between the individuals of a group (here between the municipalities of the same space. It is calculated by dividing the weighted standard deviation by the mean.

different social situations from one municipality to the next. Following this (but with 10 points less) are the centers of large urban areas, which are also confronted with strong sociospatial inequalities followed closely by all the municipalities outside the catchment area.

Consequently, there are three categories of spaces: namely, the greater French periurban ring, large French conurbations and rural areas. The common feature of these three categories is that they group together municipalities that are extremely disparate in terms of the wealth of their inhabitants.

In contrast, the centers and the periurban rings of small cities, as well as the centers of medium-sized cities, are more homogeneous.

	Average 2018 CV
Paris-periurban ring	33.2
700 pole-center	23.3
Outside catchment areas	21.6
700-periurban ring	19.5
200-700 periurban ring	19.3
200-700-pole-center	19.1
50-200-periurban ring	15.2
50-periurban ring	11.9
50-200-pole-center	10.5
50-pole-center	7.4
Total	24.8

Table 1.3. *Communal inequalities within each territory (coefficient of variation)*

COMMENT ON TABLE 1.3. *The coefficient of variation (CV) between municipalities was first calculated for each of the French catchment areas, and then we calculated the average of these CVs for each category of catchment area. The centers containing only one municipality (and whose CV = 0) were removed from the calculation so as not to introduce bias to the analysis (source: author's calculations and production based on population censuses and tax department).*

Figures 1.4 and 1.5 detail these results. The Île-de-France region stands out with a very high territorial inequality result, in both the central municipalities, as well as the large outer suburban areas. Among the large urban areas outside of Île-de-France, Metz, Nancy and Dijon also show high rates of inequality between the municipalities in the center and those in the periurban ring.

We can note that for many large catchment areas – such as Toulouse, Montpellier, Marseille, Nice, Nantes and Lille – territorial disparities are more pronounced and relatively more significant in the periurban ring. Conversely, in Lyon, Rennes, Grenoble, Rouen, Tours, Clermont-Ferrand and Avignon, inequalities are greater in the center than in the periphery. Finally, income inequalities per capita between municipalities are less pronounced in the smallest catchment areas.

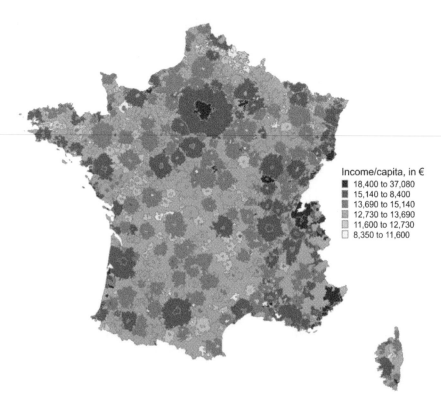

Figure 1.4. *Household income per capita in 2018 (source: author's calculations and map based on population censuses and tax department)*

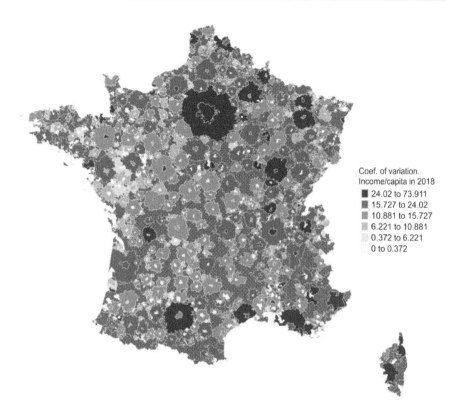

Figure 1.5. *Income disparities per capita in 2018 (source: author's calculations and production based on population censuses and tax department)*

1.3.5. *Typology of territorial inequalities*

Despite the diversity of contexts vis-à-vis spatial inequalities, certain regularities have emerged. In order to synthesize these results, we propose a typology of catchment areas constructed on the basis of a principal component analysis (PCA), then a hierarchical ascending classification (HAC). This results in four main types of catchment areas (see Figure 1.6).

First, we can note the areas that have an income higher than the national average, which are made up of centers that are generally richer than the periurban rings (type 1/C1, in orange). Île-de-France is emblematic of this type, but so are Bordeaux, Basque country, part of the Côte d'Azur and the areas bordering Switzerland.

We then have a type that concerns many medium- to large-sized areas. This type is characterized by rather high incomes per capita, but it is the periurban rings that are home to the better-off households (type 2/C2, in blue). Finally, types 3 (C3, in green) and 4 (C4, in pink) are characterized by smaller areas with lower incomes. The difference between these two stems from inequalities within the periurban rings, which are higher in type 3. This type is also overrepresented in the northeast quarter of France. These territories are known to be the country's former industrial territories, often accumulating negative social and economic indicators.

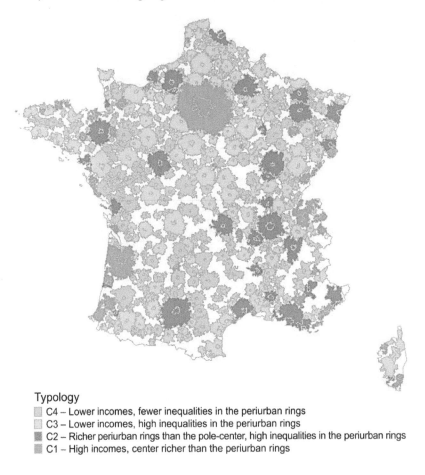

Typology
- C4 – Lower incomes, fewer inequalities in the periurban rings
- C3 – Lower incomes, high inequalities in the periurban rings
- C2 – Richer periurban rings than the pole-center, high inequalities in the periurban rings
- C1 – High incomes, center richer than the periurban rings

Figure 1.6. *Typology of catchment areas by income level and territorial disparities (source: author's calculations and production based on population censuses and tax department)*

Thus, after 30 years of metropolization, France is marked by the hegemonic weight of Paris in terms of the wealth of its inhabitants. There is also a concentration of higher incomes in suburban rings and high inequalities in city centers. The rest of the chapter outlines the evolution of territorial inequalities over the period observed.

1.3.6. *Rapid growth in per capita incomes in periurban rings*

Since the mid-1980s, there has been a fairly clear correlation between volumes of income and population growth. Thus, the rate of increase is faster in the catchment areas (see Figures 1.9(A) and (B)). In terms of per capita income, positive rates of change can be observed in all types of areas, but with consistently more sustained growth in the periurban rings than in the suburbs. Per capita income is therefore both lower and growing less rapidly in the city centers. The gap between the city center and the suburbs is widening in favor of the latter, contrary to popular belief. For once, the Paris area is operating on an inverted basis: per capita income in Paris is growing much faster than in its periurban ring.

We will now discuss the data by sub-period in order to clearly distinguish the impact of the 1993 crisis from that of 2008 (see Figure 1.9(B)). The available data suggest a more marked slowdown in per capita income in 1993 than in 2008. Concerning the territorial impact, we observe, first of all, a sustained growth in per capita income in rural areas (outside the catchment area) throughout the period and low sensitivity to economic shocks. The periurban rings, outside Paris, have also seen their level of per capita income rise rapidly for more than 30 years, without any noticeable impact of the crises. Because of the structure of their inhabitants, but also because they are more residential than productive, these two types of territories are less exposed to economic shocks. On the other hand, the center of Paris shows a sensitivity to the economic situation, that is, it experiences a drop in per capita income in times of crisis and rapid growth during times of recovery. In particular, during the last period (2009–2018), the dynamic of concentration of high incomes in the capital has never been as rapid as over the last period observed, widening the gap with its peripheral territories, but also with the rest of the country. Finally, the situation has deteriorated relative to the French average in the centers of small and medium-sized towns, but also in the Île-de-France periurban ring. In the centers of large urban areas, after some difficult years following the 2008 crisis, the situation is improving and per capita income is growing at a rate comparable to the national average.

1.3.7. *Geographic inequalities in terms of income per capita*

The maps in Figures 1.11(A)–(C) show annual changes in per capita income by major period since 1984. Several lessons emerge from these maps in terms of geographic impacts.

From the beginning of the analysis period, there has been less growth of income per capita in the North and Northeast of France – although this does not include the Île-de-France and eastern border region (Alsace). These traditionally industrial areas have suffered heavy job losses since the 1970s. As such, it is evident that the crisis of 1993 hit the large metropolises in France much harder. Sometimes the loss of per capita income concerns the entire catchment area (such as in Paris, Lyon, Bordeaux, Grenoble and Strasbourg); other times, it only affects the center of the area (in the cases of Bordeaux, Marseille and Nantes, for example). The more rural areas, small and medium-sized cities of the diagonal of low-density linking the territories of the northeast to the southwest are more resilient. In these areas, a large part of household income comes from transfer income, pensions and minimum social benefits, but also from income that is more residential than productive (tourism, trade, etc.), and that was less affected by the 1993 economic crisis.

The period of economic recovery from 1994 to 2005 resulted in a faster annual increase in per capita incomes than that recorded between 2009 and 2018. The entire period clearly shows the dropout of small cities and medium-sized cities in the Île-de-France region and France's former industrial territories.

The crisis of 2008 did not have the same spatial impact as that of 1993. While the slowdown in income growth is notable, decreases are relatively rare. Only Paris and a few small, scattered municipalities are in this situation.

Finally, following the recovery period of post-2009, per capita incomes have been increasing at a rather moderate pace and are more consistent across all areas, with the exception of central Paris and the areas bordering Switzerland. In these two cases, the gap between these high-income areas and the rest continues to widen.

Let us now turn to sub-local inequalities (see Figures 1.12 and 1.13). These maps show that overall, sub-local inequalities are reduced during the crisis, but increase as soon as the recovery takes effect. Spatially, the last 10 years have resulted in an increase in inequalities between the municipalities of many suburban areas of small cities and within large metropolises (such as Île-de-France, Toulouse, Marseille, Montpellier, Nice and Dijon, for example). On the other hand, we observe a convergence of per capita income levels between municipalities in the periurban rings of medium-sized cities.

Metropolization combined with the ups and downs of the economic situation has consequently produced numerous effects vis-à-vis territorial inequalities in France. It has resulted in both a convergence of income to the benefit of the most disadvantaged territories, that is, the rural areas, and, at the same time, an increase in the gaps between the city, and between the richest city Paris and the rest of the country. There has evidently been both a concentration of wealth to the benefit of the capital and a distribution of income to lower density areas. Thus, the gap between the extremes has been maintained on the basis of an improvement in the situation of these two extremes. In the case of Île-de-France, the growth in income of periurban households is lower than in the other French periurban ring municipalities. In France, it is the periurban rings that have experienced uninterrupted regular and rapid growth in per capita income. Evidently, suburbanization, which accompanies metropolization, has helped to improve the periurban rings, which have become the preferred place to live for a large proportion of high-income households. Thus, over the entire period, the situation has been reversed between the centers and the suburb to the benefit of the latter. While per capita income was higher in the centers of urban areas in the 1980s, it is now higher in the periurban rings. In particular, it is the periurban rings of large urban areas with more than 700,000 inhabitants (excluding Paris) that have seen a rapid increase in the income of their inhabitants, attracting more and more skilled workers. The situation of the metropolises has therefore deteriorated relative to other areas. Moreover, this observation is even more pronounced in small and medium-sized cities.

Finally, local socio-spatial fragmentation is resisting, and even increasing in large urban areas. The periurban rings of Paris remain extremely unequal, with strong inequalities from one municipality to another. This is the case in the centers of large urban areas, as well as the centers of rural areas, which are similarly composed of high-income communities located in attractive rural areas, such as part of Provence, for example, but also of communities that remain extremely poor.

The metropolitan model is explicitly based on systems of flows and networks, in permanent interaction, which also explains the processes of concentration and de-concentration of income. Concentration and deconcentration play out at the same time, but not in the same places, nor with the same intensity and impacts. The metropolitan model is fundamentally a systemic model of the circulation of exogenous and endogenous wealth, resulting from productive and residential dynamics. It is this circulation of wealth that explains the geography of the territorial inequalities that we have just discussed.

1.4. Wealth circulation and the reshaping of territorial inequalities

During the 2000s, researchers in Europe were able to shed light on the impact of income circulation on local economic development processes. By revisiting the economic base theory (Sombart 1916; North 1955; Tiebout 1956), these researchers (Davezies 2008; Talandier and Davezies 2009) have helped redefine the mechanisms of territorial development. They have shown that the residential mobility and public transfers ultimately generate more income than productive and export activities alone. In terms of territorial inequalities, their work sheds light on the mechanisms of public redistribution, as well as those linked to the mobility of people.

1.4.1. *The economic base theory: an operational conceptual framework for the analysis of income flows*

In the 20th century, the economic base theory was one of the most widely used conceptual frameworks in regional and urban economics for the economic analysis of cities and their planning. This approach aims to identify the economic driving forces of a region or city (called the economic bases) in order to calculate the multiplier effects on other activities in the area (non-basic sectors) (see Figure 1.7).

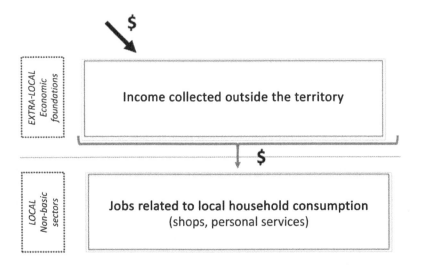

Figure 1.7. *Original principle of the base theory (source: author's own representation in accordance with Sombart (1916))*

1.4.1.1. *Foundations of the base theory*

Although it remains unclear what the origins of the base theory are, many agree that Sombart was the first to formalize and apply the theory (Krumme 1968). He developed his analytical framework in order to understand the economy of the medieval city, distinguishing between the *Städtebildner* (town builder) and the *Städtefüller* (town filler): the former brought in external income, and the latter worked to satisfy local needs. Formulated from the outset in terms of the circulation of income, the base theory has almost always been applied to employment data. Sombart built his model of the medieval city by associating the economic base with the flows of imported wealth (taxes and fees, rent collected by landowners, student expenditures, income of authors, etc.) and was the first to do so. But when he made his first calculations for Berlin in 1927, he limited the basic sector to manufacturing activities and considered the share of jobs dedicated to exporting industrial activities to be a good "approximation" of the number of *Städtebildner*.

In the second half of the 20th century, the theory was at the heart of numerous controversies, the most famous being North and Tiebout's opposition from 1956 to 1962. Relatively abundant literature, both old and recent, traces the essence of these debates (Richardson 1985; Krikelas 1992; Kilkenny and Partridge 2009; Vollet et al. 2018). Finally, it was not until the early 2000s that this theory was applied to all income flows and not only to jobs in exporting.

1.4.1.2. *The base theory revisited*

From the 1990s onwards, the center of a number of productive activities has been based on the profits generated by metropolization (Krugman 1991). As we have seen, these processes have been accompanied by profound change in society, lifestyle and relationship to space. In parallel to a concentration of high value-adding productive activities in urban areas, the rise of individual mobility in individual countries, but also in European countries, the aging of the population, the growth of unemployment and transfer incomes will all gradually lead to a disconnect between the geography of production and that of consumption. These processes can be observed in most industrial countries, albeit at different levels (Talandier and Davezies 2009). The processes of spatial concentration of value added in cities are accompanied by a reformulating of the spatial distribution of household income. An "invisible" circulation of income takes place (Davezies 2008) between spaces.

The economic base theory allows us to better define the mechanisms of this redistribution. In 2003, Davezies differentiated between four economic bases calculated not in terms of jobs, but rather, in terms of income. He therefore returned to the original definition of the model. He distinguishes:

– the private productive base or export base, which includes income from production and exporting activities and financial flows, such as capital gains and a share of property income;

– the residential base, which includes pensions, the wages of migrants who reside in the territory but do not work there and the expenditures of tourists;

– the public base, which includes the salaries of public officials;

– the social base, which includes transfer incomes.

The initial calculations were made at the level of French employment areas and urban areas based on the 1999 data (Davezies 2004). The results highlight the diversity of local economic driving forces and, in particular, the preponderant weight of the residential base. Following this initial work, other authors have enriched the model and improved the calculation methods. Talandier (2007) introduced health care reimbursements, in order to better define the health and social base, and developed a new calculation methodology applicable to the scale of living territories, with the aim of covering the entire national territory. Following this and taking the case of Switzerland into account, Segessemann and Crevoisier (2013) put forward the notions of local residential economy and urban residential economy, whereas Ruault (2018) expanded the tourist base to include the expenditure of visitors or transient consumers at the scale of the Île-de-France departments. In the United Kingdom, Nesse (2014) studied more specifically the impact of non-market bases on the development of territories. Figure 1.8 provides an overview of these different works.

All of the studies that draw on Davezies' economic bases confirm the importance of residential, tourism and redistributive drivers for local economies. These results can be observed in France (Davezies 2008; Talandier 2013), Switzerland (Segessemann and Crevoisier 2016), Belgium (Carlier et al. 2006; De Keersmaecker et al. 2007), Portugal (Guimarães 2014) and in South American contexts, such as Brazil (Favareto and Abramovay 2009). In the case of France, the latest estimates show that the residential base amounts to 40% (on average) of urban areas' (e.g. catchment areas) income from outside their boundaries. The social base has as much weight as the productive base, that is, nearly 25% (Talandier 2016). Finally, the public base is just over 10%. These averages hide important inequalities. In some territories, the flows of redistribution (residential base) and public (public and social base) far exceed these rates. The work carried out in France has also shown that these mechanisms allow many non-metropolitan areas (rural areas and small towns) to maintain dynamic economic activity (Talandier 2007). In some cases, the residential economy and social income are the only external income flows available to the most vulnerable territories.

Metropolization and Territorial Inequalities 25

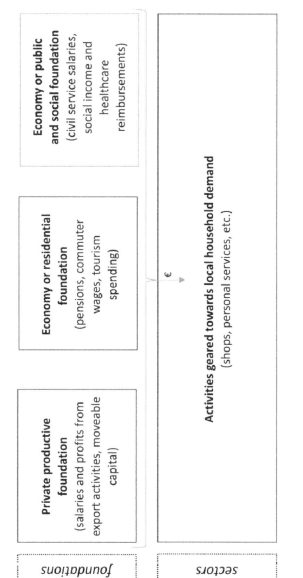

Figure 1.8. *The base theory revisited in the 2000s (source: author's own schema/diagram/representation)*

Finally, we have looked in more detail at the geographical origins and destinations of the wealth flows in order to analyze these processes in more depth. These analyses highlight the existence of productive residential systems (PRSs), which redraw the geography of wealth flows and largely explain the dynamics observed in terms of territorial inequalities.

1.4.2. Productive residential systems

The concept of PRSs is based on the observation of interdependencies between the territories of the residential economy and the receiving territories. The three "origin-destination" databases available to us to break down these flows are:

– the flows of workers between their home and workplace;

– the residential mobility of retirees during the last five years prior to the population census survey date;

– the database linking the municipality of the main residences of the owners of secondary residences (the municipality of the secondary residences also being known)[7].

1.4.2.1. The influence of residential flows from metropolises

If all territories are potentially producers and receivers of residential flows, we can note that, whatever the flow in question (commuters, retirees or secondary residents), the large and medium-sized French cities are the main producers and receivers of these flows. A size effect partly explains these results, but not exclusively. As such, it is metropolises in France that produce almost all residential flows. Three quarters of the residential flows studied here are produced by only 7% of French municipalities, all of which belong to metropolises (and not to their periurban rings or to rural areas).

In order to take into account the different types of metropolises – the largest ones, as well as those that are more average-sized in terms of the number of jobs or inhabitants – we have selected 130 urban clusters. The analysis is therefore based on 130 PRSs defined by the residential flows of metropolises and all the municipalities

---

7 These three types of flows do not cover the whole of the residential economy, since only second homes (for tourism) are taken into consideration. These flows are nonetheless representative of the main tourist exchanges between the territories. We obtain a correlation coefficient of 0.7 between the number of hotel rooms per municipality and the number of second homes, and a correlation coefficient of 0.5 between the number of camping sites and the number of second homes (calculated according to INSEE).

of France potentially receiving them. Each PRS is named after the metropolis that defines it. The 130 metropolises selected account for half (52%) of the French population and cover 5% of the national area. In addition, these urban areas represent more than two-thirds of the salaried jobs in the INSEE's productive sphere. Lastly, eight out of 10 executive jobs are located in these areas. These "productive" cores are also structurally less "residential" than the rest of the country, since they are home to only 52% of the working population and 62% of employment, 36% of the flow of retirees and barely 17% of secondary residences.

In order to think in terms of revenue, these flows of people have been converted into monetary flows and supplies[8]. The calculations showed that commuting is behind the 70 billion euros in circulation per year, which mainly benefits the periurban rings. These monetary flows represent the equivalent of 17% of the income of households in metropolises, received by households working in these centers but living outside of them. These mechanisms therefore largely explain the findings of the previous section. Urban sprawl has generated a massive shift in household income in favor of cities' suburbs. Mobility between home and work is therefore the source of more than 70 billion dollars of wealth flows between territories, independent of any public mechanism or any other form of economic activity.

In less than five years, it has also been calculated that more than 400,000 retirees have left one of these 130 metropolises (i.e. 7% of retirees), including nearly 150,000 in the case of Paris (i.e. more than 10% of its retirees). Income flows of 6 billion, or a loss of 1.4% of the income of the sending metropolises (a loss of 2 billion for Paris, 1.3% of household income). The method of calculation underestimates the amount of these flows, insofar as we are working on the migration of retirees over the last five years alone, and not on a stock of retirees actually "lost" or "gained" over a longer period. The monetary masses would then be much larger.

Finally, nearly 1.3 million households in the 130 metropolises have a second home outside it, that is, 9% of households. For Paris, this rate reaches 12% of households. These secondary residences generate annual monetary flows of 25 billion euros each year, which benefits the municipalities receiving the PRSs. Note that 25 billion euros represents a loss equivalent to 6% of the income of households in metropolises. In the case of Paris, this amounts to 11 billion euros spent outside the territory each year, or 6.5% of household income. Naturally, the income flows generated by tourism are much greater.

---

8 All the details of the approach are available in the book dedicated to productive residential systems (Davezies and Talandier 2014).

Together, on the scale of the 130 PRSs studied, these three flows topped more than 100 billion euros in 2008. This sum is equivalent to more than a quarter of the household income in the metropolises studied. This wealth circulates and reshapes territorial inequalities, benefitting the suburbs and even rural areas. These results could lead us to believe that a form of vampirization of productive spaces by residential spaces was at work. However, we shall see that by better understanding the PRSs, we can see several types of relationships emerge between cities and their "hinterland", as well as particularly interesting logics of reciprocity.

1.4.2.2. *Four types of PRSs*

To do this, we will use two indicators:

– A measure of intensity (or relative weight of the flows produced or received). The aim is to study what these flows represent in the sending and receiving of local economies.

– A range measurement (or average distance weighted by the flows). This involves calculating the average distance of production and reception of flows to better understand the relations with the hinterlands of each center[9].

Several results are highlighted and reveal the diversity of the PRSs, first of all according to the type of flow considered and the variable observed (intensity or scope). Finally, four main families of PRSs stand out:

– Extensive and intense PRSs: Paris is characterized by large residential flows to the rest of France.

– Extensive but *not* very intense PRSs (such as Lille and Strasbourg): these generate, for example, residential flows that benefit the rest of France but that are not very intense.

– Compact PRSs (including Rennes, Nantes and Montpellier): these generate significant flows of income that primarily benefit the surrounding territories, that is, the hinterland of these centers. The circulation of wealth is local.

– Short-range and low intensity PRSs: these are metropolises located in rural departments (such as Mende and Albi). Here, residential flows benefit nearby areas even if they have relatively low intensity.

It is evident that there is a capacity for redistribution vis-à-vis metropolises to the rest of the territories. This capacity varies according to the context: some large urban

---

9 The hinterlands were defined as all the municipalities located less than one hour from the city center of the urban area.

areas generate significant residential flows, and others less so. The distance is also a determining factor in identifying the geographical scales of these redistributions.

1.4.3. *PRSs and territorial development*

This work has allowed us to examine the impact of these PRS types on the socioeconomic development of the territories, leading us to ask: would certain configurations be more favorable than others for the metropolises and their hinterlands? To this end, three main findings emerged from the calculations.

First, we have shown that there is a positive and significant correlation between local urban dynamics and the intensity and compactness of the flows studied. More specifically, changes in population, net migration, employment or even in inhabitants' income are positively correlated with the small scope and high intensity of the PRSs. This is the case for cities in the West and the South of France (such as Nantes, Rennes, Montpellier, Bordeaux, Toulouse, etc.), as well as for smaller cities (such as Annecy) where many retirees have left the metropolis but remain in the same area. Many households own a second home, located (on average) less than 140 km away from their primary residence. The compactness of the PRS (high intensity and short range) is accompanied by real socioeconomic dynamism in the territories. The circulation of wealth that takes place via the mobility is played out "locally" and allows for a redistribution of wealth to the territories "around" it, along with an overall increase in the territory's income. We observe less monetary evasion for the entire system.

The second point concerns the territorial reciprocity that links the metropolises to their hinterlands. Indeed, in the PRSs and compact systems – that is, in spaces where we have observed a significant circulation of residential income within a limited radius – the hinterlands have their own development driving force. In these compact and intense PRSs, cities send massive and more significant income flows to their hinterland. However, the primary source of income for the hinterlands does not come from this local redistribution, but from external flows that these suburban areas attract because of their amenities (including, but not limited to, their residential ones). For example, in the areas surrounding Rennes, Nantes and Toulouse, the countryside benefits from significant flows of wealth coming from these cities, however, these flows do not constitute their primary source of external income. These hinterlands benefit (thanks to their own assets) from residential income from all over the national territory and beyond from tourists or international retirees, and are also equipped with a local productive system. Thus, we are witnessing a form of "happy marriage" between two factors, each contributing in their own way to the development and well-being of the whole.

On the other hand, these processes are not at work in other territories. In the hinterlands around the Paris region, or even around Strasbourg or Lille, the flows of residential income that the large metropolises send to the surrounding countryside are weak, but, unlike the previous case, they constitute their main source of external residential income. They are penalized for their lack of amenities. They are less attractive vis-à-vis the urban dwellers of the region and more generally vis-à-vis the "rest of the world". Wealth circulation systems are functionally much weaker and less structured than those measured in compact and intense PRSs.

Finally, the third point relates to the common destiny shared by both metropolises and their hinterlands. More specifically, we have observed variations in population, net migration, employment in metropolises, urban areas, as well as in their hinterlands. The analysis of the respective dynamics of these intertwined spaces did not show any divisions or fractures between the centers and the suburbs. All is not well, however, since we observe territories that are dropping out, but this is then as true for the "urban" or central part of these vast PRSs as for the suburban areas. Conversely, at least when one of these develops or displays signs of "good territorial health", another tends to also be doing well. Is territorial reciprocity within these large areas of attractiveness then the result of constructed local strategies or the sole fact of assets or attributes more favorable at the start? Other work, carried out with local authorities (Talandier and Tallec 2020), leads us to think that the activation of these interterritorialities (Vanier 2010) by local actors, sometimes supported by national policies, is essential to guarantee a form cohesion between cities and their hinterland. Our experience of working with local authorities leads us to note that if a local construction of these reciprocal links is possible, it nevertheless remains and in many territories it should at least be deepened. In contrast, we have also observed that in territories largely with productive, residential and tourism assets, the lack of coordination between local intermunicipalities could result in real socioeconomic difficulties for the whole territory. Additional work on this more political dimension of the dynamics of co-development of cities and hinterlands remains necessary, particularly with regard to the embryonic actions that are emerging in this direction (reciprocity contracts, metropolitan pacts, territorialized food projects, etc.).

1.5. Conclusion

The issue of territorial inequalities is at the heart of urban planning and cohesion policies. Their development depends both on macro socioeconomic dynamics, policies implemented at different levels of governance (from the municipality to Europe), but also, as we have seen, on individual residential strategies. The interactions between these three factors are many and varied, both in terms of time and space. The study of territorial inequalities is plural and requires an exchange of perspectives and interaction between different scales of analysis.

In this chapter, we wanted to trace both the major socioeconomic developments that have strongly influenced the relationship of people to space and led to profound changes in terms of spatial inequalities. Over the past 30 years, these dynamics have played out in terms of metropolization. The concentration of part of the wealth, particularly productive, in the world's major cities has had contrasting effects on non-metropolitan areas. Public redistribution, but also private, through household mobility, has afforded many so-called "suburban" areas sustained per capita income growth. Thus, the outer suburbs (not including Île-de-France) at present have the highest incomes per inhabitant. Rural areas have experienced, along with Paris, the greatest increases in income per capita.

On the other hand, the city centers (including in medium-sized cities) are experiencing a relative decline compared to other spaces. In addition, the gap between Paris and its suburbs has been widening, especially over the past 10 years. Within these spatial categories, the situation is obviously not homogeneous and multiple counterexamples illustrate the possibility of deviating from or contradicting the model entirely. However, it is interesting that the representations of the territorial divide, namely hyper-bourgeoisized city centers surrounded by impoverished suburban areas, are far from being a dominant model. In fact, it would appear that the French urban system embodies the opposite. More specifically, our work shows that it is in terms of complementarity and reciprocity that city-countryside relations are played out. The productive competitiveness of metropolises is not enough to ensure sustained and harmonious socioeconomic development. The model of metropolises which gain by the cumulative effect of growth and development, dragging down peripheral territories under perfusion, is outdated. Metropolitan construction requires taking into account the territorial reciprocity of flows. This requires diversification of local economies, work on anchoring activities, but also support for inter-territorial policies. Territories that manage to offer local productive, residential, recreational and tourist functions maximize the circulation of local wealth and minimize the risk of spatial fractures between the center and the suburbs. In these territories, you can live, train, work and have fun, but you can also spend your holidays and retirement there. In this sense, medium-sized cities have not had their last word. They offer a possible reconnection of the productive-residential logics that metropolization had caused to dissociate. The compactness of territorial systems would be a source of socioeconomic dynamism, but also perhaps of levers of change to initiate a socially and spatially united ecological transition.

1.6. Appendices

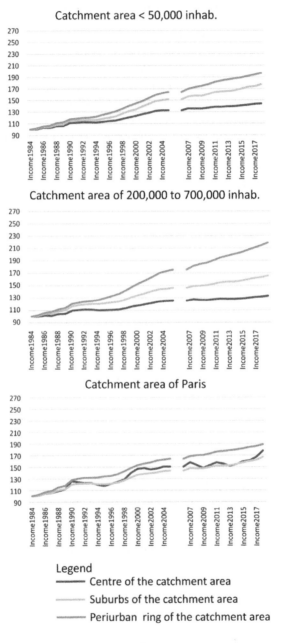

a)

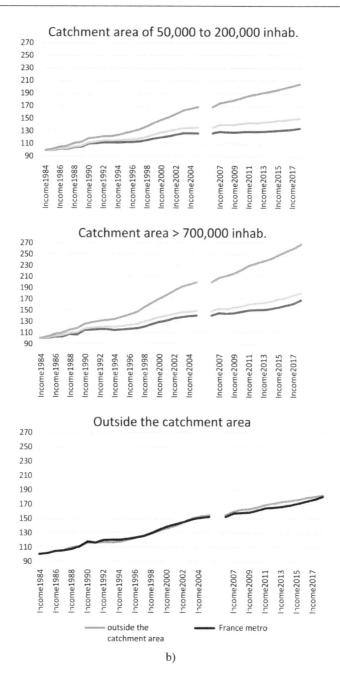

Figure 1.9. *Change in tax-reported household income since 1984 by type of territory (source: author's calculations and graph)*

34 Territorial Inequalities

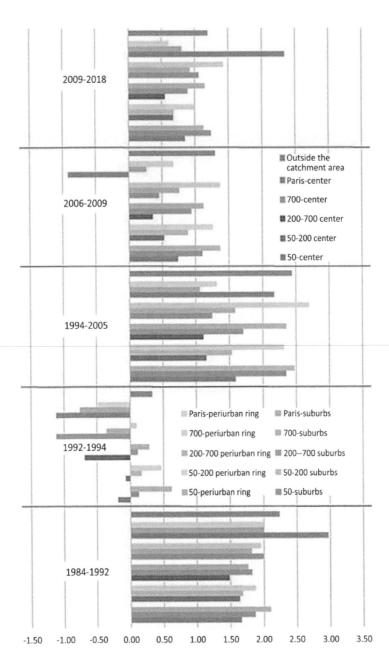

Figure 1.10. *Annual change in per capita income by time period and type of space (source: author's calculations and graph)*

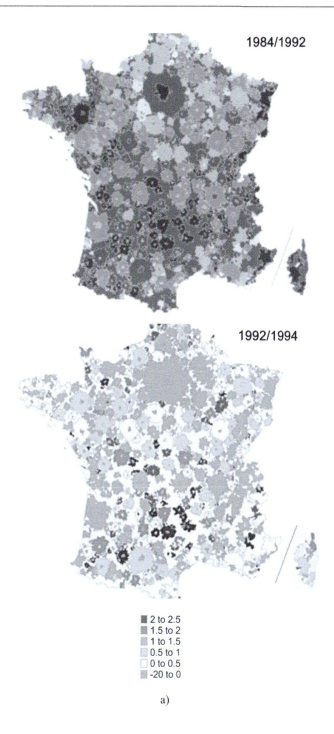

a)

36 Territorial Inequalities

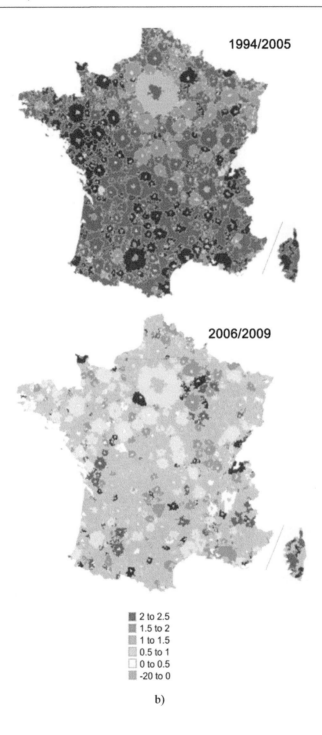

b)

Metropolization and Territorial Inequalities 37

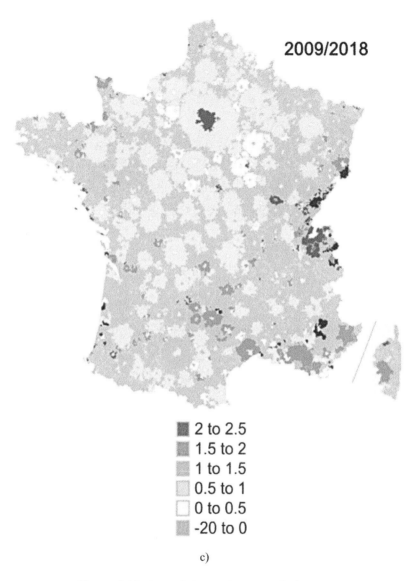

Figure 1.11. *Annual change in per capita income in % since 1984 (source: author's calculations and map)*

38   Territorial Inequalities

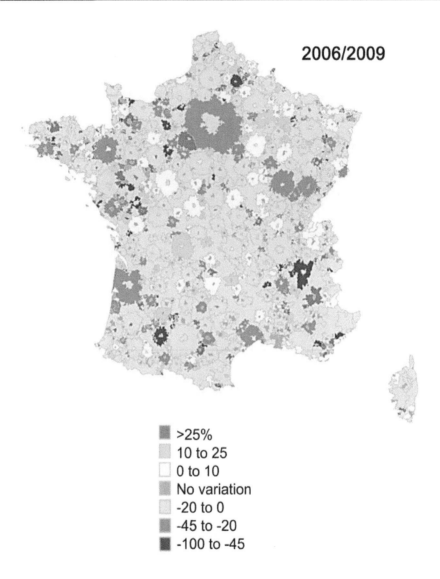

Figure 1.12. *Development of the coefficient of variation during the 2008 global financial crisis (source: author's calculations and map)*

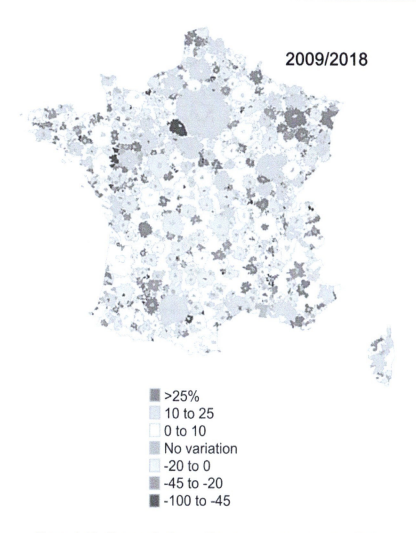

Figure 1.13. *Changes in the coefficient of variation since the 2009 economic recovery (source: author's calculations and map), 2009/2018*

1.7. References

Ascher, F. (1995). *Métapolis : ou l'avenir des villes*. Odile Jacob, Paris.

Ascher, F. (2001). *Les nouveaux principes de l'urbanisme. La fin des villes n'est pas à l'ordre du jour*. Éditions de l'Aube, La Tour d'Aigues.

Blumenfeld, H. (1955). The economic base of the metropolis: Critical remarks on the "basic-nonbasic" concept. *Journal of the American Institute of Planners*, 21(4), 114–132.

Carlier, E., Dawance, J., Barthe-Batsalle, H., Bellayachi, A., Harou, R., Neri, P., Servais, M. (2006). L'économie résidentielle en Wallonie. In *Travaux de recherches de la Conférence Permanente du Développement Territorial. Étude IV : L'économie résidentielle*. Brussels.

Davezies, L. (2004). Temps de la production et temps de la consommation : les nouveaux aménageurs des territoires ? *Futuribles*, 295, 43–56.

Davezies, L. (2008). *La République et ses territoires. La circulation invisible des richesses*. Le Seuil, Paris.

Davezies, L. and Talandier, M. (2014). *L'émergence des systèmes productivo-résidentiels. Territoires productifs-territoires résidentiels : quelles interactions ?* La Documentation française, Paris.

De Keersmaecker, M.L., Bailly, N., Barthe-Batsalle, H., Bellayachi, A., Carlier, E., Neri, P., Rousseaux, V. (2007). Economie résidentielle et compétitivité des territoires. *Territoire(s) wallon(s)*, 21–34, Special edition.

Favareto, A. and Abramovay, R. (2009). Surpreendente desempenho do Brasil rural nos anos 1990. Work document/Programa Dinámicas Territoriales Rurales. *RIMISP-Centro Latinoamericano para el Desarrollo Rural*, 32, 71 [Online]. Available at: https://www.rimisp.org/wp-content/files_mf/1366376963N32_2009_FavaretoAbramovay_SurpreendentedesempenhoBrasilrural90s.pdf.

Florida, R. (2002). The economic geography of talent. *Annals of the Association of American Geographers*, 92(4), 743–755.

Florida, R. (2014). *The Rise of the Creative Class*. Basic Books, New York.

Gabe, T.M. and Abel, J.R. (2016). Shared knowledge and the coagglomeration of occupations. *Regional Studies*, 50(8), 1360–1373.

Greenhut, M.L. (1959). An empirical model and a survey: New plant locations in Florida. *The Review of Economics and Statistics*, 41(4), 433–438.

Guilluy, C. (2014). *La France périphérique. Comment on a sacrifié les classes populaires*. Flammarion, Paris.

Guimarães, M.H., Sousa, C., Dentinho, T., Boski, T. (2014). Economic base model for the Guadiana estuary, Portugal an application for Integrated Coastal Zone Management. *Marine Policy*, 43, 63–70.

Kilkenny, M. and Partridge, M.D. (2009). Export sectors and rural development. *American Journal of Agricultural Economics*, 91(4), 910–929.

Krikelas, A.C. (1992). Why regions grow: A review of research on the economic base model. *Economic Review*, Federal Reserve Bank of Atlanta, July, 16–29.

Krugman, P. (1991). Increasing returns and economic geography. *Journal of Political Economy*, 99(3), 483–499.

Krumme, G. (1968). Werner Sombart and the economic base concept. *Land Economics*, 44(1), 112–116.

Levine, M.V. (2004). La classe créative et la prospérité urbaine : mythes et réalité. In *Conférence INRS-Urbanisation, Culture et Société*, Montreal.

Lévy, J. (2013). *Réinventer la France. Trente cartes pour une nouvelle géographie*. Fayard, Paris.

Malanga, S. (2004). The curse of the creative class. *City Journal*, 14(1), 36–45.

Nesse, K. (2014). Expanding the economic base model to include nonwage income. *Journal of Regional Analysis and Policy*, 44, 93–108.

North, D.C. (1955). Location theory and regional economic growth. *Journal of Political Economy*, 63(3), 243–258.

Orfeuil, J.P., Ripoll, F., Hancock, C. (2015). *Accès et mobilités : les nouvelles inégalités*. Infolio, Paris.

Polzin, P.E. (2001). Why some states grow faster than others: New growth models for state economic policy. *Growth and Change*, 32(3), 413–425.

Richardson, H.W. (1985). Input-output and economic base multipliers: Looking backward and forward. *Journal of Regional Science*, 25(4), 607–661.

Ruault, J.F. (2018). Beyond tourism-based economic development: City-regions and transient custom. *Regional Studies*, 52(8), 1122–1133.

Rutland, T. and O'Hagan, S. (2007). The growing localness of the Canadian city, or, on the continued (ir)relevance of economic base theory. *Local Economy*, 22(2), 163–185.

Scott, A.J. (2008). Human capital resources and requirements across the metropolitan hierarchy of the USA. *Journal of Economic Geography*, 9(2), 207–226.

Segessemann, A. and Crevoisier, O. (2013). L'économie résidentielle en Suisse : une approche par les emplois. *Revue d'économie regionale urbaine*, 4, 705–735.

Segessemann, A. and Crevoisier, O. (2016). Beyond economic base theory: The role of the residential economy in attracting income to Swiss regions. *Regional Studies*, 50(8), 1388–1403.

Sombart, W. (1916). *Der moderne Kapitalismus. Historisch-systematische Darstellung des gesamteuropäischen Wirtschaftslebens von seinen Anfängen bis zur Gegenwart*. Duncker & Humblot, Berlin.

Talandier, M. (2007). Un nouveau modèle de développement hors métropolisation. Le cas du monde rural français. PhD Thesis, Université Paris XII Val de Marne.

Talandier, M. (2013). Redefining the in-place economy and women's role in the local economy of highland areas. *Journal of Alpine Research*, 101(1) [Online]. Available at: https://journals.openedition.org/rga/2033.

Talandier, M. (2016). Mutations des systèmes territoriaux. Vers un modèle résidential-oproductif. Thesis, Université Grenoble Alpes.

Talandier, M. and Davezies, L. (2009). *Repenser le développement territorial ?* Éditions PUCA, Paris.

Tiebout, C.M. (1956). Exports and regional economic growth. *Journal of Political Economy*, 64(2), 160–164.

Vollet, D., Aubert, F., Frère, Q., Lépicier, D., Truchet, S. (2018). The importance of integrating supply-side factors in economic base models. *Growth and Change*, 49(1), 203–222.

2

Inequalities in Territorial Development: Enigmas and Threats

Laurent DAVEZIES
CNAM, Paris, France

2.1. Introduction

We do not understand anything anymore! While in France, the people of the "peripheral" territories occupy the traffic circles to protest against the "abandonment" of the state, the "bankruptcy of solidarity" and "fiscal injustice". At the same time, large and rich regions of neighboring countries, such as Flanders, the Basque Country, Catalonia or "Padania", are protesting on the contrary to free themselves from the burden of national solidarity with their poor counterparts.

On one side, we observe violent demonstrations in the name of "abandoned" territories; on the other, movements for the self-determination of the rich regions. The main cause of these paradoxes is in fact a widespread confusion about these territorial issues, both conceptually and statistically. We hear both, and from a reliable source, that territorial inequalities are increasing and decreasing, that national public budgets are redistributing "backwards" from poor regions to rich regions, or "forwards" from rich to poor. Poverty would be reduced when income inequality and increases vice versa.

Some of the metropolises are a veritable rapture of the country's economic activity, while others are, on the contrary, a sort of "golden goose" for their regional and national environment. Rural areas are said to be abandoned and forgotten on the road to development, even though they have experienced an economic, social and even demographic revival over the past 20 years.

More generally, the issue of decentralization and the organization of states with several territorial levels of democratic administration is not the subject of any common doctrine in Europe (or elsewhere). We have no common model, stable and combining territorial autonomy and solidarity, to offer to countries in which inter-territorial conflicts are not limited to a few blows of the stick between Flemings and Walloons, but can degenerate into murderous conflicts, as we have seen, close to home, in ex-Yugoslavia and in many other places in the world. The new nationalism that is emerging today, particularly in the rich regions, and which leads to the fragmentation of nations, is for some part of the continuity of legitimate struggles for the fundamental rights of self-determination, and for others part of a calamitous movement of the rise of territorial egoism and the rejection of inter-territorial solidarities put in place by the national progressivism of the past decades.

These are all questions around and based on territorial inequalities which the territories present to us today. To try to shed light on them, we will begin by looking at the dynamics of development inequalities (see section 2.2), then the mechanisms of territorial cohesion at work (see section 2.3), and finally the current risks of a reappraisal of these cohesion systems (see section 2.4)[1].

2.2. The evolution of development inequalities

The concern for territorial development is a recent phenomenon. According to the lexicometric software Ngram Viewer, the term has experienced a sudden and sharp increase in its online presence across all French publications since 1980. Prior to this, the term "local development" emerged in the 1970s in the English literature.

Indeed, it is since the wave of decentralization of the 1980s, in France as in most industrial countries, that the responsibility for regional and local development has been entrusted to regional and local authorities. However, there is still no set standard definition for the term "territorial development" and local or regional development mean different things to different people.

---

1 This text provides an overview of the matter for educational purposes and is mainly based on various publications of the author.

2.2.1. *How should local or regional development be defined?*

For some, territorial development is measured by the capacity of the territories to generate wealth (added value of companies) and so gross domestic product (GDP) per inhabitant or per job is used to measure this. For others, territorial development concerns the social health of the population, measured primarily by the income of the inhabitants and more broadly by human development indicators (HDI). Thus, two major concepts, productive development and human development, coexist in the minds of territorial experts and territorial actors.

2.2.1.1. *Territorial productive development*

The proponents of a productive definition of development – that is, most economists and international institutions – have until only recently held the view (and many of them continue to) that there is no need to choose between GDP and income or human development because the former determines the latter: naturally, there can be no income and no public services without GDP.

Before today, it was this GDP approach that dominated in institutions and the literature. But the use of HDI – thanks to authors such as Amartya Sen, or, in France, Jean Gadrey or Florence Janny-Catrice – has made strong progress over the last 10 years. The Organization for Economic Cooperation and Development (OECD), for example, has recently set up a center for monitoring the HDI of the territories of its member countries.

The European Commission has done much to establish regional GDP as the master indicator of human development, which is its main eligibility criterion for regional aid. However, nowhere in its political and administrative documentation does it provide a formal definition of what it means by "development". Rather, this is implicit: in many reports (such as periodic reports on the regions and reports on cohesion), regional development is discussed in terms of GDP per capita and then, on the basis of this data alone, make income assessments on the territories (rich or poor) and consequently, on their development.

In short, there is some confusion between GDP and income, which is evident at the European Commission and in the work of many economists. Since, at the national level, there is neither household income nor human development without wealth creation, GDP is rightly viewed as a key factor in national development and therefore in regional development as well.

But what is true for nations is unfortunately not so for sub-national, regional and even more local spaces. At the national level, GDP feeds the entirety of household income. This is far from being the case in sub-national territories. Firstly, the geography of added value is different from the geography of labor income because of (i) commuters, who work in one territory yet live in another (e.g. 8% of the wage bill in the Île-de-France region is paid to workers who work there but live elsewhere); (ii) capital income, which is largely paid to natural or legal persons who live far from the place of production, in France or abroad (e.g. via English pension funds); (iii) the mountain of compulsory taxes on wealth creation, both fiscal and social, which results in a geography of public and social spending which is completely different from that of taxes and wealth creation. The last point includes the salaries of 4 million public employees, the pensions of 16 million retirees and multiple social benefits (health, family, minimum income, etc.). In total, all of these public and social expenditures have amounted to about 57% of French GDP (before experiencing a considerable increase as a result of the Covid-19 pandemic).

The geography of income (an indicator for assessing human development) is different from that of wealth creation. For example, today, the Île-de-France region generates 31% of national GDP but its households have only 22% of the gross disposable income (GDI) of the country's households. This nine-point difference should not be overlooked. To varying degrees, the same kind of gap can be found in a large number of European regions. On the one hand, this is case with regions that have a higher (national) GDP per capita index than GDI, as in the London region (with respective indices of 176 and 137 in 2017), Lombardy (133 and 123), the Community of Madrid (136 and 126), the Stockholm region (136 and 112) and the Stuttgart region (135 and 117). But there are also, conversely, regions with a low GDP per capita index that have a higher income index, such as Languedoc-Roussillon (73 and 89), Wales (72 and 82), Sicily (61 and 72) or the German region of Mecklenburg-Vorpommern (69 and 85) (Talandier 2009).

A true model of cohesion is thus emerging specific to developed countries. We may call it a "Western model of territorial cohesion". This model (although it is also found in countries such as Japan and Korea) is found everywhere in Europe and the United States, as well as in Canada and Australia: the share of the wealth that these countries generate (GDP), which returns in the form of income to households in the regions, decreases throughout these countries. The graph in Figure 2.1 shows what appears to be a common pattern in industrialized countries, which is not (as of yet) found in industrializing countries, such as China, India or Brazil (Davezies 2015).

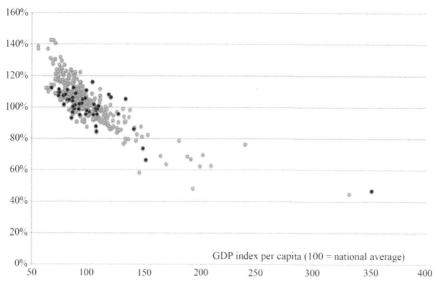

Figure 2.1. *The homogeneity of interregional mechanisms of economic solidarity in Europe and the United States in 2011 (264 regions from 21 European countries and 51 US states) (source: Davezies 2015). For a color version of this figure, see http:// www.iste.co.uk/talandier/territorial.zip*

Despite all of this evidence (Wishlade et al. 1998), GDP remains the master indicator vis-à-vis regional development[2]. We may wonder whether or not there are ideological reasons for this: GDP is more compatible with a Protestant austerity and work ethic, whereas income is more in line with spending and enjoyment. Is GDP preferred because it embodies the fruits of labor?

2.2.1.2. *Human development*

On the other hand, HDIs were first used in poorer countries, notably by the United Nations' (UN) agencies. In these countries, monetized measures do not accurately address the crucial human development problems at stake: access to food,

---

2 In spite of the great uncertainty in the conventions adopted for its calculation, particularly with regard to the regionalization of the added value of multi-territorial enterprises, the inclusion of real and fictitious rents, the treatment of inter-mediation banking activities as if they produced value added as if they produced value added, the regionalization of the value added of the public sector (which sells nothing), etc.

education and drinking water, etc. HDIs are now increasingly being utilized in industrialized countries.

The works of Jean Gadrey and Florence Jany-Catrice have shown in a striking way the mismatch of the two approaches to economic development (Gadrey 2005), that is, from the perspectives of GDP or HDI, respectively. Their "social health indicator" (SHI) is constructed from a dozen indicators (unemployment, wage inequality, work accidents, poverty, housing, etc.). In their ranking of regions, the two authors show that the Limousin region ranks first nationally in SHI and 18th in GDP per capita. The Île-de-France region is first for GDP per capita and 15th for the SHI.

Could the Limousin development model be the "right model" of regional development (and it is striking to note that, until the last few years, the voters of this region have given in less than elsewhere to the temptation of voting, protesting, for the lepéniste party)? If this is the case, then the model should be generalized to the other regions. But if all the regions in France adopted this model and had the same GDP per capita as Limousin, then France would instantly and suddenly fall into a recession with a 20% drop in GDP. Ultimately, this would massively set back the territories in terms of development, including Limousin!

Here, we can clearly see the difference between national and local development issues. This is one of the major blind spots in the principle of decentralization: contrary to what decentralization postulates, the sum of local or regional interests does not equate to the national interest. Regional or local development has been decentralized, it is in the hands of elected territorial actors whose mandate it is to prioritize the local and regional interest. But, as we have seen, what is "good" for local or regional constituents may be untenable if it were generalized to the national level.

As such, we once again fall back into the generalized bias that pollutes many territorial analyses and consists of viewing each territory as a small autonomous nation (Béhar 2004)[3]. On the side of human development and particularly regional and local household income, it is clear that most of it derives from inter-territorial monetary circulation mechanisms. It is the capacity to capture income from the outside, even more than to generate it through productive activity, that it makes for the human development of the territories (and which explains the flattering position of Limousin in terms of the SHI).

---

3 Besides, many local and regional actors already behave as if their territory was indeed a small nation!

It is therefore necessary, contrary to a macro-economic approach of the nations, to make a formal distinction between the territorial processes of growth (of GDP) and development (of income and other social indicators)[4]. Yet, this is generally not done.

The new economic geography, which dominates the current intellectual landscape (with authors such as Paul Krugman), rather exacerbates this confusion. Indeed, it is presented as "the" theory of territorial development when in fact it is a theory of growth which integrates the territorial factor (which is already remarkable). It forgets or ignores the monetary circulation linked to non-market mechanisms which, however, is the source of most of the income of the territories (there is not a single French region – and probably European – in which wages private sector have an amount greater than the sum of retirement pensions and public salaries).

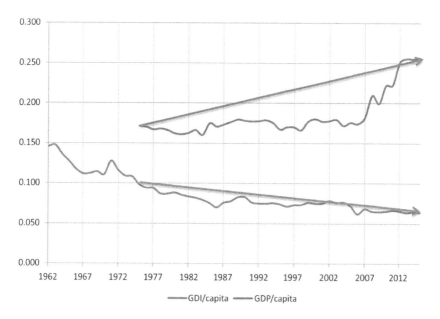

Figure 2.2. *Changes in coefficients of variation (standard deviation/mean) of gross income (GDI) per capita and GDP per capita (22 former regions), France, 1962–2015 and 1975–2015 (source: Insee). For a color version of this figure, see http://www.iste.co.uk/talandier/territorial.zip*

---

4 However, in some nations with many multinational companies, this distinction makes sense: for example, in Ireland over the past decades, where GDP grew much faster than people's incomes because of capital flight from foreign-owned companies.

This results in territories with high growth and low development as well as those with high development and no growth. It is through this lens that we must analyze territorial inequalities and their development. It is therefore meaningless to state that interregional inequalities are increasing or decreasing. We must first clarify whether we are talking about growth or development, since they are not the same thing: in France, interregional inequalities in GDP per capita are increasing at the same time as those in GDI per capita are decreasing. Indeed, this has been the case for some 40 years (see Figure 2.2).

On the eve of the Covid-19 pandemic, we were at a historical high point of productive inequalities (in GDP) and a historical low point in inter-regional income inequality! Many of the people, actors and institutions who are alarmed by the territorial divide only see the widening of inequalities in GDP per capita and not the fact that in terms of human development, we are actually in the process of repairing it.

2.2.2. *The widening of productive inequalities*

Since 1980, it is the most developed regions that have had the strongest dynamic of wealth creation: in 1980, the Île-de-France contributed 27% of national GDP. In 2017, with an unchanged population weight, it contributed 31% meaning that 4% of national GDP has shifted from the provinces to the Paris region. We note (see Figure 2.2) that the post-crisis period of 2008 led to an acceleration in the widening of these inequalities.

This concentration mechanism benefits the most developed regions and disadvantages the more peripheral regions in most industrialized countries. For example, between 2009 and 2017, the Flemish region increased from 57.6% to 58.5% of Belgian GDP and the London region (population of 9 million) increased from 21.7% to 23.6% of UK GDP, while Scotland fell from 8% to 7.5%. Lombardy rose from 21.2% to 22.1% of Italy's GDP, while Sicily fell from 5.6% to 5.1%. In Spain, Madrid and Catalonia have increased their weight, while Andalusia has slightly shrunk; in Germany, the regions of Bavaria and Stuttgart have increased their weight, while poor regions such as Mecklenburg-Vorpommern have seen their weight in German GDP decrease.

In France, the inequalities in GDP (coefficients of variation) between the French regions are sharply rising. Over 25 years (from 1990 to 2015), this coefficient has risen from 0.21 to 0.26, that is, an increase of 23%.

2.2.3. Reducing inequalities in territorial income

The issue of per capita income inequality is not without its paradoxes. Figure 2.1 shows that interregional inequalities in GDI per capita have been declining steadily since at least the 1960s. Yet this point is rarely raised in political debates on "land use planning".

But the evolution of income inequalities (i.e. incomes declared to taxes) between French territories is very different according to the geographic scale in question: on small geographic scales (i.e. among the regions, departments or urban areas of a country), these inequalities are reduced, whereas on large scales (e.g. between municipalities of the same of the same metropolis or between the districts of the same of the same municipality), they are growing. In response to the question, "are disparities in income per capita between territories increasing?", the most thorough answer would be that "it depends on the geographical scale".

Between 1999 and 2015, inequality measured by the coefficients of variation of reported income per capita decreased by 24% in the 22 regions of metropolitan France, by 13% in the 96 departments and by 7% between the 304 employment areas, but increased by 13% among the 770 urban areas.

At the local level, within large urban areas, income inequality in income per capita between municipalities is erratic: between 1999 and 2015, it increased in the metropolises of Lyon, Aix-Marseille and Lille, but decreased in Greater Paris and in the metropolises of Toulouse, Nice, Nantes, Rennes and Strasbourg.

Inequalities are increasing at certain scales and decreasing at others because the mechanisms of their formation are not the same. The smaller the territory (and so the larger the geographical scale), the more population inflows and outflows result in population changes and the more inhabitants' incomes are affected by and depend on these shifts. They are not the same inhabitants at the beginning and end of the period. The larger the geographic scale, the less this effect is present, and the more income variation is driven by economic mechanisms.

Most of the residential migration takes place through intraregional redistribution of the population with residential mobility affecting the social specialization of municipalities. The evolution in the average income of the municipalities' inhabitants will largely depend on the nature of these sociodemographic changes (ghettoization, gentrification, concentration of wealthy populations, etc.).

2.2.4. Territorial inequalities do not equate to social inequalities

It is thus perfectly possible to imagine that the social situation of all the inhabitants of a country remains unchanged and to observe, despite everything, an increase in interterritorial inequalities. The simple fact that rich people leave poor territories for richer territories and vice versa for poor people living in rich territories accentuates the social specialization of territories. In Table 2.1, a poor person leaves A for B and a rich person leaves B for A, which in year 2a increases the average income gap between A and B from 133% to 163%: an increase of 22% (albeit in the absence of change in social inequality).

Year 1		
	Territory A	Territory B
No. of rich inhabitants	5	2
No. of poor inhabitants	2	5
Total income	6,000	4,500
Average income	857	643
Difference between A and B	133%	

Year 2a		
	Territory A	Territory B
No. of rich inhabitants	6	1
No. of poor inhabitants	1	6
Total income	6,500	4,000
Average income	929	571
Difference between A and B	163%	

Year 2b		
	Territory A	Territory B
No. of rich inhabitants	6	1
No. of poor inhabitants	1	6
Total income	6,600	4,600
Average income	943	657
Difference between A and B	143%	

Table 2.1. *Example of the impact of residential mobility on interterritorial inequalities in per capita income*

Better still, we can imagine a scenario where social inequalities are reduced (year 2b), with an increase in the income of the poor from 500 to 600 euros, while that of the rich remains at 1,000 euros. The same type of residential mobility – as in the scenario for year 2a – with the cross-migration of a poor person and a rich person, will finally, here again, result in an increase in interterritorial inequality. In this example, the reduction of social inequality does not prevent the widening of inequality between rich and poor territories.

We must therefore not automatically assume from the widening of inter-municipal inequalities in per capita income that this equates to a deteriorating social situation for populations living in the poorest areas. The change in the average income of a poor municipal area may well be due to the fact that its least penalized inhabitants have left and been replaced by much poorer new arrivals (Davezies 2012). In this case, all the inhabitants are better off: those who leave as well as those who arrive. At a certain point, even the fact that the average income of a disadvantaged municipality is falling can be a positive sign, indicating that public policies have enabled certain inhabitants to improve their situation and leave the municipality.

On the other hand, the fact that the average income of a poor municipality starts to increase, reducing its inequality with other municipalities, is not necessarily good news for its poor population: it may simply mean that its population is changing as a result of gentrification. Inequalities at the local level vary somewhat erratically, with the expansion of wealthy territories "eating into" into poor municipalities (e.g. in Montreuil or Bagnolet, in the poor department of Seine-Saint-Denis, or in the poor municipalities of the rich department of Hauts-de-Seine), while elsewhere, the effects of social specialization among poor sectors play a decisive role (e.g. elsewhere in Seine-Saint-Denis, such as in Stains, La Courneuve or Blanc-Mesnil).

2.2.5. Policies for the "neighborhoods" or for the people?

In terms of the objectives and evaluation of public policies, we must distinguish between territorial inequalities and those affecting people, because the negative change of a territory (i.e. a decline in households' average income) can coincide with an improved social situation of the population that lived there at the beginning of the period (a percentage of which has since relocated elsewhere). Steering policies by the evolution of the average income of the inhabitants of the areas eligible for these policies, while their population is constantly changing, is an illusory treatment of the spatial question. As in the myth of Sisyphus, the public money poured into these neighborhoods has not helped to narrow the average income gap with the rest of the country. Nonetheless, it may have helped to reduce income inequality between households.

This transformation of the settlement of the sensitive urban zone (SUZ) is happening equally or more rapidly than in the rest of the country, with the same propensity for residential mobility than the national average, while the housing status in these neighborhoods (massively social) tends to be a hindrance to residential mobility. These neighborhoods function as gateways, not barriers (Davezies 2011).

Is urban policy a new way of throwing public money down the drain? Yes, as we have seen, if their aim is to move toward the "equality of territories". Yet, this is unlikely to be the case when their aim is to improve the situation of the most vulnerable populations: they are effective where these policies improve the situation of the inhabitants and allow them to leave these neighborhoods. We must distinguish between the SUZ (i.e. the means) and the population that lives there (i.e. the target of public policy). It is not possible to evaluate these policies using, for example, successive captured photographs of a neighborhood whose population is constantly changing. Rather, it is a matter of carrying out analyses on the follow-up of cohorts of inhabitants who are or have been concerned by the neighborhood.

In order to appreciate the positive aspects of the city's policy, this requires an understanding of the social characteristics of population flows (i.e. inflows and outflows), but these data are not available in the French statistical system. However, the data do exist (and can be easily anonymized) in the form of administrative data held by databases of social security organizations. It is striking to note that in a privatized social data management system, such as Dunn & Bradstreet in the United States, this type of data, especially when processed by cohorts, is more easily accessible to researchers than in the French public system.

For years, the government has promised to provide detailed analyzes of the routes of population cohorts passing through the territories of urban policy, without seeing any results coming from these efforts. This means that we still do not have access to the necessary detailed data (including the income level of mobile populations in particular) which would allow us to measure and compare the different neighborhoods the respective weights of the two effects which can be the origin of the rise in inter-municipal inequalities: (i) the social specialization of territories through mobility and (ii) the variation in the income of immobile populations (Reynard 1995)[5].

2.2.6. Inequality and poverty

In social and territorial analysis, it is often thought that alleviating poverty involves overcoming income inequalities. Unfortunately, here again, there is widespread confusion. It is often observed that when income inequalities increase, poverty decreases; conversely, when inequalities decrease, poverty increases. Contrary to what seems to be obvious, whoever goes hunting for poverty wastes their bullets by shooting at inequality!

---

5 An earlier study by Insee Rhône-Alpes tackled this question and showed the role of mobility in the widening of inter-municipal inequalities. It did not deal with income, but with the detailed social categories of the populations migrating within Greater Lyon.

This paradoxical phenomenon can be observed on a global scale: according to INSEE, inequalities in household living standards (income per consumption unit) mostly fell between 2007 and 2017, despite the macroeconomic turbulence of 2008 and 2011, with the Gini coefficient falling from 0.292 to 0.289. This is certainly a marginal change and is far from the notorious "explosion of inequality" that is so often invoked. At the same time, poverty (i.e. the number of people living in poverty) has increased significantly. Between 2007 and 2017, regardless of the definition of the poverty line (at 40, 50, 60 or 70% of the median income), the number of people living in poverty increased: 3.1% of the population lived on an income 40% below the median income in 2007, 3.5% in 2017. At less than 60% (the convention generally used), the number of people living in poverty has increased from 13.4% to 14.1%, and at less than 70%, the number of people living in poverty increased from 21.5% to 22.1%.

In short, inequality is decreasing, yet poverty is increasing. As we have said above, income inequality is decreasing "in spite of" crises and especially the 2008–2009 recession. But could we instead say that inequality has been reduced "thanks to" these crises?

Indeed, in general, during a recession, the potential loss in income for the "rich" is much greater than that of the "poor", who in any case have an income slightly above the poverty line. When the rich fall, it is from above, but the poor do not (although a small loss of income can affect a poor person much more severely than a larger loss for a rich person). In these periods, inequality therefore tends to decrease, while the poverty rate tends to increase since even a small drop in income can push many ordinary people into poverty. In 2007, 8% of the country's population had incomes of 60–70% of the median income, which means that there were about 5 million people living just above the poverty line (at 60%). Many of whom fell into poverty as a result a minor dip in their income following the recessions of 2008 and 2011.

In times of growth, the opposite is true: the rich have a greater capacity to get richer compared to the poor, and income inequalities increase at the same time as the poverty rate falls. For example, in the boom period of 2015–2016, the poverty rate fell slightly.

Returning to the matter of territories, we can examine this phenomenon in municipalities in the Île-de-France region. Table 2.2 shows changes in the inhabitants' declared income around the 2008 recession and the 2014–2016 recovery period for three rich areas (Saint-Cloud, 16th arrondissement of Paris and Neuilly-sur-Seine) and poor areas (Montfermeil, Clichy-sous-Bois and La Courneuve).

56   Territorial Inequalities

Constant euros (millions) in 2015	2005	2006	2007	2008	2009	2010	2007-2009, recession	2014	2015	2016	2014-2016, growth
St-Cloud	787	992	1,085	1,016	967	1,033	-11%	994	1,028	1,195	20%
Paris, 16th arrondissement	6,637	8,288	8,658	7,904	7,405	7,980	-14%	7,676	8,042	8,119	6%
Neuilly-sur-Seine	2,672	3,278	3,605	3,316	3,064	3,290	-15%	3,160	3,325	3,386	7%
Montfermeil	231	291	294	292	293	305	0%	301	301	308	2%
Clichy-sous-Bois	171	214	213	209	209	211	-2%	214	213	209	-3%
La Courneuve	236	299	303	301	305	309	1%	326	330	333	2%
3 rich municipalities	10,095	12,558	13,348	12,236	11,436	12,303	-14%	11,830	12,395	12,700	7%
3 poor municipalities	638	804	810	802	807	825	0%	841	844	850	1%
Euros par habitants											
St-Cloud	26,338	33,196	36,325	34,008	32,359	34,572	-11%	32,514	33,618	39,064	20%
Paris, 16th arrondissement	38,782	48,435	50,594	46,188	43,274	46,634	-14%	45,540	47,712	48,170	6%
Neuilly-sur-Seine	43,271	53,090	58,374	53,699	49,615	53,282	-15%	51,557	54,241	55,244	7%
Montfermeil	9,136	11,522	11,644	11,554	11,599	12,082	0%	11,209	11,199	11,466	2%
Clichy-sous-Bois	5,740	7,177	7,171	7,021	7,020	7,108	-2%	7,277	7,229	7,094	-3%
La Courneuve	6,222	7,873	7,961	7,930	8,029	8,118	1%	7,539	7,646	7,706	2%
Rich	38,422	47,796	50,800	46,568	43,523	46,825	-14%	45,426	47,594	48,765	7%
Poor	6,860	8,642	8,709	8,624	8,676	8,871	-0.4%	8,453	8,483	8,541	1%
Income/capita Rich/poor	5.6	5.5	5.8	5.4	5.0	5.3		5.4	5.6	5.7	

Table 2.2. *Changes in income inequality in rich and poor municipalities. Selected municipalities: years of crisis (2007–2009) and recovery (2014–2016)*

During the 2008–2009 recession, the impact on the income of the poor municipalities was much greater than on that of the rich ones: overall, in constant euros, −14% for the former and −0.4% for the latter, all for a practically unchanged population over such a short period. In short, inequality fell considerably during the crisis: between 2007 and 2009, the average per capita income of the three wealthy territories fell from 5.8 times to 5 times that of the three poor territories. But at the same time, the (slight) decline in per capita income in poor municipalities necessarily led to an increase in the number of inhabitants living below the poverty line.

In a period of great turbulence, alternating phases of growth and recession, we are thus witnessing a cross-play of inverse variations in inequality and poverty.

2.2.7. *A reduction in territorial inequalities in terms of income*

A major paradox, often mentioned but rarely understood, is that while inequality in terms of GDP per capita has been rising, interregional inequality in terms of GDI per capita has been steadily declining since the 1980s (and even since the 1960s).

Figure 2.2 shows the changes in inequality (coefficients of variation) in GDP and GDI per capita between French regions over this period.

While the enormous restructuring of our productive system has redistributed the cards of comparative territorial advantages, as we have seen above, to the benefit of the richest territories this productive territorial divide has not been accompanied by a territorial divide in household income, despite which is so often deplored.

While we hear everywhere, especially in recent months, a long complaint from "abandoned" territories, about a territorial divide suffered by households in peripheral territories, we are surprised to note that the interregional disparities in total disposable income (gross domestic income) or declared income per inhabitant, but also the interdepartmental disparities in declared income, have on the contrary been gradually reduced and for a long time.

Between 1990 and 2015, as noted above, inequality in terms of GDP per capita increased by 23%, and inequality in terms of disposable income per capita decreased by 18%.

This pattern of declining income inequality (including all income after redistribution, even if not taxed) between regions can also be observed vis-à-vis inequality in declared household income (GDI, gross domestic income) between the 22 former regions, the 96 departments and the 348 employment areas (see Table 2.3).

22 regions	1999	2006	2011	2015
Standard deviation	1,175	1,331	1,355	1,334
Average	9,362	13,043	13,888	14,039
Var coef.	0.126	0.1021	0.0975	0.095
Var. in coef. Var		-19%	-4%	-3%

96 departments	1999	2006	2011	2015
Standard deviation	1,664	2,042	2,169	2,170
Average	9,461	13,134	13,976	14,135
Var coef.	0.176	0.1555	0.1552	0.154
Var. in coef. Var		-12%	0%	-1%

348 EA	1999	2006	2011	2015
Standard deviation	1,432	1,755	1,972	2,017
Average	9,157	12,789	13,654	13,828
Var coef.	0.156	0.137	0.144	0.146
Var. in coef. Var		-12%	5%	1%

Table 2.3. *Changes in inequality in declared income per capita between regions, departments and employment areas (EA) in constant euros for years 1999, 2006, 2011 and 2015. These are measured by coefficients of variation (standard deviation/ mean) (source: according to DGI). For a color version of this table, see: http://www. iste.co.uk/talandier/territorial.zip*

2.3. Public mechanisms for territorial cohesion

The reasons for the decline in territorial inequalities in income which more than offsets the increase in inequalities in added value are well known and are due to the fact that household incomes now depend more on public and private circulation and on the capture of income than on the creation of wealth in their territories (Davezies 2008).

With the rise of public funds for decades and with public expenditure that reached 57% of the value of GDP on the eve of the health crisis, these redistribution mechanisms have not stopped strengthening, in particular since the beginning of the 1980s, with the growing influx of resources from deficits and debt.

We will not return here to the mechanisms of private circulation of income on the territories: (i) the growing dissociation between the places of production and domiciliation of income through commuting; (ii) the residential mobility of retirees; (iii) tourism expenditure (i.e. in the territories of "uncounted residents") and the difference between the residential and "present" population (Davezies 2008).

2.3.1. *Redistribution mechanisms for public funds*

The most important – and yet, at the same time, the most ignored – cohesion mechanism (at least in France) is that linked to public levies and expenditure, and their balance in the territories. Some territories contribute more to public and social budgets than they benefit from, and others, conversely, are net beneficiaries in these games.

An important point of difference between regional GDP and regional income is due to these public transfers. Moreover, measuring them is fraught with conceptual and statistical difficulties that are certainly significant, but not insurmountable.

The issue of the impact of levies and expenditures of public budgets and social budgets is far from being clearly established by the theory.

– Which and what types of territories bear the burden of corporate taxes? Employees, consumers or owners of capital?

– Who benefits from the President's salary? Everyone? The voters?

– What is the meaning of the term "benefit of public spending"?

With Mushkin (1957), we must distinguish an approach *flow* (where the expenditure is located) from that of the *benefit* (who has benefited from the expenditure).

In short, there are several, or even many, acceptances of what redistribution can be between the territories, induced by public budgets.

2.3.2. *Interterritorial redistribution linked to social welfare budgets*

These difficulties may, perhaps, explain why there have been no studies on the interterritorial redistributive effects of public budgets. In past decades, the only attempt was in 2015 and involved solely addressing social welfare, for which the amount of expenditure equivalent to 31% of GDP, but not the 57% of total public and social spending. This study, which was conducted by the French High Council for the Financing of Social Welfare (*Haut Conseil au financement de la protection sociale 2015*), aimed to measure the impact of social welfare budgets (levies and expenditures) on income inequality between departments.

It is clear from this that the poorest departments benefit from very large transfers through social welfare. For example, in the Ardennes or Haute-Marne, social welfare spending is twice as high as social security contributions. But this is only an estimate, since the report does provide detailed data on social welfare levies and expenditures for each department. As such, it is impossible to make a precise assessment of the redistributions. Only 574 billion euros of resources have been departmentalized for 641 billion euros of expenditure.

This difference is due to the fact that a certain number of social protection resources are not localizable: 42 billion euros in financial and non-financial costs on the expenditure side and 114 billion euros in imputed social contributions, government contributions and miscellaneous income.

With such an unbalanced balance and with expenditures 12% higher than pre-tax, it becomes difficult to attribute a transfer to this accounting imbalance or to the economic reality of the gap between contribution and benefit (and we do not know where this 12% was financed!). This is all the more surprising since in all such studies conducted around the world on these issues, the primary condition for estimating transfers is to balance the budgets, by integrating "non-localizable" budget items and also deficits, when they exist, by adopting and applying conceptually robust localization conventions.

Table 2.4 compares the weight of the (former) regions in the resources and the (localized) use of social welfare. Without offering a precise measure of the redistributive effect, this table shows that Île-de-France is the main source of transfers, followed by Rhône-Alpes, while the regions that benefit the most are those with the most severe social problems: Languedoc-Roussillon, PACA and Nord-Pas-de-Calais. If we look in more detail at the scale of departments, the effects of transfers are much more powerful: we find differences comparable to those mentioned above for the Ardennes and Haute-Saône in departments such as Aisne, Creuse, Haute-Marne or Pyrénées-Orientales.

	Social protection resources in millions of euros	Social protection resources in % total metropolitan France	Social protection jobs in millions of euros	Social protection jobs in % total metropolitan France	(ii)-(i)/(i) in %
Île-de-France	168,290	29.3%	114,558	17.9%	-11.4%
Rhône-Alpes	58,621	10.2%	62,952	9.8%	-0.4%
Corsica	2,410	0.4%	3,419	0.5%	0.1%
Alsace	15,916	2.8%	18,504	2.9%	0.1%
Champagne-Ardenne	10,513	1.8%	13,064	2.0%	0.2%
Pays de la Loire	29,833	5.2%	34,710	5.4%	0.2%
Franche-Comté	8,425	1.5%	11,393	1.8%	0.3%
Haute-Normandie	14,570	2.5%	18,538	2.9%	0.4%
Limousin	4,949	0.9%	7,954	1.2%	0.4%
Basse-Normandie	10,883	1.9%	15,050	2.3%	0.5%
Auvergne	9,851	1.7%	14,092	2.2%	0.5%
Midi-Pyrénées	23,742	4.1%	29,606	4.6%	0.5%
Poitou-Charentes	13,157	2.3%	18,182	2.8%	0.5%
Burgundy	12,291	2.1%	17,406	2.7%	0.6%
Picardy	12,952	2.3%	18,760	2.9%	0.7%
Centre	19,134	3.3%	26,067	4.1%	0.7%
Brittany	24,756	4.3%	32,690	5.1%	0.8%
Aquitaine	26,262	4.6%	34,778	5.4%	0.9%
Lorraine	15,408	2.7%	23,093	3.6%	0.9%
Nord-Pas-de-Calais	29,574	5.2%	38,869	6.2%	1.0%
Provence-Alpes-Côte d'Azur	43,176	7.5%	56,185	8.8%	1.2%
Languedoc-Roussillon	19,167	3.3%	29,980	4.7%	1.3%
Metropolitan France	573,880	100.0%	640,852	100.0%	0.0%

Table 2.4. *The regionalization of resources and uses of social welfare, 2013*

2.3.3. *The redistributive effects of public budgets between regions*

To find a study on the redistributive effects of public budgets on the incomes of French regions, we have to go back to the 1990s! The study (Wishlade et al. 1998) on France (and six other large European countries) was conducted by two teams from the universities of Créteil (l'Œil) and Glasgow (EPRC) for the European Commission as part of the preparation for the first report on cohesion, which dates back to 1997. The method proposed in the 1996 EPRC-Œil report consisted of calculating all the conceptually possible scenarios for the distribution of taxes and expenditure between regions by randomly combining the different impact concepts. Using computer technology, it was possible to calculate a sample of thousands of random allocation scenarios (for the two families of approaches: "flow" and "benefits") and then to analyze the concentration. Fortunately, the latter turned out to be very strong, which showed that, whatever the definition adopted, the status of the regions (whether beneficiary or contributor) was practically the same, which made it possible to estimate the transfers by the median balance of the thousands of scenarios.

This study provided an initial estimate of the interregional transfers induced by the public budgets and social budgets of seven major European countries for 1993[6]. In 2003, during the preparation of the third "cohesion report", the European Commission commissioned a team led by Ian Begg (London School of Economics) to prepare a report on the same subject (Begg 2004). In its conclusions, it confirms that the results of the 1998 EPRC-Œil report remain relevant, but it does not update the results of the EPRC-Œil report. Instead, it only suggests (somewhat incorrectly with the term "redistribution") an analytical study of the regionalization of certain public spending[7]. It should be noted that this work has provided the Commission with proof that national budgets in Europe are powerful machines for interregional cohesion and in truth, the main ones: national interregional transfers for peripheral regions are 50 times higher than European interregional transfers.

This was not, however, the Commission's initial conviction. In preparing the first report on cohesion (in 1996), it had instead planned to show that national public budgets redistribute resources from poor to rich regions and that the Commission was the only body capable of implementing genuine cohesion policies through its regional policy. The EPRC-Œil report (and later the "Begg report") set the record straight by sounding the death knell for this thesis and the communications strategy set down in the cohesion report. It is a reminder of what had already been shown 20 years earlier by the MacDougall report (1977), which measured the sharp reduction in inequality in the 1970s as a result of national budgets in four major European countries (Germany, France, Italy and the United Kingdom), as well as in Australia, Canada and the United States.

National budgets transfer significant amounts of money from rich to poor regions in the seven European countries studied in the EPRC-Œil report. For example, the

---

6 Germany, Spain, France, Italy, Portugal, Spain, Sweden and the United Kingdom.
7 Redistribution is not the result of expenditures or taxes separately, but that of the balance between the two.

report found that the Île-de-France or the London region, respectively, had a net contribution to the income of the other regions of their country of around 10% of their GDP, Madrid by 9%, Lisbon by 2% and Lombardy by 12%[8]. Conversely, these income transfers represented a contribution of around 14% of the GDP of Andalusia, 17% of that of Sicily and almost 10% of that of Languedoc-Roussillon!

All of this means that, contrary to what the Commission (and a large number of experts, civil servants and elected representatives) thought, most of the territorial rebalancing effects implemented by public policies in Europe are the result of national policies. When the Commission implements 0.4% of European GDP in its regional policies, all the public funds of the various European countries mobilize around 50% of Europe's GDP and operate colossal transfers of income between regions, within national borders.

For the seven large European countries studied in 1993, the 29 richest regions richest regions (i.e. net contributors to national public budgets) represented 55% of the population of the seven countries, 69% of their total GDP and transferred ECU (European Currency Unit) 128 billion, or 4% of their GDP, to their less developed counterparts[9].

Thus, the reduction of inequality in regional income and the compensation of the mechanisms of geographical polarization of activities resulting from the game of the market are much more the work of national governments than of European policies. The first report on cohesion (in 1996) had to integrate these results, and in particular the fact that this mechanism makes it possible to reduce on average by nearly 30% the economic inequalities between the regions of these countries. Today, the main (and almost the only) system for creating European cohesion (i.e. for implementing redistributions) are still the national budgets of Member States.

2.3.4. *Fragmented European cohesion*

At the same time, evaluating interregional transfers has made it possible to take into account the fact that the various national cohesion systems are unequal on a European scale. The cohesion effect of existing public budgets in Europe does not

---

8 The low relative net contribution of "Lisbon and Tagus" is due to the fact that this region is large, not limited to the wealthy Lisbon urban area, and that a large part of its territory is underdeveloped.

9 The richest regions therefore transfer an average of 4% of their GDP to the poorest regions within the same country; "poor" regions for which, this time, these transfers represent an average of 8% of their GDP!

cross national borders, because the bulk of public funds is national and not European. It is a well-known mechanism: the more a system is decentralized, the less redistribution occurs between populations and areas. The European Union (EU) functions in this respect as a very decentralized space. This is one of the major differences with the United States, whose federal budget induces large implicit transfers between all of the states. There is concrete solidarity – financial and public – between Massachusetts and Alabama. There is no such solidarity between Hamburg and Naples or Dublin, except for the few thousandths of European GDP dedicated to European regional policy.

While the arithmetic average of the coefficients of variation of the 20 European countries in 2011 was 0.32 for regional GDP per capita, the same coefficient calculated for all the European regions was 0.49 (compared to 0.39 in the United States). For household income per capita, the average of the coefficients for the 20 countries was 0.13, but the coefficient for the 267 regions was 0.28 (compared with 0.17 in the United States).

We see that the mechanisms of interregional cohesion in the European countries are powerful within each of these countries, but the differences in the level of development between these countries and the absence of a significant mechanism of cohesion integrated at the European level have led to a large part of the equalizing power to be lost on a European scale. Finally, income inequalities between European regions are a little more than one and a half times lower than those of GDP, whereas they are more than twice in the United States. We have, on the one hand, a Europe with a Community budget – until recently banned from deficit – weighing around 1% of European GDP and less than 2% of European taxpayers' taxes, and, on the other hand, a federal budget weighing a quarter of the American GDP and where 66% of the taxes go to the federal budget (which practices generous deficits).

The United States has not, like Europe, inscribed the question of "cohesion" in the stone of its institutions. They have never had a regional policy or a Ministry of Cohesion and are often considered to embody the "ruthless universe" of the market. Certainly, the fact of being truly united (having a federal budget and having no brakes on mobility between states) allows them to do better than Europe in terms of cohesion, which speaks a great deal of cohesion (with a General Directorate for Cohesion), but which is based only on a segmented network of national systems of unequal and impervious territorial cohesion. There is more talk of love than there is proof of it.

2.3.5. Unequal treatment of equals

The fact that the main public mechanism for European cohesion is implemented at the national level ultimately results in a paradoxical mechanism at the European scale: regions that are equal in terms of their level of development (measured by GDP per capita) are not treated equally by their respective national budgets. Table 2.5 gives some selected examples of regions in this situation.

Regions that are relatively rich in their national context may at the same time be relatively poor regions in the context of Europe or in another country. For example, the richest regions in Spain or Portugal subsidize even poorer regions in their respective countries, whereas they would be net beneficiaries if they were in a richer country. Table 2.5 gives some examples of regions with different levels of development (GDP), but treated unequally by their national budgets.

Table 2.6, for a more recent year, does not deal with redistributive transfers (which have not been recalculated for over 30 years!), but instead with the differences between GDP and GDI mentioned above. From the point of view of the underlying mechanisms, these differences are very similar to the redistributions between regions.

	Transfer (flow) in % of regional GDP	Transfer (flow) in ECU/capita	GDP ECU/capita
Lisboa e V.T.	-2%	-190	10,207
Brandenburg	17%	1,800	10,637
Wales	8%	930	11,734
Aragon	-3%	-380	11,776
Pais Vasco	-9%	-1,080	12,347
North	9%	1,180	12,433
North West	4%	550	12,507
Catalonia	-5%	-675	12,658
West Midlands	1%	75	12,722
East Anglia	-3%	-360	14,140
Languedoc-R.	9%	1,270	14,500
Tuscany	-7%	-1,050	15,450
Brittany	3%	395	15,621
Midi-Pyrénées	3%	870	15,842

Table 2.5. *European regions equal in terms of GDP per capita are treated unequally by national budgets, selected regions, 1993 (source: EPRC-Œil 1998)*

COMMENT ON TABLE 2.5.– *The table reports on interregional income transfers implemented by public budgets and also shows the interregional income transfers implemented by national public budgets, estimated, according to the conceptual distinction proposed by Mushkin (1957), from a "flow" perspective (another calculation, which produced similar results, was carried out from a "benefit" perspective).*

We see, for example, that in 2011 at the same level of GDP per capita, Catalonia "lost" income in relation to its GDP index, while Schleswig-Holstein in Germany, gained income. In short, Europe functions as a large, highly decentralized country with a very small central government. Public finance and fiscal federalism theorists know that the more decentralized a country is, the less resources are redistributed among its populations and territories.

In his political economy textbook, Musgrave (1989) states that if allocative public policies are to be implemented as close as possible to the territories (in accordance with the principle of subsidiarity), redistribution policies (such as stabilization) should be implemented at the highest possible level of government. In essence, local redistributive policies lead to social and spatial fragmentation and the undermining of redistribution mechanisms.

This principle can be explained schematically (see Table 2.7) through the comparison of two local authorities, one rich and the other poor. In each of the two municipalities, local tax is levied on a proportional basis (rate of 10%) and local budget expenditure is distributed on an equal basis. We see that this mechanism makes it possible to redistribute income from the rich to the poor in each of the municipalities. In the poor community, individual 5, who is the richest, has a net contribution to local solidarity of 2, to the benefit of individual 1. In the rich community, individual 10, the richest, also has a net contribution of 2 to the benefit of individual 6.

Everything would be fine if individual 5 and individual 6 did not have the same level of income: the richest of the poor and the poorest of the rich! Naturally, individual 5 will relocate to the rich community. The following year, once individual 5 has left, the poor territory will be even poorer and the amount of public expenditure per capita will decrease. The social specialization of the territories and interterritorial inequalities will have increased. This kind of "vote with your feet" mechanism is largely responsible for the high social and spatial segregation in American cities. Local redistribution can be associated with injustice and increased inequality. Here, we are talking about interpersonal redistribution, since the redistributive effects of business taxes – the old business tax or the current CVAE – do not pose this kind of problem. This point must be borne in mind at a time where taxes on households are increasingly being substituted by taxes on companies.

	Region (NUTS 2)	In euros GDP euro/capita 2011	In euros GDI euro/capita 2011	GDP euro/capita 2011 (national index)	In national index GDI euro/capita (national index)	GDI/GDP ratio (national index)
Bulgaria	Yugozapaden	8,800	7,600	191	128	67%
Slovakia	Východné Slovensko	8,700	8,800	56	77	139%
Romania	Bucuresti – Ilfov	15,500	10,300	239	183	76%
Spain	Extremadura	15,700	11,100	71	77	109%
Poland	Mazowieckie	15,700	13,100	181	142	79%
Hungary	Közép-Magyarország	16,200	10,600	188	129	69%
Italy	Campania	16,000	11,200	62	70	112%
Portugal	Lisboa	22,500	15,500	136	127	94%
Germany	Thüringen	22,000	16,600	71	86	121%
Greece	Attiki	24,800	15,200	153	126	82%
Germany	Leipzig	24,600	16,500	79	85	108%
Spain	Cataluña	26,600	16,600	120	115	96%
Germany	Schleswig-Holstein	26,800	19,500	86	101	117%
Spain	Comunidad Foral de Navarra	29,100	18,700	131	129	99%
Austria	Niederösterreich	29,400	20,600	85	105	124%
Spain	Comunidad de Madrid	29,600	17,500	133	121	191%
The Netherlands	Gelderland	30,100	14,200	87	101	116%
Spain	País Vasco	30,500	19,500	137	135	98%
Germany	Rheinhessen-Pfalz	30,500	20,300	98	105	107%
Czech Republic	Praha	31,200	13,500	209	132	63%
Finland	Länsi-Suomi	31,700	14,700	88	92	104%
Slovakia	Bratislavský kraj	31,500	16,000	202	141	70%
Belgium	Prov. West-Vlaanderen	31,800	17,500	99	104	105%

Table 2.6. *European regions with high levels of GDP per capita, but different levels of income (GDI) (source: Eurostat)*

So, as difficult as it is to accept for many local "left" elected officials, we should not implement (too explicitly) redistributive local policies. This should be left essentially to the central government. Indeed, redistribution only avoids such adverse effects when the cost to the "rich" of avoiding taxes is greater than the amount of the net contribution. It is easy to move from one municipality to another, more complicated to move from one region to another and very difficult to move from one country to another.

2.3.6. The "Catalonia" effect

As we have said, Europe functions as a very decentralized system, in which the local authorities – in this case, the nation states – have strong redistributive policies. We find the same pattern as in the case of local redistributive policies mentioned above. Let us take the case, which is not extreme, of Catalonia and Midi-Pyrénées, based on data from the EPRC-Œil study. An average Catalan produced 13,000 ECU of GDP in 1993. The difference between what the region's inhabitants contribute to the Spanish budget and what they receive from it is 700 ECU per capita. The average Catalan has therefore "lost" in this budget game and has subsidized the poorest regions of Spain. At the same time, an average inhabitant of Midi-Pyrenees produces about 16,000 ECU (of GDP). But since, in France, the Midi-Pyrenees is a rather poor region, its net benefit to the state budget is approximately 900 ECU, financed by richer regions, starting with Île-de-France. At the end of the day, the average Catalan is left 1,500 ECU worse off by the end of the redistribution.

Unfortunately, more recent figures are not available to evaluate these interregional budget transfers. However, these mechanisms are still at work today. In 2017, for example, Eurostat data show that the Catalans' share of Spanish household income (18.3%) is lower than their contribution to the country's GDP (19.1%). The opposite is true for the inhabitants of the former Midi-Pyrénées (4.4% of French household income for 4.2% of GDP). The result is that while Midi-Pyrénées has a GDP per capita that is only 5% higher than that of Catalonia, its inhabitants have an income that is 13% higher than that of the Catalans. Finally, in this GDP-income game, the inhabitants of Catalonia "lose" 750 euros and those of Midi-Pyrenees "gain" 1,000 euros. Obviously, the processing of these data on GDP and income cannot replace a precise calculation of the redistributive effects of public and social budgets, but it allows us to grasp a good part of it, and in particular, its general meaning.

This mechanism, which is still found today throughout Europe (see Table 2.6), strongly contradicts the stated objectives of harmonization and cohesion. Rather, it is a mechanism of "fragmented cohesion". Treating equals unequally appears unfair.

Inequalities in Territorial Development: Enigmas and Threats 69

Year 1

Poor city A

	Pre-tax income	10% tax	Public spending (budget/S)	Pre-tax income and spending	Balance sheet
Person 1	20	2	4	22	2
Person 2	30	3	4	31	1
Person 3	40	4	4	40	0
Person 4	50	5	4	49	−1
Person 5	60	6	4	58	−2
Budget		20			

Rich city B

	Pre-tax income	10% tax	Public spending (budget/S)	Pre-tax income and spending	Balance sheet
Person 6	60	6	8	62	2
Person 7	70	7	8	71	1
Person 8	80	8	8	80	0
Person 9	90	9	8	89	−1
Person 10	100	10	8	98	−2
		40			

Year 2

Poor city A

	Pre-ax income	10% tax	Public spending (budget/S)	Pre-tax income and spending	Balance sheet
Person 1	20	2	3.5	21.5	1.5
Person 2	30	3	3.5	30.5	0.5
Person 3	40	4	3.5	39.5	−0.5
Person 4	50	5	3.5	48.5	−1.5
Budget		14	14		

Rich city B

	Pre-tax income	10% tax	Public spending (budget/S)	Pre-tax income and spending	Balance sheet
Person 5	60	6	7.7	61.7	1.7
Person 6	60	6	7.7	61.7	1.7
Person 7	70	7	7.7	70.7	0.7
Person 8	80	8	7.7	79.7	−0.3
Person 9	90	9	7.7	88.7	−1.3
Person 10	100	10	7.7	97.7	−2.3
		46	46		

Table 2.7. *The effects of redistribution mechanisms of income by local budgets*

What consequences can be expected from this difference in treatment between regions with a comparable level of development (in terms of GDP) such as Catalonia and Midi-Pyrénées? Not much, at least in the short term. The average Catalan should in theory "vote with their feet" – in accordance with the model of "fiscal federalism", as we have seen in the diagram of Table 2.7 – and settle in a region of a country where, with equal income, they would be a net beneficiary rather than a net contributor. But in practice, this is not the case: rather, we observe very low permanent migrations between European countries. The reason for this is the very weak long-term integration of European markets, compared to that in the United States, as evidenced by the fact that trade between European nations tends to be intra- rather than inter-industry (government statistics 2017)[10]. The Italians buy cars from the French, who buy cars from them. If there were "American-style" integration with a sharing of specializations between the EU's territories (like aeronautics in Seattle, IT in California, advertising in New York, etc.), we would record residential mobility of the same intensity as in the United States. Research on transport economics has shown that three quarters of the interterritorial exchanges expected from the gravity model are "blocked" by national borders in Europe (Dia Solvera 1995).

If Europe did not have its linguistic and cultural barriers, and if it had realized its project of a large integrated market, surely our Catalan would take advantage of the freedom of movement, effective today within the EU, to settle in Toulouse. But in today's Europe, "voting with one's feet" would be too expensive.

Paradoxically, therefore, it is the non-achievement of the objective of the single market which constitutes one of the best protections against the risks of imbalance, in terms of the relocation of people and activities, introduced by this biased system of European cohesion based on national public budgets with unequal redistributive powers. The two major European objectives – and of which we affirm the equal importance – of economic integration and cohesion interact in a singular way: indeed, it is the failure to achieve the first that protects us from the adverse effects of the second!

But there is, suddenly, another type of effect which can lead to imbalances in this system of "fragmented cohesion". Rather than mobility of factors of production, and particularly of labor, which we may think will remain permanently limited, this unequal treatment of equal regions can result in a calling into question of the entire national public redistribution system.

---

10 In the 1990s, the annual flow of interstate migrants to the United States comprised approximately 2.5% of the American population, that is, more than the average weight of the population (of the countries of Europe of the 15 at the time the stock of foreign nationals of another country of the EEC!). In 2017, Europeans living in France represented only 2.6% of the French population.

2.4. The risk of rejecting intranational solidarities

So, our Catalan will not "vote with their feet", but this is not the last word on the matter. The awareness and the measure of the status of net contributor to the Spanish interregional solidarity, and hence to European cohesion, have progressed in the region over the years and are giving rise to a questioning of the mechanisms of re-distribution between the country's regions. Catalonia first negotiated and obtained from the Spanish government that part of the national tax levy be allocated to the Catalan budget, which reduced the region's net contribution to solidarity, but essentially maintained it.

If Catalans cannot escape this system of forced solidarity, as we have seen, by leaving the region, one solution would be for the whole of Catalonia to "vote with their feet" and separate from Spain to become an independent country. In recent years, the pro-independence movement has repeatedly stressed the 17 billion euros in transfers financed by Catalonia *from* the public budgets to the poorer regions of Spain. During the revolutions that have marked history, we have seen arguments that were a little more sublime. We smile when we hear Catalans say that in the future they would prefer to play the game of European redistributive solidarity rather than the Spanish one[11]. We can understand them, given that there is practically no system of Euro-Mediterranean redistributive solidarity!

In a context of proliferation of autonomist or independentist movements in Europe and across the world, the arrival of large wealthy regions is giving weight to the thesis of national fragmentation and the questioning of the "Western model of national cohesion". These regions have significant political standing and economic strength, affording them the means to achieve what other poorer regions have been trying in vain to achieve for decades. The success of their project (and we are not far from it in Scotland as in Catalonia) would complete the opening of the Pandora's box of the fragmentation of nations.

It is already half-open. Indeed, if we limit ourselves to European cases (in the broadest sense), since 1990, nearly 30 new countries have appeared: the Czech Republic, Slovakia, the break-up of Yugoslavia into seven independent countries (for the time being), and the break-up of the USSR into 15 countries, not to mention the emergence of Novorossia in the Donbass region of eastern Ukraine, which has been in the news since 2014. Other examples of self-proclaimed states not recognized by the UN include Transnistria, the Republic of Nagorno-Karabakh, the

---

11 The author of these lines had, for example, a debate on RFI with a Catalan militant of the independence, however university professor, developing without blushing this particularly specious argument.

Dniester Republic of Moldova, Abkhazia, the Republic of South Ossetia and the Turkish Republic of Northern Cyprus.

In Europe, we perhaps consider ourselves to be sufficiently "civilized" and informed by our recent history to be able to prevent these territorial conflicts from intensifying. Yet, only a little more than 20 years ago, the wars in Yugoslavia caused more than 150,000 deaths and the displacement of four million people. The bloody Irish Troubles, which only really calmed down after the 2007 agreements, are now on the verge of restarting, with new demands for independence and unification of the two Irelands following Brexit. Likewise, activists in the wealthy Basque country have only recently stopped the armed struggle.

Faced with these movements, neither the European countries nor the EU administration have a clear, common and stable doctrine. In the Yugoslav affair, the major European countries even threw oil on the fire, with pro-Croat Germany pushing for the fragmentation of the country and pro-Serb France defending its unity. The EU seems not to want to recognize Scotland as a member country (even if its independence is motivated by the refusal of Brexit?) or even an independent Catalonia. But three quarters of European countries recognized the independence of Kosovo in 2008[12]. Old habits die hard!

In many parts of the world that were struggling against colonial oppression in the 20th century, the principles of self-determination and the principle of self-determination and that of peoples was clearly legitimate, particularly in the colonies where "indigenous" populations did not enjoy citizenship rights. But the matter is now politically more complicated, with demands for independence from thriving territories with full democratic rights. This is the case with many of today's European regionalist movements, which are based on identity, cultural or ethnic considerations, as well as purely economic ones.

2.4.1. *The revolt of the rich regions*

In Western Europe, the Scots, Catalans, Basques, Northern Italians and Belgian Flemish have lately been the topic of much debate.

All of these movements, which are difficult to classify into two distinct categories, variously combine two political forces: on the one hand, the promotion of a valuable identity that is, however, curbed or oppressed by the national power; on the other

---

12 The Helsinki agreements, signed in 1975 by, among others, all the current member states of the EU (except Andorra) was however clear as to the principle of territorial integrity.

hand, a more or less explicit territorial egoism with a growing refusal to share its wealth with the other components of the nation. In an earlier article (Davezies 2003), it was proposed that a distinction should be made between "pre-national" and "post-national" conflicts. Pre-national conflicts are the result of regions with a strong identity and have historically been reluctant to join a national grouping, for example, Corsica, Northern Ireland, Scotland, Brittany or the Basque Country. This category also includes many of the territories of the former Yugoslavia and the former USSR. These regions are sometimes wealthy, but more often than not they are still poor (in comparison to the rest of the country), yet they are alike in their reluctance to see their particular identity drowned in the national melting pot.

Post-national regionalist driving forces are found in regions, generally rich and net contributors to national budgets, which wish, based on the more or less clear reality of a regional cultural or linguistic identity, to free themselves from the "ball and chain" of national budgets and solidarity: Belgian Flanders, Greenland, Italian "Padania", Catalonia, the Spanish Basque Country or Scotland (which thinks it is richer than it is!)[13]. Yesterday, the fragmentation in the violence of the Yugoslav federation took place with a succession of the republics in decreasing order of income (and net contribution to the federal game of income redistribution of income) (Boniface 1999). What distinguishes today's movements from those in the past is the fact that it is the wealthy regions that are demanding more autonomy (from federalism to independence) because they simply no longer need the poor regions, which together with these wealthy nations have "made the nation" up to now.

These claims are aimed directly at the cohesion model that our European "social market economy" allows: the powerful redistribution mechanisms linked to public budgets and social budgets allow a territorial rebalancing of household incomes in all European countries, while the creation of wealth (i.e. the GDP) tends to be concentrated in the most developed and wealthy territories. In short, as we have seen, there has been a reduction in intraregional income inequalities while at the same time an increase in interregional GDP inequalities for many decades.

In the 40 European regions, according to the nomenclature established by the European Commission in 2015, the national GDP per capita indices (on average more than of more than 50% higher than the average GDP per capita of their respective countries), their national per capita income indices are on average 25%

---

13 We have seen that Scotland's GDP per capita is lower than that of the United Kingdom, but Scottish independents believe that an independent Scotland would be richer with the North Sea oil fields. Regardless of the legal issue of the ownership of these fields, the oil (of which the price has collapsed) is of poor quality and requires very costly processing in a global context where fossil fuel usage is being re-evaluated broadly.

lower. Among these 40 regions, the following are leaning toward independence: the Flemish province of Antwerp, the "Padanian" provinces of Bolzano, Trentino, Valle d'Aosta, Lombardy, Catalonia and the Basque Country in Spain. In Scotland, only the Eastern-Scotland region has a per capita GDP index that is barely above the average UK index (but to reiterate, the Scots argued for independence on the basis that they would be richer than the UK!).

On the other hand, if we consider the 40 poorest regions in Europe (excluding the French overseas territories), there are no significant regionalist movements. They have on average a national GDP per capita and an income index that is only 13% lower. These rich territories tempted by one form or another of secession had played the game of solidarity with the poorer regions as long as they benefited from it. Globalization, the change of the great industrial cycle and the end of a form of "territorial Keynesianism" have melted away these benefits.

2.4.2. Questioning the cohesion model

Today, the global organization of production, the generalized economic competition of nations with nations and territories with territories, and the asymmetry of systems of formal solidarity (powerful within nations, we have seen, but almost non-existent between them) all discredit the idea of international and intranational interterritorial solidarity. While global market integration has taken place by erasing national borders, the redistributive component of our economies has not followed and remains confined within national borders. Even the European administration, which only has the word "cohesion" in its mouth, only implements interregional transfers of a derisory amount (less than 0.5% of European GDP). As a result, a poor region such as the Alentejo essentially receives transfers from the (fairly poor) region of Lisbon and not from the (rich) regions of Île-de-France or from Bavaria.

"European cohesion" has little to do with Europe and is in fact nothing more than the addition of disparate national cohesion and is achieved at the cost of a strong inequality of treatment between regions: as we have seen, the wealthy regions of poor countries are net contributors to intranational transfers, whereas at the same level of development, they would be net beneficiaries in a wealthy country. This bias, which is unfavorable to them in the mechanisms of "European cohesion", figures prominently in the arguments of the Catalan independents.

In this context, the strategy of "every man for himself" is gaining ground. For the rich regions, it is better to keep for themselves the means of investment necessary to face up to global competition rather than subsidize poor and uncompetitive regions. And this is all the more true since there is no longer any point in helping them.

2.4.3. *Wealthy regions independent of poor regions*

Indeed, a new cycle of immaterial production has replaced, in industrial countries, the activities of material production. In the past, material production was widely shared between regions: here, design and management, there, production and, elsewhere, component suppliers. The production of a car involved a large number of facilities in a large number of regions (rich and poor). Industrial production was thus a vast affair of inter-industrial relations and inter-territorial interdependencies – in the hierarchical mode of head and legs, of course, but which still allowed for cooperation and interaction between the regions.

With the shift to globalization, these intranational interterritorial productive cooperations are being challenged first by the growing recourse to low-cost labor countries.

On the other hand, the new "hyperindustrial" system (as defined by Veltz (2017)), which deals more with information than materials (including in material production with the digitization of industry) and concentrates, even hyperconcentrates, in the densest and richest territories in which it is self-sufficient. Between 2008 and 2018, about three-quarters of the 300,000 net creations of private salaried jobs in the digital sectors, technical studies and superior business consulting were the work of only about 15 of French municipalities, in four major cities of the country (according to Acoss). In short, the major productive centers have less of a need of the rest of the country.

Finally, globalization calls into question the idea of "territorial Keynesianism", whereby wealthy regions are subsidized through redistributive transfers from poor regions that were their clients. Everyone won: for example, in Italy, the North subsidized the South, which drove Fiats and Piaggios manufactured in the North. Today, the South buys German, Korean or Japanese cars and scooters, and Fiat and Piaggio sell mostly outside Italy. The virtuous solidarity-trade link is broken. Once again, wealthy regions no longer need the poor regions[14].

---

14 In Mexico, the Secretary of the Budget of the State of Nuevo León, the largest net contributor to the country's budget, gave a speech during the OECD's evaluation interviews of Mexican territorial policies that was particularly explicit on this problem: as long as the Mexican economy remained largely closed to foreign trade, until the mid-1980s, redistributive transfers from Nuevo León to other regions of the country were significantly translated into purchases by these regions from Nuevo León firms. The interregional trade-socio-solidarity relations followed a Keynesian logic that was broken by the opening of the borders to international trade in the 1980s. The net beneficiary regions now buy from abroad, while the net contributor regions suffer from international competition. It is on this discourse, which is not scientifically proven – the figures put forward are unverifiable – that the secessionist arguments of the "border states" of northern Mexico were based.

Behind all these economic upheavals, the arguments of a new territorial egoism no longer whispered, but erected as a political slogan and capable, as we have seen, of mobilizing large coalitions in our European regions as elsewhere in the world. These new regionalist ideologies, based on the beautiful ideas of "short circuits", of a return to a democracy closer to the citizen and bringing to the pinnacle the fashionable concept of "common good", too often allowed to make up in a flattering way what is basically only a prosaic "ideology of the pocket calculator".

2.5. References

Begg, I. (ed.) (2004). The impact of Member State policies on cohesion. Background study for the 3rd Cohesion Report, European Commission, DG Regio, Brussels.

Béhar, D. and Estèbe, P. (2004). Développement économique : la fausse évidence régionale. Analyse des schémas de développement régionaux. *Les annales de la recherche urbaine*, 101, 41–49.

Besnainou, D. and Davezies, L. (1998). *Regional Development and Structural Policies in Mexico.* OECD, Paris.

Boniface, P. (1999). La planète "balkanisée". *Le Monde*, 4th of September.

Davezies, L. (1999). Un essai de mesure de la contribution des budgets des pays membres à la cohésion européenne. *Économie et prévision*, 2–3(138–139), 178–196.

Davezies, L. (2008). *La république et ses territoires. La circulation invisible des richesses.* Le Seuil, Paris.

Davezies, L. (2015). *Le nouvel égoïsme territorial. Le grand malaise des nations.* Le Seuil, Paris.

Davezies, L. and Estèbe, P. (2011). Le sas ou la nasse : les deux visages de la Seine Saint Denis. Report, ANRU.

Davezies, L. and Rekacewicz, P. (2003). Régions contre États-Nations. In *L'Atlas du monde diplomatique*, Achcar, G., Gresh, A., Radvanyi, J., Rekacewicz, P., Vidal, D. (eds). Le Monde diplomatique, Paris.

Diaz Olvera, L., Le Nir, M., Plat, D., Raux, C. (1995). Les effets frontières : évidences empiriques et impasses théoriques, collection. Report, L.E.T, Lyon.

Dougall, M. (1977). Rapport du groupe de réflexion sur le rôle des finances publiques dans l'intégration européenne. Report, CEE, Brussels.

Haut Conseil au Financement de la Protection Sociale (2015). Rapport sur l'impact de la protection sociale et de son financement sur la redistribution territoriale des revenus. Report, Haut Conseil au Financement de la Protection Sociale.

Houard, N. (ed.) (2012). *Politique de la ville. Perspectives françaises et ouvertures internationales.* La Documentation française, Paris.

Musgrave, R. and Musgrave, P. (1989). *Public Finance in Theory and Practice.* McGraw Hill, New York.

Mushkin, S. (1957). Distribution of the federal expenditures among the states. *The Review of Economics and Statistics*, 39, 193–213.

Nicot, B.H., Wishlade, F., Davezies, L., Yuill, D., Taylor, S., Prud'homme, R., EPRC (Wishlade, F., Yull, D., Taylor, S.), L'OEIL (Davezies, L., Nicot, B.H., Prud'homme, R.) (1998). Economic and social cohesion in the European Union: The impact of Member State's own policies. *Regional Development Studies 29*, Office for Official Publications of the European Communities, Luxembourg [Online]. Available at: https://dumas.ccsd.cnrs.fr/LABURBA/hal-01138700.

Reynard, R. (1995). Villes-centre, banlieues : les écarts se creusent. *Lettre de l'INSEE Rhône-Alpes.* Report, 23.

Statistique publique (2017). Le chiffre du commerce extérieur. *Études et éclairages*, 71 [Online]. Available at: http ://lekiosque.finances.gouv.fr.

Talandier, M. and Davezies, L. (2009). *Croissance et développement territorial. Un examen des phénomènes et des représentations dans les pays industriels.* Éditions PUCA, Paris.

Veltz, P. (2017). *La société hyper-industrielle. Le nouveau capitalisme productif.* Le Seuil, Paris.

Wishlade, F., Davezies, L., Yuill, R., Prud'homme, R. (1998). Economic and social cohesion in the European Union: The impact of Member State's own policies, regional development studies. European Commission, Brussels, 29.

3

Which Geographical Figures Should Be Mobilized Against Particular Territorial Inequalities?

Xavier DESJARDINS[1] and Philippe ESTÈBE[2]
[1] *Médiations, Sorbonne Université, Paris, France*
[2] *Acadie, Paris, France*

3.1. Introduction

Territorial unity is a vital issue for nation states, one that is compounded by the fact that this unity is never self-evident[1]. To endure this, national unity must demonstrate a specific advantage by creating a distinction between the inside and outside. This specific advantage obviously involves the rights on which citizenship is based, the driving forces of which are firstly civic rights then social rights. Even if the results are imperfect and are the subject of much debate, this project can easily be expressed in terms of public policy objectives: the reduction of income gaps, access to decent living conditions, equal opportunities and the capacity to act. The problem is much more difficult vis-à-vis the territorial issue. France is made up of various territories – consolidated, acquired, annexed or even attached – and so it is necessary to demonstrate the advantages of being part of it, or else secessionist sentiments may

---

1 This text is a heavily edited version of a paper presented at the *Festival international de géographie de Saint-Dié-des-Vosges* in 2018.

arise. Today, nation states are potentially fragmented because of secessionist movements. Indeed, among the 28 Member States to become part of the United Nations (UN) since 1990, 15 are European! In addition, secessionist tendencies are strong, particularly in Spain, the United Kingdom, Moldova and Belgium. Across the continent, governments must express their concern for the condition of the territories they govern and establish alliances with localized alliances to ensure the unity and cohesion of the nation as a whole.

How can the unity of a territory be ensured? When the term "territories" is used in contemporary French political debates, it is used to refer to small or medium-sized, low-density local authorities, which are presumed to be in a state of social and economic difficulty, perhaps even "abandoned". By extension, in political-administrative language, the term "territories" refers to any territory out of the larger cities governed by an interminicipal body called a *métropole*. It is more common for the plural to be used to designate smaller entities rather than the singular: for example, culture versus cultures, history versus histories and land versus lands. Consequently, the idea has gradually emerged that territories are both part of and in tension with the territory (as a singular unit). In other words, the territory designates the national space, that is, the territories and its components. As such, we are faced with the following recurring questions: does the development of the territory necessarily equate to the development of its territories? Is promoting the equality of citizens necessarily the same as promoting the equality of territories?

In this chapter, which focuses on the case of France, we will analyze three territorial inequalities that have been the driving force (at least, in terms of their existence having been denied) behind long-term public policies since the French Revolution: the Saint-Malo-Geneva line, the rural-urban divide and provincial France. While other representations and geographical discourses exist of course to denounce unbearable inequalities (notably between France and the conquered regions outside of Europe), we have chosen to isolate these three, because they continue to infuse, quietly and sometimes unconsciously, contemporary public action.

Firstly, we will highlight the writings, maps or figures that have exposed, with the greatest repercussion – but not always with scientific rigor – a territorial difference deemed as harmful. We then review some of the public policies that these discourses have inspired and attempted to identify their main effects. What are the social and political systems that lead to a representation of a territorial difference as being perceived as an inequality? How are actors, over a period of time, brought together to work on mitigating it? Finally, what effects do such policies produce in the region over time?

3.2. The Saint-Malo-Geneva line

The intervention of the geographical map into French public debate can be dated quite precisely as reported by Roger Chartier reports in an article in *Lieux de mémoire* (Chartier 1997). In 1822, the Italian geographer Adrien Balbi drew up a table comparing the number of students enrolled in each of the academies with the total population. In 1823, the geographer Conrad Malte-Brun, commenting on Balbi's results, pointed out the existence of two Frances:

> If we separate France into two parts, one in the North and the East/the Northeast, the other in the South and the West/the Southwest (excluding, if one so desires, Paris), we will have very different results [...] In the first group, which includes twelve academies, for every thousand men, one hundred and twenty-three boys go to school; in the second, with thirteen academies, only forty-nine [...] Public education in the South and West/the Southwest of France is to that in the North and East/the Northeast as 1 is to 2 ½ (Chartier 1997).

As such, geography and statistics formed a lasting relationship, the legacy of which would be prolific.

3.2.1. *An obscure and enlightened France*

Charles Dupin, mathematician and politician, popularized the Saint-Male-Geneva line using pioneering statistical cartography work, and in doing so, invented the choropleth map.

Dupin did not only draw upon Malte-Brun's work; he systematized it. As an (albeit unknown) inventor, he imagined that each department could be assigned a value in a figurative sense. This innovation was considerably forward-looking. He went further. Firstly, he gave a name to the fracture: "Notice, from Geneva to Saint-Malo, a sharp and blackish line separates the North from the South of France" (quoted in Chartier (1997)). Secondly, he qualified this fracture, with "enlightened France" in the North, and "obscure France" in the South. Finally, he compared the level of education and development, showing that Northeastern France was (in general) richer, more industrious and more inventive. To do this, he made a large number of cross-references between various statistical series, in keeping with the spirit of the times and the passion for these emerging materials.

On closer examination, Dupin's map does not quite oppose Northeastern France with Southern France, but rather identifies an "enlightened" crescent that joins the

English Channel to the Mediterranean and a diagonal that connects Brittany to the Massif Central.

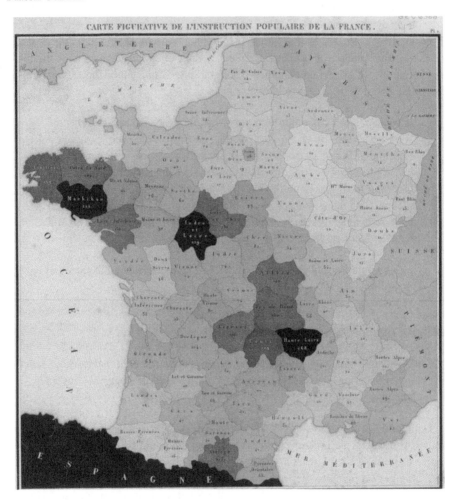

Figure 3.1. *Charles Dupin's map published in 1826 (source: Wikipedia)*

However, the Saint-Malo-Geneva line was to become an image and acquire a performative dimension. It first opened a philosophical-political debate: should the government be judged by its capacity to equalize the conditions of life and to converge the territories toward the same development model? Dupin was convinced of this. He believed without a doubt that Northern France was superior to Southern France. In passing, he raises a question that will also have a remarkable posterity:

according to him, the superiority of the North over the South does not reside so much in the high level of education as in the fact that a greater number of schoolchildren produces tougher competition for access to higher education and more generally to positions of authority. In other words, the lag in development in the South of France was due to a lack of competition. Equality of conditions or equality of opportunities? Without these situations being explained, the debate was launched.

The general consensus regarding a single model of development was challenged by many of Dupin's followers.

Based on the *Compte général de l'administration publique*, in 1832, the lawyer Guerry published an article in the *Revue encyclopédique,* entitled "Statistique comparée de l'état de l'instruction et du nombre de crimes" (Comparative statistics on the state of education and the number of crimes). In the article, he not only exposed the weaknesses of the Saint-Malo-Geneva line, but also demonstrated that the North's superiority was not so clear-cut to establish in consideration of the crime rate and that, in any case, there was no obvious correlation in the level of education. Furthermore, while retaining the Saint-Malo-Geneva line, he reversed its values: he no longer separated enlightened France from obscure France, but rather, a France of toil and pain (in the North) from a France of health and joy of living (in the South). Here again, the foundations were laid for a long-lasting debate, still ongoing even today: does the equality of the conditions of life suppose the homogeneity of the development model? A century and a half later, Laurent Davezies, Magali Talandier, Jean Gadrey and Fabienne Jany-Catrice continue to fuel this debate (Davezies and Talandier 2014; Gadrey and Jany-Catrice 2016).

Even if it is not patent geographers who are at the origin of this debate, it is based on the diffusion of geographical techniques and on the use of the map as an instrument for measuring differences and inequalities between territories[2]. After Dupin, maps multiplied, supporting or not the division North/South division of the country. It has been said that this division was performative. It participates, indeed, in an awareness of the "French territory", as well as in a form of obligation of equalization of conditions in the whole of the national space.

It is the "territorialized" resurgence of a revolutionary debate, a question raised by Condorcet in the early years of the French Revolution, that of the abstract citizen and the situated citizen: in their geography, their social relations, their capacities, their social relations, their material and financial capacities. This is a question that

---

2 Thanks be to Adrien Balbi. Often, the Italians have cast a glance on our isthmus much more relevant than ours. Let us think of the *Commentaires sur la guerre des Gaules.*

Hannah Arendt (1967) would take up again a century and a half later, comparing the French and American revolutions.

According to Arendt, the American Revolution was (wisely) content to extend political rights, because the founding fathers were well aware of the aristocratic dimension of the representative system[3]. According to her, the social dimension of the French Revolution opens an infinite credit: if the revolutionary project is confused with that of the equality of conditions, it indexes the public policies on this only objective. For Arendt, this original mark is a factor of permanent frustration: the equality of conditions never being reached, it opens to citizens and territories an infinite line of credit on public policies. However, we can also think that the egalitarian project is an extraordinary driving force, as soon as the State in one way or another takes it on as its main mission. This tension between the equality of conditions and the equality of territories has crossed over from the political history of France to our present day.

3.2.2. From map to policy

From this perspective, Dupin was encouraging a dynamic already at work: the generalization of primary education. His words made this clear:

> If the government wishes to increase its resources and to collect with greater and greater ease the billions that France pays today, to increase even if necessary this mass of taxes. Let it therefore promote popular education everywhere, and subsequently all the other branches of education (Dupin 1827).

The development of education continued throughout the 19th century, and the French Republic institutionalized its gradual standardization between the middle of the 1830s and the end of the 1860s (Prost 1993).

Perhaps it is necessary to recall the stages. From the 19th century, we remember the laws of Jules Ferry in the 1880s on free, secular and compulsory education yet we often forget that the implementation of these laws was made possible by the remarkable constancy of governments, from the July monarchy to the Republic, to generalize and unify education and instruction throughout the country. It is also rarely remembered that religious congregations have contributed greatly to this, especially among girls and in the poorest territories.

---

3 See the *Federalist Papers,* where Jefferson and Hamilton set out their views on the aristocratic character of the representative system/representative system of government.

In 1833, the Guizot law required each municipality with more than 500 inhabitants to open a public school for boys; in 1850, with the Falloux law, this obligation included a public school for girls. The law passed by Victor Duruy authorized municipalities to finance schools for the poor on a voluntary basis. Following the measures implemented under the July Monarchy and the Second Empire, the primary school enrolment rate was 86% for the whole of France in 1876. Although Brittany and the center of the country still remained under-schooled, the Saint-Malo-Geneva line had been crossed: Hérault and Haute-Garonne achieved an enrolment rate of 100% (Briand 1995). In 1875, 78% of men and 66% of women were able to sign their own names in the marriage register. Ferry's improvements were mainly of two kinds: school became free (in 1881) and compulsory until the age of 13 (in 1882). In 1911, 96% of young people aged 20–24 years old were literate. It was only after World War II that secondary education progressed with the advent of free education and family allowances.

The result of this policy was evident on the eve of the First World War: regional contrasts in education and health were barely perceptible along the Saint-Malo-Geneva line at the time of conscription (Boulanger 1998). Over the decades, public policies on education and family investment proved that Dupin's opponents were right: today, the Saint-Malo-Geneva line has not disappeared, the positions of the territories it delimits have been reversed. Education was not the only factor, economic changes, in particular the disappearance of mining and manufacturing activities in former industrial regions had a huge impact to such an extent that a "inverted France" was in the 1980s (Uhrich 1987).

3.2.3. *A paradoxical ingratitude?*

Administering over a vast and sparsely populated country like France requires a considerable financial effort on the part of public authorities. Indeed, providing a comparable level of education costs more in sparsely populated areas. It takes more buildings and more staff to reach the same number of students as in densely populated areas. Even today, despite the laments that follow the closure of a classroom or school, this form of settlement leads to the fact that the least densely populated territories are the best equipped with teachers, meaning there is an invisible transfer of finances taking place from the big cities to the most rural territories. For every 1,000 students (all years combined), there are between 50 and 55 teachers in the departments of the inner suburbs of Paris and 98 in Lozère![4]

---

4 Insee, 2013.

In 2014, the map of the average cost of a high school student showed that the greatest collective effort was made in the least densely populated regions, the famous diagonal of the void and in the overseas territories.

In metropolitan France, Auvergne (52 inhabitants per km^2), Limousin (43 inhabitants per km^2) and Corsica (36 inhabitants per km^2) are at the top of the podium, with costs ranging around €9,000 per student, compared to just under €7,500 in Île-de-France. This is the result of a process that has developed over nearly two centuries and, after primary education, has succeeded in including secondary education, and then higher education. The last notable event was the "University of the Third Millennium" plan at the end of the 1990s, which provided several medium-sized cities with higher education institutions[5].

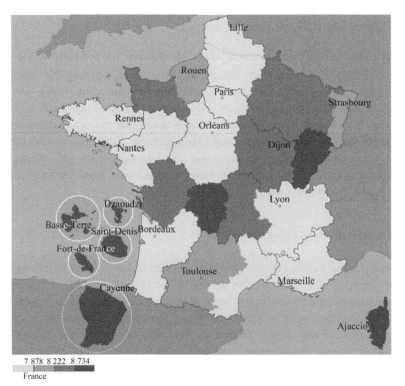

Figure 3.2. *Average expenditure per high school student in 2014 (€/student) (source: Observatoire des territoires). For a color version of this figure, see http://www.iste.co.uk/talandier/territorial.zip*

---

5 Baron, M. (2004). La Formation supérieure en régions (France). *Cybergeo: European Journal of Geography?* DOI: 10.4000/cybergeo.2575.

However, this considerable effort did not eradicate inequalities linked to population density. In 2019, a study by the French Ministry of Education showed that on average, high school students had to travel 3 km to get to school (Maugis and Touahir 2019). This average evidently encompasses very different situations: the deviations from this average are obviously very significant between Paris and the rural departments. If they are better endowed per capita, high schools are further away for many. This may explain the feeling of abandonment or being forgotten.

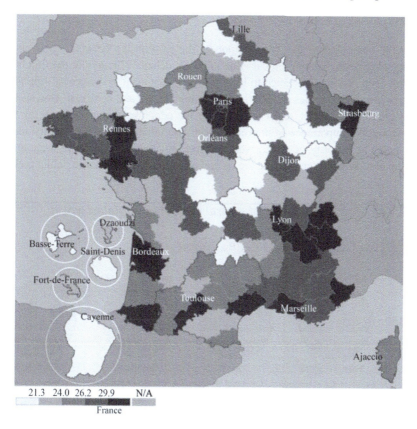

Figure 3.3. *Share of higher education graduates in the population aged 15 and over (2017) (source: Observatoire des territoires, Insee). For a color version of this figure, see http.//www.iste.co.uk/lalandier/territorial.zip*

But there is a second, even more problematic paradoxical effect. The transformations of the economy have passed by; the acquired mobility has freed us from the territories of our birth and from our cultural and family constraints. Many studies show that territorial mobility is a precondition for social mobility. In fact, the results are there: the values delimited by the Saint-Malo-Geneva line have been permanently reversed.

Is this inversion the distant product of Dupin's map? The inversion of the values delimited by the line shows that territorial inequalities and that the maintenance of a homogeneous national space is a permanent construction site.

3.3. The countryside and the city

At the beginning of the Third Republic, the relationship between cities and the countryside became a key political issue in public debate. Throughout the first half of the 19th century, France seemed to have grown accustomed to the central role played by Parisian revolutionaries in ushering in regime change and upheaval. However, the presidential vote in 1848, and even more so the adoption of the plebiscite of 1851, underscored the importance of the rural world. The inhabitants of the countryside, the overwhelming majority of which were farmers, emerged as a political force and up until the First World War, became the central protagonists of territorial public policies.

3.3.1. *The long persistence of a rural densely populated world*

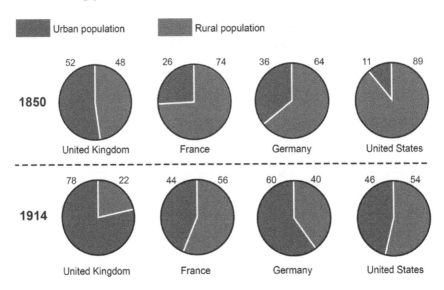

Figure 3.4. *Urban and rural population change and rural population in four countries (source: INSHEA–SDADV 2010–2011). For a color version of this figure, see http://www.iste.co.uk/talandier/territorial.zip*

France covers the largest area of Western Europe and, until the end of the 18th century, was the most populated European country (with about 28 million inhabitants). Unlike southern European countries (such as Spain and Italy), it does not have a desert.

At the beginning of the 19th century, in contrast to the situation of its neighbors, France underwent a demographic transition: infant mortality decreased, life expectancy slowly increased, but the birth rate stagnated and even decreased. However, all of its neighboring countries saw their respective populations increase. At the end of the 19th century, the French population was overtaken by that of England and Germany and caught up by Italy. From that point onwards, these countries reached population densities about twice as high as that of France. This phenomenon explains the permanence of a large "rural" population in France, in contrast to its neighboring countries. In 1914, 44% of the French population lived in rural areas compared with 22% in the United Kingdom, where 78% of the population already lived in cities. It was not until the 1970s that France caught up – a century after the United Kingdom!

Three factors explain this long duration of "rural living" in France. Firstly, demographic stagnation does not encumber the agricultural production space: you can live in the countryside and share the land without necessarily needing to leave to live better. However, this does not mean that the French remained stable (and many works testify to this) but these were temporary and seasonal movements. The "rural exodus" only began (slowly) from the second half of the 19th century[6].

The second factor is economic. The sale of Church property reinforced the (already ancient) tradition of peasant ownership, which reduced the dependency of rural producers on a land owner[7]. In the 19th century, many French people (as a 1970s slogan put it) "lived and worked in the country". The mass of "peasants" (Marx 1969) was a characteristic feature of French society and quite different from England, Germany or northern Italy. In England, restrictions on communal access and the rise of the factory system (Mokyr 2001) accelerated the urban concentration of the labor force. Even if the Italians considered themselves "behind", industry was organized around the large cities of the "industrial triangle", with Genoa, Milan and Turin at the top. Finally, due to political fragmentation, Germany's polycentric

---

6 Planhol (1994). See the section devoted to the exodus rural exodus.
7 The 1862 agricultural survey counted 1.8 million owner-operators, 1.9 million smallholders who also worked on other people's land, nearly 600,000 sharecroppers, and 2.9 million "farmhands" and seasonal workers. Cited in Hérault, B. (2016). *La population paysanne : repères historiques*. Centre d'études et de prospective, Ministère de l'Agriculture, de l'Agroalimentaire et de la Forêt.

structure facilitated the development of a network of industrial cities where, in the course of the 19th century, large and medium-sized companies, a regional banking system and vocational schools were concentrated.

In France, the process of worker concentration is late, apart from a few rare cities (Paris, Lyon, Lille). The development of industry largely took place outside the big cities, where the workforce would work on a contract-basis or would combine their labor with agricultural activities (Trempé 1971). On the other hand, the development of large-scale industry from 1850 did not upset the traditional urban economy: craftsmanship remained very present in the heart of cities, which did not have the same transformative effect as industrialization in German or English cities.

Thirdly, from then on, the countryside retained much of its autonomy in comparison to the cities. Rather, the latter did not contribute to the running or organizing of their territory and instead experienced a rather slow and uneven population and economic growth for the reasons explained above. Because of the dispersion of the population, the State had organized, since the Revolution and especially the First Empire, a tight territorial grid based on small and medium-sized cities: county towns, sub-prefectures and prefectures.

This administrative network formed the real political geography of the country, even if the revolutionary changes in Paris governed the great breaths of the century until the Second Empire. This network was also the social and economic geography, that of the notables, the peasants, the craftsmen and the agents of the State.

The plebiscite of 1852 proved the strength of this profound country: the countryside and the small towns voted massively in favor of the re-establishment of the Empire, whereas the big cities were more inclined to vote against it[8]. So much so that from 1871 onwards, the nascent Republic understood that if it wanted to last, it not only had to develop primary education, but also win the hearts and minds of the peasantry, which had established itself as a political force. Indeed, peasants made up nearly 50% of the working population in 1876. Hervieu and Viard (2001) show how, with the impetus of Léon Gambetta, the Third Republic afforded the countryside a privileged status[9]. On the one hand, a state within the State was created with a Ministry of Agriculture that centralized all the functions to the countryside, including the administration, economy, infrastructure, education and agricultural

---

8 A massive 96% voted in favor. Since only the "yes" ballots were printed, voters had to bring the "no" ballots themselves.
9 Several speeches by Gambetta were devoted to the peasant question: Bordeaux (June 26, 1871) and Auxerre (June 1, 1874) (see Vigier 1991, pp. 7–12).

research. On the other hand, communal fragmentation was conserved by the law of 1884.

From then on, the marriage of the Republic and the countryside began. With it, the Republic brought three advantages: political autonomy (with the law of 1884), the protection of agricultural outlets (thanks to the "Méline" tariffs that were named after the Minister of Agriculture) and connectivity (with an ambitious policy establishing communication networks).

3.3.2. *The marriage of the Republic and the countryside*

The communal law of 1884 is considered as one of the founding pillars of republican liberalism. Ozouf-Marignier and Verdier (2013) show that the law of 1884 ushered in a long period of stability for the municipality system.

The number of municipalities decreased steadily during the 19th century as a result of mergers of municipalities deemed unviable by the prefects, absorption of peripheral municipalities by large cities, sudden drops linked to the annexation of Alsace-Moselle by Prussia. From 1880 onwards, this number stabilized at 36,000, then rose to 38,000 (when Alsace-Moselle was annexed to France) and remained stable until 1970. After this date, it decreased following the 1972 law on mergers of municipalities. The law of 1884 thus led to a virtual freeze on the communal map for almost a century.

The law of 1884 created an equality in law between all these "territories". With the exception of the city of Paris, which was under state supervision, all of the other municipalities enjoyed the same status. Consequently, the same power structure and the same legal capacities were found everywhere. The municipalities had a quasi-sovereignty thanks to the so-called "general territorial competence" clause. Article 61 of the 1884 communal law states that: "The municipal council shall regulate, by its deliberations, the affairs of the municipality". In other words, the municipality is not a specialized administrative body, but can know and deal with any subject of communal interest, that is, within the limits of the law and jurisprudence, municipalities have the freedom to do anything.

Thus, France (according to Jean Viard's formula) gave more power to the territory than to the people. In fact, the rural world benefited from a distortion of representation that was reflected until recently at all levels. At the local level, the maintenance of the 36,000 municipalities (and 38,000 from 1919 to 1970) gave an overwhelming influence to the rural world. The mayors were first overwhelmingly notables, merchants and eventually, particularly after the Second World War, farmers (Laferté 2019).

In small municipalities, the members of the municipal council more or less represented the heads of the land-owning families. Thus, a large number of the municipalities functioned as assemblies of co-owners where building rights were afforded. This is still present today in the urban planning of small municipalities.

This political weight of the municipalities is felt at all levels of political administration. The developments – at first modest then exponential – of inter-municipality remain firmly anchored to their communal base. In fact, it was not until the early 2000s that (if not in law) unanimity was required for any decision, which obviously afforded considerable weight to small municipalities[10].

The traces of this can still be seen today whereby the general councils (which became departmental councils), despite the changes in the electoral map, are still fierce defenders of the rural areas because of the voting system. Their fields of action give them an eminent role in the field of planning and rural development. While they all claim to be protectors of the arts and industry, they are above all the advocates and supporters of the agricultural world. At the regional level – a newcomer, given the long history of territorial institutions – the concern for balance is constantly displayed by the regional plans of development, which most of the time translates into strategies targeted at medium-sized cities and small cities. This is often reflected in targeted strategies for medium-sized cities and small towns, which are seen as a counterweight to metropolitan domination (Béhar et al. 2021). At the national level, via the Senate, national representation is clearly tilted in favor of the rural world. At the European level, the common agricultural policy absorbs more than a third of the community budget: France has played an essential role in this assumption of responsibility by the EU vis-à-vis agricultural issues (Noël 1988)[11].

In short, rural and agricultural areas enjoy a very special status in France, a legacy of this founding pact with the Third Republic, the traces of which in national representation and in public policies at all levels are still perceptible today. This political status, acquired under the Third Republic, has led to the emergence of powerful pressure groups from the rural world who today exert a decisive influence on the public policies in the direction of the territories, whether it is the *Association des maires de France* (AMF) (Le Lidec 2003), the *Fédération nationale des*

---

10 Guéranger, D. and Lesage, F. (2011). *La politique confisquée : sociologie des réformes des insti-tutions inter-municipal institutions*. Éditions du Croquant, Vulaines-sur-Seine.

11 The continuities are astonishing from Méline to the European Economic Community.

syndicats d'exploitants agricoles (FNSEA) or the less well-known *Fédération nationale des collectivités concédantes et régies* (FNCCR).

3.3.3. Solidarity through networks

Maintaining the 36,000 municipalities perpetuated for a century entity that did not all have, far from it, the financial and technical means for their political autonomy.

Equality of rights did not entail equality of abilities. Political choices legitimized institutions many of which did not have the means for practical autonomy. The extreme political fragmentation had the mechanical effect of highlighting the glaring inequalities between the territories. The republican system was not satisfied with a system that did not ensure equality of conditions and abilities. All the more so since the pact between the peasantry and the Republic only held – Gambetta, Freycinet or Méline, among others, being convinced of this – while the latter proved to be equal to the promise of equality.

Beyond agricultural policies, national solidarity was manifested with regard to rurality by an active policy of regional planning in the territory (the governments spoke about "equipment" until the creation of the DATAR in 1963) through the networks.

At the end of the 19th century, cities were developing and certain observers were beginning to speak of rural depopulation. From that time, voices called for "industrial decentralization" to prevent overpopulation in cities and maintain the urban-rural balance[12]. The "Freycinet plan", launched by the Ministry of Public Works in 1878, aimed to open up the whole country and connect all of the sub-prefectures and as many of the district administrative centers as possible to the rail network. To this end, it planned 16,000 km of which 8,700 lines of local interest[13]. Nine hundred and sixty-four municipalities were connected to the network. The plan also included a river and port section[14]. A monumental effort was made over 20 years, resulting in an increase in the population of small towns and large villages

---

12 See Efi Markou's thesis: Markou, E. (2019). La Décentralisation industrielle en France dans le premier XXe siècle : du mot d'ordre réformateur à l'aménagement du territoire. Sociology PhD Thesis, under the direction of André Grelon, defended at EHESS on 16 December 2019, volume. 2, notably via its presentation by Christian Topalov in: Topalov, C. (2020). En lisant les thèses et les HDR. *Entreprises et histoire,* 98, ESKA, 173–182.

13 Mayeur, J.-M. (1973). *Les Débuts de la IIIe République*. Éditions du Seuil, Paris.

14 The river component provides for the improvement and interconnection of more than 14,000 km of canals (the "Freycinet gauge" locks) and the creation of 1,900 km of additional canals.

(which is a premise of the rural exodus). By 1914, France was covered by 49,000 km of railroads[15].

The continuity of the network policy in favor of the rural world was also manifested in a spectacular way by the development of electrification. At the beginning, the new technology was only able to support very localized networks, servicing districts or small towns from a hydroelectric or thermal power station. The 1906 law provided a framework for local practices and established electricity distribution as a municipal public service. During the interwar period, the technological advancements facilitated access to electricity and the interconnection of networks. With the help of a national policy, the percentage of municipalities with electricity went from 20% in 1918 to 96% in 1937. This movement was driven by inter-municipal unions, which really took off during this period.

This development of production and distribution fostered an increased economic integration of the sector, which resulted in the sector being organized into a few large groups of regional and then national size. However, the pricing system remained fragmented, with considerable price variations from one municipality to another. François-Mathieu Poupeau shows how the *Fédération nationale des collectivités concédantes* (FNCCR), created in 1934 and supported by rural elected officials, played a decisive role in the development of vast unions capable of confronting the powerful concessionary companies and in the search for ways to achieve solidarity between cities and the countryside[16]. The creation of EDF in 1946 reinvigorated the debate, which, this time, took place on a national scale: should we move toward a unified tariff for the whole country? Was this pricing a commercial tool or a public policy tool? A signal to the user of the cost to the community? The debate was difficult and the changes were slow, but in the end, it is the FNCCR that emerged victorious by first imposing an equalization at the departmental level, then by negotiating the principle of a universal tariff with EDF (1965). This came into effect for the entire country until 1990, partly due to the nuclear program that diversified the sources and locations of production. The law on the modernization of the public service (February 10, 2000) includes the principle of equalization set down in Article 2.

---

15 Enough to go around the world, we were still taught in elementary school in the past. The current network is 31,000 km long. We can refer to the cartographic work of Etienne Auphan on the network in 1911 (Auphan 2002).

16 Poupeau, F.-M. (2007). La Fabrique d'une solidarité nationale. État et élus ruraux dans l'adoption d'une péréquation des tarifs de l'électricité en France. *Revue française de science politique*, 5, 599–628.

In this debate, which ends with three interlocutors – the State, EDF and the FNCCR – the cities, particularly the largest ones, are absent. This is understandable: they are the big losers in the system, since it is partly their users (in good marginalist reasoning) who finance the single network tariff. Thus, EDF and the public company that manages most of the communal networks, Enedis, which is a subsidiary of EDF, are not only producers and distributors of energy, they are also operators of a considerable monetary redistribution toward the inhabitants of the rural world and small towns.

3.3.4. *Cycles of inequality*

In this section, we shall not repeat the relative marginalization of the countryside and its inhabitants as the cities grew in power in the post-war period. The sequence is well known: economic specialization of rural areas in agricultural production, withdrawal from industrial activities, concentration of productive forces in cities, etc. Even if Laurent Davezies (2021) has shown that until recently the income of rural inhabitants was increasing at the same rate or even faster than that of urban dwellers, the fact remains that today, the countryside has lost its strategic place. This is logical: planning and developing the countryside in the 19th and early 20th centuries was in fact equivalent to planning and developing the country. Given today's population distribution, the rural space has become residual (which does not mean that it is empty, that is why there is a problem).

The massification of services and the development of new techniques systematically highlight the inequalities linked to the contrasts of density. Let us take two examples.

Firstly, the business model for high-speed rail lines is based on serving densely populated areas in order to maximize the average train load and reduce the number of stops. In less than 30 years, France has been equipped with a high-speed network linking the country's main cities. This network allowed Pierre Veltz to conclude that a "metropolis" is emerging, made up of a network of large cities that are linked (both to one another and to Paris)[17]. Of course, this colossal effort has been made at the expense of investing in and maintaining "everyday trains", in spite of the investments made by the regional councils. But above all, this high-speed network produces a hierarchical connectivity that marginalizes rural areas and medium-sized cities (Emangard and Beaucire 1985). In terms of relative distance-time, today, rural areas are less well connected to the national network than they were at the beginning

---

17 Veltz, P. (2013). *Paris, France, monde : repenser l'économie par le territoire*. Éditions de l'Aube, La Tour d'Aigues.

of the 20th century. The national territory of France in 1914 was larger and the time-distances were longer, but it was more "egalitarian" than the contracted space-time of 2022.

Secondly, the asymmetric digital subscriber line (ADSL) and then the very high-speed digital subscriber line (VDSL) have given a second life to the traditional telephone network. But, unlike telephone communications, the quality of the signal depends on the distance between the user and the switch box. The VDSL speed drops rapidly from 100 Mbit/s to less than 40 Mbit/s where the user is more than 2 km away from the sub-distribution box. The alternative using satellite communications allows for more powerful and stable speeds provided that the user is located in an area covered by 4G, etc. In fact, the deployment of these technologies once again creates inequalities comparable to those which arose during the electrification process between the two world wars.

It is the well-known paradox: technological developments are constantly redrawing the lines of territorial inequalities. The most densely populated areas are always one step ahead of the less densely populated areas, and even if the gap is gradually closing – often thanks to the invisible redistributions carried out via the networks – the rural inhabitants often feel "forgotten" because they benefit with delay from networks whose deployment owes much to national solidarity.

3.4. The Paris–countryside divide

Jean-François Gravier (1947), a geographer, called attention to this significant geopolitical divide in his book *Paris et le désert français*, which is also known as *Quand Maurras rencontre Staline* (*When Maurras Met Stalin*). Little criticized by geographers at the time of its publication, it was to become important for the territory in the 1950s and 1960s. It was probably read by politicians more so than by geography professionals.

3.4.1. *The meeting of Maurras and Stalin*

Gravier made a clear statement of the way in which Parisian hypertrophy killed France by sucking up and concentrating the wealth and the living forces. In his book, Paris is accused of failings and immorality: it exhausts the country and kills its inhabitants, it benefits from an outrageous share of public money, even though it costs the nation more than the rest of the territory, the birth rate is lower in Paris than in the countryside, etc. His argument is well known and has already been subject to much analysis (Marchand 2001). The author's high praise of small and medium-sized cities and rural areas owes much to his Maurrassism and to the fact that his professional life began under the Vichy government, notably in the Alexis Carel center: named after a winner of the Nobel Prize in Physiology or Medicine and notorious eugenicist. A brilliant controversial figure, Gravier was able to embody the strongest contradictions, being both a supporter of decentralization and a strong centralized state; a Maurrasian, nostalgic for the old regime and its local liberties while admiring the Soviet planning, a Malthusian and natalist. He perfectly embodied a synthesis of French tensions. His analyses, based on a retrospective reading of the inter-war period, came into play precisely at the moment when they were beginning to be disproved.

If we accept a little simplification, Gravier's thesis is based on a few postulates:

– the population does not change much, the demographic growth population growth is low;

– the production of wealth is proportional to the population;

– therefore, if the population does not change and the wealth is proportional to the population, it must be shared equitably among the different territories;

– this perspective is beneficial for the cities, Gravier considers that they should not exceed an optimal size that he does not specify;

– thus, the territory takes precedence over the populations; equipping the territories with an egalitarian objective allows it to equalize the capacities and contribution to national wealth.

Obviously, we cannot rely on the spontaneous movement of populations, and even less so on the market, to bring about this rebalancing. A strong state is therefore needed, capable of effecting, even in an authoritarian manner, a different distribution of the population. Soviet-esque planning, which already fascinated the modernist fringe of the Vichyites[18], becomes, in the words of Gravier, a necessary instrument for the realization of this oxymoron: in order to decentralize, we need a strong State[19]. In other words, the territories must be forced to become autonomous.

The strength of Gravier's work is that it does not stop at denunciation and incantation: it outlines a concrete program for a policy of territorial development. He advocates the creation of 16 regions headed by a super-prefect and points out the

---

18 Voldman, D. (1997). *La Reconstruction des villes françaises de 1940 à 1954 : histoire d'une politique.* L'Harmattan, Paris. Historical works have clearly shown the continuities between Vichy and the Fourth Republic in terms of economic and urban planning.

19 Gravier proposed (among other things) to relocate 2 million Parisians.

need for a "Greater Paris" limited to 5 million inhabitants. He wants France to develop a multipolar organization like Germany and thinks that Aix-en-Provence or Poitiers could become the French Oxford and Cambridge. More generally, he develops an "urbaphobia" that is part of a long tradition, as traced by François Ascher (1998) in *La République contre la ville*. As Joëlle Salomon-Cavin (2005) puts it, "[t]he city is going badly, let's change the city".

This "urbaphobia" is not unique to France: Salomon-Cavin and Bernard Marchand show that this ideology is widespread. It is underpinned by a common argument, that is, the predatory nature of cities, their tendency to prevent the development of their surrounding territories, the unhappiness and misery that they generate among their inhabitants as opposed to the balance of a territory meshed with villages and small towns and medium-sized cities where authenticity, tradition and roots are expressed.

This strand of thought is not only transnational, but also crosses time periods. We find it today in certain ecological (Faburel 2019) and political (Guilluy 2014) texts. It has come to be identified, via the *Gilets jaunes* (yellow vests) movement in particular, with the struggle for social equality. The equality of territories is therefore, now and always, the basic condition for the equality of people. It is therefore not only a question of territorial balance and state attention to the "forgotten" territories; it is also, in a certain way, the salvation of humanity that depends on the reduction of the size, influence and activity of cities, Paris in the first place. For its misfortune, Paris not only symbolizes the centralization that would have done so much harm to the country, but also crystallizes all anti-urban ideologies.

In his book, Gravier invites Maurras and Stalin. Maurras for the celebration of the province, of its truth and its roots, as opposed to the Parisian octopus engendered by revolutionary ideology and the Republic that followed in its footsteps; Stalin for the steering of a powerful planning held in a firm hand by an unquestioned central authority, working for the common good. Published in 1947 by a somewhat unknown/small publishing house (Le Portulan), the work went relatively unnoticed. It was only following the editions published by Flammarion (1950, 1958 and 1972) that the work became known as "the bible of the planning" (Marchand 2021). This is indeed strange insofar as, in 1950 and even more so in 1958, the postulates of Gravier's reasoning are almost all disproved.

According to demographers, population growth took off again in 1942 (we wonder how, from his position at the Carel Institute, Gravier did not see this happening); productivity and wealth produced per capita and per job the post-war years; urban concentrations, and especially the Paris region, have a higher productivity than less dense and contribute more intensively to national wealth.

These facts, which were already known in 1950, did not prevent the political and administrative pilots of regional planning from seizing upon Gravier's work and establishing it as a kind of standard.

3.4.2. Would France have won against Paris?

The translation of Gravier's work into public policy is part of a national strategy of the territory that contributes to redraw the geopolitics of France. Industrial decentralization was initially driven by the *Direction générale de l'équipement national* (DGEN), then by the *Délégation à l'aménagement du territoire et à l'action régionale* (DATAR)[20]. We may also note in passing the appearance of the word "development" in the political-administrative lexicon.

This policy is based on two systems: the *authorization system*, which limits the creation of business premises in the Paris region, and the *zonal bonus system*, which encourages companies to establish themselves in regions with a low level of industrialization. The policy achieved impressive results: between 1955 and 1975, 3,000 decentralization operations led to the creation of 400,000 jobs in the provinces. The Paris region's share of manufacturing production fell and the region lost 35,000 industrial jobs (Aydalot 1985). The automobile industry is a particularly striking example: in 1960, 60% of the workforce was located in the Paris region; by 1974, only 40% workforce was located in the Paris region. In the same period, the growth of the Paris region declined sharply and the mid-level movements began to be reversed.

Would France have won against Paris? "Victory is in the blink of an eye", said Rémy Prud'homme, Philippe Rochefort and Philippe Aydalot (Prud'homme 1974; Prud'homme et al. 1975; Aydalot 1978). This demonstration is in three steps.

On the one hand, Rémy Prud'homme shows that the voluntary action carried out by DATAR is marginal compared to the overall movement of companies relocating. Not only did most of the decentralizations of establishments take place before the creation of DATAR, but they occurred in non-prime areas. In fact, industrial

---

20 This is another remarkable effect of continuity between the Vichy regime and the Fourth Republic, the DGEN having been created in 1942, already with the ambition of piloting a policy of industrial decentralization.

decentralization, as Aydalot also remarks, mainly occurred in the Paris Basin, so that the manufacturing sites were not too far from the decision-making centers. He then emphasizes that this decentralization has mainly consisted of the relocation of production units, and has led to the creation or relocation of low-skilled jobs while tertiary centers have been developing in Paris. He points out the limits of the policies practiced by DATAR by showing that the growth of industrial employment is more strongly linked to endogenous factors (e.g. the development of companies already located in the region) than exogenous factors (e.g. the decentralization of establishments) and underlines the marginal weight of bonuses in the location decision. By way of example, he cites the director of a Motorola company, recently established in Toulouse: "We chose Toulouse because we found a good university and cheap labor there. Bonuses were a welcome gift".

On the other hand, Prud'homme, Rochefort and Nicol examine the impact of public budgets public in terms of interregional redistribution. After some difficult (but pioneering) calculations – due to the limited availability of statistics – they conclude that public budgets play an important role in interregional redistribution. To this end, they show that the Paris region is the clear loser in the game of monetary circulation via public budgets, whereas Picardie, Haute-Normandie and Rhône-Alpes are rather disadvantaged, and all the others receive more than their contribution to public revenues[21]. Yet they also show that these transfers are linked to automatic operating expenses (civil servants' salaries, pensions, social welfare, etc.). In other words, a territory-blind fiscal policy is much more redistributive than an explicit spatial policy.

Lastly, Aydalot shows that industrial decentralization is a natural process in the Fordist capitalist system. On the one hand, it occurs even in countries that do not pursue a voluntary land-use planning policy (in the United States and Germany in particular). On the other hand, it is the consequence of industrial concentration, which sees small and medium-sized units absorbed by large industrial groups that alone have the means to invest in the requirements of Fordism, that is, mass production and mass consumption. From then on, he notes, the decentralization of production units corresponds to a rationalization of costs. Companies are looking for "cheap" labor (as the director of Motorola in Toulouse puts it) and are relocating manufacturing units that do not require high qualifications and can employ newcomers to the labor market: farmers "liberated" from the toil of the land, young women entering the labor market, undemanding workers, weakly unionized and

---

21 This is a truth that is constantly being rediscovered, and which is immediately refuted by tests that call this type of calculation into question.

"hard at work", he says, ironically quoting the brochures of the expansion committees.

In doing so, industrial decentralization does not in any way contribute to the rooting of industry in the territories. On the contrary, it contributes to its deterritorialization, and through this, it is not the horizontal links between companies that develop, but the vertical links between relocated establishments and their head office (which for the most part remains in Paris). These industrial decentralizations contribute to a certain convergence of living standards between regions and cities and (according to a retiree) above all, these contribute to the spatial division of labor and the social specialization of territories[22].

Finally, far from emancipating the "provinces" this process extends the hold of the Paris region on the rest of the national territory. Although it lost 35,000 blue-collar jobs between 1955 and 1975, it gained 330,000 service jobs during the same period. Paris accentuated its dominance in the density of executives, engineers, researchers, etc. And, because of the relocation of production facilities, in 1975, more than 4 million jobs located in the provinces were now dependent on Paris. Industrial decentralization, a largely spontaneous movement, is actually helping to increase the influence of Paris over France, much more than it is reducing it.

In practice, this decentralization operation will only have accompanied the process of "metropolization". This manifests itself in particular by a specialization of territories and by the industrial "degreasing" of the Paris region which is no longer the industry of yesteryear, but which became, in the words of Beckouche and Damette (1992), "the heart of the French productive system", following a process of specialization in three dimensions: socio-professional specialization through decrease in the number of workers and the domination of engineers, technicians and executives; sectoral specialization by maintaining a small number of branches with a high level of skills (defense electronics, IT, aeronautics), functional specialization with the sharp reduction in execution, storage, distribution and above all production jobs for the benefit of the abstract functions of direction, management, commerce, marketing, design and research.

The irony is that medium-sized cities, once attractive for low-skilled manufacturing activities, are now threatened by globalization which, from the 1980s

---

22 This is still true today: the share of workers in the labor force is inversely proportional to the size of the municipality. In 2014, the importance of unskilled workers was higher, the greater the distance from large cities. They represented only 5% of jobs in central cities of more than 100,000 inhabitants, compared to 12% in the urban and small areas, and 13% in the municipalities far from the cities. Source: Insee Première, No. 1, 674, November 2017.

onwards, has resulted in companies looking beyond France for the same conditions (i.e. cheap land and labor). The specialization of manufacturing activities and the vertical dependence of factories no longer provide sufficient protection for medium-sized cities. In practice, the 1990s and 2000s saw a gradual specialization of medium-sized cities in "residential" activities, with a strong focus on personal services, including healthcare. Ironically, the process of specializing the Paris region in the higher tertiary functions constituted, in the 1990s, the springboard for its gradual emancipation from the national economy.

3.5. Conclusion

Over the last 20 years, we have witnessed the sedimentation of these fractures with shifts. The St-Malo-Geneva line still exists, but its values are now reversed: northern, eastern and the center of France, while still more industrialized than the rest of the country, are all losing jobs and inhabitants at an almost constant rate, while western and southern France are experiencing positive economic and demographic growth rates. The "metropolises" with the best performance in terms of employment, population and income are located in a vast "peripheral" crescent that links Rennes to Lyon, passing through Nantes, Bordeaux, Toulouse, Montpellier and Marseille-Aix. It has taken almost 200 years for the diagnosis of Baron Dupin to be reversed (CGET 2018).

The debate on the city–countryside relationship has returned, with more or less the same terms as at the end of the 19th century, that is, services and networks. The question of networks still concerns access to public transport, the development of daily trains, but above all, access to very high-speed digital networks, considered today as the main lever for territorial development. The topic of collective service coverage has become prominent following successive reforms of state services (Courcelle et al. 2017).

The Paris/province tension has shifted, or rather, it has become generalized. It has taken a more radical turn, referring to the tension between the big cities (now referred to as "metropolises") and the rest of the territory (for which the neologism "peripheral France" is increasingly used) (Guilluy 2014). Some research (including by several of the co-authors of this book) demonstrates the effects of "horizontal" redistribution between large cities and territories, whereas others show that the structural problems of poverty, unemployment and loss of population are linked to regional characteristics more so than the size of the city. As a result, large cities are often contrasted with medium-sized cities or small towns (Desjardins and Estèbe 2019), particularly at the time of the *Gilets jaunes* crisis, despite studies which show the more social than territorial springs of the inequalities denounced (Delpirou 2018).

The permanence of these fractured interpretations is partly due to the permanence of deep and persistent structural problems, partly to recurrent fantasies in the public debate and the unthinking of public policies planning policies. A review of past interpretations of these fractures allows us to see that two factors have always been present to facilitate their passage from an analytical approach to the insertion in a political project.

First of all, these fractures have always been conceived as temporary: in this sense, they are fractures that, like in bones, can resolve themselves if they are well treated. To insist on the Saint-Malo-Geneva line is to distance ourselves from an interpretation of France of the Ancien Régime (the France of the provinces) as well as that of the civil wars during the revolutionary period (with the conflict in the Vendée in particular). To speak of a division between cities and the countryside, or of the opposition between Paris and the provinces, is to assert the unity of the nation, since it leads to making urban and Parisian questions also rural questions.

Secondly, managing these inequalities has always been possible because of a fairly broad objective alliance between social and territorial interests and economic actors. Erasing the Saint-Malo-Geneva boundary makes it possible to extend economic and social progress to the whole country. Reducing Parisian industrial employment at the time of Fordism amounts to favoring the competitiveness of the territory. Bringing networks to the countryside means promoting agricultural and industrial development.

Rather than trying to weigh up the reciprocal analytical merits of the different readings of the divides, should we not look more precisely at the forces capable of joining forces to produce new policies to fight against territorial inequalities?

3.6. References

Arendt, H. (1967). *Essai sur la Révolution*. Gallimard, Paris.

Ascher, F. (1998). *La république contre la ville : essai sur l'avenir de la France urbaine*. Éditions de l'Aube, La Tour-d'Aigues.

Auphan, E. (2002). L'apogée des chemins de fer secondaires en France : essai d'interprétation cartographique. *Revue d'histoire des chemins de fer*, 24(25), 24–46.

Aydalot, P. (1978). L'aménagement du territoire en France. *L'Espace géographique*, 7(4), 245–253.

Aydalot, P. (1985). *Économie régionale et urbaine*. Economica, Paris.

Baron, M. (2019). La formation supérieure en régions (France). *Cybergeo: European Journal of Geography*. doi: 10.4000/cybergeo.2575.

Beckouche, P. and Damette, F. (1992). Le système productif en région parisienne : le renversement fonctionnel. *Espaces et sociétés*, 66(1), 235–254.

Béhar, D., Czertok, S., Desjardins, X. (2021). *Faire région, faire France. Quand la région planifie*. Berger-Levrault, Boulogne-Billancourt.

Boulanger, P. (1998). Géographie historique de la conscription et des conscrits en France de 1914 à 1922 d'après les comptes rendus sur le recrutement de l'armée. PhD Thesis, Université de Paris 4.

Briand, J.P. (1995). Le renversement des inégalités régionales de scolarisation et l'enseignement primaire supérieur en France (fin XIXe – milieu XXe siècle). *Histoire de l'éducation*, 66(1), 159–200.

CGET (2018). Rapport sur la cohésion des territoires. Report, CGET, Paris.

Chartier, R. (1997). La ligne Saint-Malo-Genève. In *Les lieux de mémoire*, Nora, P. (ed.). Gallimard, Paris.

Courcelle, T., Ygal, F., Taulelle, F. (eds) (2017). *Services publics et territoires : adaptations, innovations et réactions*. Presses universitaires de Rennes.

Davezies, L. (2021). *L'État a toujours soutenu ses territoires*. Le Seuil, Paris.

Davezies, L. and Talandier, M. (2014). *L'émergence de systèmes productivorésidentiels : territoires productifs, territoires résidentiels, quelles interaction ?* La Documentation française, Paris.

Delpirou, A. (2018). La couleur des gilets jaunes. La Vie des idées [Online]. Available at: https://laviedesidees.fr/La-couleur-des-gilets-jaunes.html.

Desjardins, X. and Estèbe, P. (2019). *Villes petites et moyennes et aménagement territorial – Éclairages anglais, allemands et italiens sur le cas français*. Éditions PUCA, Paris.

Dupin, B.P.C.F. (1827). *Forces productives et commerciales de la France*. Bachelier, Paris.

Emangard, P.H. and Beaucire, F. (1985). Du bon et du mauvais usage des gares T.G.V. dans les régions traversées. *Géocarrefour*, 60(4), 359–373.

Faburel, G. (2019). *Les métropoles barbares*. Le Passager clandestin, Paris.

Gadrey, J. and Jany-Catrice, F. (2016). *Les nouveaux indicateurs de richesse*. La Découverte, Paris.

Gravier, J.F. (1947). *Paris et le désert français : décentralisation, équipement, population.* Le Portulan, Paris.

Guilluy, C. (2014). *La France périphérique : comment on a sacrifié les classes populaires.* Flammarion, Paris.

Hervieu, B. and Viard, J. (2001). *L'archipel paysan : la fin de la république agricole.* Éditions de l'Aube, La Tour d'Aigues.

Laferté, G. (2019). Du notable à la petite bourgeoisie. Sociologie des élus ruraux du Châtillonnais (XIXe–XXIe siècle). *Études rurales*, 204, 42–64.

Le Lidec, P. (2003). Les maires dans la République. L'Association des maires de France, élément constitutif des régimes politiques français depuis 1907. *Annuaire des Collectivités Locales*, 23(1), 647–654.

Marchand, B. (2001). La haine de la ville : "Paris et le désert français" de Jean-François Gravier. *L'information géographique*, 65(3), 234–253.

Marx, K. (1969). *Le 18 Brumaire de Louis Bonaparte.* Éditions Sociales, Paris.

Maugis, S. and Touahir, M. (2019). Indice d'éloignement pour les établissements scolaires. Report, Ministère de l'Éducation nationale et de la jeunesse, Paris.

Mokyr, J. (2001). The rise and fall of the factory system: Technology, firms, and households since the industrial revolution. *Carnegie-Rochester Conference Series on Public Policy*, 55, 1–45.

Noël, G. (1988). La participation de la France aux stratégies d'organisation internationale de l'agriculture. *Économie rurale*, 184(1), 63–70.

Ozouf-Marignier, M.V. and Verdier, N. (2013). Les mutations des circonscriptions territoriales françaises. Crise ou mutation ? In *Mélanges de l'École française de Rome – Italie et Méditerranée modernes et contemporaines.* École française de Rome.

Planhol, X. (1994). *Géographie historique de la France.* Fayard, Paris.

Prost, A. (1993). Pour une histoire "par en bas" de la scolarisation républicaine. *Histoire de l'éducation*, 57(1), 59–74.

Prud'homme, R. (1974). Critique de la politique d'aménagement du territoire. *Revue d'économie politique*, 84(6), 921–935.

Prud'homme, R., Rochefort, P., Nicol, C. (1975). La répartition spatiale des fonds budgétaires. *Revue d'économie politique*, 85(1), 38–59.

Salomon Cavin, J. (2005). *La ville, mal-aimée : représentations anti-urbaines et aménagement du territoire en Suisse.* Presses polytechniques et universitaires romandes, Lausanne.

Trempé, R. (1971). *Les mineurs de Carmaux, 1848-1914*. Éditions ouvrières, Ivry-sur-Seine.

Uhrich, R. (1987). *La France inverse ? Les régions en mutation*. Economica, Paris.

Vigier, P. (1991). La République à la conquête des paysans, les paysans à la conquête du suffrage universel. *Politix. Revue des sciences sociales du politique*, 4(15), 7–12.

4

The Periurban Question

Éric CHARMES
EVS, ENTPE, Vaulx-en-Velin, France

4.1. Introduction

In France, one of the most common territorial divides separates the working-class suburbs of the large metropolises and their gentrified centers. Over the past decade, however, another divide has emerged in public debate, pitting supposedly left-behind rural areas and small cities against metropolises that are seen as the winners of globalization. In France, the essayist Christophe Guilluy has helped draw attention to this divide. He has had great political (rather than academic) success (Charmes 2014) with the notion of "peripheral France", which refers to the struggling territories that are far away from the metropolises (Guilluy 2014). This understanding of the territory – which contrasts metropolises with other territories – echoes others outside of France, in connection with the distribution of so-called "populist" votes (Broz et al. 2021). This interpretation of territorial fractures has the advantage of going beyond the classic rural urban divide to associate small and medium-sized cities with the countryside and set them against the metropolises. The difference is significant: while France has several hundred cities, only a dozen or so can claim the status of metropolis (at least in geographical terms and in meeting the criteria of size and the presence of functions typical of metropolises)[1]. The opposition between peripheral France and the metropolises continues, however, to mix very disparate territories, and does not make it possible to understand the long-established blurring of relations between cities and the countryside. This blurring is particularly intense in the periurban rings, that is, in the rural areas that surround cities and metropolises and are integrated into the functional systems constituted by the latter (Nilsson et al. 2013).

Behind periurbanization is an old dream, formulated more than a century ago by one of the historical figures of urban planning, Ebenezer Howard: to marry the advantages of the city with those of the countryside. With the development of transport and remote communication, this dream has become a reality for many: it is possible to live in the countryside, while commuting regularly to the city. This may require long commutes to work, especially around the largest metropolitan areas. But this seems to be acceptable for the households that, year after year, move to small towns and villages surrounding cities. This is how villages close to large cities can attract senior executives and be at the heart of metropolization, far from the supposed plight of "peripheral France". Conversely, some periurban villages have become places of relegation and social suffering. This is especially true for low-income homeowners who are forced to move away from their place of work to find affordable housing and whose transportation costs can become too high. This was one of the key drivers of the *Gilets jaunes* movement, which emerged in the fall of 2018 following the announcement of an increase in fuel taxes (Kipfer 2019; Jeanpierre 2020).

Thus, if the old opposition between villages and cities is largely obsolete, it is not clear whether the opposition between metropolises and peripheral France can replace it. This chapter, after defining and geographically characterizing periurbanization in France, examines the sociological and political changes in the countryside. It will then turn to the case of medium-sized cities, many of which are now dominated by their periurban rings, before considering the opposite situation of large metropolises, where the periurbs are often seen as a place of relegation. In the face of these conditions, the chapter ends by examining the available policy options, following two main paths: the first is to supplement the right to the city with the right to the village; the second is to

---

1 The geographical definition of metropolization is the subject of much debate, but based on the criteria of size and concentration of certain professionals (senior private sector executives, intellectual professions), France has a dozen or so metropolises. For the sake of simplicity, and in accordance with the criteria used by Insee in France, metropolitan areas are defined here as those with more than 700,000 inhabitants (see Box 4.1 for definitions and Table 4.1 for numbers). In France, smaller cities have a government called "Metropolis". In this case, the status comes from the French organization of intermunicipalities and is *not* geographic (Charmes 2019).

modulate or even revise the critique of urban sprawl to take better advantage of the intermingling of the rural and the urban brought by periurbanization.

4.2. Periurbanization in figures and tables

While the press regularly insists that the world is becoming increasingly urbanized, some geographers are calling attention to the new appeal of the countryside and even go so far as to speak of an "urban exodus". This is particularly the case in France (Merlin 2009), where many cities are losing inhabitants and many young households with children are leaving metropolises and moving to the countryside, which, in France, often means moving to a small municipality. Indeed, France counts 35,000 municipalities for a population of 67 million inhabitants. Thus, since the 1960s, a large number of small municipalities have seen their population grow steadily. Most stayed small however, growing from a few hundred inhabitants to more than a thousand – so much so that today, nearly a quarter of the population lives in a municipality with fewer than 2,000 inhabitants[2]. This living situation is highly valued: many see it as an asset to live in what they call a "village"[3]. Covid-19 has greatly reinforced the significance of these discourses (Milet et al. 2023).

However, talking of an urban exodus is questionable. First of all, several French metropolises, such as Bordeaux, Nantes, Rennes, Lyon and Toulouse, remain very attractive and are experiencing significant population growth (+1.1% per year between 2011 and 2016 for the Lyon Metropolis, compared to +0.4% on average for France as a whole). Their high rent and real estate prices do not dissuade households from moving there.

Then, and above all, the world of the metropolises and that of the countryside largely overlap. This overlap is at the heart of the notions of "urban areas", redefined as "city catchment areas" since 2020 (see Box 4.1). These areas are made up of a "center" and a "ring". The notion of a center, based on the criteria of density and contiguity of built-up areas, corresponds fairly well to the common definition of a city:

---

2 Unless otherwise indicated, the demographic data in this chapter is all taken from the latest Insee census, noting that the census is "rotated" by four-year periods and that the most recent year available at the time of writing is 2018. If the figures are for another year, the date is specified.

3 A "village" can refer to various realities. For example, up until 2020, Insee distinguished between rural municipalities and urban municipalities from a threshold of 2,000 inhabitants for the main agglomeration (i.e. continuous built-up areas). But in current vocabulary, the term village can be applied to much more populated entities, particularly near large cities, where the name village underlines a rural anchorage, in opposition to the neighboring city. Consequently, some municipalities of 10,000 inhabitants can claim to be villages (Amarouche and Charmes 2019).

buildings built up around a center. However, the center is only part of a city catchment area[4]. To define the latter, Insee includes the municipalities under the influence of the center, which is established above a threshold of 15% of the active population working outside the boundaries of the municipality concerned and in the center. The municipalities thus identified form a ring. This ring may be described as periurban when it is included in a catchment area with more than 50,000 inhabitants[5].

> Until 2020, the zoning proposed by the French National Institute of Statistics (Insee) was specific to France. Some of the maps proposed in this chapter are based on this zoning, called "urban areas zoning"" (*zonage en aires urbaines* (ZAU)). In 2020, Insee adopted a new zoning, called "city catchment areas zoning" (*zonage en aires d'attraction des villes* (ZAAV)). While slightly different, this new zoning is based on the categories and nomenclature used by Eurostat and the OECD to define functional urban areas (FUA) and cities (Dijkstra et al. 2019).
>
> Like the ZAAV, the ZAU identified "centers" (*pôle*), consisting of a core municipality and the suburbs agglomerated to it, as well as "rings" (*couronnes*), which build on the metropolis. A center and its ring form an urban area – a concept that has been replaced by that of city catchment area with the ZAAV. One of the main differences between the ZAAV and the ZAU is that the latter does not take into account density, and in particular, the 1,500 inhabitants per km² criterion used by the ZAAV to define the centers. The ZAU favored a criterion of built-up continuity – a rather loose criterion that led to the delimitation of more extensive centers than in the ZAAV (built-up continuity was established from a distance of less than 200 m between two buildings). Moreover, in the ZAU, centers were considered urban when they gathered 10,000 jobs, whereas in the ZAAV, the classification of a city catchment area is determined by its population. Thus, in the 2010s, while Insee identified 241 urban areas in France (Brutel and Lévy 2011), it now distinguishes 699 city catchment areas: Paris, 13 metropolitan, 47 large, 126 medium and 512 small (see Table 4.1). This classification is slightly different than that in functional urban areas, since Eurostat identifies areas with a center of more than 50,000 inhabitants as such (the center is then called a "city"). With this criterion, Eurostat identified 85 functional urban areas in France.
>
> Another major difference concerns the defining of rings. In the ZAAV, rings are defined on the basis of their dependence on the center (*pôle*) and measured by a commuting rate to the center of more than 15%. In the ZAU, this threshold was set at 40%. However, it was used in an iterative fashion: an initial calculation was used to define a first ring of municipalities; a second calculation, based on the center plus the periurban ring thus defined, extended the ring and so on, until the perimeter was stabilized. Consequently, when a secondary center (a town or even a city) was integrated

---

4 Only the essential elements of the definitions are presented here. For more details, see Cusin et al. (2016) and Aragau (2018).
5 This threshold is not explicitly used by Insee, but set for this chapter in line with the previous zonings used by Insee (see Box 4.1).

into a periurban ring, during the next iteration, the municipalities linked to this secondary center were in turn integrated into the ring. Thus, the further we moved away from the center of an urban area, the less direct dependence on that center was shown. As a consequence, these municipalities became more dependent on the intermediary of a secondary center (which constituted the main center of daily life for the inhabitants of the surrounding area). Unfortunately, the ZAAV, like the functional urban area zoning, obliterates this reality, defining rings only by their direct dependence on a center. This is particularly regrettable for metropolises, given that polycentrism is an essential part of metropolization (Hall and Pain 2006).

However, for a given city, the perimeters of the areas defined by the ZAU and ZAAV are quite comparable (Genevois 2018). As such, in 2015, the urban area of Paris had 12.5 million inhabitants when its catchment area had 12 million inhabitants. For a city like Lorient, in Brittany, the resulting populations were almost equivalent in 2015, with 218,000 inhabitants on one side versus 220,000 on the other. In a few cases, the gap is more substantial. This is particularly true for Lyon, whose urban area had 2.3 million inhabitants compared with 2 million for its catchment area.

Box 4.1. *French and European zonings*

These rings do not correspond to the common image of the city: similar to what some American geographers call the "exurbs" (Berube et al. 2006), they mostly resemble the countryside (Figure 4.1). The inhabitants themselves are surprised when they discover that their municipality is periurban. They consider themselves, not without reason, to be living in the countryside, near a large city of course, but in the countryside nonetheless. In fact, in the former zoning in urban areas (see Box 4.1), nearly two-thirds of French farms (in terms of number as well as surface area) were located in the periurbs[6]. Likewise, according to this zoning, more than half of the periurbanites resided in municipalities that Insee classified as "rural", that is, whose main built-up area had fewer than 2,000 inhabitants (Aragau 2018). Yet, this definition of rurality was rather restrictive: in Great Britain, for example, all spaces located outside centers of more than 10,000 inhabitants are classified as rural[7]. With such a threshold, 95% of the inhabitants of the French periurbs would have been classified as rural dwellers.

The periurban rings of the cities have significant demographic weight (see Table 4.1). They account for more than two-thirds of the population. They are one of

---

6 According to data from the Ministry of Agriculture, published in *Agreste Primeur*, No. 299, 2013 (it should be noted that the definition of the periurbs used in this publication is slightly more extensive than the one used here).
7 Based on Office for National Statistics categories.

the main places where the French population lives. They have almost as many inhabitants as all of the metropolitan areas (i.e. those with more than 700,000 inhabitants). In contrast, small and very small cities (whose area has fewer than 50,000 inhabitants), as well as the countryside outside the catchment area of a city, account for only 18.9% of the population.

Figure 4.1. *Charny, in Seine-et-Marne, 50 km from the center of Paris, a municipality of 1,200 inhabitants with a landscape typical of the eastern quadrant of Paris' periurban ring (source: Charmes (2007)). For a color version of this figure, see http://www.iste.co.uk/talandier/territorial.zip*

Figure 4.2. *Auxerre, a medium sized urban area*

COMMENT ON FIGURE 4.2.– *In the middle, the three municipalities of Auxerre, which form the metropolis (pôle urbain), with their built-up spaces in continuity with each other. These three municipalities have 42,000 inhabitants, less than half of the 92,000 inhabitants of the urban area. The 50,000 inhabitants of the periurban ring are scattered in 65 municipalities (map established according to the 2010 ZAU).*

Type of areas	Number of spaces	Number of municipalities	Population		Share of periurban rings in the population of the area
			Number of inhabitants	Distribution (%)	
Paris metropolis	1	1,929	13,025,000	19.5	19.1
Other metropolitan areas (excluding Paris) with 700,000 or more inhabitants	13	2,733	13,137,000	19.7	48.1
Large areas of 200,000 to less than 700,000 inhabitants	47	5,698	15,732,000	23.6	53.9
Medium areas of 50,000 to less than 200,000 inhabitants	126	7,824	12,295,000	18.4	59.6
Small areas of less than 50,000 inhabitants	512	7,852	8,126,000	12.2	
Municipalities outside city catchment areas	–	8,932	4,467,000	6.7	–
All French municipalities	699	34,968	66,781,000	100	42.6

Table 4.1. *Types of space with their share in the French population, according to the 2020 city catchment areas zoning (ZAAV)[8]*

Within the individual areas considered on their own basis, the periurbs also have significant demographic weight. In most medium-sized city catchment areas, the large majority of the population is periurban (see Figure 4.2). This also applies to

---

8 The table is based on data presented in *Insee Focus*, No. 211, 2020.

some metropolises: for example, in Rennes, the largest city in the Brittany region whose catchment area has 740,000 inhabitants, nearly two-thirds (or 472,000) live in the periurban ring. In the largest metropolises, periurbanites represent a smaller share of the catchment area population (19.1% in Paris). But in absolute terms, the numbers are high. Around Paris, there are about 2.5 million periurbanites.

4.3. The revitalization of the countryside

Periurbanization is the main source of dynamism in the French countryside. The villages and small towns that are experiencing the most remarkable demographic growth are generally in the process of periurbanization, on their way to integrating a catchment area. The periurbanization of a municipality is the result of two different processes, with the arrival of young households from a neighboring city in which they continue to work, on the one hand, and households already established in the municipality that go to look for a job in this neighboring city, without moving there, on the other hand. Since the 1960s, the number of villages that have been revitalized in this way has increased steadily; it is as if a wave of population growth is spreading to the countryside around the large cities. Regularly, cities and metropolises integrate new rural areas into their orbit. The catchment area of Toulouse is a good example of this geographical mechanism: although in the early 1960s, the ring did not encompass any municipalities, it included 197 in 1990, 270 in 1999 and 380 in the 2010 zoning (Bonnin-Oliveira 2012).

It may seem appropriate to speak of an urban exodus insofar as the families that carry the demographic growth in periurban villages seek to leave the city to settle in the countryside. At the same time, these families do not just settle anywhere, but choose to do so in the countryside close to a city, in order to continue to benefit from the latter's resources. In many cases, they remain dependent on the city for an essential aspect of their daily lives: employment. On the other hand, the rural exodus is slowed down because rural people can find a job in a nearby city. In this case, the revival of the countryside is only the extension of the area of influence of large metropolises. The countryside is revitalizing itself by becoming urban, following the model of generalized urbanization put forward by Lefebvre (1970).

A few figures make it possible to specify the influence of periurbanization from among the dynamics that affect rural areas. Insee has divided metropolitan France into some 1,900 "daily life areas", which are areas where it is possible to satisfy the essential needs of daily life. A distinction can be made between predominantly urban areas, organized around a large or medium-sized city, and predominantly rural areas. According to the work of Pistre (2011), 40% of the latter are not very attractive: they are home to low-income populations and are located far from the major cities. Of the 60% of rural daily life areas that are attractive, 80% are periurban. The 20% that are not periurban attract mostly tourists and second-home owners. These figures confirm that rural revitalization is essentially linked to the extension of the area of influence of cities. The transformations carried out by the "neo-rural" (Sencébé 2004) (i.e. people who move to the countryside to work and adopt a rural lifestyle) certainly exist. Their numbers are even growing (Grimault 2020). This being the case, the renewal of neo-rurality remains limited, both sociologically and geographically.

Not all of the revitalized countryside is just urban: around the largest cities, it can even be metropolitan. The idea of a metropolitan countryside may seem like an oxymoron, but in the villages located a few dozen kilometers from Paris, daily life is much more metropolitan than in many French cities. To the west of the French capital, in the department of Yvelines, the population of many of the villages is dominated by executives – some of whom work, for example, in the La Défense business center, which is one of the largest in Europe. These executives, who claim to live in the countryside, regularly take advantage of the infrastructures and cultural resources of Paris. In the center of France, in the cities of a few tens of thousands of inhabitants that used to radiate out to hundreds of small towns and villages (as prefectures for example), daily life is much less metropolitan. The cultural offer exists, but is limited; it is also impossible to take a direct flight abroad and the "creative classes", whose presence is a marker of metropolization, are almost absent (Martin-Brelot et al. 2010).

Thus, the contradictions between discourses that emphasize the expansion of the urban realm (Brenner 2014) and those that insist on the urban exodus are only apparent. In terms of demographics, some rural areas are indeed showing signs of vitality, with the arrival of many households. At the same time, this revitalization is based on the development of mobility (especially by car) and the improvement of communication (including developments in teleworking as a result of the Covid-19 crisis). It results from the expansion of cities catchment areas. In most cases, villages are revitalized as they become part of a city's orbit; those who move into these villages are primarily urbanites, with lifestyles that are not easily distinguished from those of the inhabitants of metropolises.

By meeting in the periurbs, cities and countryside have hybridized (Vanier 2016): they have composed a new world. The interdependence of cities and the countryside is not new, but up until the 1960s, the two formed very distinct social worlds. The countryside was made up of relatively similar, self-contained villages from which most people rarely moved (Morin 2013). These villages were juxtaposed in a hierarchical system, dominated by the cities, which were the places where commercial exchanges took place. However, since the 1960s, this territorial system has progressively lost its pre-eminence: the urban has spread to the rural, while conversely, the rural has become part of the daily life of urban people.

4.4. Villages: from community to club

As spaces of daily life, rural communities have lost a large part of their autonomy. Unlike the farmers of the 1960s, many of the inhabitants of the countryside depend on a metropolitan area on a daily basis for work, leisure or consumerism. At the same time, the villages have diversified, distinguishing themselves from each other by offering a particular way of life, which households enjoy according to their tastes and, even more so, their financial capacities (in the periurban ring of Paris in 2020, the average price of single-family homes ranged from €1,200 to €5,000 per m²)[9].

Over the course of these changes, the relationship with the emblematic space of the countryside, the village, has been completely transformed. Local social relations have been particularly transformed, with groups that previously tended to form political communities (where people who have not chosen to live together organize the sharing of what they have in common) and that now tend to constitute residential clubs (where people who have decided to move there are united by their choice of a specific living environment).

In the 1960s, rural villages formed political communities. Without going into detail (Charmes 2009), in these villages, there was little or no discussion regarding membership or belonging: in traditional rural societies, you would rarely choose the village where you would spend your entire life. The majority of people were destined to remain in the place where they had been born for the rest of their lives. The questions people asked themselves were: how can we live together? How can we share the available resources? Who can lead their cattle to the communal pastures? The question was whether access to the pastures should be reserved for the poorest, those who did not own a field, or for the wealthiest, those whose taxes financed the municipality (Vivier 1998) And when the local rules were contested, people rarely sought to leave, but preferred to work to change the political orientations and choices of the community.

---

9 According to data posted on the real estate brokerage site Meilleurs Agents. For single-family homes in the upscale suburbs of Paris, such as Neuilly-sur-Seine, this price rises to €12,000 per m².

These lifestyles and political debates have largely disappeared from villages. As they have become periurbanized, many of these villages have become residential spaces wherein households choose to live for a few years and where they spend only a portion of their daily life. With these residential and daily mobilities, people's relationship with their place of residence has become more utilitarian and economic than political. This transformation can be found everywhere in the world: in Brazil, the United States or China, it often materializes into privately governed residential complexes, many of which are gated communities (Le Goix and Webster 2008). However, this local private governance is much less widespread in France than elsewhere, as other means exist to control and manage residential spaces. Indeed, while in many respects France deserves its image as a centralized country, this is not the case for urban planning, and in particular, for zoning and land use regulations. Even if, in recent years, there has been a recentralization, the prerogatives of the municipalities are very important. Like the others, the periurban municipalities control the rules that determine land use, between protected natural areas, agriculture, commerce, industry and housing. They can also regulate the height of buildings or density and can even impose architectural requirements, such as the type of roofing or the color of the facades. There is therefore no need to resort to private governance to control the development of periurban territories, since municipal councils are able to do this (Charmes 2011). Urban planning rules even have the significant advantage of allowing control over the use of land without having to acquire it.

Here, the small population size of periurban municipalities is a determining factor. It is indeed difficult to govern large municipalities in the same way as a private residential complex. These municipalities group together tens, or even hundreds of thousands of inhabitants. In the municipal councils, very diverse political projects confront each other, and the defense of their interests alone by the inhabitants of a neighborhood is complicated. The situation is very different in the periurbs, where most municipalities have a population the size of a neighborhood or even a city block. In urban area zoning (ZAU), nine out of 10 periurban municipalities had a population of less than 2,000. Thus, periurban municipalities can operate in a manner quite similar to a private residential complex and many do so. When a municipality is the size of a large private residential complex, and the residents are overwhelmingly homeowners (typically, 80% of residents are owners), the main political demand is focused on residential issues (Charmes 2009). In the municipality, the inhabitants ask their council to seize the tools at their disposal to manage and maintain their living environment. In addition, in the periurbs, the feeling of belonging to a particular place, distinct from the others, is favored by the limited extension of built-up areas and their surrounding by nature or agriculture (see Figure 4.1). In many periurban municipalities, buying a single-family home is thus like buying a ticket to a club: by moving into a house, we also become a member of a municipality whose inhabitants are united by their mutual enjoyment of a particular living environment.

In wealthy or bourgeois territories, decisions are quite similar from one municipality to another, falling under a form of exclusionary zoning (Schmidt and Paulsen 2009). In accordance with the club model, the municipality is concerned with access to the municipal territory via, among other things, the regulation of urban extensions. Very protective urban planning regulations are put in place, limiting urbanization to part (often less than a quarter) of the municipality's territory. This Malthusianism articulates preservation of the living environment and enhancement of real estate heritage. As a result of the real estate market, the clubs that offer the most sought-after living environment become the most exclusive and the most expensive to access. This is the reason why the chic periurban communities of large metropolises are particularly affected by "clubbisation" (Charmes 2009). In these municipalities, the increase in real estate prices is often accompanied by a drop in the number of inhabitants: as the inhabitants age and their children leave the parental home, it is not possible for new households to be accommodated for as there are few new constructions.

Of course, not all small residential municipalities surrounding the big cities have become clubs. Social logics specific to the political community are maintained and even defended (this important point will be discussed below). The club is above all an ideal-type – an abstract model that makes it possible to give meaning to the current changes and understand the transformations undergone by the rural municipalities with periurbanization. It helps to better understand the meaning of the attachment that periurban dwellers show to their village, despite the fact that their lives have become metropolitan. It also makes it possible to analyze the mechanisms that sustain inequalities between households in the periurbs. Indeed, clubbisation is linked to the constitution of a market for residential municipalities, according to a model similar to that of Tiebout (Fischel and Oates 2006), and, like many other markets, the periurban club market favors the more affluent and maintains forms of segregation (Dawkins 2005).

4.5. Unequal intermunicipal governments

Clubbisation is not a form of residential secession, but rather the opposite: it is because the inhabitants of villages close to large cities spend most of their waking life elsewhere that these villages can specialize in residential neighborhoods and become clubs. The question then arises of how best to govern the relationship between periurban clubs and the metropolises connected with them. This problem refers to the more general question of how to govern metropolises and to the fact that the dispersion of daily life over vast areas calls into question the powers of the municipalities, especially when they are small. The problem is particularly acute in France, where land use planning competences are divided between 35,000 municipalities. Thus, in France, even more than elsewhere (Cox 2010; Judd and Hinze 2018), a broad consensus has emerged in favor of expanding local governments, so that the territories of democratic debate and local public action correspond to those of everyday life. Intermunicipal governments have developed on this basis (for a comparative approach to cooperation between local governments on a European scale, see Wollmann (2012)).

Cooperation between municipalities has existed for a long time and has been implemented through special districts (*syndicats*) since 1890. However, those districts have mainly approached cooperation as something technical. Most of them were focused on the provision of a specific service or the management of a single public equipment. In 1992, a form of intermunicipal government (hereafter intermunicipality) was created to carry out projects that were debated politically. The consolidation of intermunicipality is still underway, with the municipalities progressively dispossessed of their prerogatives in favor of their intermunicipal government.

However, not all intermunicipal governments are equal, since they are organized into different categories. The various laws, which since 1992, reinforced intermunicipality, treat the municipalities in a differentiated way, with the political will to make the metropolises the dominant local governments (Le Galès 2003). In France, cooperation between metropolitan core municipalities and their suburbs has over time become a key issue. This cooperation was promoted in order to allow metropolises to change their scale of action, gain influence and increase their capacity for large urban projects, which seemed necessary in the face of competition from other large European metropolises. The current culmination of this spatial integration is an intermunicipal government called Metropolis (*Métropole*), created in 2014[10].

Outside the metropolises, intermunicipalities have developed, but they have done so in a minor form, with diminished powers and limited resources. The difference increases as we descend in the hierarchy, from the metropolises to the "community of municipalities" (*communauté de communes*), a form of intermunicipality that is both the least integrated and the most widespread in the periurban and rural areas. The low population of the communities of municipalities (around 22,000 inhabitants

---

10 This form of intermunicipality dedicated to metropolises is capitalized to avoid confusion with the geographical entities discussed so far.

on average at the end of the 2010s) severely limits the resources at their disposal. These resources are all the more reduced as, per inhabitant, the budgetary endowments by the state are significantly lower than those allocated to the metropolises on the grounds that the latter have to deal with "centrality charges" (Depraz 2020). While the communities of municipalities are granted 20 euros per inhabitant, the metropolises benefit from 60 euros, that is, three times as much[11]. Consequently, the periurban intermunicipalities are for the most part politically, administratively and financially inferior to the metropolises. Yet 26,400 municipalities and more than one-third of the French population are gathered in communities of municipalities.

Because of its technical nature, this problem is rarely discussed outside of specialist circles. However, this is one of the sources of the success of Guilluy's (2014) theses on the "peripheral France" and the opposition that has been built up in public debates between metropolises (increasingly confused with their intermunicipal governments) and the rest of the territory. Intermunicipality is not the only issue. Its organization merely reflects broader developments in public policy that have gradually become more favorable to metropolises. The change was clear under the presidency of Nicolas Sarkozy (2007–2012), the first French president since the Second World War to display local roots in the Parisian center and not in the rural world. In the name of global competition and the key role that metropolises play in it, greater economic productivity granted to these same metropolises and the rationalization of public expenditure and in search of economies of scale, the facilities and public services present in medium and small cities have been reduced, if not completely closed. These cities, along with rural areas and towns, have become the poor relations of public policies.

However, change is slow and the countryside and small municipalities did not become totally secondary players. The municipalities that join the orbit of a large metropolis are in some respects experiencing a favorable evolution. Weak political power and low budgetary resources do not prevent them from attracting households, including executives. On the other hand, the reforms promoting intermunicipality are only very gradually changing an institutional context dominated by municipal powers. Even when they are small, municipalities continue to play a decisive role in local policies.

In fact, resistance to intermunicipality is very strong. One of the critic of this change was none other than François Mitterrand (President of the French Republic from 1981 to 1995): "There are 36,000 municipalities? This is very useful. That

---

11 According to local taxation data for the year 2017 from the *Direction générale des collectivités* (Ministry of Territorial Cohesion).

makes 500,000 municipal councilors without counting, don't forget, the 500,000 others who would have liked to be. That is one million citizens who are interested in local affairs. And you want to reduce that to a quarter of professionals? You're crazy"[12]. Here, Mitterrand's point of view is close to that of Alexis de Tocqueville, who saw in local associations the places where people learn about the limits of individualism and, by extension, of the democratic spirit, about the need to negotiate and find compromises in order to not only live with others, but also carry out projects collectively (Ferraton 2004). In another register, left libertarians see in acting in common at the local level the ferments of a true democracy (we will come back to this in the following). These and other currents of thought come together to support the thousands of mayors who, more pragmatically, want to defend their prerogatives and their power to act.

4.6. When the periurbs rebel

Intermunicipality also offers some opportunities for political affirmation for periurbs, which the villages can use to unite and carry weight within their catchment area. Certainly, when they are close to a large metropolis, the "communities of municipalities" have difficulty making themselves heard, particularly because of their lesser demographic weight. Even if all of the communities of municipalities were to form an alliance, the 1,500 or so municipalities in the Paris periurban ring would (as it has already been said) only account for 19% of the total population of the catchment area. Besides, such an alliance remains highly unlikely. Paris' periurban municipalities are currently scattered in dozens of intermunicipalities and what can they do in the face of the Greater Paris Metropolis and its seven million inhabitants? The demographic differences are less pronounced for the other French metropolises, but they remain significant. In such a context, periurban intermunicipalities are often drawn into defensive postures. For example, the community of municipalities of eastern Lyon, which hosts the airport of the Lyon metropolitan region, devotes a great deal of energy to avoiding falling under the control of the Lyon Metropolis. The jobs associated with airport activity and the tax resources that result from it are indeed arousing appetites.

When cities are smaller, neighboring communities are able to be more offensive. This is particularly true for former industrial territories whose cities have been weakened by decades of deindustrialization and whose old districts, as well as social housing estates, are now impoverished. Saint-Étienne, whose center has 289,000 inhabitants, is in this situation and suffers very badly from competition from its periurban ring and its 207,000 inhabitants. Saint-Étienne has been confronted with a

---

12 Cited in Laruelle, N. (2008). Sortir de l'impasse. *Vacarme*, 42, 40–43.

form of "white flight", whereby the middle classes are leaving the city center (where households of North African origin are especially concentrated) as it becomes increasingly impoverished, to settle instead in the surrounding periurban villages (Béal et al. 2020). This competition has taken on a new dimension with intermunicipality. In 2017, three communities of municipalities in the periurbs of Saint-Etienne united to form a larger intermunicipality based in Montbrison (a town of just over 15,000 inhabitants) and sufficiently populated to take on the status, which is more favorable in terms of financial endowment by the state, of a "community of agglomeration" (*communauté d'agglomération*). This intermunicipality, called Loire-Forez, brought together 87 municipalities of which only one (apart from Montbrison) had more than 10,000 inhabitants. This intermunicipality is thus mainly made up of villages. By forming an intermunicipal alliance, the latter weighs 112,000 inhabitants, which is no longer completely negligible compared to Saint-Étienne Métropole and its 404,000 inhabitants. As such, Loire-Forez weighs all the more in the local political game as it captures a large part of the population growth, attracts the middle classes and sees employment develop, to the detriment of Saint-Étienne.

Finally, if, when directly associated with the intermunicipality of a metropolis, small municipalities are often dominated by the central municipality, they are not without means of expression. They sometimes even manage to control the political game, especially when the central municipality is in difficulty. The case of Mulhouse, a former industrial center with a catchment area of 410,000 inhabitants, illustrates this well (Miot 2016). In response to legislative changes, the intermunicipality build on the central city has been expanded, growing from 16 to 33 municipalities in 2009, and then to 39 municipalities in 2017, in a catchment area that contains 132. As a result of this change, the internal balance of the intermunicipality has shifted in favor of the small peripheral municipalities (except for Mulhouse, all of the municipalities have fewer than 15,000 inhabitants). The result is that the presidency of the Mulhouse intermunicipality passed into the hands of the mayor of Berrwiller, a periurban municipality of 1,200 inhabitants. The fact that Mulhouse is one of the poorest cities in France, while certain periurban municipalities, in particular those close to the Swiss border, are conversely among the wealthiest, is not insignificant. The mayor of Mulhouse, defeated at the presidency of the intermunicipality, was not mistaken in declaring that his eviction showed "that representatives of wealthy municipalities no longer wish to pay for the poor"[13].

---

13 Comments published in *L'Alsace*, December 18, 2016 ("M2A, les dessous d'une crise").

4.7. City life in the countryside: an unequal dream

In medium-sized cities, where real estate pressure remains limited, large sections of the middle classes are generally able to access the periurbs. There are a few exceptions, especially cities whose hinterland is very attractive from a tourist point of view, but generally, the working classes, as long as their incomes are stable, can find accommodation in a pleasant setting without moving away from the center. The situation is different for large metropolises, whose periurban rings are highly segregated. On the one hand, executives can afford a house in a bucolic living environment, while maintaining their access to excellent educational establishments and being close to highly qualified jobs. On the other hand, working-class families have to compromise on the quality of their living environment (e.g. by settling near a troublesome industrial activity) or on the distance from their place of work.

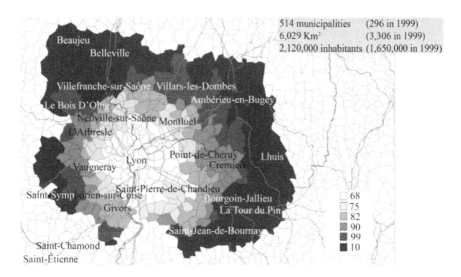

Figure 4.3. *Progressive extensions of Lyon's periurban ring (source: Lyon Metropolitan Area Planning Agency, 2011). For a color version of this figure, see http://www.iste.co.uk/talandier/territorial.zip*

COMMENT ON FIGURE 4.3.– *The different extensions of Lyon's periurban rings are delimited according to the ZUA, in force until 2020 (see Box 4.1). These extensions are due to the attractiveness of the metropolis, but also to the periurbanization of already existing villages and towns (such as La Tour-du-Pin and its 8,000 inhabitants).*

These families occupy an important place in the real estate markets of the periurban territories farthest from the metropolitan centers.[14] For example, households earning less than 2,500 euros represent about one-fifth of first-time buyers in the Lyon region (Mouillard and Vaillant 2018).[15] With the support of homeownership assistance policies (which include zero-interest loans, among other things), a couple of blue-collar or skilled employees are able to purchase a new single-family home. But in the metropolitan areas, they generally can only do so by moving away from the center.

The problem is that over time, working-class households have had to move farther and farther away to find affordable land – even up to well over 100 km in the case of Paris. Indeed, as villages become periurban, municipal land use regulations tend (as we have seen) toward the preservation of the living environment, and new housing construction is slowed down. The fight against urban sprawl has largely supported this local Malthusianism. National policies have combined with local policies to restrict the building of new single-family homes around metropolitan areas (Charmes et al. 2020). This has pushed low-income homebuyers to look further afield, in areas where rural development issues make national policies more conciliatory with respect to urban sprawl, and where local elected officials are concerned about revitalizing schools or taking advantage of increased land values. This is how the periurban rings of large metropolitan areas have expanded significantly over the decades, as illustrated in Figure 4.3. This model is not unique to France (Vyn 2012), but the periurban expansion it produces is particularly scattered in France because of the influence of small residential municipalities in local politics.

Over the course of the 2000s, this expansion has led to the emergence of a new form of precariousness (Charmes 2021) powered by the cost of travel (which can become very high). The only available report on the cost of housing and travel for households according to their location and income is out-dated (based on surveys conducted in the early 2000s) and covers only the Paris region, Île-de-France (Coulombel and Leurent 2012)[16]. It does, however, give an idea of what is at stake in transportation in terms of social equity: on average, low-income homebuyers in

---

14 The data that we have does not allow us to quantify precisely.
15 This threshold corresponds roughly to the upper limit of the third decile of households, classified according to their income per consumption unit, as defined by Insee in 2015 (see "Les niveaux de vie en 2015", *Insee Première*, no. 1665, September 2017). The region considered here is the Rhône-Alpes region (before the merger with the Auvergne region).
16 This assessment also suffers from significant limitations, particularly for small periurban municipalities: the figures are based on extrapolations whose statistical robustness is severely limited in the case of small municipalities.

rural municipalities spend more than 40% of their income on travel, while this figure falls well below 10% for residents of the central city, Paris, whose incomes are much higher[17].

These inequalities are the downsides to the revitalization of the countryside brought about by metropolitanization and the fact that, through daily mobility, households can access the resources of a city while residing in rural territories or in small towns. As the periurban rings have expanded their reach into the countryside, the distances traveled daily have increased and transport costs have risen with it. A multi-speed periurban territory has developed, with inner rings on one side and outer rings on the other. Thus, the duration of commutes between home and work is multiplied by almost two between the periurban ring closest to Paris and those furthest away (Berger et al. 2015). The distant periurban does not wear its name for nothing!

4.8. The *Gilets jaunes* crisis

These inequalities are aggravated by differences in the capacity of local governments to act. In the periurbs, they are generally unable to implement significant transport policies (Le Breton 2019). These inequalities are also exacerbated by national policies that concentrate public facilities and public services in metropolises (Taulelle 2012). Studies have indeed established a link between the rate of loss of these services and facilities at the communal level and the intensity of mobilization during the *Gilets jaunes* protests, one of the most significant social movements of the last few decades in France (Algan et al. 2020). Over the course of its duration, the protests took on an urban dimension with, among others, demonstrations on the Champs-Élysées in Paris. Initially, however, in fall 2018, the movement took shape a good distance away from the metropolises on roundabouts (Jeanpierre 2020).

Other inequalities are related to underdeveloped municipal services and facilities, particularly before and after school care. When you have to leave at 6:30 a.m. to get to work on time, childcare is a major concern. The longer the commute, the more difficult and costly childcare is to organize. And here again, the most low-income first-time buyers are over-represented among those whose needs are both the highest and whose access to services are the most degraded.

---

17 As stated above, rural municipalities are those whose main built-up area has less than 2,000 inhabitants.

Figure 4.4. *Grouping of Gilets jaunes around a roundabout during the first day of national mobilization (November 17, 2018). Photograph taken in La Tour-du-Pin, in the outer periurban ring of Lyon (source: author, 2018). For a color version of this figure, see http://www.iste.co.uk/talandier/territorial.zip*

In addition to the costs of housing, mobility or childcare, there are also various other expenses that reduce the amount of money left over to live on, such as telephone, Internet and television bills (Martinache 2019). Thus, once mandatory expenses have been paid, households whose adults have stable jobs and are paid just above the minimum wage (SMIC) can be categorized as poor and yet still be able to access property[18]. In France, with a poverty threshold established at 60% of the median income, a household composed of a couple with two children under the age of 14 is poor below a monthly income of 2,150 euros[19]. Because of the higher costs of transport, this threshold is much higher for low-income homebuyers in the periurbs.

Let us repeat, periurban populations are very diverse and not all are in difficulty (Dodier et al. 2012). Many people living in the periurbs are executives and do not encounter major difficulties in making ends meet (especially since they also tend to live in the periurbs closest to metropolitan centers and with the best facilities), and, among the low-income earners in the periurbs, many work close to home.

---

18 Set at 1,219 euros net (after mandatory contributions) in 2020.
19 This is the disposable income after taxes and payment of social benefits. Based on 2018 data presented by the *Observatoire des inégalités* (online).

Households of local origin often have family members nearby to help them, especially with childcare, and in general, many are satisfied living where they live.

Many, however, feel threatened – only getting by on overtime, with missed vacations and other hardships (Rougé and Bonnin 2008). They worry that their expenses will increase while their incomes stagnate. At the same time, they deplore the decline of public services (even if their presence remains significant, the dynamic is negative). And even when the end of the month is not too difficult, they judge what they see around them severely, worrying about their children, or revolting about the difficulties of a young couple who has just bought a house and cannot meet the expenses, despite working extra hours. Life's accidents are also the talk of the town: when they see the often devastating consequences, the inhabitants of the periurbs are made acutely aware of the fragility of their own situation. The *Gilets jaunes* crisis is largely the result of the anger generated by these life experiences and the anguish they cause. The increase in fuel taxes that sparked the movement was simply the straw that broke the camel's back (Jeanpierre 2019).

In fact, since the early 2000s, there have been several signs of the difficulties and dissatisfactions among the inhabitants in the periurban rings' fringes, in particular the very high electoral scores of Jean-Marie Le Pen's National Front, and then of Marine Le Pen's National Rally (Rivière 2008). These electoral results underlined the growing resentment toward a "system" that pushes those who want to buy a house outside of the big metropolises and that, at the same time, concentrates investment in the heart of the metropolis where the most affluent reside, and far from the modest populations that populate the small towns, the rural areas and the distant periurbs. It is true that France has long favored rural areas, and in many respects, they are still better equipped than large metropolises, for instance in terms of sports facilities (Lévy 2019). However, when it comes to the perception of inequalities, perspectives count for a lot. And, in this respect, it is rather the feeling of "neglect" that dominates (Taulelle 2012).

This sentiment is interpreted in various ways. Some emphasize that moving to the periurbs remains a choice and point to the responsibilities of those who complain (Levy 2007). This perspective will be detailed later in this chapter. Others (Ripoll and Rivière 2007; Lambert 2015) see low-income suburban households as victims of the capitalist system, which hijacks the aspirations of the working classes for its own benefit. This perspective is in line with the work of Bourdieu (1980), who studied homebuying by working-class households in the late 1980s. Within this framework, some intellectuals have proposed to respond to the *Gilets jaunes* crisis by activating the right to the city, proposed at the end of the 1960s by Lefebvre, and still relevant in critical urban thinking[20].

4.9. From the right to the city to the right to the village?

Ensuring the right to the city in the periurbs can meet certain demands, such as easier and less expensive access to resources of the metropolises, particularly their jobs. Appropriate transportation policies can reduce the cost of mobility, whereas regional planning policies can help to reduce the distance between homes and jobs or shops (Korsu et al. 2012). Invoking the right to the city also seems relevant to the needs of early childhood, after-school care and sports activities.

However, as attractive as it may be, the idea of the right to the city comes up against the expectations and wishes of those concerned, which Lefebvre considered essential to pay attention to. Many of the expectations of the inhabitants of the urban countryside are out of step with the ideals of the right to the city, especially since not all of them live there by default. Many live there because it is their "home", that is, the place where their parents live. In other words, the countryside is their universe of reference, not the city. As for those who come from a city, their arrival is not only constrained by the cost of land, it is also guided by their desire to live a "quiet" life in the country, away from the large metropolises and their hustle and bustle – a desire no doubt reinforced by the Covid-19 pandemic[21]. In this context, the development of public transport is not always desired. For many periurbanites, improving bus service risks bringing the urban agitation from which they wanted to escape to their doorstep. How then can we defend a right associated with a world from which the main people concerned keep their distance, preferring to define themselves as country people? Should we not rather speak of a right to the countryside, a right to the village (Landy and Moreau 2015; Charmes 2019)?

---

20 Henri Lefebvre coined this notion in his eponymous book, published in 1968. He wonders about the splintering of the city and its dissolution in the urban. Faced with this observation, he proposes a reconquest of the city, based on a right to not only live in a city rather than in an urban magma, but also to benefit from a pleasant living environment and have access to its resources. The right to the city is also, and this is an essential element, a right to have a voice and be able to act on our environment in an autonomous way (Costes 2011).

21 To read the press, interest in the countryside is on the rise. However, recent research showed no signs of a flight away from the metropolises (see Milet et al. (2023)). It seems rather that the countryside near the metropolises, and therefore the periurban rings have gained attractivity.

But is a right to the village not a reactionary right, that is, a right to withdrawal, and thereby contrary to Lefebvre's intentions? To understand the situation and its political stakes, the focus has to be shifted from a critic of homeownership and its social ills. Rather, attention has to be refocused on those who are satisfied with their lot in order to find clues on the political expectations of periurbanites. Before returning to local households, those who become periurbanites without changing "home", we will focus on the case of those who come from cities. To this end, the historical link between periurbanization and the emergence of the "new middle classes" warrants attention. In the 1970s, with the development of public services (notably, in welfare, education, health and culture), the middle classes were enriched by a new group, made up of people with university degrees but without managerial roles, that some sociologists called the "new middle class" at the time (Bidou 1984). The political orientations of this group were varied, but some of its members played a decisive role in the consolidation of what was then called the "second left", that is, a reformist, non-working class left-wing movement.

At that time, a significant share of the new middle classes settled in the working-class neighborhoods of the city centers, resulting in their gentrification. This is well known, but it is often forgotten that the new middle class also contributed to periurbanization, or what some English geographers have called "rural gentrification" (Phillips 1993). By settling in the countryside around cities, many were not only aiming for ownership of a single-family house, or even a rural way of life (Bidou 1984). They were also seeking to realize a political project – in particular, to rediscover an authentic social life and gain control of their living environment. For this, the village and the small town were considered suitable, because they were on a human scale and controllable by means of action accessible to the middle classes.

Social relations also seemed to be warmer there, oriented by the desire to work together, unlike cities where social relations seemed to be dominated by anonymity and indifference. The new middle class' desire to cooperate was reflected by the creation of associations of all kinds, such as those for the protection of the environment, the enhancement of heritage, sociocultural animation or, quite evidently, the defense of the living environment.

With these new middle classes, the periurbs contributed to the "pink wave" of the municipal elections of 1977, with many municipal councils passing into the hands of the reformist wing of the Socialist Party (Jaillet and Jalabert 1982). This wave has since subsided and the periurbs have redefined their place to the right or far right of the political spectrum. Nevertheless, the ideas that brought it remain present. Buried in abstention, they can be revived (Girard 2017). The right to the village can contribute to this (Landy and Moreau 2015). Today, it could be defined as a right to organize at the local level, with relative autonomy from higher levels of government, whether metropolitan or state. It would be a right to the concrete experience of acting in common.

Such a right presents opportunities to deal with some of the problems encountered by low-income periurban households (Fleury 2014; Bühler et al. 2015). At the scale of a village, cooperation makes it possible to organize childcare after school, develop carpooling or set up local food distribution channels (Ripoll 2010). Of course, not every problem can be solved locally and independently. As far as metropolitan logics are concerned, however, a village can be a mobilization base for claiming, for asserting rights to services or equipment. Mobilizations to defend schools and post offices against threats of closure are an illustration of this (Taulelle 2012).

In a less defensive register, and more open to questions that go beyond local contexts, the village can also be the place where an overall transformation of society is prepared. Its small size makes it conducive to experiments in radical democracy, where everyone is invited to deliberate and take part in decisions on the subjects that concern them. As such, in some small municipalities, the keys to the town hall have been entrusted to co-legislative teams that strive to involve the whole population in important decisions (Dugrand 2020). In addition, the village level appears to be the appropriate place to build commonality (Cossart and Sauvêtre 2020), where the metropolitan lifestyle breaks up the collectives, by sending each one back to their individuality. Among the radical left, which is experiencing a growth in its followers in France, and its supporters of libertarian municipalism (as defended by Bookchin (2015)), the village is often put forward as the appropriate scale for developing interstitial strategies of social change (Rivat 2017; Jeanpierre 2020)[22]. Compared to clubbisation, these trends remain admittedly marginal and are more visible in isolated countryside than in the periurban rings of metropolises. Nevertheless, these movements are significant enough to build a political project on them, which could therefore be embodied in the right to the village.

4.10. The moral devaluation of the periurbs

The relationship between metropolises, large cities and the territories that surround them is not always considered in terms of inequalities, but also in moral terms. The critic of periurban life as an illusion is often grounded on the idea that

---

22 The term "interstitial strategies" should be understood here in the sense of Wright (2010).

metropolises are the ideal place to live, and this for not only material but also moral reasons. Admittedly, for some years now, voices have been raised to depreciate the moral value of life in metropolises, especially in ecological terms[23]. The Covid-19 pandemic has reinforced these critics. However, for the time being, they remain a very small minority and in France, as elsewhere, the lifestyles specific to metropolitan centers exert a strong symbolical and moral dominance (Bisson et al. 2020). Consequently, the qualities of the periurbs are being frequently questioned on the basis that life in large metropolises is more beneficial both for individuals and in a collective sense.

This moral perspective is supported in France by the geographer Lévy's (2013) theory of the "urbanity gradient". This theory is very influential and is part of an international trend of thought that postulates that large metropolises, because of their density and variety of populations, allow for greater exposure to difference and offer incomparable opportunities for intellectual stimulation and open-mindedness. This theory is attractive to those who appreciate the atmosphere of large cities (Lofland 1998; Frug 2001), and its success seems to be partly due to the fact that it has come to provide an advantageous moral justification for so-called "back-to-the-city" movements and the gentrification of working-class neighborhoods of large metropolises (Vermeersch et al. 2018). Graduates of the "Brahmin left" (Piketty 2020) who are driving working-class people out of the big cities can take comfort in praising the social mix and highlighting their open-mindedness (which usually finds its limits when it comes to schooling children).

In any case, as with the suburbs before them, periurban territories are the objects of a strong political and sociological critique (Vermeersch et al. 2018). As such, they are considered to be places where private interests are exacerbated to the detriment of collective interests – for example, residents prefer private gardens to public squares, their own cars to public transport, etc. – and where materialist consumerism takes precedence over spirituality – for example, residents prefer the soothing comfort of their home over arousing their curiosity by wandering around public spaces. These oppositions are the basis of the contempt of certain intellectual elites for mass-produced single-family houses. This contempt, which is present to varying degrees across the world (including in the United States, where a tradition of criticism of *suburbia* was inaugurated by Whyte (1956) with the publication of *The Organization Man*), is particularly widespread in France.

The criticism was increased tenfold by the rise of environmental issues and the related critic of urban sprawl, questioning single-family housing and automobile

---

23 One pamphlet has particularly made its mark: *Les Métropoles barbares* by Faburel (2019).

mobility. Indeed, in a typical small periurban municipality, more than 90% of the housing is single-family and almost all travel is done by car. These characteristics raise well-established ecological problems, which hardly need to be emphasized. In the debates on ecological transition, the periurbs therefore seem to be less virtuous than metropolises that are well served by public transport and well equipped with services, meaning that it is possible to make a large proportion of daily trips without a car.

The dominance of these critical views on the periurbs explain the initially very reserved reception given to the *Gilets jaunes* by intellectuals (Jeanpierre 2020)[24]. At the beginning of the protests, before a part of radical left rallied to the movement, many intellectuals looked with distrust at a movement whose protagonists complained that they could no longer fill their gas tanks. Asking for financial support to maintain practices that are disastrous for the environment did not really seem justified, especially since this was coming from people living in areas where the far-right National Rally regularly leads in elections (Lévy 2019).

4.11. From urban sprawl to the revitalization of the countryside: toward a reversal of the stigma?

This moral questioning, based on the critique of single-family housing and automobile mobility, is more delicate when, as this chapter has just done, the gaze is focused on the rural dimension of the periurbs and on the importance of villages. In the collective imagination, the village enjoys a rather positive image, as a place of strong sociability, less marked by anonymity and more united. In addition, as we have seen, the countryside is considered as the place of a possible political renewal, favorable to the common, compared to metropolises dedicated to consumerism and capitalist accumulation (Zask 2016; Faburel 2019). The moral debate on the periurban question thus takes on another dimension when we insist on the fact that judgments about the periurbs are also about the countryside. This recalibration of the question is all the more necessary since the settlement of the periurbs is not limited to the countryside. Periurbanization does not take place on greenfield land. This is one major difference between France and other countries (such as Australia or the southern and western states of the United States) where urban sprawl is advancing on little-occupied or even uninhabited land. The French periurbs are not pioneer territory, only populated by families coming from large metropolises. As we have said, many families have strong local connections, with their residential and professional careers confined to a relatively small area, that is, a quadrant of a

---

24 For an exception, see Coquard (2018).

periurban ring[25]. In general, periurbanization helps the inhabitants of rural areas to stay in the place where they used to live, since instead of moving to find a job, they can simply commute to the neighboring metropolis. The importance of this mechanism for periurbanization is difficult to quantify, but the further we move away from the hearts of the metropolises, the more it predominates. This greatly contributes to the working-class character of the periurban ring's outer fringes. Indeed, the households kept in place are rather modest, mirroring the dominant social characteristics of rural areas.

This means that the distance to the place of employment does not depend solely on the residential trajectories of modest first-time buyers from the metropolises; it is also necessary to consider the households that are already there. However, the proposals often made do not meet their expectations. Following the *Gilets jaunes* movement, researchers (Lambert et al. 2019) have insisted on the need to limit the supply of single-family homes in the periurbs (by combating urban sprawl) and promote the construction of accessible housing in the heart of metropolises (through densification). For periurban households, such policies seem particularly unfair. Indeed, why should they have to oblige certain restrictions for the benefit of the metropolises? Elected officials think the same. For many rural municipalities, the arrival of periurbanization is above all an opportunity to put an end to demographic decline or stagnation in order to regain dynamism. Faced with periurbanization, municipalities believe they have a right to development, if only in the name of defending rurality. For them, the policies against urban sprawl are a form of dispossession and a denial of their right to welcome new inhabitants and even to have a voice on their future (Charmes et al. 2020).

The limits put on single-family homes construction is all the more difficult for distant periurban rings that it may freeze any new construction. In areas where buyers are low-income and land is relatively inexpensive, the single-family home is the crux of the real estate market. Indeed, this type of housing is by far the least expensive to build (Bouteille and Cavailhès 2016). In relaxed markets, where land is cheap, building dense housing is too expensive to be economically viable (Vilmin 2012). Thus, preventing the construction of single-family homes in order to fight urban sprawl is tantamount to hindering the reception of new households by rural communities.

The social and ecological problems raised by periurbanization are major, but it is not certain that a critique calling into question the very existence of certain

---

25 In the periurban quadrant northeast of Lyon, only 20% of total moves between 2008 and 2013 were by households from the Lyon metropolitan area (source: SCoT BUCOPA, as approved in 2017).

periurban territories is likely to lead to a satisfactory political compromise. Yet such a compromise seems possible, including on an ecological level. The construction of single-family houses poses many problems, however, these can be mitigated – for example, by promoting vegetable and fruit production in private garden (Janin 2020). More generally, the hybridization between city and countryside brought by periurbanization is favorable to the construction of a more ecological relationship with food and the environment (Church 2015). In addition, the periurbs have many resources for the ecological transition, some of which are necessary for large cities. Metropolises and cities need their periurban rings to build greater autonomy on a regional scale to work like a bioregion (Newmann and Jennings 2008; Magnaghi 2020). Water management, for example, is only possible on the scale of vast metropolitan regions, including the periurbs. The same is true for improving food self-sufficiency, or for reaching the objective of net zero carbon emissions (this objective is difficult to achieve by any cities without including agricultural land and forests in the area considered for the balance).

In short, when the rural dimension of the periurbs is taken seriously, it becomes more difficult to condemn it on the basis of the perspective of the ecological argument. It is indeed difficult to pretend that the countryside is an environmental horror and that its revitalization is a problem, such that its repopulation should be prevented. Instead, it sounds more appropriate to consider the environmental assets of the countryside, of which there are obviously many.

4.12. Conclusion: beyond "peripheral France"

More than 50 years later, Lefebvre's (1970) first intuitions must be reiterated: the old opposition between cities and countryside is largely outdated. The periurban territories show why. The periurban is the countryside placed in the orbit of a city, the hybridization of the urban and the rural. This phenomenon is now massive. Since the end of the 1960s, increasing numbers of city dwellers have settled in villages or small towns while continuing to work in their city. Consequently, the cities have gradually extended into their rural outskirts, the difference between the periurbs and the countryside becoming above all landscape, mainly a matter of the living environment. The periurban countryside now encompasses more than one-third of the French population.

This is why the settlement of the countryside is not limited to poor and elderly people in isolated rural areas where demography is at a low. Although many rural areas face difficult situations such as these, the part should not be mistaken for the whole story: the countryside does not only welcome the working-class populations, the rural areas close to cities are often home to middle-class households and sometimes even very well-off families, as in the west of Paris.

From this perspective, the opposition drawn between metropolitan France and peripheral France (which generally includes the countryside) hinders our understanding of periurbanization. This is evidenced by the intense debates on the place of periurban spaces in the geography drawn by Christophe Guilluy[26]. These spaces can be placed on either side of this divide. In the periurban rings of the largest cities, some villages attract executives and are at the heart of metropolitan France, while others, further away and more popular, seem more likely to be included in so-called peripheral France. Moreover, in the latter, the territories that have the most difficulty are often in the center of a medium-sized city, while the municipalities that do the best are periurban villages.

This attractiveness of the countryside neighboring the cities has upset the political relations between the cities and their surrounding territories. In large metropolises, the periurban population remains a minority, but the situation is different in medium-sized city catchment areas, where they are often the majority. In terms of the number of municipalities, the balance tilts even more clearly in favor of periurbs and this is beginning to be felt in the government of cities. In some cases, a periurban village has taken over the intermunicipality. In others, the central municipality continues to dominate its intermunicipality, but its situation is not better when the nearby periurban rings turn away from it and develop their own intermunicipalities.

Of course, the relationship between the countryside and cities cannot be reduced to simple competition. Cooperating with their rural surroundings, cities can establish new relationships with agriculture and nature, and build new pacts. To this end, numerous exchanges and discussions are currently taking place, some of which are formalized in "reciprocity contracts" (Doré 2019). This search for partnerships is unfortunately hampered by a form of demonization of the periurbs, with the focus on the fight against urban sprawl.

The attention paid to votes in favor of the extreme and populist right also maintains a negative vision of the periurbs. The initial reactions to the *Gilets jaunes* movement clearly demonstrated this bias. However, the periurbs are far from being locked into a form of cultural backlash (Norris and Inglehart 2019). They are sometimes carriers of social innovations. Villages can be places where mutual cooperation takes place and a sense of commonality is built. The initiatives that are

---

26 Christophe Guilluy's statements were rather ambiguous in his early writings. Over the course of his research, he has clarified his position in a way similar to the one presented here.

emerging here and there are the beginnings of establishing a right to the village. This right could be opposed to the current dominant trend of clubbisation, which is particularly prevalent in periurban areas around large cities. The right to the village could also help guide action to benefit low-income and poor households, for example, those who do not have access to a car. In any case, it could be a solution to the tensions made visible by the *Gilets jaunes*.

4.13. References

Algan, Y., Malgouyres, C., Senik, C. (2020). Territoires, bien-être et politiques publiques. *Les notes du Conseil d'analyse économique*, 55 [Online]. Available at: https://www.cae-eco.fr/Territoires-bien-etre-et-politiques-publiques.

Amarouche, A. and Charmes, E. (2019). L'Ouest lyonnais et la lutte contre l'étalement urbain. Le "village densifié" comme compromis entre une politique nationale et des intérêts locaux. *Géoconfluences* [Online]. Available at: http://geoconfluences.ens-lyon.fr/informations-scientifiques/dossiers-regionaux/lyon-metropole/articles-scientifiques/villages-densifies-lutte-etalement-urbain.

Aragau, C. (2018). Le périurbain : un concept à l'épreuve des pratiques. *Géoconfluences* [Online]. Available at: http://geoconfluences.ens-lyon.fr/informations-scientifiques/dossiers-regionaux/france-espaces-ruraux-periurbains/articles-scientifiques/periurbain-concept-pratiques.

Béal, V., Cauchi-Duval, N., Gay, G., Morel Journel, C., Sala Pala, V. (2020). *Sociologie de Saint-Étienne*. La Découverte, Paris.

Berger, M., Bouleau, M., Mangeney, C. (2015). Les périurbains franciliens : vers de nouveaux comportements de mobilité ? *EchoGéo*, 34 [Online]. Available at: http://journals.openedition.org/echogeo/14399.

Berube, A., Singer, A., Wislon, J.H., Frey, W.H. (2006). *Finding Exurbia: America's Fast-Growing Communities at the Metropolitan Fringe*. The Brookings Institution, Washington.

Bidou, C. (1984). *Les Aventuriers du quotidien. Essai sur les nouvelles classes moyennes*. PUF, Paris.

Bisson, B., Charmes, E., Kennedy, L., Pinson, G., Tallec, J. (2020). La mort de l'urbain et le règne de la (grande) ville ? In *Pour la recherche urbaine*, Adisson, F., Barles, S., Blanc, N., Coutard, O. (eds). CNRS, Paris.

Bonnin-Oliveira, S. (2012). Intégration des espaces périurbains à la planification métropolitaine et recompositions territoriales : l'exemple toulousain. PhD Thesis, Université de Toulouse, Toulouse.

Bookchin, M. (2015). *The Next Revolution: Popular Assemblies and the Promise of Direct Democracy*. Verso Books, New York.

Bourdieu, P. (1980). Un signe des temps. *Actes de la recherche en sciences sociales*, 81(82), 2–5.

Bouteille, A. and Cavailhès, J. (2016). Quels surcoûts de construction ? *Revue foncière*, 12, 6–10.

Brenner, N. (2014). *Implosions/explosions. Towards a Study of Planetary Urbanization*. Jovis, Berlin.

Broz, J.L., Frieden, J., Weymouth, S. (2021). Populism in place: The economic geography of the globalization backlash. *International Organization*, 75(2), 464–494.

Brutel, C. and Levy, D. (2011). Le nouveau zonage en aires urbaines de 2010 – 95 % de la population vit sous l'influence des villes. *Insee Première*, 1, 374.

Bühler, E.A., Darly, S., Milian, J. (2015). Arènes et ressources du droit au village : les ressorts de l'émancipation dans les campagnes occidentales au 21ᵉ siècle. *Justice spatiale*, 7 [Online]. Available at: https://www.jssj.org/article/arenes-et-ressources-du-droit-au-village-les-ressorts-de-lemancipation-dans-les-campagnes-occidentales-au-21eme-siecle/.

Charmes, E. (2007). Les périurbains sont-ils anti-urbains ? *Les Annales de la recherche urbaine*, 102, 7–18.

Charmes, E. (2009). On the residential "clubbisation" of French periurban municipalities. *Urban Studies*, 46(1), 189–212.

Charmes, E. (2011). Ensembles résidentiels privés ou municipalités exclusives ? Le débat sur le gouvernement local privé revisité au travers des cas de la France et des États-Unis. *Cahiers de géographie du Québec*, 55(154), 89–107.

Charmes, E. (2014). Une France contre l'autre ? *La Vie des idées* [Online]. Available at: https://laviedesidees.fr/Une-France-contre-l-autre.html.

Charmes, E. (2019). *La revanche des villages. Essai sur la France périurbaine*. Le Seuil, Paris.

Charmes, E. (ed.). (2021). *L'éloignement résidentiel. Vivre dans le périurbain lyonnais*. Autrement, Paris.

Charmes, E., Rousseau, M., Amarouche, M. (2020). Politicizing the debate on urban sprawl: The case of the Lyon metropolitan region. *Urban Studies*, 58, 12.

Church, S.P. (2014). Exploring urban bioregionalism: A synthesis of literature on urban nature and sustainable patterns of urban living. *Sapiens*, 7, 1.

Coquard, B. (2018). Qui sont et que veulent les "Gilets jaunes" ? *Contretemps* [Online]. Available at: https://www.contretemps.eu/sociologie-gilets-jaunes/.

Cossart, P. and Sauvêtre, P. (2020). Du municipalisme au communalisme. *Mouvements*, 1, 142–152.

Costes, L. (2011). Le droit à la ville de Henri Lefebvre : quel héritage politique et scientifique ? *Espaces et sociétés*, 140(141), 177–191.

Coulombel, N. and Leurent, F. (2012). Les ménages arbitrent-ils entre coût du logement et coût du transport ? Une réponse dans le cas francilien. *Economie et Statistique. Insee*, 457(458), 57–75.

Cox, K.R. (2010). The problem of metropolitan governance and the politics of scale. *Regional Studies*, 44(2), 215–227.

Cusin, F., Lefebvre, H., Sigaud, T. (2016). La question périurbaine : enquête sur la croissance et la diversité des espaces périphériques. *Revue française de sociologie*, 57(4), 641–679.

Dawkins, C.J. (2005). Tiebout choice and residential segregation by race in US metropolitan areas, 1980–2000. *Regional Science and Urban Economics*, 35(6), 734–755.

Depraz, S. (2020). Justice spatiale et ruralité. Thesis, Université Paris Nanterre, Paris.

Dijkstra, L., Poelman, H., Veneri, P. (2019). *The EU-OECD Definition of a Functional Urban Area*. OECD, Paris.

Dodier, R., Cailly, L., Gasnier, A., Madoré, F. (2012). *Habiter les espaces périurbains*. Presses universitaires de Rennes, Rennes.

Doré, G. (2019). Quelles coopérations entre les métropoles et les territoires ruraux en France ? Les pactes État-métropoles et l'expérimentation des contrats de réciprocité. *L'Information géographique*, 83(4), 55–78.

Dugrand, M. (2020). *La Petite République de Saillans. Une expérience de démocratie participative*. Éditions du Rouergue, Rodez.

Faburel, G. (2019). *Les métropoles barbares : démondialiser la ville, désurbaniser la terre*. Le Passager clandestin, Paris.

Ferraton, C. (2004). L'idée d'association chez Alexis de Tocqueville. *Cahiers d'économie politique*, 46, 45–65.

Fischel, W.A. and Oates, W.E. (eds) (2006). *The Tiebout Model at Fifty: Essays in Public Economics in Honor of Wallace Oates*. Lincoln Institute of Land Policy, Cambridge.

Fleury, A. (2014). Le périurbain, des pratiques solidaires en émergence. In *Pratiques et politiques de la ville solidaire*, Rousseau, M., Béal, V., Faburel, G. (eds). Éditions PUCA, Paris.

Frug, G.E. (2001). *City Making*. Princeton University Press, Princeton.

Genevois, S. (2018). Intérêts et limites du zonage en aires urbaines. *Géoconfluences*.

Girard, V. (2017). *Le vote FN au village. Trajectoires de ménages populaires du périurbain*. Éditions du Croquant, Vulaines-sur-Seine.

Grimault, V. (2020). *La renaissance des campagnes*. Le Seuil, Paris.

Guilluy, C. (2014). *La France périphérique : comment on a sacrifié les classes populaires*. Flammarion, Paris.

Hall, P.G. and Pain, K. (eds) (2006). *The Polycentric Metropolis: Learning from Mega-city Regions in Europe*. Routledge, London.

Jaillet, M.C. and Jalabert, G. (1982). Politique urbaine et logement : la production d'espace pavillonnaire. *L'Espace géographique*, 11(4), 293–306.

Janin, P. (2000). Retrouver les sols. In *Capital agricole. Chantiers pour une ville cultivée*, Rosenstiehl, A. (ed.). Pavillon de l'Arsenal, Paris.

Jeanpierre, L. (2020). Des ronds-points à la mairie. *Revue projet*, 1, 55–59.

Judd, D.R. and Hinze, A.M. (2018). *City Politics: The Political Economy of Urban America*. Routledge, London.

Kipfer, S. (2019). What colour is your vest? Reflections on the yellow vest movement in France. *Studies in Political Economy*, 100(3), 209–231.

Korsu, E., Massot, M.H., Orfeuil, J.P. (2012). *La ville cohérente. Penser autrement la proximité*. La Documentation française, Paris.

Lambert, A. (2015). *"Tous propriétaires !" L'envers du décor pavillonnaire*. Le Seuil, Paris.

Lambert, A., Dietrich-Ragon, P., Bonvalet, C. (2019). Des femmes et des ronds-points. *AOC* [Online]. Available at: https://aoc.media/analyse/2019/01/23/femmes-ronds-points/.

Landy, F. and Moreau, S. (2015). Le droit au village. *Justice spatiale*, 7 [Online]. Available at: https://www.jssj.org/article/le-droit-au-village/.

Le Breton, E. (2019). *Mobilité, la fin du rêve ?* Éditions Apogée, Paris.

Le Galès, P. (2003). *Le retour des villes européennes*. Presses de Sciences Po, Paris.

Le Goix, R. and Webster, C.J. (2008). Gated communities. *Geography Compass*, 2(4), 1189–1214.

Lefebvre, H. (1968). *Le droit à la ville*. Anthropos, Paris.

Lefebvre, H. (1970). *La révolution urbaine*. Gallimard, Paris.

Lévy, J. (2007). Regarder, voir. Un discours informé par la cartographie. *Les Annales de la recherche urbaine*, 102, 131–140.

Lévy, J. (2013). *Réinventer la France*. Fayard, Paris.

Lévy, J. (2019). L'abandon des territoires périurbains est une légende. *La Gazette des Communes* [Online]. Available at: https://www.lagazettedescommunes.com/603895/jacques-levy-labandon-des-territoires-periurbains-est-une-legende/.

Lofland, L.H. (2017). *The Public Realm: Exploring the City's Quintessential Social Territory*. Routledge, London.

Magnaghi, A. (2020). The territorialist approach to urban bioregions. In *Bioregional Planning and Design*, Fanfani, D. and Matarán Ruiz, A. (eds). Springer, Berlin.

Martin-Brelot, H., Grossetti, M., Eckert, D., Gritsai, O., Kovacs, Z. (2010). The spatial mobility of the "creative class": A European perspective. *International Journal of Urban and Regional Research*, 34(4), 854–870.

Martinache, I. (2019). L'impouvoir d'achat. Quand les dépenses sont contraintes. *La Vie des idées* [Online]. Available at: https://laviedesidees.fr/L-impouvoir-d-achat.html.

Merlin, P. (2009). *L'exode urbain : de la ville à la campagne*. La Documentation française, Paris.

Milet, H., Maisetti, N., Simon, E. (2023). *Exode urbain. Un mythe, des réalités*. PUCA, POPSU, Paris.

Miot, Y. (2016). Le rôle du facteur démographique dans les processus de décroissance urbaine. Le cas de trois villes de tradition industrielle française. Report, Espace populations sociétés.

Morin, E. (2013). *Commune en France : la métamorphose de Plozévet*. Fayard, Paris.

Mouillard, M. and Vaillant, V. (2018). L'accession à la propriété des ménages pauvres et modestes. *L'observatoire de l'immobilier du Crédit foncier*, 97, 34–47.

Newman, P. and Jennings, I. (2008). *Cities as Sustainable Ecosystems: Principles and Practices*. Island Press, Washington.

Nilsson, K., Pauleit, S., Bell, S., Aalbers, C., Nielsen, T.A.S. (eds) (2013). *Peri-urban Futures: Scenarios and Models for Land Use Change in Europe*. Springer, Berlin.

Norris, P. and Inglehart, R. (2019). *Cultural Backlash. Trump, Brexit, and Authoritarian Populism*. Cambridge University Press, Cambridge.

Phillips, M. (1993). Rural gentrification and the processes of class colonisation. *Journal of Rural Studies*, 9(2), 123–140.

Piketty, T. (2020). *Capital and Ideology*. Harvard University Press, Cambridge.

Pistre, P. (2011). Migrations résidentielles et renouveaux démographiques des campagnes françaises métropolitaines. *Espace populations sociétés*, 3, 539–555.

Ripoll, F. (2010). L'économie "solidaire" et "relocalisée" comme construction d'un capital social de proximité. Le cas des AMAP. *Regards sociologiques*, 40, 59–75.

Ripoll, F. and Rivière, J. (2007). La ville dense comme seul espace légitime ? Analyse critique d'un discours dominant sur le vote et l'urbain. *Les Annales de la recherche urbaine*, 102, 120–130.

Rivat, M. (2017). *Ces maires qui changent tout : le génie créatif des communes*. Actes Sud, Arles.

Rivière, J. (2008). Le vote pavillonnaire existe-t-il ? Comportements électoraux et positions sociales locales dans une commune rurale en cours de périurbanisation. *Politix*, 83(3), 23–48.

Rougé, L. and Bonnin, S. (2008). *Les "Captifs" du périurbain 10 ans après : retour sur enquête, espaces sous influence urbaine*. CERTU, Lyon.

Schmidt, S. and Paulsen, K. (2009). Is open-space preservation a form of exclusionary zoning? The evolution of municipal open-space policies in New Jersey. *Urban Affairs Review*, 45(1), 92–118.

Sencébé, Y. (2004). Être ici, être d'ici : formes d'appartenance dans le Diois (Drôme). *Éthnologie française*, 34(1), 23–29.

Taulelle, F. (2012). *Le délaissement du territoire : quelles adaptations des services publics dans les territoires ruraux ?* Presses universitaires du Mirail, Toulouse.

Vanier, M. (2016). Mutation des territoires, sur la piste des hybrides. In *L'Hybridation des mondes. Territoires et organisations à l'épreuve de l'hybridation*, Gwiazdzinski, L. (ed.). Elya, Grenoble.

Vermeersch, S., Launay, L., Charmes, E., Bacqué, M.H. (2018). *Quitter Paris ? Les classes moyennes entre périphéries et centres*. Créaphis, Grâne.

Vilmin, T. (2012). Les trois marchés de l'étalement urbain. *Études foncières*, 157, 27–33.

Vivier, N. (1998). *Propriété collective et identité communale. Les biens communaux en France de 1750 à 1914*. Publications de la Sorbonne, Paris.

Vyn, R.J. (2012). Examining for evidence of the leapfrog effect in the context of strict agricultural zoning. *Land Economics*, 88(3), 457–477.

Whyte, W.H. (1956). *The Organization Man*. Simon & Schuster, New York.

Wollmann, H. (2012). Local government reforms in (seven) European countries: Between convergent and divergent, conflicting and complementary developments. *Local Government Studies*, 38(1), 41–70.

Wright, E.O. (2010). *Envisioning Real Utopias*. Verso, London.

Zask, J. (2016). *La démocratie aux champs. Du jardin d'Eden aux jardins partagés, comment l'agriculture cultive les valeurs démocratiques*. La Découverte, Paris.

5

The European Union: Territorial Inequalities and Development Policy

Frédéric SANTAMARIA
Pacte, Université Grenoble Alpes, France

5.1. Introduction

This chapter draws on the example of the European Union (EU) to address the theme of this book, territorial inequalities, in a transnational context. While this example does not exhaust the question of transnational cooperation in development, it is nevertheless relevant in several respects. Indeed, the EU is an area of strong regional integration compared to other such spaces in the world, and it is based on a set of political and legal institutions that implement transnational actions and policies, especially in the field of reducing territorial inequalities.

Furthermore, beyond the EU's initial aim of ensuring peace in Europe, European construction also corresponds to a desire to promote a development model, that is, a "European model of society" (Faludi 2007; Davoudi 2009). This model involves the implementation, sometimes laborious and often judged to be very imperfect, of a certain solidarity, which is expressed either on an ad hoc basis or through long-term policies carried out at the European level, aimed at reducing inequalities in development by acting mainly at the territorial level. More generally, this expression of European solidarity corresponds to a political objective (Coman et al. 2019)

For a color version of all figures in this chapter, see http://www.iste.co.uk/talandier/territorial.zip.

aimed at promoting the feeling of a common belonging to a transnational space encompassing a number of socioeconomic, demographic, spatial and institutional differences.

Although long associated with the period of prosperity that Western Europe experienced after the Second World War, European construction no longer seems to be the development framework that will allow European countries to maintain their position alongside the large economic powers (i.e. the United States, China), even though certain European territories are experiencing the most negative effects of globalization. Today, this situation challenges the legitimacy of the European construction and its institutional form, the EU. The latter faces criticism both in terms of its ability to intervene to ensure the prosperity and protection of European citizens, but also with regard to its legitimacy to intervene in national affairs. This crisis of legitimacy was accentuated by the difficulties of European countries to agree to manage the effects of the financial crisis of 2008 and, subsequently, to ensure the recovery of European economies, then, finally, by the exit from the UK from the EU (2020) following the results of the 2016 referendum. This has jeopardized the major argument which has justified European construction since its beginning: that is, cooperation between states aimed at ensuring their collective prosperity as well as a certain standardization of the living conditions of European citizens regardless of the state in which they live.

In several respects, this situation can be considered paradoxical. Indeed, the EU remains a space wherein wealth inequality between individuals is less pronounced than in other major economic areas of the world. Moreover, at the territorial level, although significant differences in wealth and development can be observed within the EU, the EU area appears to be relatively homogeneous on a global scale.

Moreover, the question of development, which is tied to that of reducing inequalities between Europeans and between territories, is a constant political concern for the EU, expressed both in the political choices negotiated between Member States and in the substantive policies it implements at the EU level. Even if the EU's political decisions have undergone significant changes since the 2000s, the link between development and inequality, particularly territorial inequality, is still an objective of EU action that goes back to the early days of the EU. While the issue of economic development has been at its center since its beginning, it is not the only one: following the Treaty of Rome (1957), the issue has been articulated in terms of reducing inequalities within the new area of cooperation then established[1].

---

1 The preamble to the Treaty of Rome mentions the need for the founding states "to strengthen the unity of their economies and to ensure their harmonious development by reducing the differences between the various regions and by mitigating the backwardness of the least favored".

Moreover, if the initiators of European construction thought that cooperation alone via the Customs Union and the positive effects that it would produce in terms of economic development would suffice to bring about standardized development on the scale of all the countries concerned, it appeared, from the beginning of the 1960s, that if nothing is done, territorial inequalities will tend to be accentuated because of the competitive situation in which areas that are unprepared to face it are now placed.

Nevertheless, it was not until the mid-1970s that a solidarity mechanism was implemented between Member States through the establishment of a fund, the European Regional Development Fund (ERDF), to compensate for development inequalities between European regions. Yet, it was not until the end of the 1980s that a real European policy for regional development was established with a dedicated policy, that is, regional policy. Regional policy, or cohesion policy as we know it today, is part of the perspective of what was established at the end of the 1980s, even if multiple changes in orientation and modus operandi have since taken place. These changes, as we will see, generate tension between the EU's initial objective of compensating for inequality and that of boosting the competitiveness of the European economy.

However, the objective of compensating territorial inequalities has never disappeared from the European agenda. Even today, the largest share of the funds dedicated to cohesion policy is dedicated to the regions seen as lagging behind in their development. Moreover, cohesion policy has come to include environmental and social dimensions into its objectives, despite having undergone significant changes in its orientation toward support for economic development. Beyond cohesion policy, certain sectoral policies, such as the Common Agricultural Policy (CAP), also provide support for territorial development[2].

Thus, despite changing policy objectives and their consequences for substantive EU policies, the EU still offers its members a number of policies and funding geared toward reducing inequality through intervention in the EU territories. From this point of view and on a global scale, the EU appears as a singular model of transnational cooperation, as most other instances of transnational cooperation are more concerned with facilitating the implementation of their trade agreements

---

2 The CAP makes it possible to finance territorial development projects in rural areas, particularly by way of the Leader program. Some actions supported by the European Investment Bank are also part of the EU's approach to territorial development and the reduction of territorial inequalities.

through development projects (e.g. with the construction of major transport infrastructure) rather than the issue of development in generally speaking[3].

The EU appears to be relatively exemplary in its political action to reduce inequality in developing dedicated substantive policies, a situation that is also part of a context of lesser territorial inequalities on a global scale. This observation must be qualified; however, because these policies remain limited, particularly in terms of the budgetary effort made, but also because they appear to be a field of tension – both political and theoretical/conceptual – between contradictory political ambitions that blur the objectives pursued at the EU level in this area. This has been particularly evident over the last 15 years and can be explained by two major developments:

– at the level of the general functioning of the EU, the federalist dynamic of the project has gradually lost steam, giving way to a clearer intergovernmental mode of functioning. This situation is linked to institutional changes as well as the financial weight of the states in the financing of the EU[4];

– from the perspective of the actions carried out from the EU, the objective of a better equilibrium of wealth within the EU has faded away in favor of a search for economic development economic development aiming at a boosting the competitiveness of the European economy. This is particularly evident in the EU's development choices, both through the major political choices established by intergovernmental activity – the Lisbon Agenda, Europe 2020 – as well as through the redefinition of the objectives of substantive policies, such as the cohesion policy.

The tensions between Member States regarding political and financial arbitrations at the time of the negotiation concerning an important area of intervention relative to the overall EU budget led to a form of "compromise" supposed to articulate the maintenance of the objectives of reductions in inequalities and the introduction of new targets to support the competitiveness of the European economy. This situation may help to explain the contradiction between the relative exemplary nature of the EU and the strong criticisms leveled at it in general, regarding its action in reducing inequality, particularly territorial inequality.

---

3 See, on this subject: Richard, Y. and Mareï, N. (eds) (2018). Aménagement. In *Dictionnaire de la régionalisation du monde*. Atlande, Neuilly-sur-Seine.

4 The Maastricht Treaty (1993) opened up new fields of intervention for the EU, but these have not been institutionalized at the European level. Within the EU, these fields are therefore dealt with on an intergovernmental register (see on this subject: Bickerton, C.-J., Hodson, J., Puetter, U. (2015). The new intergovernmentalism: European integration in the post-Maastricht era. *Journal of Common Market Studies*, 53(4), 703–722). Moreover, the largest share of EU funding now comprises of transfers from Member States to the EU (see section 6.2.4).

This situation raises a series of issues that appear to limit European action in the fight against territorial inequality. These limits relate to political choices, the nature of the development supported by the EU, and therefore to the objectives pursued, the expected effects and, in relation to the objectives, the real effects of the actions carried out.

In addition, the European institutions and, in particular, the European Commission concerned with legitimizing their actions beyond political choices mobilize the science to support the choices made and evaluate the effects of policies, all in a context of transnational debates which, while being rich, do not always allow for greater clarity regarding the theoretical and conceptual frameworks that could guide the action of the actors involved in implementation.

In this situation, both constrained and somewhat confused, the EU's legitimacy is at risk in terms of its promise standardize living conditions across Europe. While certain recent initiatives – such as those following the 2008 financial crisis (the "Juncker plan") or during the 2020 health crisis (the "recovery plan") – have created a form of solidarity between states, the EU still seems far from being able to define a new development model taking into account the "new great transition" (Farínos-Dasí 2020).

5.2. Inter-territorial inequalities in the framework of European construction

5.2.1. *The reduction of territorial inequalities as a fundamental building block of the European project*

European construction is historically part of an integration process with a strong economic component (i.e. establishing the common market and a single currency). From the point of view of the rest of the world, the economic challenge is that of a common organization, the most effective possible, to ensure the international economic position of Europe. Within Europe, integration presupposes that the idea that obstacles to the movement of people, goods and services should be lifted or at least reduced. This can be done by standardization or implementing common rules (those of the single market, for example) as well as through actions aimed at creating a common space by acting on its spatial organization (e.g. integrated transport).

The EU today operates from the founding values that justified the European project: the preservation of peace, equality and solidarity, economic development, political and social human rights that constitute so many European "public goods" (Fitoussi et al. 2007). The reference to these founding values and the ambition to create a common European identity imply the search for a certain homogenization of the living conditions of Europeans. This necessitates the reduction of inequality between individuals, which is at the heart of the "European model of society" (Faludi 2007; Needham and Hoekveld 2013). This model can be defined, as opposed to the North American model and, to a certain extent, the British model, as that of a regulated market economy and an extensive social welfare system which offers significant assurances against economic insecurity and social inequality (Davoudi 2009).

In the European context, where the attachment to places is reputedly stronger than in North American societies, the territorial dimension of the model in question arises with a certain acuity: it is not only a question of aiming to reduce inequalities between individuals, but also to ensure that, regardless of where they live, Europeans can benefit from comparable living conditions and access to resources (education, employment, information and communication, etc.). This idea is ultimately opposed to the liberal model whereby regulation involves the mobility of individuals who are supposed to move, particularly to central regions, to ensure their prosperity. This refers to the idea of territorial solidarity, which is expressed through the search of a better spatial balance and greater "territorial cohesion", and introduced into the European vocabulary by the Treaty of Amsterdam (1997) and by the most recent treaty, the Treaty of Lisbon (2009).

Thus, while competition between territories within the single market tends, systematically, to reinforce inequalities, the EU has, since the 1990s, set itself the objective of ensuring a "balanced development" of the community space (Dühr et al. 2007). This is through a voluntarist understanding of polycentrism as an orientation aimed at counterbalancing the monocentric character of the European space organized around the "Pentagon" – a space with a high concentration of populations and wealth delimited by the cities of London, Paris, Munich, Hamburg, Milan – by supporting the development of metropolises which can contribute, on different scales, to a better structuring of the EU's territories (Élissalde et al. 2008; DATAR 2010). In this sense, polycentrism appears to be the means for a more balanced development of the European space.

However, since its inclusion in the treaties, "territorial cohesion" has become the preferred concept to denote the EU's action in the field of territorial development and the reduction of territorial inequality. It appears as the territorial expression of one of the founding societal principles of European construction, that is, of solidarity (Bourdin et al. 2020). This notion of territorial cohesion of a political nature has been the subject of an abundant literature aimed at determining its meaning. It is presented both as an objective to be achieved and as a means to achieve the objective in question; thus, the objective of territorial cohesion is primarily to ensure a balanced distribution of activities and people (Faludi and Peyrony 2011). From this point of view, it is supposed to be a response to the problem (raised earlier) of the balanced development of the European space.

If, from an analytical point of view, the reduction of territorial inequality can be seen as a constitutive element of the European project, its inclusion in actions and substantive policies is relatively recent.

5.2.2. *An early awareness for a late political consideration*

At the end of the Second World War, the question of cooperation between European countries became an important element of relations between states within the European continent (with the creation of the Council of Europe in 1949)[5]. Some European states expressed a desire to move beyond the traditional form of cooperation between states and to combine some of their policies, particularly in the economic sphere (European Coal and Steel Community 1952). They thus inaugurated what would henceforth be called European integration.

In this context, the Spaak Report (1956), which laid the foundations for the Treaty of Rome (1957), that is, the founding treaty of the European Economic Community (EEC), was a major step forward. In particular, the treaty is concerned with supporting six of the most disadvantaged countries in Europe: Belgium, France, Germany, Italy, Luxembourg and the Netherlands. The Treaty of Rome mentions the need for the newly established EEC to ensure "harmonious development by reducing the differences existing between the various regions and by mitigating the backwardness of the less favored" (preamble) and confers on this organization the task: "to promote throughout the Community a harmonious development of economic activities, a continuous and balanced expansion, an increased stability, an accelerated raising of the standard of living and closer relations between its Member states" (Article 2 of the Treaty of Rome).

However, while no operational mechanism related to these objectives was established at the time, the territorial inequalities have been a persistent issue since the origins of European construction. In 1961, at a conference on regional economies organized by the European Parliamentary Assembly, Robert Marjolin,

---

5 The Council of Europe was originally created by 10 European states and has gradually expanded to include almost all European states. Today, it is a reference institution for the promotion of pluralist democracy and human rights; the member countries undertake to respect its founding principles.

the first vice-president of the European Commission, emphasized in his introductory report that the common market was of greater benefit to the already highly developed parts of the European area than to the disadvantaged regions[6]. During the 1960s, several proposals to ensure European territorial solidarity emanating from European institutions would remain a dead letter (Drevet 2008). These proposals were met with hostility from the Member States, which did not want to mobilize specific financial resources to carry out regional actions that would, moreover, be regulated at the European level. Little progress was made during this period, and it was only after long negotiations that the European Regional Development Fund (ERDF) was created in 1975. However, we cannot refer to this as a true European policy, because at that point in time, this common fund was managed by the Member States that had allocated the funding according to their national priorities in terms of regional aid (Drevet 2008). It was not until the end of the 1980s, with the 1988 reform of the regional policy, that a real European orientation was defined. Several elements contributed to the rise of regional policy: a significant increase in its allocated budget, the definition of strategic orientations at the community level, broken down into objectives, and a European zoning of the areas receiving funds[7]. The programming period for of European funds, which began in 1989 (1989–1993), thus established a new conception of the implementation of regional aid with a clearer European flavor; the zoning system enabled the EU to take control, as it were, of the spatial distribution of regional policy funding to aid the territories that needed it the most[8]. As such, the end of the 1980s marked the beginning of a period that lasted until the mid-2000s (corresponding to the programming period for European funds 2000–2006), during which regional policy appeared to be an expanding policy whose European nature was more clearly affirmed. From the mid-2000s onwards, there have been a number of important changes in terms of the objectives pursued by the EU, notably through the cohesion policy. The objective of reducing territorial inequality has not, however, been contested.

---

6 "[…] the net result of the common market, in the absence of an active regional policy, would probably be for the peripheral regions a faster progress than that which has been theirs up to now, without however closing the gap which separates them from the central regions, it is not excluded, in truth, that this gap increases in certain cases" (European Commission (1961). Conférence sur les économies régionales. In *Services des publications des Communautés européennes*, Luxembourg).
7 The objective zonings were defined according to socioeconomic measures at the municipal level and, according to the level of difficulty of the defined zones, each zone then fell under a different "objective" of the regional policy.
8 The cohesion policy funds correspond to a total amount for a period of 7 years. The use of these funds is therefore spread over several years, and the term "programming period" is used to describe the period during which the funds will be used.

5.2.3. *Maintaining the objective of reducing territorial inequalities in spite of major change*

During the 2000s, the debates surrounding the EU's action in reducing territorial inequalities gave rise to major changes in cohesion policy, both in terms of its objectives and its modus operandi. In general, these debates were concerned with maintaining the economic position of the EU in terms of globalization. From an internal EU point of view, the "great enlargement" of 2004 and 2007 raises questions about the spatial reorientation of cohesion policy funds. Finally, the 2008 financial crisis challenged, even more acutely, the choices of the EU regarding its development model.

In 2002, the report by the economist André Sapir, which had been commissioned by the European Commission, strongly called into question the principles on which regional policy was based, in particular that of aid for regions whose development was lagging behind. Placing themselves in the perspective of making Europe regain its lost growth by pursuing the objectives set by the Lisbon strategy (2000), the authors of the report considered that Europe's money would be better invested in the regions most likely to develop it, that is to say, the most dynamic regions. They therefore called for a significant reduction in the funds devoted to regions in difficulty the EU-15 Member States and a more massive investment in the new Member States, while leaving them the choice of their allocation. Contested within the European Commission itself, the report did not have, at least explicitly, political consequences. However, it is clear, through this example, that from the beginning of the 2000s, two essential concerns overlapped: on the one hand, the new spatial configuration of Europe and, on the other hand, boosting the competitiveness of the EU on a global scale (Faucheur 2017).

This situation had an impact on the discussions on the reform of regional policy for the period 2007–2013. Following tough negotiations concerning the budget, the Member States finally agreed on an upper limit (0.37% of EU GDP) and then on a relative decrease in spending allocated to this policy (0.35% in 2013 compared to 0.46% in 1999). The reform is also reflected in a change in objectives accompanied by an end to zoning, with the entire territory of each European region becoming, from then on, eligible for European funds. Consequently, this change reduced, a priori, the ability to target areas that were most behind in terms of development or in most difficulty[9]. The three new objectives – "convergence", "competitiveness" and "cooperation" – appear to be the result of political choices in the context which presided over the negotiations: the "competitiveness" objective refers to the concern

---

9 It should be noted, however, that regions may choose to allocate funds on a territorial basis, as the Île-de-France region has done to the regional areas north of Paris struggling the most.

to be able to invest in all regions of EU countries that already have levels of development at least in line with the European average, thus echoing an objective centered more on the overall competitiveness of the EU than on overcoming inequalities between European territories[10]. Nevertheless, the "convergence" objective, which concerns the new accession countries or emerging states, underscores the importance that the EU attaches to helping these parts of Europe to catch up economically[11]. In order to ensure a regional distribution of European funding, the EU distinguishes three categories of regions according to their relative level of wealth, measured by gross domestic product (GDP) per capita. Through these categories, maximum levels of cofinancing are determined for each category of regions[12].

The 2014–2020 programming period for the EU cohesion policy funds falls took the same perspective as the previous programming period. However, the two objectives of "convergence" and "competitiveness" were then replaced by an encompassing wording, "investment for growth and employment", again testifying to the importance of European competitiveness.

The current programming period (2021–2027) of European funds for cohesion policy does not introduce substantial changes in the methods of allocation; the regional distribution of funds is organized around the three main categories of regions and the principle of relative levels of cofinancing (see Figure 5.1):

– 40% for the *"most developed regions"* with a GDP per capita of more than 100% of the European average;

– 60% for *"regions in transition"* whose GDP per capita is between 75% and 100% of the European average;

– 85% for the *"least developed regions"* with a GDP per capita of less than 75% of the European average.

---

10 On this point, Jacques Robert and Moritz Lennert noted in 2012 that "The EU Commissioner for regional policy, Danuta Hübner, [...] urges a "paradigm shift" in the definition of cohesion policy, calling for a dynamic process of empowerment helping overall European *economic growth and competitiveness*" (Robert and Lennert (2012, p. 13)). Author's emphasis.

11 The "territorial cooperation" objective is new, as it enshrines, within the framework of the general European guidelines, the experience of one of the community programs previously included in the Interreg programme for cooperation between European territories (cross-border, interregional, transnational, etc.).

12 European money mobilized under the regional policy intervenes by co-financing operations conducted in its name. The EU then intervenes to support national funding according to the principle of additionality; this European principle states that EU funding is additional to, and not a substitute for, funding already provided at sub-European levels (states, regions, etc.).

The European Union: Territorial Inequalities and Development Policy   153

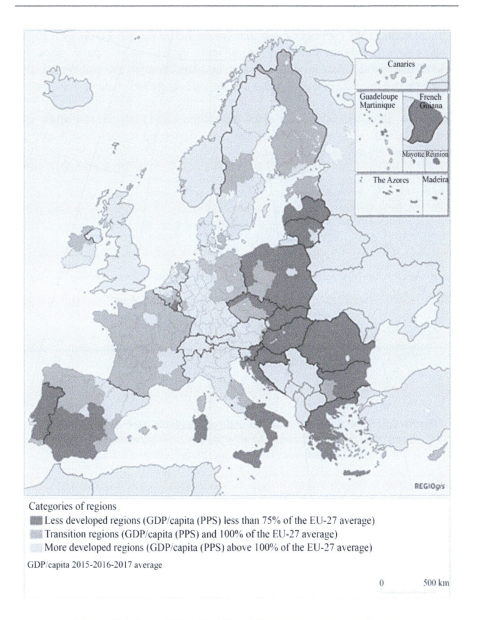

Categories of regions
■ Less developed regions (GDP/capita (PPS) less than 75% of the EU-27 average)
■ Transition regions (GDP/capita (PPS) and 100% of the EU-27 average)
  More developed regions (GDP/capita (PPS) above 100% of the EU-27 average)
GDP/capita 2015-2016-2017 average

Figure 5.1. *Map of the eligibility of European regions under the 2021–2027 cohesion policy (source: European Commission)*

In addition to the European funds that can be utilized by all European regions (such as the ERDF or the European Social Fund), the EU has also put in place, in view of the "great enlargement", a budget envelope through the Cohesion Fund (with a maximum cofinancing of 85%) that provides additional funding for regions belonging to countries whose gross national income is less than 90% of the EU average (i.e. all new member states since 2004, Greece and Portugal) and which has been maintained ever since. Therefore, the "least developed regions" and those "in transition" are eligible for all three funds.

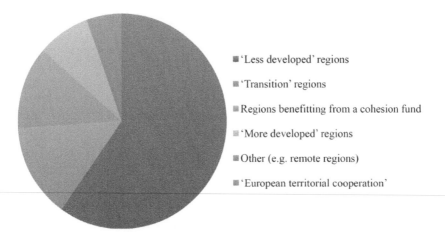

Figure 5.2. *Breakdown of structural funds of the 2021–2027 cohesion policy according to the three categories of regions eligible under the cohesion fund, and European territorial cooperation (source: EUR-Lex)*

The share of funding devoted to cohesion policy is about one-third of the European intervention budget, which makes it, alongside the CAP, a major EU policy. However, while its share of the EU's regular budget is continues to grow, there has been a slight decrease in the absolute terms of the amounts allocated to cohesion policy excluding funding for the recovery plan), with the budget falling from around 350 billion euros in the period 2014–2020 to 330 billion euros in the period 2021–2027[13]. While this situation can be explained by the end of the British

---

13 Between 2020 and 2023, the Cohesion Policy will be given an additional *47.5 billion* in the framework of a specific initiative of the European recovery plan aimed at addressing the consequences of the health crisis in Covid-19, that is, the Recovery Assistance for Cohesion and the Territories of Europe (REACT-EU). These funds aim to provide financial support to project leaders to contribute to the economic recovery.

contribution to the EU budget following Brexit, it can be interpreted as a common desire to (at the very least) maintain the importance of the cohesion policy among other EU policies.

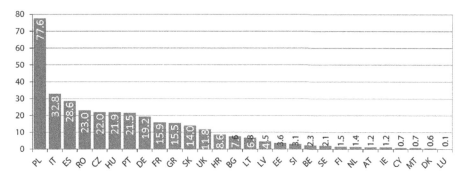

Figure 5.3. *Distribution of the total budget allocation of the structural funds of the 2014–2020 cohesion policy by member state (source: European Parliamentary Research Service 2014)*

Moreover, despite these changes, the principle of European solidarity is still expressed from a budgetary point of view through a classic mechanism: if all countries contribute to the EU budget, some Member States receive more money from the EU than they pay to it; and conversely, some Member States pay more money than they receive. In European vocabulary, we may refer to them as "net contributors" and "net beneficiaries", respectively. This principle of redistribution is at the heart of the cohesion policy. By measuring, for the year 2020, the ratio between the share obtained by each country under the cohesion policy in relation to its contribution to the total EU budget, this solidarity is clearly expressed vis-à-vis most of the countries of Central and Eastern Europe (e.g. Lithuania, Hungary, Latvia, Poland, Croatia, Estonia, Slovakia, Czech Republic, Romania, Bulgaria and Slovenia), but also vis-à-vis Greece and Portugal. Most of the wealthiest EU15 countries are those whose cohesion policy funding relative to their contribution to the overall EU budget is below the average share (35%) of inflows of cohesion policy vis-à-vis the average contribution of states to the EU budget. Thus, the principle of European solidarity effectively takes shape through this mechanism of budgetary redistribution.

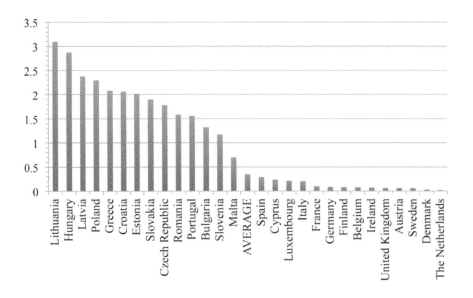

Figure 5.4. *Ratio (multiplied by...) of contribution to the EU budget to the share received from cohesion policy by Member State in 2020 (source: European Commission)*

5.2.4. Substantive policies

The EU has institutional and financial instruments enabling it to implement actions intended to lead to a reduction in the development inequalities between European countries and regions, and to promote regional development, as well as the cooperation and networking of European territories, in order to enable common achievements or sharing of experiences in terms of planning and development.

At the heart of this action is the cohesion policy. The EU mobilizes, under this policy, a relatively large budget compared to the total EU budget for European policies (1,074 billion euros for the period 2021–2027[14]), amounting, for the period 2021–2027, to 330 billion euros distributed in various funds (ERDF, European Social Fund, Cohesion Fund, etc.)[15]. The implementation of actions financed by the

---

14 750 billion, financed by loans and grants, under the European recovery plan set up in the wake of the Covid-19 health crisis, called next-generation EU.

15 The cohesion policy is also financially supported by the European Investment Bank that grants loans to certain actions subsidized by the European policy, particularly in the struggling territories.

EU is negotiated with the Member States for the funding period through national agreements which are translated at sub-national levels through regional and local programs, and transnational cooperation programs.

Beyond the cohesion policy, other EU actions are likely to play a role in reducing territorial inequalities at the EU level. This is the case for certain sectoral policies, distinct from the cohesion policy. The so-called policy of trans-European networks cofinances, based on political choices, the creation of material and immaterial networks with a continental vocation with a view to interconnection. Beyond the objective of the technical and economic integration of networks on a continental scale, this policy also aims to better connect certain European territories that are little or poorly served in a logic of promoting polycentricity to EU scale. In another area, the second pillar of the CAP makes it possible to finance, at the local level, development actions in rural areas.

5.2.5. *The EU in the world: a relatively homogeneous space*

Compared to the rest of the world, the EU area appears relatively homogeneous in terms of measuring differences in wealth and "quality of life". Of course, the point here is not to consider whether the EU action presented above explains this situation, but rather to note that it is part of a relative context of lesser disparities. This context does not prevent actions seeking to counterbalance territorial inequalities in development from taking place; it is in this respect that the EU seems to be an example on a global scale.

At the EU level, compared to the rest of the world, the data on GDP per capita (see Figure 5.5) and the human development index (HDI) (see Figure 5.6) show a certain homogeneity of national situations.

Even if significant differences in terms of HDI can be noted (see the world ranking in Table 5.1) between the EU Member States in northern and western Europe, on the one hand, and the Baltic countries and certain ones in southern, central and eastern Europe, on the other hand, all of the countries that make up the EU are, according to the United Nations Development Programme (UNDP) categories, at a "very high" level of development (see Table 5.1)[16]

---

16 Very high HDI: 1–0.800; high HDI: 0.700–0.799; medium HDI: 0.550–0.699; low HDI: 0.350–0.549.

158   Territorial Inequalities

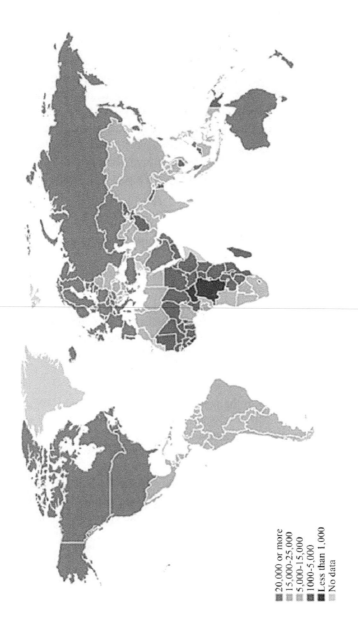

Figure 5.5. *GDP by country in purchasing power parity in 2017 (source: IMF 2017)*

The European Union: Territorial Inequalities and Development Policy   159

Figure 5.6. *HDI in 2018 (source: UNDP –2018)*

EU countries	HDI (2017)	World ranking (189 countries)
Ireland	0.938	4
Germany	0.936	5
Sweden	0.933	8
Netherlands	0.931	10
Denmark	0.929	11
Finland	0.92	15
Belgium	0.916	17
Austria	0.908	20
Luxembourg	0.904	21
France	0.901	24
Slovenia	0.901	25
Spain	0.891	26
Czech Republic	0.888	27
Italy	0.88	28
Malta	0.878	29
Estonia	0.871	31
Greece	0.87	31
Cyprus	0.869	32
Poland	0.865	33
Lithuania	0.858	36
Slovakia	0.855	38
Latvia	0.847	41
Portugal	0.847	42
Hungary	0.838	45
Croatia	0.831	46
Bulgaria	0.813	51
Romania	0.811	52

Table 5.1. *HDI of EU countries in 2017 (source: UNDP 2018)*

In a report published by the World Inequality Lab (Alvaredo et al. 2018), the authors show that Europe[17], in a context of strong increases in global income inequality from the 1980s to 2016 (the date of the latest data processed by the

---

17 The study takes into account the countries of western and eastern Europe, excluding Ukraine, Belarus and Russia.

report), stands out from other major geographical or national groupings (such as North America, China, Russia, Sub-Saharan Africa, Brazil, India and the Middle East) by having the lowest income inequality[18] in 2016. Moreover, over this period, the evolution of income inequality underwent the least amount of change in Europe: the share of the wealthiest 10% of the population rose from 32% to 36%, while at the same time, this share increased by 13%, from 34% to 47% for the United States and Canada combined, for example. Lastly, Europe's situation is also unique in terms of the share of income held by the lowest 50% of income earners and that held by the top 1% of income earners. Indeed, while this share is almost stable (i.e. a share going from 10% to 12% for the top 1% of income earners and from 23% to 22% for the bottom 50% of income earners) over the period, we see the opposite evolution elsewhere, particularly in the United States. This evolution takes the form of a scissors diagram, with the top 1% of income earners going from a little more than 10% of the national income to a little more than 20% over the period, while the bottom 50% of income earners went from more than 20% to about 13% over the same period. In the end, the authors deem the European model to be the most redistributive model, with the incomes of Europeans rising the most after taxes and social benefits.

However, these findings do not prejudge the intensity of territorial inequalities within the EU, which European political action intends to tackle. In this respect, despite a rather enviable general situation on a global scale and the political and operational consideration of this issue by the European institutions, the EU's action and its effects remain limited, both because of the European policies themselves and because of the way in which the EU operates more generally.

5.3. The limits of EU action in the fight against territorial inequalities

5.3.1. *Significant wealth inequalities at different levels within the EU*

Measured through GDP per capita by Eurostat, wealth inequality within the EU can be studied at different scales[19]. At the national level, there is a difference in wealth between countries in the east and west and, to a lesser extent, between those in the north and south of the EU (see Figure 5.7).

---

18 Measured by the share of the richest 10% in national income: 37% in Europe, 41% in China, 46% in Russia, 47% in the United States/Canada/North America, 55% in Sub-Saharan Africa, Brazil and India, and 61% in the Middle East.
19 Eurostat is a Directorate-General of the European Commission responsible for statistical information at the community level.

162   Territorial Inequalities

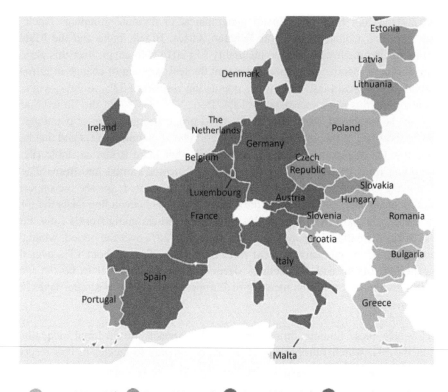

● From €14 to 23k   ● From €23 to 28k   ● From €28 to 37k   ● More than €37k

Figure 5.7. *The GDP per capita of EU countries in 2018 in terms of purchasing power standards (PPSs) (source: Toute l'Europe)*

EU countries	GDP/in PPS
Luxembourg	75,600
Ireland	53,200
Netherlands	37,500
Austria	37,100
Denmark	36,500
Sweden	36,100
Germany	35,800
Belgium	34,200
Finland	31,700

Country	GDP per capita (PPS)
France	30,300
Average	*28,900*
Italy	28,000
Malta	27,700
Spain	26,700
Czech Republic	25,700
Slovenia	24,400
Cyprus	24,000
Slovakia	22,500
Portugal	22,400
Lithuania	21,900
Estonia	21,700
Poland	20,200
Hungary	19,800
Greece	19,300
Latvia	18,900
Croatia	17,500
Romania	17,200
Bulgaria	14,200

Table 5.2. *GDP per capita in PPS by country of the EU 27 (source: Eurostat 2017)*

Beyond the somewhat crude representation in Figure 5.7, the values of GDP per capita at the national level (see Table 5.2) corroborate and clarify the general observation, while accounting for the magnitude of wealth inequalities between EU countries and between the large geographic subgroups that they constitute. As such, we can see that all of the countries with GDP per capita that is below the average GDP per capita in purchasing power standard (PPS) – 28,900 euros – are located in the south and east of the EU area[20].

---

20 The purchasing power standard (PPS) is an artificial currency unit that eliminates differences in price levels between countries. Thus, one PPS allows the same volume of goods and services to be purchased and services in all countries. This unit allows meaningful volume comparisons of economic indicators between countries (Insee definition).

164 Territorial Inequalities

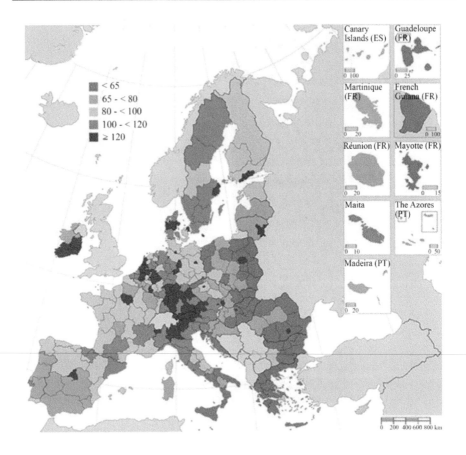

Figure 5.8. *GDP per capita in PPS at the regional level in 2019 (percentage of EU average, EU27 = 100) (source: Eurostat 2021)*

The data proposed by Eurostat at the regional level reinforces the observation of an East–West/North–South divide. At present, the situation of the European regions in terms of their relative wealth appears to be contrasted (see Figure 5.8). The central and eastern European countries that are the most recent to join the EU (i.e. the 13 countries that have joined since 2004) have regional GDPs per capita that are almost 75% below the EU average. Most of the southernmost regions also rank below 75% of the average. In contrast, most of the regions in the western, northern and central EU-15 Member States have GDP per capita levels that are almost always above 75% of the average to well above the average.

Rank	Country	Region	GDP/per capita in 2019 (base 100)
1	Luxembourg	Luxembourg	260
2	Ireland	Southern	240
3	Czech Republic	Praha	205
4	Belgium	Brussels-Capital	202
4	Ireland	Eastern and Midland	202
5	Germany	Hamburg	195
6	France	Île-de-France	178
7	Germany	Oberbayern	173
8	Netherlands	Noord Holland	170
9	Denmark	Hovedstaden	167
10	Sweden	Stockholm	166
11	Slovakia	Bratislavský kraj	162
12	Poland	Warszawski stołeczny	160
12	Romania	București-Ilfov	160
13	Netherlands	Utrecht	158
14	Germany	Stuttgart	157
15	Italy	Province of Bolzano	155
16	Germany	Darmstadt	154
17	Austria	Salzburg	151
17	Hungary	Budapest	151

Table 5.3. *The 20 regions with the highest GDP per capita (in PPS, EU-27 = 100) (source: Eurostat 2021)*

However, the categories in Figure 5.8 obscure differences in wealth between different European regions (see Tables 5.3 and 5.4). For instance, the average GDP per capita of the 20 richest regions is four times higher than that of the 20 poorest regions. While a large majority of the richest regions are in Western Europe, the majority of the poorest regions are in the countries of central and Eastern Europe (e.g. Bulgaria, Hungary, Poland, Romania and Slovakia). In the south, Greece is now among the five poorest regions in the EU.

Beyond this observation at the European level, there are also significant differences between regions within EU countries (see Tables 5.3 and 5.4 and Figure 5.8). These differences are particularly marked in some central and eastern European countries, where the capital regions – where the country's wealth is concentrated – are quite distinct from other regions in terms of their GDP per capita levels that are at or even above the EU average. Although the contrast is less striking, this can also be observed for case of southern European countries, such as Greece and Portugal. There are also regional differences in Spain (notably in the Madrid region and Catalonia), and in France, particularly between the capital region and other regions of the country.

Rank	Country	Region	GDP/per capita in 2019 (base 100)
1	France	Mayotte	32
1	Bulgaria	Severozapaden	32
2	Bulgaria	Severen tsentralen	35
3	Bulgaria	Yuzhen tsentralen	37
4	Bulgaria	Yugoiztochen	40
5	Bulgaria	Severoiztochen	41
6	Romania	Northeast	44
6	Greece	Voreio Aigalo	44
7	Greece	Anatoliki Makedonia, Thraki	45
8	Hungary	Észak-Alföld	47
8	Greece	Ipeiros	47
9	Greece	Dytiki Ellada	48
9	France	Guyana	48
10	Hungary	Észak-Magyarország	49
11	Poland	Lubelskie	50
11	Poland	Warmińsko-mazurskie	50
11	Hungary	Dél-Alföld	50
11	Slovakia	Vychodné Solvensko	50
12	Poland	Podkarpackie	51
12	Greece	Thessalia	51

Table 5.4. *The 20 regions with the lowest GDP per capita (in purchasing power standards, EU-27 = 100) (source: Eurostat 2021)*

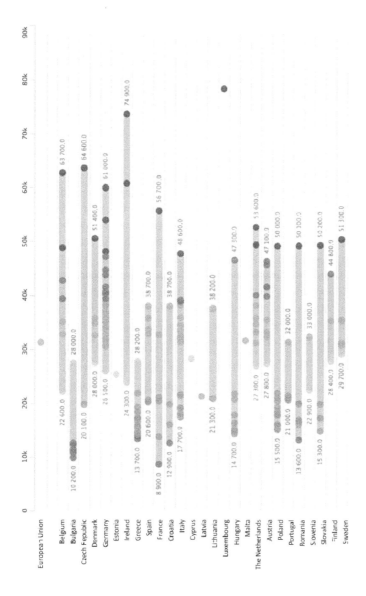

Figure 5.9. *Regional inequalities in GDP per capita in PPS by region in 2019 (in percentage of the EU-27 average, EU-27 = 100) (source: Eurostat)*

Figure 5.9 provides a clearer picture of regional inequalities within EU countries. This graph provides information on the national differences between regions and on the relative position of the regions in terms of wealth in relation to the GDP per capita of each country compared to the EU average (base 100). Most countries experience strong regional polarizations in terms of wealth regarding the capital region, the extent of which can be, however, more or less significant, while their other regions are practically all below the average national GDP per inhabitant. This situation concerns several EU countries – such as Bulgaria, Denmark, France, Greece, Hungary, the Netherlands, Poland, Portugal, the Czech Republic, Romania, Slovakia, Sweden – regardless of being a part of the major intra-European geographical groups or not.

There are therefore significant spatial discontinuities in wealth between large subsets of European countries, particularly between Member States in eastern and western Europe, but also within many of these countries. If these discontinuities testify to a certain inertia linked to the economic history of Europe, they proceed, in a very marked way, from the most recent enlargements to the countries of central and eastern Europe. Consequently, in the context created by the accession to the EU of new countries whose national wealth is relatively low, the initial objective of regional policy, then of cohesion policy, that of reducing disparities in levels of development of European regions, is put to the test, even questioned. Admittedly, it is not possible for the cohesion policy to eradicate all territorial inequalities, but rather it can aim to mitigate them in a dynamic of support for convergence as defined by the EU. However, on this point too, EU action has its limits.

5.3.2. *The 2008 financial crisis and the challenge to convergence*

In this area, convergence refers above all to the area of public finances and the macroeconomic standardization necessary to ensure a stable foundation for the single currency (i.e. the euro). However, it applies to other areas of European action, including the cohesion policy; in particular, to the cohesion policy (Dicharry et al. 2019). It therefore also shares the objective of reducing inequality in terms of the levels of development of European countries and regions (Élissalde et al. 2008).

At the EU level, convergence is measured by the convergence of GDP per capita in PPS of the different regions of the Member States. However, until 2008, convergence in this area was indeed taking place. Of course, this situation cannot be attributed solely to the actions carried out under the cohesion policy, but given the time, we can say that its objectives were clearly reflected in the figures and that, in the extent of its resources, it should therefore contribute to it.

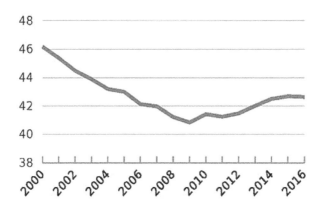

Figure 5.10. *Convergence of GDP per capita (source: OECD, Economic surveys: European Union, 2018 – OECD 2018)*

Figure 5.10 shows a decrease in wealth inequalities between European regions from the early 2000s until 2009, then a significant increase in these inequalities between 2009 and 2016. Admittedly, the level of inequality is not at the same as in 2000, but the mere fact that these inequalities are increasing calls into question the EU's objective of reducing inequalities in regional wealth and, consequently, the action of cohesion policy. While this trend can be explained by the accession of Romania and Bulgaria (2007), the two countries which encompass the poorest regions of the EU, it is mainly explained by the effects of the economic crisis of 2008 (financial crisis), the trend reversing more frankly after this date, from 2009.

Beyond the general trend illustrated in Figure 5.10, the 2008 crisis also had the effect of accentuating inequalities between European regions in terms of their respective varied capacities for economic "resilience", which do not completely overlap with the major cleavages of wealth within the EU. Indeed, if southern European countries (such as Greece, Spain and Portugal) have been particularly affected, the situation is more contrasted in central and eastern Europe, that is, if we were to compare the situations of different countries (e.g. Poland vs. Croatia), or even within the countries of this part of the EU (e.g. within Bulgaria). In addition, certain regions of Western Europe, particularly the United Kingdom, were also affected by the 2008 crisis[21].

The authors of a study released in April 2019 on income inequality in Europe (Blanchet et al. 2019) have shown that in general, and over a longer period of

---

21 ESPON, Cardiff University (2014). *Economic Crisis: Resilience of Regions – Scientific Report.* Luxembourg, Cardiff.

analysis, the EU is far from having fulfilled its promise of "convergence" between the different European economies. Indeed, while there has been some convergence (see Figure 5.11) between the large geographic areas that made up the EU-15 (i.e. northern, western and southern Europe), even in the 1990s there was evidence of divergence. While the average per capita income of eastern European countries has increased faster than that of western European countries since the early 2000s, this has not made up for the initial lag of the former communist countries. The authors also point to the consequences of the 2008 financial crisis, which has had very different repercussions from one country to another. In Spain, Portugal, Greece and Italy, the average income per capita has decreased (Dicharry et al. 2019). Conversely, Scandinavian countries saw their average income grow faster than the average rate, even though they already belonged to the circle of the most well-off countries. The authors of the study conclude that net transfers of income between EU countries are more favorable to rich countries than to poor countries, even when taking into account the net contributions of income from different states to the European budget.

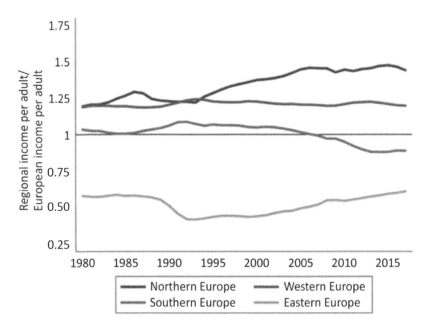

Figure 5.11. *Average income of European regions compared to the 1980–2017 average (source: Blanchet et al. 2019). Between 1980 and 2017, the average income of a western European citizen remained about 20% higher than that of an average European*

All of these elements make it possible to establish a mixed, even critical assessment of the European situation with regard to territorial inequalities. This situation may explain why the EU's action in terms of reducing territorial inequalities faces challenges from certain European political actors as well as certain experts. The debate around the effects of the cohesion policy is certainly not recent, but even if it is part of a context of complex developments over the long term, it has been revived by the various crises experienced by the EU since the late 2000s.

At the heart of this debate, cohesion policy is particularly in the spotlight, since it represents the EU's political action in relation to its objective of reducing territorial inequalities. However, in addition to the territorial effects of major macro-economic phenomena, the European ambition that is embodied by the cohesion policy seems to go far beyond the scope of the policy's actual capabilities.

5.3.3. *Beyond the financial and political framework of the EU's action to reduce territorial inequalities*

In order to establish its legitimacy, which today is the subject of much debate, the EU must, in order to justify its action with the Member States and European citizens, display ambitious objectives which go beyond its real capacity to act, in particular through its substantive policies. This contradiction is likely to explain its current difficulties as a result of successive and consecutive crises, such as the 2008 financial crisis, the 2015 migration crisis, Brexit in 2016, the Covid-19 pandemic in 2020, etc. Cohesion policy can, from this point of view, appear as an illustration of this contradiction, because although it absorbs a large part of the EU intervention budget, the sums involved remain limited. The recurrent debates around questions of EU financing make it possible to underline the difficulty of conceiving, between Member States, European solidarity, particularly in its territorial dimension.

Overall, the funding mobilized by the EU is very limited, as it is conditioned by a rule of capping own resources of 1.40% of the EU's gross national income. At present, the total budget of the EU (which contributes to the operation and financing of European policies) represents only about 1% of the GDP of the EU-27. For the period 2021–2027, it amounts to 1,074 billion euros. By comparison, in 2019, the total revenue of in the EU-27 amounted to 46.2% of the GDP of the Member States.

For example, in France, the net expenditure of the general government budget (operating and investment) amounted to more than 386 billion euros in 2018 alone[22].

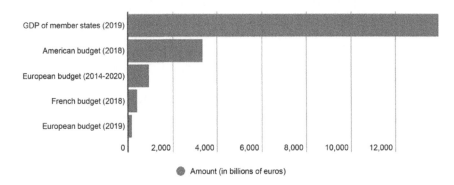

Figure 5.12. *Comparison between the European budget, the French budget, the American budget and the GDP of the Member States (source: Toute l'Europe (2020). Le budget de l'Union européenne [Online]. Available at: www.touteleurope.eu/actualite/le-budget-de-l-union-europeenne.html [Accessed 3 September 2020].*[23]

Despite these relatively small amounts, the financing of the EU is the subject of intense discussions among Member States in regular negotiations to establish the budget for 7 years. These negotiations are now crucial to the EU's ability to implement its policies, since the direct contribution of the states (the so-called "GNI resource") to the EU budget has been steadily increasing since the late 1980s. At the end of the 1980s, the direct contribution of the states represented just over one-tenth of the financing, compared to almost one-third from customs duties and agricultural levies (the so-called "traditional own resources") and more than half from VAT-based own resources. This situation has gradually changed: at present, and depending on the year, the share of "gross national income resources" is between two-thirds and three-quarters of the budget, "traditional own resources" around 15%, and VAT resources around one-tenth (see Box 5.1).

In terms of evolution, although between 1989 and 2013 there was an increase in cohesion policy expenditure in absolute terms, their relative share in relation to EU GDP stagnated, or even decreased slightly. This increase in absolute value is

---

22 Source: Eurostat (2020). Statistiques sur les finances publiques [Online]. Available at: https://ec.europa.eu/eurostat/statistics-explained/index.php?title=Government_finance_statistics/en#Revenueand_d.C3.A9public_government_expenditure [Accessed 3 September 2020].

23 This is an indication, as these amounts are difficult to compare due to the very different jurisdictions involved.

particularly noticeable from 2004, as a result of needs of the countries of the "great enlargement", which resulted in an increase of approximately one-fifth of EU population, but only 5% of its GDP (Creel and Levasseur 2004). However, since then, the budgetary effort has stabilized at around 0.4% of EU GDP.

> The EU's revenue mainly comprises its own resources and a small share of miscellaneous revenue (i.e. contributions from third countries to certain European programmes, fines imposed on companies that violate European competition rules, etc.).
>
> – The EU's "traditional own resources" consist of customs duties levied on imports into the EU of products from third countries and taxes on imports of agricultural products covered by the CAP;
>
> – the "VAT resource" is generated by a uniform rate for all Member States, with a standardized base;
>
> – the "GNI resource" corresponds to the contributions of each Member State calculated according to their shares in the European gross national income.

Box 5.1. *How is the EU budget replenished?*

In addition, the action of the cohesion policy and its expected outcomes cannot be separated from the effects of EU legal acts and certain initiatives taken within the framework of other sectoral areas of EU action that are likely to produce territorial effects that may be contradictory to the objective of reducing territorial inequalities[24]. For example, the liberalization an EU-wide basis of transport, questions the ability of Member States and/or their regions to articulate the European provisions with the objective of equitable transport services in their territory, in particular through the granting of subsidies to railway lines that are not very profitable or not at all[25]. In the area of sectoral policies, competition policy limits, in the name of maintaining the fairest possible competition between European companies, the ability of Member States to support companies, even if they are located in territories in socioeconomic difficulty. For example, in 2007, the French government had to review, in order to comply with European competition rules, its zoning of territories in difficulty in which companies could benefit from financial

---

24 In this respect, European law includes two levels of legal rules:
– regulations, that is, European legislation of direct application in all Member States simultaneously: "European laws";
– directives, that is, general legal guidelines leaving it up to the Member States to choose the methods of application on their territory.
25 Various European provisions (including directives and regulations) support the liberalization of the of the rail transport market, especially since the end of the 2010s.

support to maintain or even develop their activity[26]. This revision, which is still in force today, has resulted in a very significant reduction in the surface areas of the zones concerned by the aid.

These two examples illustrate the potential contradiction between, on the one hand, the objectives of cohesion policy, and, on the other hand, certain actions carried out in other areas of the EU's activities.

However, the territorial effects of EU actions in sectoral areas are generally little studied, even though there are studies and tools[27], notably those financed under the European applied research program ESPON[28], which make it possible to measure certain territorial effects of European decisions or sectoral policies. This work and these tools mobilize various evaluation methods applied to certain sectoral domains (e.g. transport and agriculture) or certain legal provisions (e.g. directive on air quality) and generally focus on an evaluation of the potential effects of measures planned at the EU level (evaluation ex ante) and little on the effects of provisions already in place. Finally, it is only within the framework of the cohesion policy itself that the outcomes of EU actions are really taken into account because of the obligation, under the European regulation on the European Structural and Investment Funds (ESIF) to produce, every three to four years, a "report on cohesion"[29]. This report is designed to make it possible to assess the progress made as a result of cohesion policy and to suggest the ways in which actions can be

---

26 So-called "regional aid zones".

27 For an update on the state of research on territorial impact assessment, see: Medeiros, E. (ed.). (2020). *Territorial Impact Assessment.* Springer, Cham. For tools and methods specifically developed within the ESPON program, see: ESPON (2010). *Territorial Impact Package for Transport and Agricultural Policies.* ESPON, Luxembourg [Online]. Available at: www.espon.eu/programme/projects/espon-2013/applied-research/tiptap-territorial-impact-package-transport-and [Accessed 9 October 2020.] This report proposes a method for the ex-ante evaluation of the territorial impact of different European policy orientations in transport and agriculture; ESPON (n.d.). *ESPON TIA tool* [Online]. Available at: www.espon.eu/tools-maps/espon-tia-tool [Accessed 9 October 2020]; ESPON (2011). Assessment of regional and territorial sensitivity [Online]. Available at: www.espon.eu/programme/projects/espon-2013/applied-research/arts-assessment-regional-and-territorial-sensitivity [Accessed 9 October 2020]. This report examines the territorial impact of one of the provisions of the EU Air Quality Directive; it is a rare example of ex-post evaluation in a specific field.

28 ESPON: The European territorial observatory network is a programme funded by the European Commission within the cohesion policy and which proposes studies and tools for the analysis of European territories and their evolution.

29 The FESI/ESIF is the name given to a set of EU intervention funds: the ERDF, the ESF, the European Agricultural and Rural Development Fund, the development (EAFRD) and the European Maritime Affairs and Fisheries Fund (EMAF).

implemented. But this evaluative approach is not based on a systematic methodology, the "cohesion reports" being essentially contingent political documents aimed at steering the cohesion policy over time by attempting to influence the Member States as to the use European funds at the national level (Élissalde and Santamaria 2013).

Cohesion policy therefore mainly supports the evaluation of the territorial effects of European action, even though its financial resources are limited and its implementation depends largely on the Member States, in accordance with the European principle of subsidiarity (Rivière 2020)[30].

Finally, this process of evaluation, particularly pertaining to the cohesion policy, cannot be approached without taking into account the domestic political choices of the Member States. In this respect, the example of Ireland's trajectory since its accession to the EU offers an interesting example of the difficulty in distinguishing between the effects of cohesion policy and the effects of purely domestic choices. In the early 1990s, its GDP per capita was at a level comparable to that of Spain. Between 1987 and 2000, Ireland's GDP grew by 140%, while that of the EU-15 grew by only 35%. As of 2017, it ranks second in the EU in terms of GDP per capita in PPS[31]. In attempting to explain this spectacular evolution, economists point to three key reasons (Jouen 2012):

– a low corporate tax regime that has allowed a massive influx of foreign direct investment;

– reform of the education system;

– a social consensus to counterbalance, through household income tax, the low tax rate on businesses, and to accept profit sharing favorable to businesses to support employment[32].

---

30 Legal concept of EU primary law (enshrined in the treaties) that applies to cohesion policy and involves collaboration between the EU and the Member States for its implementation at the territorial level. Thus, while the broad guidelines of cohesion policy are set at the European level, the national and sub-national variations and the policy's actual implementation, although negotiated with the EU, are the responsibility of the Member States.

31 Source: Eurostat.

32 In the early 1990s, the Irish unemployment rate was between 14% and 16%. It was 5% in the 2000s. After a sharp increase after the banking and financial crisis of 2008, it was around 5% at the end of 2019.

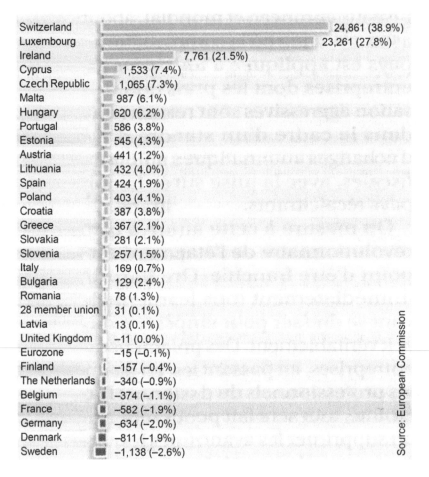

Figure 5.13. *The reality of fiscal dumping in the EU 28 in 2012 (and Switzerland) (source: Alternatives économiques)*

These national orientations were coupled with various territorial development programs, which benefited from relatively significant contributions from the ERDF and the ESF from the end of the 1980s, and from the Cohesion Fund until the mid-2000s. However, this example shows that it is the national context and the integration of Ireland into the single market that can explain the changes observed. As such, the Irish case shows the multidimensional nature of the springs of a national trajectory within the EU, as a result of economic and political decisions taken at the level of the government of the country and by the membership of the country. The Irish case highlights the importance of national choices in terms of taxation, in particular that which concerns companies and the phenomenon of tax competition within the EU which raises questions, both directly (lack of harmonization of rules) and indirectly (differential effects of fiscal dumping on national economies), the objective of convergence. The Irish case also introduces an abrupt and sudden inequality between sub-national territories that depends on national tax decisions; the evaluation of the cost for the territories of the non-coordination of tax policies between Member States still to be done.

Evaluating the effects of EU actions on the reduction of territorial inequalities is not an easy task, since many factors that are external to the policy in question interfere. While correlations between European investment and regional growth rates can sometimes be established, the chain of causality is subject to numerous factors specific to the Member States (Dicharry et al. 2019). Therefore, any evaluation remains, at best relative, and at worst, riddled with biases whose share and magnitude are difficult to measure.

Finally, limiting the scope of the EU's action on reducing territorial inequalities to the cohesion policy alone can only lead to a misunderstanding: both in terms of the resources, it has at its disposal to achieve its objectives and because other factors intervene in the trajectories of the Member States and their territories. This situation calls into question the effectiveness of EU action, if not its credibility, then its legitimacy, especially since it seems to be pursuing contradictory objectives.

5.3.4. *Major conflicting objectives*

Changes in the orientations of the cohesion policy from the mid-2000s until today raise questions about the nature of this policy which, broadly speaking, aims to both increase the convergence between European countries – by reducing inequalities in the wealth levels of European countries and regions – (see section 5.3.2) and boost the economic competitiveness of the EU. Cohesion policy then becomes the center of this assembly which must both guarantee more equality between European countries and regions while supporting the economic competitiveness of the EU in order to support its growth (Waterhout 2008).

In reality, the articulation between these two orientations is reflected, from the 2007 to 2013 period, by the addition to the "convergence" objective of a "competitiveness" objective. Then for the period 2014–2020, and again for the period 2021 2027, these two objectives disappear in favor of a single and unequivocal wording as to its objectives: "investment for growth and employment"[33]. Even if the main beneficiaries of the European windfall remain the

---

33 For the periods 2014–2020 and 2021–2027, cohesion policy was organized around two objectives: the one mentioned in the body of the text and the objective resulting from the previous period of "territorial cooperation".

"less developed" regions, support for productive investment likely to ensure both growth and European competitiveness is gradually taking precedence over action aimed at rebalancing wealth between European territories (Evers 2012; Faucheur 2017). As such, cohesion policy seems to be shifting from a policy aimed at reducing inequality between countries and regions to one aimed at promoting growth potential, regardless of a country's location within the EU. However, if European leaders strive to demonstrate, if not complementarity, at least non-contradiction between the traditional objective of cohesion policy and support for competitiveness, certain territorial trends observed at EU level and within certain countries demonstrate the contradictions that can appear in terms of development trajectories[34]. Thus, the situation of very strong polarization of wealth observed in the regions of the capitals of the countries of Eastern Europe, which are also major beneficiaries of the cohesion policy, raises questions, beyond the financing that the EU provides, the influence of the latter on the territorial consequences of the promotion of competitiveness (Bourdin 2018). At the level of the EU itself, the possibility for all European regions to have access to European funds also raises the question of the ability of the already most prosperous regions and states to mobilize EU money to derive an even more substantial comparative advantage. On the other hand, the decline noted in certain countries in southern Europe, particularly after the 2008 crisis, can be attributed to the multiple difficulties encountered by all (e.g. Greece) or part (e.g. Italy) of their regions in enrolling in this logic of competitiveness even accompanied by more generous European funding.

In addition, this desire to support European competitiveness both at EU and territorial level via part of the financing of the cohesion policy is based on an injunction from the European authorities for innovation and economic specialization. It was therefore a matter of translating a sectoral concept into a spatial context by linking the EU strategy for innovation to cohesion policy. In concrete terms, the EU has asked European regions, ahead of their regional programs for the implementation of European funds for the period 2014–2020, to define a "smart specialization" strategy that would enable them to find their own path of development, while strengthening their competitiveness – and therefore entering into competition with others – based on the resources at their disposal. Consequently, this community policy has moved away from its traditional objective of promoting territorial cohesion. In addition, it was also based on the assumption that each European region would be able to establish, based on its resources and

---

34 Among others, we can quote Danuta Hübner, the European Commissioner in charge of regional policy from 2004 to 2009: "As we need to target the endogenous development of European regions, we have further oriented our policy towards investments providing the highest returns in terms of promoting the competitiveness of European regions. *Thereby we have put competitiveness and cohesion* objectives *on the same track*" (emphasis added).

specificities, a path of development enabling it to enter into European, if not global, economic competition. However, as shown by Bourdin et al. (2020), this ambition exceeds the capacities of European project engineering, the quality of governance and the R&D potential of the regions most in difficulty, even though some of them are still struggling to put implementation of catch-up strategies.

Beyond the territorial consequences of this support for competitiveness, this situation reveals the effects of intergovernmentalism: on the one hand, some Member States have an interest in maintaining the solidarity logic of cohesion policy, because it is economically favorable to them; on the other hand, the choice to support competitiveness allows certain governments to raise their national political options at the European level while subverting, in substance, the objectives of financial redistribution which are unfavorable to them. Between these two centers, the postures can also vary according to the situation of relative wealth of the country and the development options taken at the national level. In addition, for some Member States, complying with European competitiveness objectives is their guarantee of remaining in the category of "good students in the class" and thus justifying the funding granted to them. This situation reveals, once again, a political problem in terms of the legitimacy of European action and, by extension, that of the EU, which then appears as the recording chamber of the balance of power between the Member States, casting doubt on the ideal of cooperation that the EU is supposed to embody. Under these conditions, we can understand why the European institutions today inspire great skepticism in national public opinion, even in those who were very "Europhile" a short time ago; a fortiori, such a concrete and politically sensitive subject as the reduction of territorial inequalities doesn't seem to lower this feeling[35].

In addition to the weakening of the redistributive dimension of cohesion policy due to an orientation toward the objectives of growth and competitiveness, the EU's ability to adjust its intervention territorially remains vague, partial and ambiguous.

5.3.5. *A territorial approach of imperfect inequalities*

From the mid-1980s, geographers, specialists in regional planning and, to a lesser extent, those in regional development, constantly stressed the shortcomings of regional policy in terms of its consideration of development issues (Jouen 2012).

---

35 For example, a review of regular Eurobarometer polls shows that while in the early 1990s almost 70% of Italians considered the EU to be "a good thing for their country", making them the most "Europhile" of the EU peoples, the same institute now (2019 results) ranks Italy among the countries with the lowest trust in the EU.

The territorial dimension refers here to the idea of adjusting the policies carried out by the EU to better correspond to the characteristics of European territories, that is, a process of territorialization of policies which is based on their coordinated and integrated implementation at territorial level. Following a long process of legitimizing this approach initiated in the early 1990s outside the European institutions by the Association of European Regions, it seems to have found its consecration in the Lisbon Treaty through the reference to territorial cohesion[36]. However, up until now, the territorial dimension of cohesion policy has been expressed in a partial and sometimes ambiguous way.

At the end of the 1980s, the EU identified *"regions* which suffer from severe and *permanent natural* or demographic *disadvantages"* which cover three different situations, which can be also all combined within the same area:

– rural areas suffering from population decline and low density;

– the "outermost regions," such as the five French overseas departments of Saint-Martin, the Azores, Madeira and the Canary Islands;

– European islands and Arctic areas.

These regions benefit from additional financial contributions under the cohesion policy in order to implement projects adapted to their situation aimed at compensating for situations which place them, de facto, in a situation deemed to be unequal in comparison to the rest of the EU: natural and climatic conditions, remoteness and insular nature limiting development capacities. However, this recognition, which is set down in treaties, does not result in permanent aid schemes because their terms are renegotiated before each cohesion policy programming period.

European territorial cooperation which aims, at different scales, to solve common spatial problems also contributes to the territorial dimension of cohesion policy. However, apart from the fact that they only concern, by definition, certain European areas, the share of the budget devoted to them remains limited with regard to the other objectives of the cohesion policy. Under the 2014–2020 programming, new provisions, which have been extended for the 2021–2027 period, have been introduced in the rules governing the cohesion policy relating to a new tool for implementing the funds: integrated territorial investments (ITI). This tool, designed for local actors, aims to allow for the implementation of local development policies on the basis of a global territorial project taking into account its own problems,

---

36 See "territorial cohesion" in Elissalde et al. (2008).

defining sectoral actions articulated between them and mobilizing, hence, different types of investments and funding sources. This new cohesion policy tool arises from a report submitted to the European Commissioner in charge of cohesion policy (Danuta Hübner) in 2009 by the Italian politician Fabrizio Barca. The latter was then campaigning for a so-called "place-based" approach (or *approche territoriale*", i.e. "territorial approach", in French). Based on the idea that each territory, according to its capacities, is able to ensure its own development, this approach would allow a better allocation of the budget while responding, by effects of aggregation, to the economic and social objectives of the EU as a whole. While the ITIs constitute a tool of territorialization stemming from a global reflection on the way of articulating the objectives of the cohesion policy to the territories, their application at the scale of local territories is partial and the financing at stake relatively limited[37].

In addition to the precedent of the implementation of European pilot programs for urban spaces in the late 1980s[38], the EU authorities have been trying, since the end of the 1990s, to promote the "urban dimension"[39] of the cohesion policy. Starting from the observation of the importance of cities for the organization and development of the EU space, several European Commission initiatives have attempted to adjust cohesion policy specifically to urban issues, such as support for the competitiveness of cities in a context of global urban competition, the fight against poverty and social exclusion in certain neighborhoods and specific environmental problems. The aim is to improve the articulation of EU-funded policies within urban areas. This reflection resulted, until the 2007–2013 programming period, in the development and dissemination of framework documents[40] aimed at guiding, in the form of

---

37 The maximum budget dedicated to ITI for the period 2014–2020 is 5% of the ERDF. For example, in 2014, only 10 of the 26 French regions included this type of measure in their regional programs.

38 Urban pilot projects from 1989 onwards, followed by the URBAN I (1994–1999) and II (2000–2006) programmes of Community interest to support, via the ERDF, actions in the fields of employment, urban regeneration, the environment, etc., in urban areas with socioeconomic and environmental problems. These programs disappeared during the programming period of 2007–2013.

39 The expression is in quotation marks, as it is the one used by the European authorities. For a definition of the "urban dimension", see pages 73–79 in Élissalde et al. (2008).

40 European Commission (1997). *La question urbaine. Orientations pour un débat européen. Cadre d'action pour un développement urbain durable dans l'Union européenne*. European Commission, Brussels; European Commission (2005). *La politique de cohésion et les villes : la contribution des villes et des agglomérations à la croissance et à l'emploi au sein des régions*. European Commission, Brussels; European Commission (2007). *La dimension urbaine des politiques communautaires pour la période 2007–2013*. European Commission, Brussels.

recommendations[41], the use of European funds for urban areas, and the creation of a Euro-Mediterranean database – the Urban Audit project[42] launched in 2007 – designed to provide better knowledge of the socioeconomic characteristics of European cities. At the intergovernmental level, the Leipzig Charter was adopted in 2007 and sets out the political guidelines that the Member States have set themselves for the sustainable development of European cities, in which they undertake to pursue common objectives.

As a long-standing concern, but ultimately only supported by framework documents, the "urban dimension" seems to have gained more substantial recognition through the adoption of the Urban Agenda for the EU (or Pact of Amsterdam) during the informal meeting of EU ministers in charge of urban issues on May 30, 2016. The Urban Agenda paves the way, through the implementation of action programs which will be the subject of financing under the funding already provided for the cohesion policy, to a greater intervention of the latter in favor of the cities. As such, over the 2014–2020 period, the European Commission expected that at least 50% of ERDF funds would be invested in urban areas, which constitutes a considerable share of the cohesion policy funding[43]. However, the share devoted to integrated strategies, that is, those that include a strong territorial reflection, only amounted to 10 billion euros over the period. In addition, beyond the reminder of the main orientations concerning action on cities, the 12 action themes selected fall under an approach that is a priori rather sectoral (i.e. sectoral policies) in economic, transport, social and environmental matters: employment and training for the local economy; digital development; innovation and accountability in public procurement; urban mobility; inclusion of migrants and refugees; poverty; housing; sustainable land use; adaptation to climate change; energy transition.

The difficulty in promoting the territorial dimension of the cohesion policy can also be explained by the challenge of integrating sectoral policies at the European

---

41 Communication from the Commission (2006) on Cohesion Policy and cities presenting 50 recommendations to urban actors.

42 The Urban Audit, launched by the European Commission is coordinated by Eurostat under the aegis of the Regional Policy Directorate. It involves the national statistical offices and aims, in particular, to measure the quality of life in 79 cities of the EU (in 2015) through various indicators.

43 Source: European Commission (n.d.). Politique régionale, InfoRegio, article développement urbain [Online]. Available at: http://ec.europa.eu/regional_policy/fr/policy/themes/urban-development/ [Accessed 10 October 2020].

level, as a result of competition between the various sectoral directorates of the European Commission, which would view negatively the advent of a hegemonic cohesion policy claiming to ensure, at the territorial level, the articulation of different European policies (transport, environment, agriculture, etc.). In addition, the ministers of the Member States in charge of sectoral policies tend to consider this approach as a threat to their ability to act freely in their area[44]. This situation also reflects the difficulty of taking into account the territorial dimension of development when the issue is less pressing, for the countries in greatest difficulty, that of territorial inequalities than that of economic development on a national scale.

Finally, an approach adjusted to territorial realities would imply a common understanding of the notion of "territory" that is mobilized within the framework of development policies. However, for reasons that relate to the political organization, the history of each country, as well as to differences in tradition in terms of intervention in space or simply semantics, this territorial approach is not shared on a European scale, neither between development actors nor between European experts and researchers interested in these questions. As such, some researchers promote an approach that would make it possible to overcome institutional territories that are too restrictive (Faludi 2016) and deemed irrelevant for carrying out development actions. Consequently, they are arguing for a flexible adjustment of intervention spaces (soft spaces) according to the actions to be taken (Allmendinger and Haughton 2009; Walsh et al. 2012; Stead 2014; Allmendinger et al. 2015). However, as attractive as it is, this approach risks coming up against the reality of institutional territories which often remain the framework for action by Member States and subnational actors (Santamaria and Élissalde 2018).

EU action in reducing territorial inequalities is therefore based on fluctuating and uncertain foundations due to its transnational nature. Faced with this situation, the EU is trying to establish its action, in this field among others, by mobilizing scientific knowledge. However, the political context of the reflection disturbs the possibilities of analysis, blurs the theoretical and conceptual reflection, which prevents, in short, the clarification on a scientific basis of the objectives and the

---

44 In this respect, both the Territorial Agenda (2007) and the Territorial Agenda 2020 (2010) appear, up to now, to be the expression of political will on the part of certain governments to try to orient cohesion policy toward a more territorial approach. More recently, the Territorial Agenda 2030, approved by an informal Council of Ministers responsible for spatial planning, territorial development and territorial cohesion on December 1, 2020, under the German presidency, have come to pursue the same objective: to strengthen the consideration of the characteristics of the territories for the implementation of sectoral policies by insisting on the necessary cooperation between actors, between territories and in the development of integrated strategies at the territorial level.

operating modes of the action of the EU in favor of the reduction of territorial inequalities.

5.3.6. *A scientific approach lacking clarity*

In general, the EU is a major producer of concepts that are supposed to qualify and guide its action. These notions may be specific to the EU or derived from concepts borrowed from various disciplinary fields, which are more or less adapted to the EU's political and operational needs. This production corresponds to the need to identify an original action of its own, allowing it to establish a form of legitimacy, if not outside the Member States, then at least alongside them. However, the EU is relatively weak in terms of its own capacity to design political actions.[45] Therefore, in a search for legitimacy, it mobilizes, in its own way, the resources of science in general, and in the field of its action to reduce territorial inequalities territorial inequalities in particular[46].

However, in this field, it must be noted that beyond the political watchwords that are expressed through a certain number of notions – either directly produced at the political level and "scientificized" (e.g. territorial cohesion), or transferred from the scientific sphere to the political field (e.g. polycentrism) – the difficulty of defining the latter from a scientific point of view poses a major problem: defining exactly what we are talking about.

The cornerstone of action on the reduction of territorial inequalities since its legal consecration, the concept of "territorial cohesion", constitutes, among others, a good example of the problem raised above[47]. Indeed, researchers have different interpretations of this notion (see Box 5.2). Likewise, when it is used in the context of studies commissioned by the European Commission, particularly in the ESPON

---

45 In this regard, Faludi (2010) points out the lack of expertise within the European Commission in the fields of planning and territorial development and the need to rely on external experts.

46 The political scientists Cécile Robert and Antoine Vauchez consider that the EU, and in particular the European Commission, has tried, since the beginning of the European construction to support the European legitimacy and its action by mobilizing scientific legitimacy, in particular by constructing a set of "scientific avatars" defined as "scholarly constructions built by, with and for practice" (Robert and Vauchez 2010, p. 89) and which ultimately constitute as many sui generis doctrines.

47 For examples of scientific concepts adjusted to EU policy objectives, see: Élissalde, B. and Santamaria, F. (2018). The circulation of concepts and how they are received by those involved in planning: The instance of the concepts of European spatial planning. In *Territorio y Estados*, Farínos Dasí, J. and Peiro, E. (eds). Tirant Lo Banch, Valencia.

program, it gives rise either to a purely formal treatment, perhaps showing the researchers' embarrassment with this political notion, or to a diversity of approaches that is somewhat troubling for the potential recipients of the commissioned studies (see Box 5.3).

> Without claiming to exhaust all the approaches that have been formulated, here we shall propose a typology of the attempted definitions.
>
> An "exegetical" approach suggests an analysis of the notion to both clarify and enrich its meaning. The notion of territorial cohesion is then interpreted both as the historical search for a more balanced development of the European space, on the one hand, as well as a reference to the need to better ensure the coherence of political decisions at different levels, on the other hand.
>
> A "normative" approach that consists of providing a definition of territorial cohesion based on a proposed quantified measure of what it could be. In this regard, the ESPON applied research project *Territorial Impact Package for Transport and Agricultural Policies* (ESPON 2010) proposes a model for assessing territorial cohesion based on three general components: "territorial quality" (quality of life and work, standard of living, access to services of general interest and knowledge), "territorial efficiency" (efficiency of resources, competitiveness and attractiveness, internal and external accessibility) and "territorial identity" (social capital, know-how, specificities and specializations, comparative advantage).
>
> A "Weberian approach" involves, in a way, returning the notion to its "producer" by proposing an alternative interpretation[48]. Thus, Grasland and Hamez (2005) have proposed different measures of territorial cohesion by referring to different political documents that set out the EU's intentions for the development of its territory. The authors show that the expectations of these documents refer to a choice of different measurement variables, which lead to relatively spatially contrasted results in terms of measuring territorial cohesion (at the regional level). In this way, the researchers intend to raise awareness of the fact that measures are relative to the political and intellectual frameworks from which they derive.

Box 5.2. *Different scientific interpretations of the notion of "territorial cohesion"*

While territorial cohesion provides a good example of the scientifically unstable nature of a key notion of EU action in reducing territorial inequalities, this

---

48 We qualify this approach as Weberian in the sense that it intends, a priori, to separate the academic and political spheres while referring the question of choice to the latter. It is thus defined by the authors cited.

observation can be generalized to most of the notions used in the framework of cohesion policy. If this situation poses the problem of the contribution of research to the establishment of the action carried out by virtue of territorial cohesion, it also questions the capacity of the European message to be understood by the infra-European actors who implement their actions with funding from Europe.

> On reading the various thematic study reports of the ESPON program carried out over the period 2006–2013, the question of the relationship between the theme dealt with and the objective of territorial cohesion constitutes an important element of the program's specifications. However, there is a great diversity in ways of approaching the notion. Thus, while some reports make good use of the concept of territorial cohesion, their authors do not give a precise definition of it, and it is sometimes difficult to know what the authors mean by it. Researcher Nathalie Bertrand from the *Institut national de recherche en sciences et technologies pour l'environnement et l'agriculture* notes, in an expert report on an ESPON project dealing with rural areas in Europe that it is difficult to know what exactly the authors are aiming for: is it "cohesion" between rural areas and other areas, or "cohesion" within rural areas?[49]
>
> Some reports present a general definition of the concept that refers to the "exegetical" approach (see Box 5.2): territorial cohesion being defined as a goal to be achieved, that of a balanced development and the reduction of regional inequalities using the means of a better coordination of sectoral policies within the territories.
>
> Finally, territorial cohesion is the subject of attempts to measure that vary naturally with the themes studied, but which nevertheless testify to the variety in the way of approaching the question through this prism. The combination of indicators varies from one study to another, mobilizing in a variable way indicators such as the unemployment rate, infant mortality, the measurement of homicides and suicides, educational levels, income inequalities, life expectancy, literacy rate, GDP in PPS, etc. It can be seen that the same expression ultimately covers different measurement proposals. Admittedly, the areas (employment, health, education, income) targeted to measure territorial inequalities are often the same, but the variables chosen differ from one report to another.

Box 5.3. *Territorial cohesion in the ESPON reports*

For Cécile Robert and Antoine Vauchez, the politico-scientific production of the EU also refers to categories produced for practice. In the case of the implementation of a policy aimed at counteracting territorial inequalities, this idea can be compared to a scientific debate on the effects produced by the dissemination of notions on the practice of sub-national actors. The terms of the debate in question are as follows: is

---

49 The expert report is available at: https://riate.cnrs.fr/?page_id=7605 [Accessed 9 October 2020].

it necessary, in order to design and implement actions in accordance with EU Community objectives, to have clearly defined notions to which actors can refer? Or, on the contrary, does the uncertain nature of the notions at the European level allow them to be better adjusted to different territorial situations?

Some authors (Faludi and Waterhout 2002), drawing on empirical studies, hold that these notions play a role in the development of action plans despite their lack of clarity. For Andreas Faludi, the concepts mobilized by the EU have a "generative capacity" within existing policy frameworks or in the development of new policies. In the same vein, Shaw and Sykes (2004) believe that the concept of polycentrism – which they have studied – can be adapted according to the spatial contexts to which national, regional and local actors apply it. To this end, Gareth Abrahams concluded that, for these authors, it is less important to determine exactly what a concept encompasses than to identify what it produces as outcomes (Abrahams 2013). These authors are therefore arguing from a pragmatic standpoint for more notions that have a certain plasticity and that can pave the way for uses that are more adjusted to their deployment contexts (Sykes 2008).

On the other hand, other authors, such as Ann Markussen (1999), believe that vague or ambiguous concepts are difficult to put into practice and compromise the overall consistency of the actions carried out[50]. In order for concepts to be useful, they should be linked to a set of precise objectives which would allow them to be understood in the same way by the people who use them (e.g. researchers, elected officials, practitioners, and so on).

Therefore, while a "pragmatic" approach allows us to take note of the unstable nature of these concepts according to context (Santamaria and Élissalde 2015), it can also give the impression to the practitioners located at the different territorial levels of the fundamental relativity of the European orientations. This lack of clarity confuses both the scientific activity that could support the EU project in the reduction of territorial inequalities, and the message sent to the actors at national, regional and local levels in charge of implementing the actions financed by the EU. More generally, this vagueness poses the problem of the clarity of EU action vis-à-vis citizens, if not the very legitimacy of EU intervention itself.

5.4. Conclusion

Europe, and in particular the institutional cooperation embodied by the EU, is, vis-à-vis the rest of the world, but also within it, a space where territorial inequalities

---

50 Professor and researcher in regional economics at the University of Minnesota (USA).

are less. The EU has long been concerned with the issue of territorial inequalities and has directed its action to tackle this very problem.

The choices made by the EU for the new implementation period of the cohesion policy which entered into force in 2021 reveal three important elements for the future:

– firstly, the maintenance of the modalities of action that have prevailed since the end of the 2000s and the objective of providing compensation for inequalities and to support European competitiveness;

– secondly, the concern to continue the action of the EU carried out under the cohesion policy by maintaining the budget allocated to it despite the United Kingdom's exit from the EU;

– thirdly, to respond more proactively to developments in European territories since the 2008 crisis and to the challenge posed by the latest crisis, that is, Covid-19. On this point, the distribution of funds between Member States will be more favorable to certain southern Europe countries (such as Spain, Italy and Greece) whose socioeconomic evolutions have been of concern in recent years. The cohesion policy will also benefit from additional funding under the European recovery plan until 2023.

However, the changes also relate to the objectives of better management and use of funds by the beneficiaries via streamlined and simplified control procedures in particular. This situation coincides with the development of a morality of efficiency rather than solidarity over the past two decades. More generally, it testifies to the lack of strategic ambition that can be explained by the relative fading of the Directorate-General for Regional and Urban Policy (DG REGIO) and by a more sectoral approach to the action of the EU; to this end, cohesion policy seems increasingly to be a tool rather than a policy with its own objectives (Bourdin 2020). While this situation risks weakening the cohesion policy both in terms of its supposed objectives and its clarity at EU level and at national, regional and local levels, it also reveals the lack policy attention given to academic research that points to the need for more "territorially sensitive" policies (Bachtler et al. 2019). Indeed, dealing with territorial inequalities without a real territorial approach to the European area seems, in many respects, an approach that will lead to in the very least, misunderstandings, and at worst, disappointment. Without real reflection on a European scale on the territorial dimension of inequalities, no policy in this area can be adjusted as best as possible by really taking into account, from a perspective of territorial solidarity, not the imperative of competitiveness imposed on all, but pre-existing territorial differences. It is therefore perhaps less of a revolution that the EU's action in terms of reducing territorial inequalities would need than to be placed in the perspective of the dynamics initiated by European leaders at the end of the 1980s. For this, the political leaders of the EU (at the forefront of which are the Member States' heads of state and government) would have to adopt a more forward-looking approach instead of a reactive one. In other words, it would surely be useful, for the future of the European project, if ambitious initiatives (e.g. recovery plans) were not only implemented in reaction to crises.

5.5. References

Abrahams, G. (2013). What "is" territorial cohesion? What does it "do"?: Essentialist versus pragmatic approaches to using concepts. *European Planning Studies*, 22(10), 2134–2155.

Allmendinger, P. and Haughton, G. (2009). Soft spaces, fuzzy boundaries, and metagovernance: The new spatial planning in the Thames Gateway. *Environment and Planning A*, 41, 617–633.

Allmendinger, P., Haughton, G., Knieling, J., Othengrafen, F. (2015). Soft spaces: Planning practices of territorial governance. In *Soft Spaces in Europe: Re-negotiating Governance, Boundaries and Borders*, Allmendinger, P., Haughton, G., Knieling, J., Othengrafen, F. (eds). Routledge, London.

Alvaredo, F., Chancel, T., Piketty, T., Saez, E., Zucman, G. (eds) (2018). World inequality report 2018. Report, Executive Summary, World Inequality Lab.

Bachtler, J., Martins, J.O., Wostner, P., Zuber, P. (2019). *Towards Cohesion Policy 4.0: Structural Transformation and Inclusive Growth*. Routledge, London.

Blanchet, T., Chancel, L., Gethin, A. (2019). How unequal is Europe? Evidence from distributional national accounts, 1980-2017. Report, World Inequalities Lab.

Bourdin, S. (2018). Analyse spatiale de l'efficacité des Fonds structurels européens sur la croissance régionale. *Revue d'économie régionale et urbaine*, 2, 243–270.

Bourdin, S. (2020). La Politique de cohésion 2021-2027 : vers une plus grande territorialisation ? *Géoconfluences* [Online]. Available at: http://geoconfluences.ens-lyon.fr/informations-scientifiques/dossiers-regionaux/territoires-europeens-regions-etats-union/articles-scientifiques/politique-de-cohesion-2021-2027#section-1 [Accessed 10 December 2020].

Bourdin, S., Lefevre, O., Saint, F. (2020). La spécialisation intelligente, une stratégie réellement pensée pour toutes les régions de l'UE ? *Géocarrefour*, 94(3) [Online]. Available at: https://journals.openedition.org/geocarrefour/15572#quotation.

Coman, R., Fromont, L., Weyembergh, A. (eds) (2019). *Les solidarités européennes. Entre enjeux, tensions et reconfigurations*. Bruylant, Brussels.

Creel, J. and Levasseur, S. (2004). Le nouvel élargissement de l'Union européenne. *Revue de l'OFCE*, 89(2), 253–269.

DATAR (2010). *La cohésion territoriale en Europe*. La Documentation française, Paris.

Davoudi, S. (2009). Territorial cohesion, European social model and transnational cooperation. In *Planning Culture in Europe. Decoding Cultural Phenomena in Urban and Regional Planning*, Knieling, J. and Othengraffen, F. (eds). Ashgate, Aldershot.

Dicharry, B., Nguyen-Van, P., Pham, T. (2019). La politique de cohésion de l'Union européenne et la convergence économique. Bulletin de l'observatoire des politiques économiques en Europe [Online]. Available at: https://opee.u-strasbg.fr/spip.php?article407 [Accessed 30 September 2020].

Drevet, J.F. (2008). *Histoire de la politique régionale de l'Union européenne*. Belin, Paris.

Dühr, S., Stead, D., Zonneveld, W. (2007). The Europeanization of spatial planning through territorial cooperation. *Planning Practice and Research*, 22(3), 291–307.

Élissalde, B. and Santamaria, F. (2013). Harmony and melody in discourse on European cohesion. *European Planning Studies*, 22(3), 627–647.

Élissalde, B., Santamaria, F., Peyralbes, A. (2008). *Lexique de l'aménagement du territoire européen*. Lavoisier, Paris.

ESPON (2010). TIPTAP: Territorial impact package for transport and agricultural policies. Report, ESPON, Luxembourg.

Evers, D. (2012). A solution in search of a problem: A "garbage can" approach to the politics of territorial cohesion. *European Journal of Spatial Development*, 45, 24.

Faludi, A. (2007). Territorial cohesion policy and the European model of society. *European Planning Studies*, 15(4), 567–583.

Faludi, A. (2010). *Cohesion, Coherence, Cooperation: European Spatial Planning Coming of Age?* Routledge, London.

Faludi, A. (2016). The poverty of territorialism: Revisiting European spatial planning. *disP – The Planning Review*, 52, 73–81.

Faludi, A. and Peyrony, J. (2011). Cohesion policy contributing to territorial cohesion – Future scenarios. *European Journal of Spatial Development*, 43, 21.

Faludi, A. and Waterhout, B. (2002). *The Making of the European Spatial Development Perspective. No Masterplan*. Routledge, London.

Farinós-Dasí, J. (2020). Reviving the EU Project: From values to new territorial development models. *Géocarrefour*, 94(3) [Online]. Available at: http://journals.openedition.org/geocarrefour/15603 [Accessed 30 September 2020].

Faucheur, P. (2017). La Politique de cohésion comme exercice de solidarité financière européenne. *Gestion et finances publiques*, 4(4), 31–35.

Fitoussi, J.P., Laurent, E., Le Cacheux, J. (2007). L'Europe des biens publics. In *France 2012 – E-book de campagne à l'usage des citoyens*, Fitoussi, J.P. and Laurent, E. (eds). OFCE, Paris.

Grasland, C. and Hamez, G. (2005). Vers la construction d'un indicateur de cohésion territoriale européen ? *L'Espace géographique*, 34(2), 97–116.

Jouen, M. (2012). *La politique de cohésion européenne*. La Documentation française, Paris.

Markussen, A. (1999). Fuzzy concepts, scanty evidence, policy distance: The case for rigour and policy relevance in critical regional studies. *Regional Studies*, 33(9), 869–884.

Needham, B. and Hoekveld, G. (2013). The European union as an ethical community and what this means for spatial planning. *European Planning Studies*, 22(5), 1010–1026.

Rivière, D. (2020). La politique de cohésion face aux enjeux de justice spatiale dans un contexte de crise européenne. Quelques réflexions sur le cas italien. *L'Espace politique*, 40(1) [Online]. Available at: https://doi.org/10.4000/espacepolitique.8202 [Accessed 1 September 2020].

Robert, C. and Vauchez, A. (2010). L'académie européenne. Savoirs, experts et savants dans le gouvernement de l'Europe. *Politix*, 89, 9–34.

Santamaria, F. and Elissalde, B. (2015). Parlez-vous l'Européen ? Enquête sur quelques notions clés de la Politique régionale de l'UE auprès d'acteurs français de l'aménagement. *L'Information géographique*, 79(1), 55–71.

Santamaria, F. and Elissalde, B. (2018). Territory as a way to move on from the aporia of soft/hard space. *The Town Planning Review*, 89(1), 43–60.

Shaw, D. and Sykes, O. (2004). The concept of polycentricity in European spatial planning: Reflections on its interpretation and application in the practice of spatial planning. *International Planning Studies*, 9(4), 283–306.

Stead, D. (2014). European integration and spatial rescaling in the Baltic region: Soft spaces, soft planning and soft security. *European Planning Studies*, 22, 680–693.

Sykes, O. (2008). The importance of context and comparison in the study of European spatial planning. *European Planning Studies*, 16(4), 537–555.

Walsh, C., Januciak-Suda, M., Knieling, J., Othengrafen, F. (2012). Soft spaces in spatial planning and governance: Theoretical reflections and definitional issues. In *Regional Studies Association European Conference*, Delft.

Waterhout, B. (2008). *The Institutionnalisation of European Spatial Planning*. Delft University Press, Delft.

Waterhout, B. (2011). European spatial planning. Current state and future challenges. In *Territorial Development, Cohesion and Spatial Planning. Knowledge and Policy Development in an Enlarged EU*, Adams, N., Cotella, G., Nunes, R. (eds). Routledge, London.

6

Medium-sized Cities and Territorial Inequalities

Josselin TALLEC
Pacte, Université Grenoble Alpes, France

6.1. Introduction

In this chapter, we will focus on medium-sized cities – a now much-debated feature of planning policies – and the planning policies' relationship with the treatment of territorial inequalities. At the crossroads of different social movements, but also of academic works (see in this regard Authier and Bidou-Zachariasen 2017, pp. 168–169; Hamdouch et al. 2018), the debate concerning the legitimacy of medium-sized cities in order to establish the contemporary goals of planning policies – such as reducing development gaps between territories – has been driving discussions and concrete actions in the field of public action for territorial purposes for several years. The same is true of the operational expertise that characterizes the planning policies (see for example, FNAU 2020, p. 111). In these registers, the question of inequalities, in the sense of their foundations and their evolutions, occupies here a relatively central position. For example, they encompass issues of access to everyday services and common goods for the resident populations at the scale of these cities and for those living in their spheres of influence (e.g. education, health and so on), urban planning operations to revitalize city centers in the face of urban sprawl, but also reflections on new development paths which would make it possible to improve the living conditions of the populations faced with situations of urban decline

(ANCT 2021). Like the multidimensional nature of inequalities, the range of possibilities is very wide.

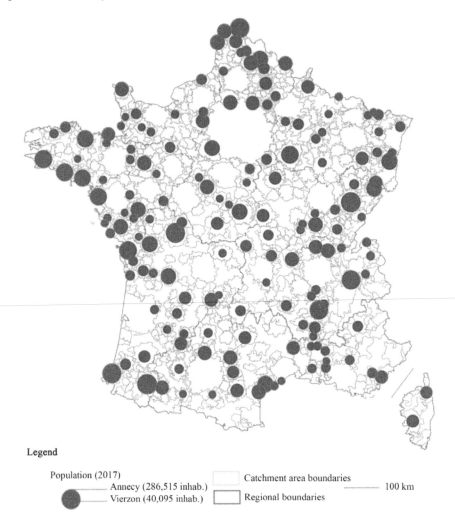

Figure 6.1. *The spatial distribution of catchment areas in medium-sized cities[1] (2021) (source: author's production). For a color version of this figure, see http://www.iste.co.uk/talandier/territorial.zip*

---

1 As mentioned in the introduction and at the scale of the French urban system, catchment areas with 30,000–400,000 inhabitants can be likened to "medium-sized cities".

But first, let us start with what a definition of a "medium-sized city" could be. Outside of the immediate sphere of influence of another city or center, a medium-sized city can be understood as an urban unit and a catchment area (according to the criteria established by Insee) which generally has between 40,000 and 300,000 inhabitants, although this demographic criterion is still somewhat vague (and even arbitrary)[2]. They form "living territories" articulated to several urban functions (e.g. economic and social) within which the daily activity of working people and households as well as businesses is organized. Nearly a quarter of the national urban-dwelling population currently reside in these 165 catchment areas, that is, a demographic mass that corresponds in size to the catchment areas of Paris and the Lyon metropolis combined (Figure 6.1)[3].

Faced with metropolization, the highlighting of a binary and a little too caricatural vision of a France at "double speed", between large cities that are winning and other territories that are losing (small and medium-sized towns, suburban spaces and rural territories), tends to crystallize a good number of debates in the political and media sphere. Social difficulties are therefore the expression of various territorial fractures. Guilluy's "peripheral France" (2014) is one of its expressions, like The Liberal Elite, opposing the London metropolis to other British territories, or The Left Behind, small "rural" towns of the United States (Wuthnow 2018). Non-metropolitan territories would thus be perceived as neglected, or at least their development trajectories (and therefore the resulting inequalities) intimately dependent on neglect at two levels. Firstly, this "left behind" (or neglected) feeling would be orchestrated by social laws producing spatial inertia, including that of the polarization of economic activity. Subsequently, this feeling would be institutionalized by mechanisms having concrete impacts on development trajectories and the increase in inequalities that can be associated with it.

The issue of public services' territorial network supports this statement (Taulelle 2012; ANCT 2020). The recent conference published by Fol (2020) on small towns also echoes this.

We will focus on the category of the "boundary object" (Trompette and Vinck 2009), which encompasses medium-sized cities at the scale of the French urban

---

2 The catchment area of a city is defined as "a group of municipalities that defines the extent of the influence of a population and employment center on the surrounding municipalities, this influence being measured by the intensity of commuting" (Insee 2020). Established in 2020 by Insee, this zoning has replaced the 2010 urban areas zoning. The components of this zoning are detailed in section 6.3.1 of this chapter.

3 These definitions are developed further in section 6.3.1 of this chapter.

system, in order to understand how spatial planning and development policies deal with inequalities, with a focus on economic issues[4].

Far from being neglected by planning policies, medium-sized cities have on the contrary been the object of cyclical interventions and interests illustrative of the different "turning points" in the objectives of planning policies. And it is perhaps benchmarks such as those of the competitiveness and attractiveness of territories, resolutely inscribed in the creation of value, which have, for a time, questioned the usefulness of this category of cities to establish the objectives of planning policies. Its coupling to various social crises (e.g. the closure of production units), the resolutely long timeframes of public action and their effects on the territories exacerbate a phenomenon of being left behind.

Between the winners (i.e. big cities and metropolises) and the losers (i.e. small and medium-sized cities), territories with increasingly divergent trajectories have taken shape. The responses likely to be provided by planning and territorial development policies are brought up for debate, and this in the face of the dissemination of development models for medium-sized cities based on the spillover capacities of metropolitan territories. However, the gradual dissemination of the principle of "territorial cohesion" – understood here as the ability to "hold together" territories with divergent but interdependent trajectories (Béhar 2019) – seems to reinstate the roles and functions that these centers can play in approaching territorial inequalities. The idea of territorial "differentiation", which is understood here in a double sense – that is, firstly, as "tailor-made", allowing the development of policies adapted to local contexts, and secondly, where the development trajectory of a territory is intimately linked relations maintained with others – can then, and in part, contribute to the development trajectory, and we will question its relevance for thinking about the treatment of territorial inequalities at the scale of medium-sized cities.

To do this, our discussion will be organized into two parts: firstly, we will contextualize the different ways in which planning policies deal with territorial inequalities; secondly, we will address the implementation of these initiatives at the level of the category of action constituted by medium-sized cities more specifically.

---

4 In sociology, the notion of a "boundary object" refers to a "malleable object that can be shaped by everyone; the library object from which everyone can extract what they need; the object that can be simplified (abstracted) or from which one ignores the properties one does not need; the interface or standard of exchange" (Trompette and Vinck 2019, p. 8).

6.2. From positions to conditions: a brief history of planning and its relationship with territorial inequalities

In their contemporary foundations, generally apprehended at the end of the Second World War, planning policies have gradually oscillated between different goals, including that of achieving "[...] a better distribution of people, according to natural resources and economic activities" (Claudius-Petit 1950)[5]. The action is openly voluntarist and its intentions, means and actors have evolved over time. Initially thought of as interventionism, regulated by the state in a territory that was then weakly decentralized, three entries, which are still probably relevant today, were the key words: repair, redistribute and encourage.

Of course, these actions are not fundamentally self-evident and are part of an evolution of social and political compromises. In the past, it was possible to reduce the issue of planning to the equipment of cities and territories, but also to material initiatives of Saint-Simonian inspiration around the networking of cities and territories. Planning was a matter of facilitating the circulation of commercial flows, information, as well as individuals (Alvergne and Musso 2009). In political economy and on the basis of a certain mercantilist tradition, it was then assumed that circulation would make it possible to achieve spontaneous economic "balances" or optimums thought out in a context of political unification of the national territory and the consolidation of "material interests in France" concomitant with the advent of industry (Chevalier 1843). A moment of expansion of economic liberalism thought of as an "equalizer" of conditions (Rosanvallon 2013) within a France made up of diversities (Braudel 1986), the arrangements that will emerge in the context of reconstruction will break with these considerations. They will carry a territorial project of national dimension with a unifying scope and conceived under the seal of "equality" between individuals and, by extension, between territories.

The following three factors are the likely origin of the relationship between planning and inequalities:

– the financial resources allocated to a public policy (including, in this context, those linked to the Marshall Plan and the Monnet Plan);

– the surges of local actors seeking to take advantage of the opportunities offered by reconstruction;

– a diagnosis (or inventory/situational analysis), discussed and debatable, built around the old adage of *Paris et le désert français* by Gravier (1947)[6].

---

5 Claudius-Petit, E. (1970). *Pour un plan national d'aménagement du territoire.* Ministère de la Reconstruction et de l'Urbanisme (MRU).

6 Xavier Desjardins and Philippe Estèbe also expand upon this point in Chapter 3 of this book.

Without going into extensive detail on these three factors, a series of guidelines and measures will be implemented in order to balance and equalize the conditions for the development of cities and territories[7]. The moment of re-construction has thus formulated windows of opportunity to solve these inconveniences in the context of an urban transition relatively recent in comparison with other European contexts and which poses bitter difficulties in the management of daily life (e.g. insalubrity and precarious housing, dilapidated and under-equipped urban and interurban transport networks and so on)[8]. Nevertheless, attention has been mostly focused on the city of Paris, which is accused of devouring most of the country's forces. A "vision" of development is for a time posed, while turning toward the correction of inequalities and the gaps of development between Paris and the "other" territories. Three other frameworks for action also coexisted for a time:

– institutions that supported and followed an interministerial and multisectoral logic (e.g. the French General Planning Commission, DATAR, created in 1963);

– actions, devices and programming objectives (e.g. legislation, deconcentration and decentralization actions, and long-term programs);

– projections, representations and "icons" that create the benchmarks of action (e.g. "the scenario of the unacceptable" published in 1971, the idea of a "metropolis of balance", established by the policy of the same name in 1963).

From now on, the different sequences of decentralization and the European integration question these past arrangements. Planning policies has now become "multilevel" and the concern for the "local" has shifted it from the planning of "the" territory to that of "territories". Even though all of the initiatives have not achieved the expected effects in terms of reducing inequalities, we will try to come back to the deeply evolving consideration of the treatment of territorial inequalities by planning policies[9]. Our discussion will draw on an approach centered on economic and productive activity.

---

7 Such as the political, populationist and even urbaphobic character of "applied geography" as popularized by Gravier. See Marchand's (2009) work on this subject.

8 Note that the urban transition (defined here as the transition from a predominantly rural population to a predominantly urban one) took place at the turn of the 1930s in France.

9 For example, the Île-de-France still accounts for nearly 30% of national GDP for one-fifth of the population. This observation can be the source of many debates on the advantages and disadvantages of this inertia (e.g. centralism, congestion effects and so on). At another scale, we can observe a displacement of these same discussions (e.g. Toulouse and the "other" territories of the former Midi-Pyrénées region).

If the question of the equality of territories seems to be gradually being called into question (Estèbe 2015), it is more generally the shift from equality of positions to equality of conditions that has emerged within planning policies, and this not without contradictions (Dubet 2011). Indeed, if the quest for equality of conditions seeks to act on the places occupied by individuals within more or less established social structures (e.g. the question of income inequalities), equality of positions agrees rather on the idea of a relative equality of opportunity where individuals must seize the opportunities capable of supporting their social mobility. In this second configuration, few questions emerge as to the openly unequal starting conditions from one social context to another. Support for the development of cities and territories can be understood on these same grounds. In the correction of territorial inequalities, two strong economic orientations have been invested in cyclically:

– The prism of redistribution and compensation generally producing explicit "territorial" discrimination (particularly through zoning) or implicit (in active or symbolic orientations). It is therefore a question of taking into account the difficulties encountered by cities and territories with the desire to overcome them. Zoning, or the fact of targeting a category of cities or territories (e.g. "city policy" (*politique de la ville*) which is targeted at so-called "problem areas"), therefore directs policy measures from the perspective of a "priority geography".

– The prism of value creation through aid to dynamic territories, but also through the construction of a territorial (and therefore development) project based on the development of territorial resources (material or immaterial) that can be qualified as "local". Behind these ambitions, it is indeed the project's ability to drive the rest of the territory(ies) which is expected at the crossroads of a development "from above" incentive and driven by state orientations and "bottom-up" development embodied by the mobilization of local actors outlining the orientations and development issues to be invested in.

We will take a "top-down" approach to describing the development movements, a time dedicated to the quest for balance and equity between and within territories. These elements can therefore show an institutionalized refusal of inequalities that may, perhaps, prove to be effective. The "turning point" in the competitiveness of planning policies thus promotes a principle of territorial concentration of investments in a reduced number of territories, a concentration that must subsequently "lead others" in the name of a runoff that is by no means spontaneous. This concentration would be opposed to a redistribution thought by the sprinkling more likely to be legitimized in period of economic growth and thus an increase in wealth. These two orientations with strong economic dimensions have served as a benchmark for planning policies in the correction of territorial inequalities. While the idea of a golden age of "equalizing" planning – formed originally – inspired this policy action (see section 6.2.1), the slowdown in economic activity from the 1970s to 1980s led to the intervention frameworks for managing crisis situations to be reassessed (see section 6.2.2). Gradually yet not without tension, the idea of the necessary territorial concentration of investments then laid the foundations for a certain unequal treatment between territories (see section 6.2.3).

6.2.1. Growth and redistribution: the idea of a certain "golden age" of planning (1950–1975)

The windfall of the reconstruction contributes to forge the representation of a territory in the grip of great imbalances and multiple "disorders" in the distribution of people and economic activities. These inequalities, which were perhaps very symbolic, then undermined French national unity. The period known as the "*Trente glorieuses*[10]", which was characterized by very strong economic growth (more than 5% per year) and a Fordist production model centered on the nation state, created the framework for government interventionism to prevail, with the state overseeing a large number of industry operators. At the same time, the institutional compromises of the post-war period (e.g. pension schemes, various social benefits, increases in wages and so on) increased domestic demand and ensured a certain prosperity for these industrial entities, which find outlets. The economic situation favored the promotion of these benchmarks of action.

The creation of the French National Land Development Fund (*Fonds national d'aménagement du territoire* (FNAT)) in 1955, coupled with an approval procedure that limited the creation and development of industrial activities in Île-de-France, was intended to limit the expansion and concentration of industrial activities in the Paris region. Growth is emerging from all sides and the idea is relatively simple: to involve in the creation of values territories previously excluded from these dynamics, without however being able to note a clear vision of the productive organization of the national space. The decentralization of productive units is the cornerstone of this system of actions. It is the organization of the national territory as a whole that counts to the rhythm of an industrial imperative that gives priority to "equipment". The development is then deeply imbued with a redistributive and equipment Keynesian dimension.

---

10 Thirty-year period in France following the end of World War Two.

Nearly 3,500 decentralization operations led to the creation of 500,000 industrial jobs (Laborie et al. 1985). The territories around the Paris region have been able to take full advantage of these operations, which have been accompanied by the gradual formation of a very pronounced Paris-province division of labor between the design, coordination and production phases. A new form of functional subordination then emerged, now industrial, confining certain territories to a relationship of renewed "domination" (apart from the decentralization of head offices and decision-making centers that were relatively weak at the time (Morvan 2004). The setups of these operations were extremely varied, as evidenced by, for example, the establishing of Moulinex in Argentan in Lower Normandy (Frémont 2005), or the Renault establishments in Cléon in Upper Normandy (Daumas 2002).

As such, interest in the urban framework of the territory only emerged at the turn of the 1960s. These include the great development plan of Paris led by Paul Delouvrier (1961) and the very emblematic and symbolic policy of balanced metropolises (*Métropoles d'équilibre*) (1963). We thus observe the desire to energize the upper stratum of the urban hierarchy of the national territory, and this, in particular, by the formation of centers of higher influence according to François Perroux's (1955) theoretical model of growth centers, within large provincial towns where forms of sectoral specialization were emerging in growth-generating niches (e.g. electronics in Rennes, chemicals and pharmaceuticals in Lyon, aeronautics and IT in Toulouse, etc.). This "qualitative" decentralization, hailing the virtues of "training" concentration and "industrializing industry", was subsequently combined with the creation and decentralization of higher education and research structures.

Between 1957 and 1977, these "implants" (Lacour and Delamarre 2006) then led to the decentralization of 17,000 tertiary jobs to the West and South-West of France by, in particular, the implementation of localization programs for research units. In the same way, medium-sized cities have obtained their own component of action on the basis of programs to improve the "living environment", programs under contract with the state. We will return to this point in the second part of this chapter. Consequently, large cities and metropolises played a decisive role in the quest for equity as well as in the economic performance of a territory that was increasingly being opened up for trade due to its being part of the European common market and whose sector policies (e.g. the European Union's Common Agricultural Policy) have significant effects on the dynamism of certain territories. The expanding industrial activity then rubbed shoulders with traditional sectors (such as the textile, metallurgy and mining industries), which encountered major difficulties from the end of the 1960s. These crises were very localized, for example, confined to the mining areas in northern France, Massif Central, Cévennes and South-East Provence, among others. The main resulting policy action thus focused on territorial discrimination through zoning without, for the moment, calling into question the organization of the national industrial fabric. Zoning, or the identifying of "target" territories for policy action, was a favorite instrument for the actors. The granting of bonuses or additional subsidies for these territories and companies was intended to deal with the difficulties that they were encountering. Equipment then rubs shoulders with support for territories that are experiencing a reduction in the industrial workforce, a situation that the two oil shocks of 1973 and 1974 considerably exacerbated. All of this helped to shine a light on the close interdependence of national industrial activity and the outside world, and thus highlighted the role of a now unavoidable player, the European Union (EU). Indeed, as we know, France is not the only European country to be a victim of this vast process. The EU, then the European Economic Community (EEC), sought to establish a community policy which notably sought to reduce "[...] disparities between the levels of development of the various regions and the backwardness of the least favoured regions" (Single European Act 1986). It is the provision in the 1975 version of the European Regional Development Fund (ERDF) which accompanies the financing and construction of major equipment and infrastructures in regions in crisis or lagging behind in development, interventions at the time the governance of the European states and regions concerned. This period contributed to forging the representations and modes of intervention of planning policies, oscillating between redistribution, compensation and concentration on the basis of reducing inequalities between territories.

6.2.2. Repairing and supporting territories "in transition" (1975–1995)

The two oil rises of the 1970s changed this situation. Economic growth was drying up and the planning model came up against imperatives and industrial organizations that the hand of the state, and more generally of public intervention, could no longer hold, but with which companies had to play on a daily basis (e.g. increase in the cost of raw materials, reduction in transport costs and so on). Above all, it was a matter of saving jobs and therefore of carrying out reconversions of territories that had been negatively affected by the closure of production units (Morvan 2004). Between 1975 and 1980, nearly 700,000 industrial jobs disappeared. To combat this, planning often became a local job defense policy. However, redistributing the fruits of growth was very difficult and the objective was rather to encourage it. To do this, territorialized measures, such as, subsidized financial aid and tax relief, were promoted. It was a question of palliating the structural deficit of territories then weakly adapted to the modes of organization of industrial activities fitting into a new international division of labor and therefore sequence of globalization. The metaphor of the "fire-fighting state" (Albertini 2006) was used for a time to evoke the structuring role played by state intervention. Indeed, the territories "driving" development were no longer the same. Large cities and regional metropolises now concentrated most of the economic dynamics (in terms of job creation, particularly in so-called innovative sectors) and approaches that aimed to equalize the territory through a quantitative deconcentration of activities that no longer appeared to be relevant because of various factors (for instance, "opportunistic" companies seeking to benefit from these subsidies without anchoring themselves strongly in the territories) (Laborie et al. 1985). These crises were no longer sectoral, but were becoming territorial and thus called for the return of interventions that would, like the metropolises of balance policy, encourage targeted interventions. Local institutional compromises then took place between industry operators, which were sometimes state-owned (e.g. Charbonnages de France and the mining industry), and national and local political actors (such as departmental authorities). For example, in 1984, 15 reconversion centers were thus set up on the basis of statistical criteria prefiguring the conditionality of aid with regard to zoning (defining the territories that could benefit from these initiatives) and therefore a territorial discrimination in order to reverse this organization of the economy–territory relations. The allocation of grants for companies that decided to establish themselves there provided a rhythm to the action (e.g. regional development grants (PAT) and current state aid for regional purposes (AEFR)). The traditional land-use planning measures persisted, but their purposes evolved. These measures were then supplemented by Act I of decentralization (1982–1983) and the implementation of state-region plan contracts involving local authorities and the state on a joint program spread over several years[11]. Local authorities (led by the regions and departments) were given regulatory powers to support the actions of the state, as well as the EU within an "integrated" regional policy. The game became more complex, and the work of coordination and guidance carried out by DATAR was transformed into a mission of "top-down" management of various and varied policies and funds.

In this highly technical game, the planning finds itself in search of a new legitimacy. The LOADT of February 1995 (Orientation law for spatial planning and development known as the "Pasqua law") brings a new stage in the implementation of planning policies which, for some of them, become "territorial policies"[12]. The question of the "territorial project" was being institutionalized and consecrated the idea of carrying out development on the basis of the valorization of local resources, that is to say endogenous development, at the rate of the signing of a contract

---

11 Law of March 2, 1982 on the rights and freedoms of the municipalities, departments and regions.
12 Law of February 4, 1995 on the orientation for the planning and development of the territory.

between the project territories (countries, regional natural parks, etc.), the state and the local authorities concerned. These local strategies contributed, at most, to organizing and considering the national territory in its diversity. The only industrial and equipment route is then no longer preferred. "[...] Act as closely as possible to act better" (Alvergne and Taulelle 2002, p. 76) sums up quite well the state of mind of a now selective territorial animation. Indeed, with the call for projects seeking the initiatives most likely to respond to the new challenges in planning, territories found themselves competing as they sought to be selected.

Over this period, it seems that planning was increasingly separated from its function of reducing territorial disparities which was replaced by that of coordinating territorial projects. We could even understand this whole period as the disappearance of a certain strategic vision of development: as a period of doubt in the face of the difficulties encountered by public policy in regulating the spatial scales within which economic activities are coordinated.

6.2.3. Animation and concentration: a shift from competitiveness to differentiation (1995 to the present)

If the question of the reconversion of certain territories, and therefore the new paths of development that could be envisaged, still arises with a certain acuity, the spatial selectivity of economic growth is confirmed and probably benefits the large cities and metropolises. Of course, growth does not automatically rhyme with development. Many non-metropolitan territories have recorded a notable improvement in their development, which can be measured on the basis of income and the invisible circulation of wealth in particular (Davezies and Talandier 2014). Spatial planning policies then embarked on a new overhaul of their interventions that various institutional reforms were to enshrine. This involved, first of all, the adoption of the LOADDT (or the Voynet law of June 1999), which sought to break with the national vision of development brought about by the Pasqua law in favor of local translations (including at the scale of living territories)[13]. This approach is found concomitant with an environmental awareness consolidated by the dissemination of the principle of sustainable development now referred to from the angle of the socioecological transition irrigating all the themes of intervention of the development and territorial development. The end of the 1990s then saw a series of initiatives that C. Lacour and A. Delamarre included in globalization, metropolization, mobility and territorial environments, which were to be anchored on metropolitan bases the vision of development. Like the policy of balanced

---

13 Law of June 27, 1999 on the orientation of the planning and the sustainable development of the territory.

metropolises, large cities and metropolises were established as the bases for the organization of national and regional economic activity. Reducing uncertainty (Veltz 1996), the articulation and dynamization of a territory's economic and social activity from the regional metropolises became, so to speak, the way forward. Mention is made of the "[...] enhancement of urban systems in global competition"[14], which would concentrate "[...] most of the opportunities for competitiveness"[15]. For Guigou (1996), this was the necessary reorientation of planning policies toward "[...] policies of structural anticipation" (ibid., p. 833), which call for a Copernican revolution in the foundations of planning policies that could not escape a European dimension that is now unavoidable. Far from being exclusive, it is this progressive shift in the scales of reference for planning actions that is now turned toward Europe and globalization that will seal a metropolitan vision.

This new establishment of the role that metropolitan areas could play in terms of territorial development explicitly raises the question of the place of French cities and regions on the scale of the EU. The adoption in 2000 of the Lisbon strategy by all the EU member states once again changed the situation. It should be remembered that the latter aimed to "make the European Union the most competitive knowledge-based economy in the world". The convergence of the French model toward these European programmatic orientations is then a period of hesitation for the missions of an administration in search of legitimacy in the face of the ups and downs of economic and industrial activity questioning the concrete usefulness of the old territorial development revenue set out in the preceding paragraphs. Consequently, the law of August 13, 2004 (Act II of decentralization) openly called for an institutional reorganization of the scales of development[16]. New competences and missions are granted to the regions which become the "territories" of the articulation of the multiple spatial and institutional scales of action, but also of the right scale within which we think we can act on territorial development. The drafting of multiple regional plans (the versions of which constitute the current SRADDET[17] or SRDEII[18] for the economic component) serve to support the coordination of the territorial development initiatives implemented by the various local authorities. It was also a period in which a relative qualitative leap in planning policies was being prepared, which would aim to translate the Lisbon strategy locally within a

---

14 Letter from DATAR, 1998.
15 Letter from DATAR, 1999.
16 Law of August 13, 2004 on local freedoms and responsibilities.
17 SRADDET: *Schémas régionaux d'aménagement, de développement durable et d'égalité des territoires* (Regional planning, sustainable development and territorial equality plans).
18 SRDEII: *Schéma régional de développement économique, d'innovation et d'internationalisation* (Regional plan for economic development, innovation and internationalization).

community space that should be organized on the basis of "regional clusters" capable of stimulating technical and technological innovation, and therefore, implicitly, the economic growth of the EU. The vocabulary of the EU, that of competitiveness and the necessary revitalization of the knowledge economy, has redirected the aims of planning policies. A relatively symbolic dimension of these "collective conversions" can be observed, in particular with the changing of DATAR to DIACT in 2006 (Interministerial Delegation for the Development and Competitiveness of Territories) and later back to DATAR (Delegation for development and regional attractiveness) in 2010 but adopting a "regional attractiveness" approach. One of the most emblematic actions of this period remains the policy of competitiveness clusters, which was implemented from 2004 to 2005 and took an approach at the intersection of industrial and planning policy. By encouraging the grouping together of public institutions (universities, research centers, etc.) and firms in the form of associations of the 1901 law type on the scale of a generally metropolitan territory (but not exclusively), it is a question of reaching a certain "critical mass" guaranteeing the production of innovative goods and services resulting from local collaborations between these different partners, but also of their international visibility. This policy of stimulation of industrial clusters, taking over from the measure of local productive systems (1999 and 2001), thus initially retained nearly 71 clusters allowing each region to promote sectors that would provide them with comparative advantages, and therefore the export capacities of the national economy. The territorial concentration of investments is central here. This policy, now reduced to 54 clusters (e.g. the Valorial cluster around the agri-food industry in Rennes and the Minalogic cluster around nanotechnology in Grenoble), operates on the basis of the call for projects, thus putting territories and their collectives in competition with one another in order to receive funding. While the effects of this policy on territorial development are still subject to various interpretations, these are essentially the hubs of metropolitan configuration – in particular Île-de-France, with seven hubs, and the Auvergne-Rhône-Alpes region (Lyon, Grenoble), but also articulated around strategic sectors (e.g. l aeronautics and space industry in Toulouse) – which have been able to take advantage of this resource allocation initiative, which is still relatively small compared to the redistribution mechanisms used by many social policies in recent years[19].

At the turn of the 2010s, new institutional advances transformed the landscape of actors, the "words" and the "ills" of development with which the stakeholders of these actions were gradually confronted. Indeed, it was a matter of highlighting in

---

[19] In this regard, see the recent evaluations carried out by France Stratégie in 2020 entitled "Les pôles de compétitivité : quels résultats depuis 2005 ?". Available at: www.strategie.gouv.fr/sites/strategie.gouv.fr/files/atoms/files/fs-2020-ns-pole-competitivite-aout.pdf.

the media sphere and the expertise of various "territorial fractures" opposing the development trajectories of large cities and metropolises to "others", namely small and medium-sized cites, rural and outer periurban areas. The development of these territories was anchored in a spiral of being stuck in limbo as a result of the commercial vacancy rate and decreasing industrial activity in many small- and medium-sized cities. In reaction and faced with the inertia of these territorialized situations, a research study on the issue of the conditions of the equality of the territories was carried out[20]. Consequently, the name for the state services in charge of planning issues changed in 2014, and became the *Commissariat général à l'égalité des territoires* (General Commission for Territorial Equality (CGET)), where the overly sectoral logic of actions would explain a large part of the origin of these situations. A more cross-cutting dialogue of policies would therefore make it possible to ward off these difficulties. But the "metropolitan" planning options that were selected were still contested or debated, as evidenced by the 2017 Senate report entitled *Aménagement du territoire : plus que jamais une nécessité* (Regional planning: A necessity more than ever), which emphasized the active metropolization of productive activity, the spillover effects of which would prove to be very selective, as they did not take into account, in their daily operations, the territories of their local environments. These spatial inertias would be the vectors of "territorial injustices" for territories that have been left behind and become the centers of mechanisms for the reproduction of social inequalities and associated determinisms. This raised questions of accessibility, spatial distribution and therefore the "network" of a whole series of public services that organize the different social times of populations (e.g. the digital, health and social divides). The same is true of territorial cohesion, which resonates with a certain acuity and calls for an overhaul of the proponents of planning, in order to "hold together" parts of a territory with divergent (or even complementary) development trajectories, so that they do not reproduce social inequalities within "shrinking" cities and territories, and those where (because of social transfers) there is development without growth.

A changing institutional context prefigured these considerations. Initially, the adoption of the NOTRe law of 2015[21], consolidated the regionalization of spatial planning and development by making the new large regions the exclusive leaders of the major orientations in planning and economic development[22]. Upstream, this advancement was expressed by the promulgation of the MAPTAM law

---

20 Report edited by É. Laurent. Available at: www.vie-publique.fr/sites/default/files/rapport/pdf/134000131.pdf.

21 Law of August 7, 2015 on the "new territorial organization of the Republic".

22 The mergers of French regions of French regions have led to the creation of 18 large regions (13 in metropolitan France and 7 in overseas France).

(*modernisation de l'action publique territoriale et d'affirmation des métropoles,* modernization of territorial public action and affirmation of metropolises), which saw the first institutional overhaul of local authorities in 2010 around the law of reform of local authorities (*réforme des collectivités territoriales* (RCT)), with the creation of a new status for "large" intermunicipalities with more than 500,000 inhabitants. This is the promulgation of the status of "metropolis", and therefore of greater capacities to act than other inter-municipal structures. This recognition of the major cities of the French urban system reshaped the practices and ways of developing with the aim of accompanying the "metropolitan fact" and the associated interterritoriality (Vanier 2015). The spirit of these institutional developments is then that of networking, in terms of intensity and capacity for connectivity of territories and activities in the service of territorial development. This other meaning of the metropolization process (Offner 2019) involves a questioning of the roles that metropolises could play in their relations with other territories on the basis of "territorial systems", for instance, as driven by an increase in populations' mobility as part of their daily practices.

By seeking to collectively define and animate complementarities or reciprocities between cities and territories that make the specificities of the development of each of these systems (e.g. food issues, mobility and transport infrastructure, economic networks), initiatives embryonic forms, such as "*contrats de réciprocité*" or "*pôles métropolitains*" (as an inter-city networking policy), outline the contours of a territorial differentiation that would break with the categorical and sectoral logics of planning (Béhar 2017; Grebot 2017; Talandier and Tallec 2020). This bet on territorial differentiation, centered on the functioning of the relations maintained between territories as a determining factor in their development, always questions the "right scale" of these spaces for negotiating flows rather than opposing stocks and is still under debate, but questions the places and functions now occupied by medium-sized cities within related spaces.

6.2.4. Differentiation at the bedside of territorial inequalities?

From the rejection to the still debated territorial inequalities, we have outlined the history of planning and its relations to cities within the French urban system and their development dynamics. From now on, it is indeed a new questioning of the roles and territorial functions which is or which would be able to play the process of metropolization in terms of territorial development which is brought to the debate. Recognition of this phenomenon and of its potential to, initially, create value by stimulating agglomeration economies and their capacities for connectivity at different scales (from the "local" territorial system to its place in globalization) should be underlined. The debate focuses on the heavy inertia to be overcome, as well as on the more or less visible bifurcations of new development paths to be accompanied according to territorial specificities, while remaining on very categorical territorial logics (for example metropolises, medium-sized cities, etc.). In fact, this logic takes little account of territorial systems, whereby the nature of one territory's relations with another will form the base of its development. In this context, a very general notion of "territorial differentiation" is emerging, which must naturally be included in territorial projects.

However, new territorial fractures are being revealed through an opposition between the big cities and metropolises and the other territories – that is to say, the non-metropolized space of which the medium-sized cities constitute one of the major symbols. This development is at the center of the second part of this chapter, whereby we will endeavor to resituate the construction of its relationship to planning and territorial development policies, and therefore to the treatment of territorial inequalities.

6.3. Medium-sized cities: a long-term figure in the planning and the treatment of territorial inequalities

Intermediate cities, cities on a human scale, ordinary cities – there are numerous expressions seeking to qualify this "[...] unidentified real object" (Brunet 1997, p. 13) that "medium-sized cities" can constitute have multiplied over the course of research on this component of urban and territorial systems or on this category of cities. This profusion of expressions naturally remains the fruit of the more general deepening of reflections on the geographical and institutional scales within which the recompositions of cities and their economic activities unfold. In common sense, it would above all be the size of cities, here reduced to the quantitative spatial concentration of populations, assets and activities, which would explain the development dynamics of these urban entities. As we know, the development trajectories of cities are not exclusively linked to their size; somewhat idealized depictions are also common. Medium-sized cities, with a less dense urban structure than that of large, sprawling and fragmented cities, are also the cities of the "middle classes" and therefore give rise to socially more homogeneous territories. These points merit further discussion.

Medium-sized cities create, in the first instance, an order of magnitude on the basis of the spatial distribution of a population stock. This magnitude, at the junction of the extremes that bound the components of each urban system (the largest and the smallest urban entity), can also refer to the category of cities with the highest frequency of distribution at the scale of an urban system. For example, in the

European context, nearly 60% of the population resides in centers with populations of less than 200,000, that is, cities that can be described as being relatively "small" (Cattan et al. 1994).

Like the very generic idea of the middle class whose porousness we agree on without excluding a certain form of social reality (Goux and Maurin 2012), it is thus relatively commonplace to state from the very first lines of work on medium-sized cities a well-known vulgate: that of the difficult, even impossible definition of this group of cities found in most urban systems (Santamaria 2000, 2012). However, these medium-sized cities are part of a twofold dynamic that is a priori contradictory, namely a movement that is fixed in a stable definition (the city) and another movement that envisages a possible expansion or growth (medium-sized) cities. These centers are thus articulated in situations inscribed in different moments of urban history that contribute to redefining the urban reality, which either does or does not characterize them in return.

To return to the analogy made between the ideas of class and medium-sized cities, their rapprochement can also be seen in their relationship to social mobility and the difficult transition between different classes that results from it. Their ability, so to speak, to negotiate their "places" in the contemporary urban system is put to the test of the contemporary organization of productive systems and their dependence on jobs or resources that only the big cities are able to supply. If we consider the notion of equality of conditions presented in the introduction, the fear of being left-behind (Taulelle 2012) therefore illustrates the growing territorial inequalities that planning policies can try to correct.

It is also often said that the diversity and variety of activities found in a city depends on its size. The evolution of their economic development would then follow certain laws of scales favorable to the production of innovations driven by the larger ones and whose hierarchical diffusion would ensure the reproduction and conservation of the initial properties and inequalities of the urban systems on the long term (Pumain 2007). These spatial irreversibilities would still leave room for a long-term adaptation of all cities to the innovations that would have emerged at first in the big cities (Paulus 2007). We would see processes linking the development trajectories of cities to the relationships and interdependencies of cities with one another. Finally, cities would gradually adapt to new forms of activity. However, studies aimed at clearly measuring the growth of French cities over the last few decades tend to influence the resonance of metropolization (Paulus and Pumain 2002). This observation is also found in the evolution of industrial activity and employment, where the evolution of the weight of workers working in industry is not determined by the demographic size of cities (Poupard 2015).

But this abandonment probably suffered by medium-sized cities unfolds in a very contemporary history. Medium-sized cities were, during the splendor of the postwar boom, considered to be "territorial filters" of economic growth within a broader movement to modernize French society (Saint-Julien 2003). This active modernization, due to being accompanied by urban policies and action dedicated to this category of cities, contributed to the initial definition of a medium-sized city. It took shape via new modes of household consumption, new relationships and practices of the population to space for cities that were catching up with a relative delay (household motorization, development of single-family homes, etc.). The development of medium-sized cities and the reduction of associated inequalities were connected to a certain increase in the power of the middle classes in French society, and more particularly, within these urban areas. The golden age of planning, mentioned in the first part of this chapter, was imbued with a certain quest for redistribution of economic growth that was emerging from all sides, would therefore be that of medium-sized cities.

At the turn of the 1970s, the loss of momentum and the refocusing on a more limited number of industries and territories, undermined this golden age which contributed to define, through the prism of strong economic growth and the smoothing of socioeconomic disparities, the expansion of this stratum of the French urban system (Commerçon 1996; Saint-Julien 2003; Santamaria 2012). How then can we conceive of the idea of a "medium-sized city" on the scale of an urban system when now nearly 92% of the population lives in an urban area (or a functional one) and therefore under the influence of a city?

As we have already stated, this same notion of the medium-sized city emerges above all as a question of urban history and social history where the equalization of the conditions of development and the repair of difficulties have been accompanied by. The qualifiers now used place them under the sign of cities cornered by a certain backwardness and dependent on relations vis-à-vis the metropolitan space. We will come back to this point over the course of the second part of the chapter. Firstly, we will define the sociodemographic magnitudes of this political object and its relationship to metropolization (see section 6.3.1). Subsequently, we will focus on the trajectories of these cities in order to outline the first milestones of deeply shifting relationships to the inequalities that now result from them (see section 6.3.2). Lastly, we will outline the attention that is paid to medium-sized cities in planning and territorial development policies (see section 6.3.3).

6.3.1. *Medium-sized cities: elements of contextualization of a stratum of urban systems*

The qualifiers cited in the introduction to this section in an attempt to define the notion of a medium-sized city from different angles present us with centers discriminated against at first sight on the basis of their demographic size. They produce, at best, metaphors for the different social, economic and geographic situations that can be discussed. In fact, there is a statistical link between the size of cities, the diversity of their activities, their influence and their development. This relationship would extend to the sources of social change, which can also be linked to the capacity of recompositions of productive activity. Indeed, the innovation capacity of cities and territories is closely linked with the agglomeration economies and therefore to the concentration of a diversity of economic activities in the same place, and the institutions supporting them.

These processes, calling back to so-called variety effects and to the economic interactions that drive them at different spatial scales, were notably introduced by Jacobs (1961). Complementary to the pioneering work of Marshall (1891), they contributed, among other things, to defining the drivers of the economic externalities generated by the concentration of activities. By analogy, we understand that compared to a large city or a metropolis, a medium-sized city's capacity for innovation or adaptation is less. Social inertia and rent phenomena, even economic lock-in resulting from the specialization of these territories would thus be legion. These phenomena therefore explain certain local difficulties.

At the scale of the French urban system, the various zonings mobilized to take into account the urban reality, the forms and the contemporary recompositions of cities (urban units, urban pole, urban areas, city catchment areas, etc.) will build a first grid in which the notion of medium-sized city is anchored. Depending on the zoning adopted, a distinct influence of urbanization will naturally be observed. Currently, there are 2,233 urban units (or cities) which show between 771 (according to the 2010 zoning) or 682 catchment areas (according to the 2020 zoning) connected to the same number of metropolises on a metropolitan scale. Consequently, and depending on the zoning, the weight of the population considered "urban" varies between 78.03%, 84.7% and 93.2% on the scale of France (i.e. there are between 48.4 million, 73.2 million or 60.2 million urban dwellers). By way of example, and if we take into account the residents of multipolarized municipalities within the limits of the zoning in urban areas of 2010, now 92% of the national population should be considered "urban". But within these movements, the 417 small centers or small urban areas represent only 5% of the urban population. The new catchment area zoning made up of 682 areas on the scale of metropolitan France contributes to a relatively similar definition and measurement of the influence of cities. In this new zoning, which seeks to standardize the territorialized statistical classifications of censuses on a European scale, in order to match the former urban areas to Eurostat's catchment areas, Insee has established five categories of catchment areas around the following demographic criteria: Paris, areas with more than 700,000 inhabitants (with the exception of Paris), those with between 200,000 and 700,000 inhabitants, those with between 50,000 and 200,000 inhabitants, and those with less than 50,000 inhabitants.

On this basis, Insee arrives at the following distribution of the French "urban" population (Table 6.1)[23].

	Number of catchment areas	Municipalities		Population	
		Number of municipalities	Distribution (in %)	Number of inhabitants	Distribution (in %)
Paris area	1	1,929	5.5	13,024,518	19.5
700,000 inhabitants or more (excluding Paris)	13	2,733	7.8	13,136,668	19.7
200,000 to at least 700,000 inhabitants	47	5,698	16.3	15,731,876	23.6
50,000 to at least 200,000 inhabitants	126	7,824	22.4	12,295,213	18.4
Less than 50,000 inhabitants	512	7,872	22.5	8,125,598	12.2
Municipalities outside the city's catchment area	0	8,932	25.5	4,466,984	6.7
All French municipalities	699	34,968	100	66,780,857	100

Table 6.1. *Distribution of municipalities and population by size of catchment area (source: Insee 2020)*

The apprehension of this urban fact by the zoning in urban areas, then in catchment areas, illustrates the relay taken by the outer periurban rings in the

---

23 For more details on the construction of this zoning, see the Insee note (2020). Available at: www.insee.fr/fr/statistiques/4806694.

urbanization of the territory[24]. Indeed, more than half of this demographic change (52.5%) is due to suburban sprawl and the extension of mobility and commuting.

As stated in the introduction, it is common to define "medium-sized cities" from the demographic thresholds of urban between 30,000 and 200,000 inhabitants (CGET 2018). However, the adoption of catchment area zoning has changed these criteria somewhat. Based on various studies, we have chosen to consider medium-sized cities as urban units with a population of between 20,000 and 200,000, corresponding to catchment areas of between 40,000 and 300,000 inhabitants. The upper category corresponding to the idea of "intermediate regional metropolises" and the lower category to small cities. Of course, there is a degree of porosity between these different categories (especially in these extremes), but we can still distinguish almost 165 catchment areas that correspond to "medium-sized cities."

If we look at the evolution of the population of the catchment areas between 1968 and 2017 (Figure 6.2), we can observe a shift in the centers of gravity of population distribution to the benefit of large cities and other metropolises[25]. The influence of Paris remained stable, but it was the areas with more than 700,000 inhabitants that were recording the highest growth rates (nearly 1% between 1968 and 2017), compared to a national average (0.65%) similar to that of Paris and the Île-de-France region. Medium-sized cities (with between 40,000 and 300,000 inhabitants) and small cities (with less than 40,000 inhabitants) were seeing their relative influence decrease.

But this quantitative shift is not entirely due to "regional" metropolises: a very limited number of urban entities are behind it. This mechanism is set in motion by a reduced number of "large" centers which switch from one category to another, explaining the dynamics of the upper fringe of the stratum of intermediate metropolises (such as Nantes, Montpellier and Rennes). In the slope of areas with more than 1 million inhabitants, this push is supported by two areas (Toulouse and Bordeaux) influencing in a non-negligible way the influence now supported by this same group.

This population growth in the upper stratum of the urban system, which can naturally be related to the process of metropolization, is based on a very limited number of centers. Thus, this observation refers, as underlined by Paulus and Pumain (2002, p. 39), to a "[...] process of hierarchical diffusion in the selective aspect of growth" illustrating that the inflections observed over recent decades do not constrain the relative stability in the position of cities in the long term.

---

24 See Chapter 4 of this book by Éric Charmes.
25 The perimeter of the analysis of catchment areas defined in 2020 by Insee services is the one used for all the periods studied.

Medium-sized Cities and Territorial Inequalities 215

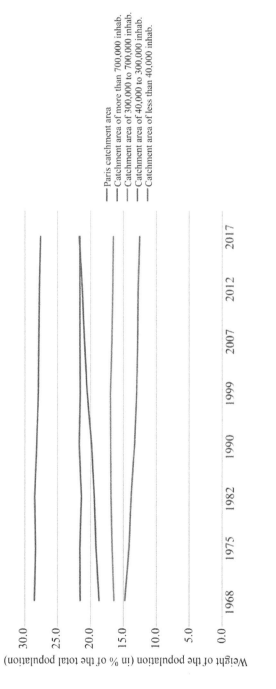

Figure 6.2. *Changes in the population weight of catchment areas (1968–2017) (source: Insee 2020). For a color version of this figure, see http://www.iste.co.uk/talandier/territorial.zip*

In these trends, medium-sized cities generally maintain their demographic size (28.2% of the urban population in 1990 compared to 27.6% in 2017). The dynamic remains present in catchment areas with a population between 200,000 and 300,000 inhabitants (+1.3% annual growth since 1999). The constancy of this dynamism subsequently seems to spread to all categories of this same stratum, with the exception of the "small" catchment areas of 40,000–70,000 inhabitants that recorded a stagnation in demographic growth between 1990 and 1999 (+0.03% per year) in contrast to now (+0.73% per year since 1999). The non-regularity of local dynamics is therefore essential in a vast global movement of stability. However, the metropolitan fact complementary to that of Paris and Île-de-France is verified. Consequently, and from a very short-term perspective, thinking about spatial planning from the angle of the "all metropolitan" can indeed constitute a credible dimension of public action, but whose usefulness for the entire national territory can be questioned.

If we focus our attention onto employment (private and public) and its evolution, these trends tend to be confirmed (Table 6.2). Between 1982 and 2017 and for all catchment areas of France's national territory, total employment grew from 19,776,844 to 24,315,363 employed persons at a rate of annual growth from one stratum of the urban system to another. Like the demographic movements described above, we observe a slight decrease in the weight of employment in Paris and the Île-de-France over the last few decades. With the exception of the "major" regional metropolises (which have catchment areas with more than 700,000 inhabitants), this inflection is also notable for all the other components. This growth in employment, which is higher than the national average and that of the other categories of cities, appears to make the large cities and regional metropolises the winners of the contemporary spatial changes in economic activity, thus pulling up the dynamics of national employment. This observation has been highlighted by Davezies (2012). But this analysis of the economic situation, which is presented as a trend, is based once again on a very limited number of urban areas (especially between 1999 and 2009), including the metropolitan areas of Toulouse (annual growth rate of about 2.8%), Montpellier (2.52%), Rennes (2.15%) and Nantes (2.14%), followed by Bordeaux (1.94%), Toulon, Marseille, Nice and to a lesser extent the Lyon metropolitan area. While the correlation between the size of centers and the dynamics of employment does not seem to be rigorous in the face of the diversity of situations, it is nevertheless clear that a small group of territories conditions the metropolitan shift of employment in its most generic form at the national level.

Catchment areas (CAs)	Annual growth rate of employment (in %)						Workforce in 1982	Workforce in 2017	Weight in 1982 (in %)	Weight in 2017 (in %)
	1975–1982	1982–1990	1990–1999	1999–2007	2007–2012	2012–2017				
CAs of Paris	0.11	0.93	−0.06	1.22	0.34	0.13	4,934,296	5,971,667	24.9	24.6
CAs of more than 700,000 inhabitants	0.83	0.98	0.88	2.05	0.81	0.64	3,832,584	5,567,366	19.4	22.9
CAs of between 300,000 and 700,000 inhabitants	0.58	0.43	0.57	1.52	0	−0.18	3,177,268	3,850,851	16.1	17.8
CAs of between 40,000 and 300,000 inhabitants	0.66	0.24	0.49	1.26	−0.02	−0.18	7,476,720	6,439,084	27.7	26.5
CAs with a population of less than 40,000	0.46	−0.09	0.30	1.21	−0.07	−0.49	2,376,176	2,486,395	11.9	10.2
Total	0.52	0.5	0.43	1.45	0.21	−0.01	19,776,844	24,315,363	100	100

Table 6.2. *Changes in employment in the catchment areas (1975–2017) (source: Insee 2020)*

For the other categories of cities, a structural decline in employment is under way. Since 2007, it has more significantly affected small and medium-sized cities, as indicated by the (large majority of) negative growth rates recorded. It is difficult to attribute these developments solely to the economic crisis of 2007–2008. Indeed, and even if the previous periods proved to be more favorable (in particular between 1999 and 2007), recompositions evolving between degradation of the productive base due to the end of a Fordist production model and growth of the residential base are active and draw new development trajectories for these cities (Talandier et al. 2016). We will come back to this point, but note that this relative stability of the demographic masses and activity ignores local dimensions that are profoundly distinct from one center to another. They suggest the existence of a "regional effect" (in the sense of their insertion in a territorial system that wins) more decisive than a single "hierarchical effect" (in the sense of the size of cities), which determines their economic trajectories (Poupard 2015; Bouba-Olga 2017). The question of their economic attractiveness and their trajectory of integration into globalization, in particular measured from foreign direct investments (FDI) – and the creation of associated activities – also suggests a diversity of situations inscribed in relatively decisive regional effects (Finance 2017).

A logic of territorial differentiation is then to be taken into account to apprehend the treatment of territorial inequalities and their relation to the economic dynamics of the territorial systems to which the cities belong (Talandier et al. 2021).

6.3.2. Medium-sized cities and a progressive differentiation of demographic dynamics and economic activity

Between 1954 and 1975, as for all cities in France, medium-sized cities recorded the highest population growth rates. This change is attributed to the rural exodus which made them into "territorial filters" of a dynamic of generalized economic growth. Following the various economic crises of the 1970s, the slowdown in economic activity had a concrete impact on medium-sized cities' development. Economic activity was being recomposed and we can observe a general deterioration in manufacturing or "concrete production" activities of around 30% of the working population between 1982 and 1999 (i.e. 1.3 million jobs). Essentially, these crises mainly affected small and medium-sized cities and those with more than 100,000 inhabitants (Fouchier 2005). Gains in productivity, outsourcing of certain tasks and functions translate these same movements being deployed in distinct geographical and sectoral configurations from one urban entity to another.

Over this period (from 1975 to 2010) of the reorganizing of production systems, the catchment areas experienced an average annual growth of 0.47%. The regional effect, detailed in particular and inscribed from the angle of "coastalization" and more generalized growth in the West and South of France, reduces the idea of a "size" effect which explain the observed trends. Between 1982 and 1999, this perspective was supplemented by higher migration balances in the catchment areas between 500,000 and 1 million inhabitants above the average (7.1% against a national average of around – 0.2%). This category of metropolises alone explains one-third of urban growth. In parallel with these larger movements, regimes of economic specialization of small and medium-sized cities, influenced by relations of "proximity-distance" vis-à-vis the nearest large city, were also at work. The effects and consequences of the metropolitan loosening of activities, probably very detailed (Levratto 2016), abound the current approach to the functioning of the national territory on the basis of multiple "urban systems" taken over and supplemented by the DATAR services, and this in a context where the urban areas of small and medium-sized cities have explained, since 1975, only 7–6% of the growth of the

French population (Berroir et al. 2012). "Regionalized" effects then emerged, whereby the place of medium-sized cities in "winning" territorial systems has influenced the trajectories of population and employment over the last decades (Figures 6.3 and 6.4).

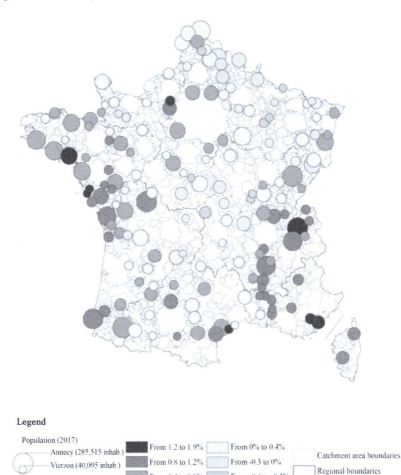

Figure 6.3. *The annual population growth in the catchment areas of medium-sized cities (1975–2017) (source: Insee 2020). For a color version of this figure, see http://www.iste.co.uk/talandier/territorial.zip*

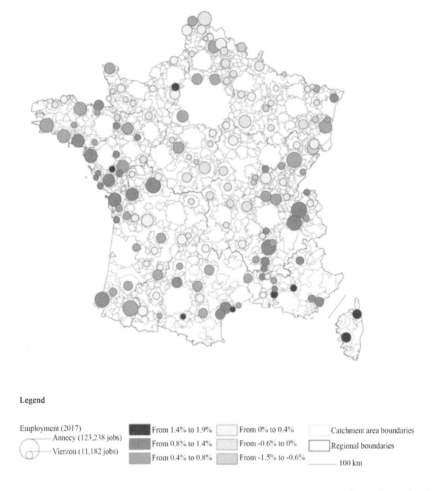

Figure 6.4. *Annual growth in employment in the catchment areas of medium-sized cities (1975–2017) (source: Insee 2020). For a color version of this figure, see http://www.iste.co.uk/talandier/territorial.zip*

6.3.3. *Medium-sized cities and the permanence of a political object for treating territorial inequalities*

With just over a quarter of the national urban population residing there, the catchment areas of Annecy (286,515 inhabitants) and Pau (279,139 inhabitants) are the "largest" medium-sized cities, whereas Pontivy (40,196 inhabitants) and Vierzon (40,095 inhabitants) are the smallest. At first glance, it is easy to see that the diversity of situations and trajectories would outweigh their uniqueness.

Nevertheless, we can see that, very subjectively, and with regard to the data presented in the preceding paragraphs, "[...] the relativity of this concept does not impede on its relevance" (Manzagol et al. 2003, p. 13) to evoke a common framework of problems related to territorial inequalities and the actions in the field of development that have the ambition to correct them. But despite all of the difficulties surrounding this definition, to speak of "medium-sized cities" is to conceptualize them chiefly as a political object of action from a historical perspective of planning. Indeed, it was the gradual shift from an economic planning to spatial planning that established a role and a function for "medium-sized cities" in a programmatic agenda of development. Their "usefulness" in dealing with territorial inequalities has consequently evolved.

On the one hand, the urban framework centered on the nation state and actions granting primacy to urban planning interventions aimed at energizing this category of city will predominate. At the turn of the 1980s and in the wave of decentralization, it was the logic of zoning that was mobilized, in order to intervene as close as possible to these "territories in difficulty". This method has been used and mobilized in a large number of mechanisms (e.g. a city policy, *politique de la ville*). Nowadays, it is the logic of "territories" that predominates.

Let us remember that the notion or the idea of a "medium-sized city", which participates in its reification as an urban and therefore territorial object, was institutionalized at the beginning of the 1970s by the conduct of a national planning component specifically aimed at the attention of these same centers: the "medium-sized city contracts" (1973). The very general regulation of the urban growth of the national territory was then at the center of this register of intervention, and the definition of these contracts prefigured the contemporary figures of an "animating state" which coconstructs and which cofinances, with the partner local authorities, a series of urban planning operations at the level of the central municipalities of the selected centers.

The "medium-sized city" also asserts itself well in advance as a geographical and institutional reality at the crossroads of two sequences of measures inscribed in the concern for the control and unification of the nation state. The first sequence of policy actions took place in the revolutionary period and involved the establishing of different administrative maps, which participated in the "historical network" of different administrative functions producing centrality (e.g. prefectures, subprefectures and the different services in related population). A first level of functional actions was thus established from the end of the 18th century on the basis of a close relationship with the surrounding "rural world" (Lepetit 1989) and on which the equipment sequence of the development was to be based on the territory after the Second World War. This "corrective" function of planning policies sought to consolidate and take over from the emblematic operations of decentralization and industrial deconcentration which affected, at first glance, these same centers (Faucheux 1959). Initiatives such as the renovation and development of public spaces and roads, the construction of community facilities and the planning of activity areas were all implemented in order to bring the local services and activities up to standard with the daily life of the inhabitants. Their aim was also to adapt these municipalities to new demands and social practices and to successfully "stabilize" the inhabitants of these centers, by providing them with the urban services and functions equivalent to large cities and regional metropolises. Indeed, migration to the "big city" has long been perceived as the "natural" and upward social trajectory for populations. However, by averting it, it then made it possible to participate in the quest for balance in the circulation and geographical distribution of people and activities. Formalized around a multi-year contract of actions with the municipalities concerned, this policy action therefore took over from the policy of balanced metropolises on the scale of another geographical level, where the spatial reference used was that of the "urban framework logic". In the words of Guichard – a former delegate of DATAR and the Minister for Regional Planning, Equipment/Public Works, Housing and Tourism, in the introduction to an issue of the journal *Urbanisme* (1973) – this "[...] urban civilization policy" was intended to rectify the "inconveniences" of urban life by outlining the intermediation functions that were at the time devolved to medium-sized cities. The passage toward a qualitative improvement of the "living conditions" of centers which would not experience the "[...] constraints and hardships of large metropolises" (Guichard 1973, p. 3) is central here.

The notion of "medium-sized city" therefore appears to be the result of a political policy that was developed during the major movements for the institutionalization of planning policies for an urbansystem in which large cities were more of an exception than the norm. Consequently, the geographical distribution of these centers dispersed over the whole of the national territory was mobilized as a factor, which made it possible to constrain "the scenario of the unacceptable" drawn up by the DATAR in 1971. The initial definition of a medium-sized city was also brought into the debate. For Guichard, it is an approach combining the systemic organization with the territory, the size of these centers and their functional dimensions thus achieving: "[...] any center with an already significant demographic weight in the population of a region, exercising diversified functions for the benefit of a sufficiently large hinterland endowed with an urban quality that ensures it a recognized influence" (ibid., p. 3). As such, it is the expansion of the question of medium-sized cities as preferred places for growth and modernity "in relation" to its area of influence (such as small cities and rural territories) that should be discussed.

The economic crises of the 1970s got the better of this orientation, which then shifted in favor of zoning and targeting interventions in territories defined as being in "difficulty". Faced with the imprint of the Fordist register of production on the scale of medium-sized cities, many centers were eligible for this type of measure. The last register at work will then be that of the logic of the territories according to territorial recompositions coupled with the reference of globalization and the quest for polycentrism on a European scale, but also in France (Baudelle and Peyrony 2007).

Upstream, decentralization and industrial deconcentration have set the pace for most of the city-level interventions perceived as "labor silos" for many industrial companies (Michel 1977; Commerçon 1996). From 1955 to 1974, these policies, driven by state subsidies, played a part in the economic and productive development of these centers.

By relying on a certain socioeconomic "proximity" with the headquarters of the decentralized units, the medium-sized cities in the Paris Basin and Seine Valley have become the main platforms of a movement that has led to the creation of 462,000 jobs as a result of 3,126 industrial deconcentration operations (Guichard 1965; IAURIF 1966). Without undermining the industrial potential of Île-de-France, the "medium-sized city" then became an "average city" (Michel 1977), whereby it is seen as a tool that makes it possible to mobilize sources of labor from a rural world in the throes of technical change and where there is potential for workers with lower social and wage requirements. The financial costs of extending certain units to the Paris region also seem to have weighed in the balance. The trajectories of these cities place them as points of support for action programs that confine these centers, according to the division of labor specific to each production unit, to production and assembly functions. For some Marxist researchers, these movements reproduce the balance of power and domination inherent to the capitalist model of production. The medium-sized city becomes "[...] deprived of all power of initiative, of all capacity for command. It can only ratify and apply decisions which, drawn up outside and above it, confine it to a role of dissemination and execution" (Michel 1977, p. 676). While the immediate interests of businesses seemed to take precedence over a more general logic of development, these initiatives helped accelerate the growth of urban society, along with a "cumulative process" of renewing economic structures (i.e. strengthening of industrial and service activities) and the sociodemographic aspects of these territories (i.e. rejuvenation and growth of executive jobs in these centers; see Santamaria 2012). Despite these units becoming the main employers of local economic activity, the other side of the coin is rooted in a more general deterioration in job qualifications compared to large cities, and this, from the end of the 1960s (Lerustre 1975). Here, the old adage of "Paris thinks and the provinces execute" finds its roots. Until 1975, the urban framework involved carrying out a series of initiatives that aimed to balance the national territory on industrial bases which would gradually move into urban planning orientations. This change appeared to be a consequence of the gradual slowdown in the economic expansion of medium-sized cities. The state then sought to combine the development of industrial and urban logics on the scale of medium-sized cities in order to ensure the extension of the initiative of "*the métropole d'équilibre*" policy. The logic of the "lowest cost" of urbanization is thus brought forward as a key argument for centers which "[...] do not know the difficulties and the additional costs that excessive urban concentration entails" (Guichard 1973, p. 4). From 1973, medium-sized city contracts were contributing to this objective by focusing on the qualitative improvement of the urban environment through qualitative means.

Subsequently, zoning and the construction of the perimeter of intervention became the main intervention measures in medium-sized cities. Faced with the strong sectoral specializations of these centers and the economic difficulties encountered, the balances negotiated during the previous period were undermined. Medium-sized cities were becoming, along with small cities, the main territories where there was a noticeable and visible decrease in employment, which led actors in medium-sized cities to reformulate traditional planning measures. The reference to the urban framework faded behind the treatment of emergencies and the local safeguarding of employment. From 1976, this was reflected by the reorienting of credits initially intended for the urban planning aspects of contracts for medium-sized cities in favor of investments to supplement the installation bonuses from which actors or industrial operators could benefit. To achieve this, various promotional and territorial marketing tools were invested in order to position the "assets" and the "strengths" of these centers which were now competing to secure economic investments (Association Bureaux-Provinces 1977). The underlying logic for this zoning served as the basis for pooling initiatives to promote and improve accessibility and the development of cities and territories broadly. However, they did not consider the role that medium-sized cities could play in terms of dealing with inequalities. The "*Pôle de conversion*" policy illustrated this turning point taking place at the intersection of the interventions of very diverse actors (such as departments, consular chambers, the EU and so on). In 1984, 15 centers defined from employment pools affected by the closure of production units were identified. Measures were implemented to modernize the sectors of activity (such as the steel industry, mining industry and so on) and industrial prospecting business operations.

Several "specialized" medium-sized cities benefited from this system (such as Roanne, Douai, Valenciennes and so on).

Following these measures, the logic of the territories was then imposed on medium-sized cities. In the movement of decentralization which recomposes the missions and the financial margins of the state in terms of development, one of the watchwords will more generally be the "pooling" of equipment and mechanisms, in order to achieve, by the cooperation between different geographically close centers, a "critical mass" that should lead to visibility of these territories and a virtuous logic of growth. Some initial experiments had already taken place toward the end of the 1980s (e.g. the "Aire 198" network for the Poitou-Charentes region (Royoux 1997)), but in particular, it was during the CIAT of November 5, 1990, that J. Chérèque, the then Minister Delegate for Planning and Industrial Reconversion, refined this idea by announcing that "it is a matter of developing, between candidate cities and a certain number of partners, cooperation projects in order to strengthen, from a European perspective, the economic competitiveness of cities and, based on this initiative, of their territory of influence"[26]. It was thought that the pooling of equipment and projects, via interurban transport networks, would broaden the relationships with other metropolises. The resulting dialogues would then make it possible to achieve economies of scale generating "network externalities" (Camagni and Gibelli 1994). Networking was done from different registers (e.g. relations and cooperation between companies, reticular systems of governance) and was structured around thematic horizons as diverse as culture and tourism, technologies of information, housing, transport and town planning, economic development, etc. Recognized and promoted by the LOADT of February 4, 1995, it is in this spirit that the actors and the centers supported 26 networks which sought to link their development to an activity, equipment or function which they lacked. The purpose of the approach was to bypass certain "size effects" and to create a framework that would be favorable to the internationalization of the development of these territories then brought about as a process explaining the inequalities observed. This policy proved not to be very effective and had little impact on the trajectory of the medium-sized cities that were invested in. Nevertheless, these ideas are experiencing a certain revival through their mobilization by the upper and metropolitan level of the urban framework, as evidenced by the successive constitutions of projects of "*Pôles métropolitains*", which would ensure a connection and therefore a shared development of metropolises with medium sized cities in their hinterlands (Talandier and Tallec 2020).

---

26 CIAT: *Comité interministériel permanent pour les problèmes d'action régionale et d'aménagement du territoire* (Permanent interministerial committee for regional action and development of the territory). Speech available at the following address: www.vie-publique.fr/discours/129374-premier-ministre-5111990-sur-la-politique-damenagement-du-territoire.

In addition to these collaborative measures, this period of development was particularly characterized by the installation and the consolidation of higher education functions on the scale of medium-sized cities. The success of two sequences of measures associating the state and the local territorial communities (the University 2000 plans between 1991 and 1995 and the U3M plan – University of the Third Millennium conducted between 2000 and 2006) shaped the contemporary university and scientific map, which now includes several medium-sized cities. These measures helped to reduce inequalities in access to higher education and also oscillated between a strategy of adapting the state's public power to the growth of student demographics and a development opportunity for these for these centers (e.g. Albi, Lorient, Troyes and La Rochelle). The close relationships with the local economic world (e.g. Lorient (Séchet 1994)) and the more global development strategies for the centers concerned have also set the pace for the trajectories of these institutions (e.g. with the creation of training programs linked to local economic sectors).

Under a productive register and toward the end of the 1990s, attention was paid to questions of industrial development through "local productive systems" or industrial districts. Nearly 160 "territorialized sectors" benefited from the financing of operations in various sectors that were intended to facilitate the development of technical and technological innovations, which would ensure their participation in the globalization of the economy. Several medium-sized cities benefited from this system, such as the *Pôle Mécanique* in Alès, the extraction and recovery of granite in Fougères, plastics in Oyonnax and Alençon, mechanics and textiles in Roanne and so on.

Oscillating between development perspectives linked to relations maintained with other territories (e.g. city network policy) or development actions that can be qualified as endogenous (e.g. local productive systems policy), the apprehension of the forms taken by the development of medium-sized cities now grants a structuring place to the logic of territories. The corrective dimension of inequalities remains eluded, or at least dependent on the conditions and capacities for linking up with other cities and territories that can lead to various forms of redistribution (and therefore equalization) supported by the dynamics of productive residential systems in which these territories participate (Davezies and Talandier 2012). This orientation was confirmed by prospective research carried out by DATAR (2010). As such, medium-sized cities are understood as spaces of intermediation that are determined by the functions of centrality supported and therefore their influence on a local space (e.g. hospital services, education and so on). These functions, admittedly weakly differentiating, constitute points of support guaranteeing a certain equality in terms of the households and working population within these territories being able to access common and public services and goods. From these reflections, four scenarios emerged:

– "uncertain communities" that are marked by strong social fragmentation;

– "green laboratories" where the proximity offered by medium-sized cities promotes initiatives in favor of the socioenvironmental transition of cities and territories;

– "interconnected satellites" that suggest a development articulated around strong relationships of complementarities between the medium-sized cities and the other territories of their respective regional environments;

– "competing specialties" where the strong specialization of these cities on a limited number of sectors of activity places them in a precarious situation regarding the economic situation.

It is therefore very difficult to reduce medium-sized cities to just one of these scenarios. Rather, their trajectories place them at the intersection, in terms of the principles of differentiation and territorial cohesion as mentioned in the first part of this chapter. But in dealing with certain crises brought to the political agenda, this has contributed to measures being implemented that have been specifically oriented toward medium-sized cities. This results in the revival of zoning (or territorial discrimination) and its underlying logic in order to overcome particular difficulties. Two policies, still in progress, can illustrate these movements: *"Action coeur de ville"* and *"Territoires d'industrie"*.

The first, promoted in 2018, is the result of a reflection held in 2016 around the revitalization of the city centers of many medium-sized cities subject to more or less pronounced decline in commercial activities, but also in their housing stock. While the reasons for these very localized territorial inequalities were based on the suburban sprawl and the development of commercial areas (and also of services) in the city outskirts, it is the symbolism of the charges and functions of centrality supported by these towns which is at stake. Various planning and animation operations of these pieces of towns are under way and supported by the state (under the granting of regimes derogating from the law, in order to accelerate the projects envisaged, the provision of engineering able to support local authorities or the reorientation of various credits toward these target territories for a provisional amount of 5 billion euros in 2020). The residential and commercial attractiveness of the 222 communities eligible for this system is the central target of this policy measure. The second policy measure, called *"Territoires d'industrie"*, targets its intervention on employment areas in small and medium-sized cities affected by major economic restructuring. One hundred and forty-eight territories are then concerned by this "pact", dedicated to the reindustrialization of the national productive base, promoted in 2018. Operating on the basis of the call for projects, the privileged scale of support is that of the industrial project, and not of the territory in these relations with "others".

While the matter of medium-sized cities has long been present in planning, metropolization is traditionally brought as the main explanatory factor for examining their roles and their functions on the scale of the French urban system. But the generalities that have been built around medium-sized cities are so totalizing and stem from multiple and diverse collective representations that it is very difficult to go against them. We can only follow them and sometimes even in a contradictory way. The same is true for the process of metropolization, which recomposes the basis of public action. As Béhar reminds us, by distinguishing the different aspects and regimes of metropolization (those of economists, sociologists and geographers), "[…] the dynamics of metropolization tend less to constitute a clearly delimited upper stratum than to recompose the interdependencies between territorial levels" (Béhar 2010, p. 119). We are therefore faced with very porous socioeconomic recompositions that determine the forms of territorial inequalities in the development of medium-sized cities. From the logic of equipment to that of "equalizing" redistribution, passing through that of territories taking shape around the principle of differentiation, the "ways of doing things" deployed with a view to reduce territorial inequalities on the scale of medium-sized cities, we see a profoundly cyclical investment in these methods. These hesitations are put in tension by the treatment of territorial abandonment, such as those observed on the scale of shrinking cities that we see, for example, the revitalization programs "*Action coeur de ville*". Nevertheless, the question of their role in the production of wealth remains. As such, we are left to wonder about their usefulness and their ability to reduce territorial inequalities in the context of the globalization of the economy, in an environment where "mundane" (but very important) functions performed by these urban entities predominate and now hold a large part of the development of these territories.

6.4. Conclusion

A relative (and debatable) "metropolitan turn" has emerged in planning policies in recent years. More or less explicitly, it examines the contribution of medium-sized cities to territorial development and, by extension, to the reduction of inequalities. A double spatial scale of action is called upon here: on the one hand, there is the national perspective which concerns the leveling of development gaps between territories; on the other hand, the local scale is invested in, which seeks to negotiate the local translations of the development trajectories of cities. The contemporary schemes for revitalizing the city centers of many medium-sized cities facing "growing" outskirts are one illustration of this.

Obviously, and in the contemporary game of productive activity, the peripheral positions of medium-sized cities would not give them the means to constitute points of support allowing them to be part of a logic of growth. At least, medium-sized cities would find themselves captive to weakly differentiating resources and inherited from the Fordist model of production heavily damaged by the globalization of the economy. But the territorial network of services to the population would place them all the same as the guarantors of a relative territorial cohesion in terms of populations' and economic actors' access to common services and common goods. A spatial division of labor would also be at work, with large cities and metropolises providing specialized services and functions (e.g. financial services). This very overhanging mechanism is nevertheless undermined by the effects inherent in the recomposition of the maps of state services (Taulelle 2012; ANCT 2020) which, beyond their symbolic function of equalizing services on the territory, have significant effects on local employment, associated incomes, and therefore development.

In the words of Santamaria (2012), "[...] it is the commonly accepted characteristics of medium-sized cities that form an obstacle to the recognition of medium-sized cities as tools for land use planning" (p. 14). It is therefore the banality of their activities and functions of medium-sized cities (but nevertheless essential to collective life) that brings their socioeconomic usefulness to the debate. As we noted in the second part of our argument, the demographic dynamics of medium-sized cities tend to show less growth than the national trend; a trend which is itself different according to regional contexts. Employment therefore follows a relatively similar trajectory, suggesting development without growth is taking place in these cities. But these long-term changes provide us with little information as to the nature of the recompositions observed (i.e. which sectors or which functions?) and their ability to support the contemporary orientations of planning and territorial development policies. The debate on the places and functions supported by these urban entities in a logic of territorial differentiation, that is to say, in a perspective of dialogue and territorial interdependencies taking shape around territorial systems, resonates as the keystone of these new perspectives that can contribute to acting on the double scales of inequalities (national and local). Detailed case studies would make it possible to both shed light on the origins and drivers of these inequalities in medium-sized cities and in their relations with other cities and territories, as well as provide the means to avoid them.

6.5. References

Albertini, J.B. (2006). De la DATAR à la nouvelle DIACT : la place des questions économiques dans la politique d'aménagement du territoire. *Revue française d'administration publique*, 119, 417–426.

Alvergne, C. and Musso, P. (2009). *L'aménagement du territoire en images*. La Documentation française, Paris.

Alvergne, C. and Taulelle, F. (2002). *Du local à l'Europe. Les nouvelles politiques d'aménagement du territoire*. PUF, Paris.

ANCT (2020). Les fonctions de centralité d'équipements et de services dans les dynamiques territoriales [Online]. Available at: https://agence-cohesion-territoires.gouv.fr/fonctions-centralite-equipements-services-dynamiques-territoriales-299.

ANCT (2021). La décroissance urbaine. Enjeux, clés d'analyse et action publique [Online]. Available at: https://agence-cohesion-territoires.gouv.fr/sites/default/files/2021-07/Décroissance_ANCT_VF.pdf

Association Bureaux-Provinces (1977). *Établissements tertiaires décentralisés*. La Documentation française, Paris.

Authier, Y. and Bidou-Zachariasen, C. (eds) (2017). Ces villes dont on ne parle pas. *Espaces et Sociétés*, 1(168–169).

Baudelle, G. (1994). Le système spatial de la mine : l'exemple du bassin houiller du Nord-Pas-de-Calais. PhD Thesis, Université Paris 1 Panthéon Sorbonne, Paris.

Baudelle, G. and Peyrony, J. (2005). *Le polycentrisme en France, cheminement d'un concept*. La Documentation française, Paris.

Béhar, D. (2010). Métropolisations : version française d'un paradigme universel. In *La France : une géographie urbaine*, Cailly, L. and Vanier, M. (eds). Armand Colin, Paris.

Béhar, D. (2017). L'aménagement du territoire : du mythe mobilisateur à la capacité transformatrice. *Pouvoirs locaux*, 110, 26–31.

Béhar, D. (2019). De l'égalité à la cohésion des territoires. Le modèle français à l'épreuve de la métropolisation. *Géographie, économie, société*, 3(21), 251–267.

Berroir, S., Cattan, N., Guérois, M., Paulus, F., Vacchiani-Marcuzzo, C. (2012). *Les systèmes urbains français*. La Documentation française, Paris.

Bouba-Olga, O. (2017). *Dynamiques territoriales. Éloge de la diversité*. Atlantique, Bruges.

Bouba-Olga, O. and Grossetti, M. (2019). Le récit métropolitain : une légende urbaine. *L'information géographique*, 82(3), 72–84.

Braudel, F. (1986). *L'identité de la France. Espace et histoire*. Flammarion, Paris.

Brunet, R. (1997). Villes moyennes : point de vue de géographe. In *Villes moyennes : espace, société et patrimoine*, Commerçon, N. and Goujon, P. (eds). Presses Universitaires de Lyon, Lyon.

Brunet, R. (2001). La France réinvestie par ses villes. *Mappemonde*, 63, 11–15.

Camagni, R. and Gibelli, M.C. (1994). Réseaux de villes et politiques urbaines. *Flux*, 16, 5–22.

Cattan, N., Pumain, D., Rozenblat, C., Saint-Julien, T. (1994). *Le système des villes européennes*. Anthropos, Paris.

CGET (2018). *Regards croisés sur les villes moyennes : des trajectoires diversifiées au sein des systèmes territoriaux*. La Documentation française, Paris.

Chevalier, M. (1843). *Des intérêts matériels en France*. Hachette, Paris.

Claudius-Petit, E. (1950). Pour un plan national d'aménagement du territoire. Report, Ministère de la reconstruction et de l'urbanisme.

Commerçon, N. (1996). Les villes moyennes. *Norois*, 171, 487–493.

DATAR (2010). *Territoires 2040 : aménager le changement*. La Documentation française, Paris.

Davezies, L. and Talandier, M. (2014). *L'émergence de systèmes productivorésidentiels*. La Documentation française, Paris.

Dubet, F. (2011). Égalité des places, égalités des chances. *Études*, 1(414), 31–41.

Dubet, F. (2017). *Le temps des passions tristes. Inégalités et populisme*. Le Seuil, Paris.

Estèbe, P. (2015). *L'égalité des territoires. Une passion française*. PUF, Paris.

Faucheux, J. (1959). *La décentralisation industrielle*. Berger-Levrault, Boulogne-Billancourt.

Finance, O. (2017). Trajectoires d'intégration des villes françaises dans les réseaux économiques et financiers des firmes transnationales étrangères. *Annales de géographie*, 718, 774–781.

FNAU (2020). Accompagner le renouveau des villes petites et moyennes. Traits d'Agence, 36 [Online]. Available at: https://www.fnau.org/wp-content/uploads/2020/05/ta-36-v4.pdf.

Fol, S. (2020). *Les villes petites et moyennes : territoires émergents de l'action publique*. Éditions PUCA, Paris.

Fouchier, V. (2005). Tendances longues de l'évolution économique des métropoles françaises. Un regard sur la notion de "taille critique". *Territoires 2030*, 1, 29–44.

Frémont, A. (2007). *Géographie et action : l'aménagement du territoire*. Arguments, Paris.

Goux, D. and Maurin, É. (2012). *Les nouvelles classes moyennes*. Le Seuil, Paris.

Gravier, J.F. (1947). *Paris et le désert français*. Le Portulan, Paris.

Grebot, B. (2017). L'alliance des territoires : penser la coopération territoriale à l'heure des réseaux ? *Pouvoirs locaux*, 111, 43–48.

Guichard, O. (1965). *Aménager la France. Inventaire de l'avenir*. Robert Laffont, Paris.

Guichard, O. (1973). Les contrats de villes moyennes. *Revue française d'urbanisme*, 136, 3–6.

Guigou, J.L. (1996). Pour une conception positive et renouvelée de l'aménagement du territoire. *Revue d'economie régionale et urbaine*, 4, 833–842.

Guilluy, C. (2014). *La France périphérique : comment on a sacrifié les classes populaires*. Flammarion, Paris.

Halbert, L. (2010). *L'avantage métropolitain*. PUF, Paris.

Hamdouch, A., Nyseth, T., Førde, A., Serrano, J., Demaziere, C., Aarsaeter, N. (eds) (2018). *Creative Approaches to Planning and Local Development: Insight from Small and Medium-sized Towns in Europe*. Routledge, London.

IAURIF (1976). *La décentralisation industrielle et le bassin parisien*. L'Institut Paris Région, Paris.

Jacobs, J. (1961). *The Death and Life of Great American Cities*. Vintage Books, New York.

Laborie, J.P., Langumier, J.F., De Roo, P. (1985). *La politique française d'aménagement du territoire de 1970 à 1987*. La Documentation française, Paris.

Lacour, C. and Delamarre, A. (2006). *40 ans d'aménagement du territoire*. La Documentation française, Paris.

Lagrange, H. (ed.) (2006). *L'épreuve des inégalités*. Presses de Sciences Po, Paris.

Le Blanc, A., Gervais-Lambony, P., Giroud, M., Pierdet, C., Piermay, J.L., Rufat, S. (eds) (2014). *Métropoles en débat : (dé)constructions de la ville compétitive*. Presses universitaires de Paris Ouest La Défense, Paris.

Lepetit, B. (1988). *Les villes dans la France moderne (1740-1840)*. Albin Michel, Paris.

Lepetit, B. (1989). Les temps de l'aménagement territorial – La formation des départements. *Annales de la recherche urbaine*, 3, 5–14.

Lerustre, P. (1975). *Le contrat d'aménagement de villes moyennes*. La Documentation française, Paris.

Levratto, N. (ed.) (2016). Analyse du lien entre les métropoles et les territoires avoisinants. Report, CGET-IDC.

Manzagol, C., Charbonneau, F., Lewis, P. (2003). Villes moyennes et mondialisation : éléments de problématique. In *Villes moyennes et mondialisation renouvellement de l'analyse et des stratégies*, Manzagol, C., Charbonneau, F., Lewis, P. (eds). Trames, Nanterre.

Marchand, B. (2009). *Les ennemis de Paris : la haine de la grande ville des Lumières à nos jours*. Presses Universitaires de Rennes, Rennes.

Marshall, A. (1861). *Principles of Economics*. MacMillan, New York.

Maurey, H. and De Nicolay, L.J. (2017). Aménagement du territoire : plus que jamais une nécessité. Report, Sénat [Online]. Available at: https://www.senat.fr/rap/r16-767/r16-7671.pdf.

Michel, M. (1977). Ville moyenne – Ville moyen. *Annales de géographie*, 478, 641–687.

Morvan, Y. (ed.) (2004). *Activités économiques et territoires : changement de décor*. Éditions de l'Aube, La Tour d'Aigues.

Offner, J.M. (2019). *Anachronismes urbains*. Presses de Sciences Po, Paris.

Paulus, F. (2007). Trajectoires économiques des villes françaises entre 1962 et 1999. In *Données urbaines*, Mattei, F. and Pumain, D. (eds). Anthropos, Paris.

Paulus, F. and Pumain, D. (2002). Répartition de la croissance dans le système des villes françaises. *Revue d'économie régionale et urbaine*, 1, 37–48.

Perroux, F. (1955). Notes sur la notion de pôle de croissance. *Économie appliquée*, 8, 307–320.

Piketty, T., Postel-Vinay, G., Rosenthal, J.L. (2006). Wealth concentration in a developing economy: Paris and France, 1807–1994. *The American Economic Review*, 96, 236–256.

Poupard, G. (2015). Développement local et emploi productif : un monopole des métropoles ? *Population et avenir*, 727, 4–8.

Pumain, D. (2007). Lois d'échelle et mesure des inégalités en géographie. *Revue européenne des sciences sociales*, 138, 57–65.

Rosanvallon, P. (2013). *La société des égaux*. Le Seuil, Paris.

Royoux, D. (1997). Réseaux de villes et logiques d'efficacité et d'équité. *Flux*, 27(28), 17–24.

Saint-Julien, T. (2003). Les villes moyennes en Europe, contextes et défis. In *Villes moyennes et mondialisation. Renouvellement de l'analyse et des stratégies*, Charbonneau, F., Lewis, P., Manzagol, C. (eds). Trames, Nanterre.

Santamaria, F. (2000). La notion de "ville moyenne" en France, en Espagne et au Royaume-Uni. *Les annales de la géographie*, 613, 227–239.

Santamaria, F. (2012). Les villes moyennes françaises et leur rôle en matière d'aménagement du territoire : vers de nouvelles perspectives ? *Norois*, 2, 13–30.

Sassen, S. (1996). *La ville globale*. Descartes, Paris.

Scott, A.J. (2001). *Les régions et l'économie mondiale*. L'Harmattan, Paris.

Séchet, R. (1994). Les délocalisations au mépris de l'université de masse ? L'essor de l'enseignement supérieur dans les villes moyennes de l'ouest. *Les Annales de la recherche urbaine*, 62(63), 93–99.

Storper, M. (2013). *Keys to the City*. Princeton University Press, Princeton.

Talandier, M. and Calixte, Y. (2021). Résilience économique et disparité territoriale. Quelles leçons retenir de la crise de 2008 ? *Revue d'économie régionale et urbaine*, 3, 361–396.

Talandier, M. and Tallec, J. (2020). Interdépendances et réciprocités entre les métropoles et leurs territoires. Une mise en perspective à l'échelle du territoire métropolitain grenoblois. In *La gouvernance des métropoles et des régions urbaines*, Demazière, C., Sykes, O., Desjardins, X. (eds). Éditions PUCA, Paris.

Talandier, M., Jousseaume, V., Nicot, B.H. (2016). Two centuries of economic territorial dynamics: The case of France. *Regional Studies, Regional Science*, 3(1), 67–87.

Taulelle, F. (2012). Ce que nous avons vu en matière de services publics dans les quatre pays de l'étude : le délaissement du territoire. *Sciences de la société*, 86, 5–14.

Trompette, P. and Vinck, D. (2009). Retour sur la notion d'objet-frontière. *Revue d'anthropologie des connaissances*, 1(3), 7–27.

Vanier, M. (2015). *Demain les territoires. Capitalisme réticulaire et espace politique*. Hermann, Paris.

Wuthnow, R. (2018). *The Left Behind: Decline and Rage in Small-town America*. Princeton University Press, Princeton.

7
Urban Segregation

Sylvie FOL[1] and Leïla FROUILLOU[2]
[1] Géographies-Cités, Université Paris 1 Panthéon-Sorbonne, France
[2] CRESPPA, Université Paris Nanterre, France

7.1. Introduction

The processes of segregation and social divisions of space in France have been highlighted by recent events, and have more broadly brought to light social inequalities and the weight of their spatial dimension. To this end, the Yellow Vests (*Gilets jaunes*) social movement (November 2018–December 2019) can be analyzed from the perspective outlined by Coquard (2019): as a consequence of the difficult living conditions of the precariat working classes of the deindustrialized countryside. Similarly, the 2020 COVID-19 pandemic both shone a light on and resulted in high inequality. While the excess mortality of certain populations according to their social class has been underlined, the crisis also highlighted the strong inequalities in housing and living conditions produced by location in the residential space, exacerbated by quarantining in domestic spaces[1]. While the negative consequences of lockdowns were much more apparent for low-income earners and women (Albouy and Legleve 2020), Bugeja-Bloch and Lambert (2020) note that lockdowns made the very high inequalities in housing between different socio-professional categories particularly visible, especially in urban spaces. In other words, the size of the living space, overcrowding, access to outdoor space, and

---

1 A study by the DREES in July 2020 highlighted very strong social inequalities vis-à-vis the risk of developing a severe form of the disease in connection with the prevalence of co-morbidities, which are very unevenly distributed between social classes.

neighborhood density are all elements that strongly distinguish households according to their social position.

The pandemic has also highlighted the role of segregation in the differences of exposure to the epidemic. For example, the media sounded the alarm about the abnormally high death rate in Seine-Saint-Denis (Camilotto 2020, published in *Mediapart*; Herzberg 2020, published in *Le Monde*), while research (Brandily et al. 2020) has shown that the pandemic's impact on mortality was twice as high in the poorest cities (based on residents' income) than in other municipalities. Another study (Amdaoud et al. 2020) concluded that the uneven geographical distribution of Covid cases and deaths associated with the pandemic may be correlated with urban population density, the share of workers in the population more generally and interdecile income differences. While the use of the concept of segregation has become much less important – as other concepts have come to shape the debate on urban inequality – we can no longer overlook, in light of these two crises, the fact that this phenomenon remains a reality and has very real consequences on people's lives.

The notion of segregation relates to many approaches and fields of research that do not necessarily refer to it explicitly. The uses of the term, which are partly dated, are part of the theoretical positions of the authors and articulated with related notions. One cannot discuss social divisions of space, relegation spaces, or ghettos and remain neutral. It results in theoretical reading grids, which can diverge slightly.

This chapter focuses on urban segregation and its place in the analysis of territorial inequalities. After showing how this concept has emerged in urban research, in France and in other countries, we shall present the analyses of the causes of urban segregation, in relation to the theoretical framework from which the work mentioned is derived. This field of research is marked in particular by debates on the methods of measuring the unequal distribution of population groups in the urban space. We shall return to these debates later. Finally, we will focus on public policies to combat these processes.

7.2. Emergence and uses of the notion of "segregation"

7.2.1. *Segregation and the ghetto in the United States*

The emergence of the notion of segregation in urban research is historically linked to that of the "ghetto" – that is, the distancing, in a delimited built space, of part of the population of a city, identified on the cultural or "ethnic" level. These categories of identification are the subject of debate in the literature, which we will return to later. There are two main concepts of what defines a ghetto, and they have left their mark on research involving urban distancing.

The first refers to the Jewish ghetto – from Venice in the 17th century to Warsaw during the Second World War. For Wirth (1956 [originally published 1928]), who devoted his thesis, entitled *The Ghetto*, to the Jewish community of Chicago's West Side, the origin of the term is uncertain. He notes the links with the Italian *gueto* and the Hebrew *get* which denote the act of divorce, or the German *gitter* ("barrier") which evokes confinement, or *gietto* (Italian) where the first Jewish community in Venice was established. For him and the first sociologists of the Chicago school, it was a question of documenting the urban processes that marked the American metropolis at the beginning of the 20th century, paying particular attention to the issues of migration and social organization. As such, he situated his analysis in a more general analysis of migrant communities: "The history of the Jews and the history of the ghetto are essentially a history of migration" (ibid., p. 301)[2]. Wirth's analysis makes the ghetto a notion of urban sociology that goes beyond the Jewish quarters of medieval Europe: "While the ghetto is, strictly speaking a Jewish institution, there are forms of ghettos that concern not merely Jews. Our cities contain Little Sicilies, Little Polands, Chinatowns and Black belts" (ibid., p. 58). The "vice areas" (ibid., p. 58) house the poor and marginalized populations of the metropolis. The big city is thus a "mosaic of segregated peoples" (ibid., p. 6).

For Wirth, ghettos exist informally, are institutionalized legally and then remain after laws are repealed[3]. In his introduction, he refers to both the regulated ("official regulation" ibid., p. 14) and "voluntarily chosen or constituted" (idem) character of these concentrations of populations in certain neighborhoods. At the end of the book, he reiterates this, saying that "there was a natural ghetto, or voluntary ghetto, before the ghetto was decreed by law [...]. And that the ghetto persists long after it has been abolished by law" (ibid., p. 295). Consequently, he conceptualizes the ghetto as being the result of a "natural" grouping and not of exclusion mechanisms[4]. This was to become central to sociological and geographical analysis in the second half of the 20th century. Moreover, living in the ghetto and belonging to the community is only one step in the residential trajectory of individuals. The ghetto

---

2 In his introduction, he compares the minority situation of the groups living in the ghettos to that of the "English in India" and the "Whites in China" without saying that the latter lived in ghettos.
3 The analysis of urban segregation therefore requires an understanding of the legislative contexts that contribute to the unequal distribution of social groups in cities, such as the creation of ghettos, segregation laws and apartheid.
4 The naturalizing vocabulary is a mark of human ecology, which thinks of human behavior on the model of plants and animals, which makes *The Ghetto* a dated text, whose "biologizing naturalism" Wacquant underlines.

provides a secure framework for the integration and then the upward social mobility of newcomers: it is a transitional space where migrants learn "attitudes related to social distance, self-consciousness and group consciousness" (ibid., p. 18) and their grouping together allows for mutual support. But "the physical distance that separates these immigrant areas from that of the natives is at the same time a measure of the social distance between them and a means by which this social distance can be maintained" (ibid., p. 294). As Cefaï (2008, paragraph 5) explains in his review of the book, which has become a classic in urban sociology, "between the boundaries of assimilation and segregation, the cycle never closes".

After the Second World War, the notion of the ghetto centered around the Black American ghetto in the United States. Although Black neighborhoods were formed in cities in the 1920s, the concentration of African American populations in inner cities became more pronounced after the Second World War: middle-class populations, who were mostly White, moved to the suburbs while Black populations migrated to the inner cities from the American South. According to Philpott (1978), using data about Chicago from the 1880s to 1930s, Black American neighborhoods differed from the European immigrant communities (which had been studied by Wirth in particular), because only a minority of these European migrants lived in these neighborhoods, which also had a high turnover rate, whereas the majority of Black Americans lived in the Black ghetto (90% lived in neighborhoods that were over 80% Black). Wacquant (2005) notes that in 1930, the all-Black Bronzeville neighborhood was home to 92% of Chicago's African American population, while the Little Ireland neighborhood was made up of 25 nationalities, with barely a third being Irish, bringing together a total of only 3% of the city's Irish-ancestry inhabitants.

Wacquant (2005) shows that while the definition of a ghetto expanded in the first half of the 20th century to refer to the intersection between an ethnic neighborhood and a poor neighborhood, it then narrowed after the Second World War, under the pressure of the civil rights movements that followed and hence came to denote the urban enclaves of the industrial centers of the North and the Midwest in which African Americans were relegated. The 1970s and 1980s were then marked, according to Wacquant, by deindustrialization and a reduction in social welfare measures, with racial domination becoming more widespread with the emergence of a Black American middle class. The term "ghetto" has sometimes been replaced in research by "inner city" or "underclass" – notions that, like "ghetto", reference both a space and a social or racial group. For Wilson (1987), "underclass" refers to a social group affected by unemployment, social isolation and deviant behavior (e.g. criminality, single parenthood and so on). Sociological research was then influenced by intense debates on the "culture of poverty", a concept introduced by Lewis (1959) to describe a series of behaviors incompatible with the social integration of individuals living in neighborhoods where poor residents were concentrated. Some authors, such as Murray (1984) and Mead (1989), attribute poverty to the policies of the "welfare state" which, through benefits allocated to the unemployed and to single-parent families, reduced the incentive to work and encouraged births outside of marriage. In response to these interpretations, Wilson's approach not only considers poverty to be the result of economic factors, but also considers it from an ecological perspective, reminiscent of the work of the Chicago school at the turn of the century: "The turn of the strength of W. J. Wilson was to propose an approach to poverty that combines spatial distance (enclavement, spatial mismatch), social (deficient networks) and cultural (deviant subcultures)" (Théry and Bonnet 2016, p. 78).

Wilson's approach has been criticized by Massey and Denton (1993) for underestimating the racial dimension and the role of segregation in his analysis, although they agree that it was indeed structural changes to the economy that pushed many Black Americans into poverty. In their view, issues related to race and racial segregation should be central to understanding the status of Black Americans and the origins of the underclass[5]. Instead, in Wilson's approach, it is class membership that is decisive in explaining the structural poverty of certain neighborhoods, which had been deserted by the Black middle classes.

While the analyses of the Chicago school at the beginning of the 20th century made very little room for social class (Chapoulie 2000), minority approaches focus on this dimension. In *Social Justice and the City*, Harvey (1973) understands the ghetto to be a solution created by the capitalist system in order to prevent solidarity within the working class[6]. As such, the ghetto is the product of structural segregation of the rich and the poor, which Marxists often call the "social division of the urban space".

For Wacquant, the 1990s corresponded to a "neutralization" in the research and public debate surrounding the concept of the ghetto, which no longer denoted a social and racial distancing, describing relations of domination, but rather a zone of concentration of poverty, without reference to its population or the institutional processes that produce it. Wacquant then proposed to construct a relational concept of the ghetto, making it possible to grasp forms of closure and urban social control by linking the understanding of the ghetto with that of other neighborhoods and the urban space in general. According to him, the ghetto is composed of four elements:

---

5 Massey and Denton also criticize analyses in terms of the "culture of poverty", a notion for which they substitute that of "culture of segregation", segregation having created the structural conditions for the emergence of a form of culture of opposition, already featured by Kenneth Clark (1989 [originally published 1965]).
6 "In a free society, competition tends to destroy castes and classes" (Park and Burgess 1921, p. 230).

stigma, constraint, spatial confinement and institutional interlocking, synonymous with the differentiation of public services (education, health, social services, security, etc.). This socioorganizational device of the ghetto maximizes the material benefits of a group (i.e. through the exploitation of a dominated group) by minimizing contact with its members. This particular form of collective violence in and through the urban space is far from the "natural" process described by Wirth, even if Wacquant emphasizes the "bifront character of the ghetto, both weapon and shield" (Wacquant 2006 p. 18), allowing the power/exploitation of the dominant, but also a certain protection for the dominated[7]. Wacquant's (2006) notion of a "hyperghetto" resituates the ghetto in an understanding of urban relations of domination. These relations are produced by the increase in urban inequalities at the end of the 20th century; a consequence in particular of the transition from an industrial-based economy to a globalized system based on services. At the same time, the withdrawal of the welfare state, institutions and public services in historic Black neighborhoods have largely contributed to the implementation of these processes[8].

The ghetto is essential for understanding the processes behind the segregation of certain populations on the basis of their "ethnic" origin, their religious affiliation and their social characteristics. Although the two notions have historically been linked, the ghetto and segregation are not synonymous. First, while poverty is a frequent feature of ghettos, it is not a required element unlike in the case of segregation. Second, segregation alone is not a sufficient element to identify ghettos: all ghettos are segregated, but not all segregated areas are ghettos, as shown by the example of gated communities, where the aggregation of residents is done in an elective mode, without stigma, and without an institutional system limiting the exit of the neighborhood for its inhabitants[9].

Unlike the "ghetto", the notion of segregation allows us to understand the divisions of the urban space in a relational way, that is, one that takes into account both the most favored and the most disadvantaged, without deciding beforehand

---

7 Clark (1989, p. 19), also quoted in Massey and Denton (1993), put forward the fact that "the invisible walls of a segregated society are not only damaging but protective in a debilitating way".

8 Massey and Denton (1993) introduce the notion of "hypersegregation", which they define as a combination of five elements: unevenness, isolation, clustering, concentration and centralization.

9 The use of the term "ghetto" to refer to the dominant classes is strictly ironic, as in Pinçon and Pinçon-Charlot's (2007) book, *Les Ghettos du Gotha*. As Wacquant (2005, p. 16) explains: "Residential segregation is a necessary but not sufficient condition of ghettoization. For a ghetto to emerge, it is necessary, first of all, that spatial confinement be imposed and that it encompass more or less all areas of existence and, secondly, that a distinctive palette of duplicative institutions that allow the group thus cloistered to perpetuate itself within the limits of the perimeter assigned to it".

whether the racial or economic or economic dimension should prevail in the analysis. In France, the use of the word "ghetto", as a notion imported from American sociology, fuels an intense debate in connection with the processes of urban segregation and the politics of the city (Gilbert 2011), as we shall see below.

7.2.2. The concept of "the ghetto" in France

At the European level, research has focused on comparing the levels of segregation between Europe and the United States. They have shown that on the whole, segregation is less prevalent in Europe than in the United States. Musterd (2005), based on a synthesis of various works, showed that the levels of racial segregation and socioeconomic segregation are on the whole lower in European cities than in American ones. However, if the Black population is not taken into account, the levels of ethnic segregation on both sides of the Atlantic are more similar. Moreover, the situations are very heterogeneous between European countries, the levels of ethnic segregation being higher in Belgium and the United Kingdom than in Germany, France or Austria. Differences are also noticeable between cities within the same country and between population groups according to their origin[10]. On the other hand, socioeconomic segregation appears to be much more prevalent in the United States than in Europe. Here again, there are differences between countries, with British and Belgian cities showing higher levels of segregation than Danish and Dutch cities. Musterd (2005) attributes the lower level of segregation in Europe to a number of structural factors: the functioning of real estate markets, which make more room for social housing in Europe, the functioning of the labor markets, public policies and, in particular, the weight of redistributive policies.

While the use of the notion of the ghetto in France has made it possible to focus analysis, since the beginning of the 2000s, on the (harmful) effects of urban segregation (Gilbert 2011), French sociologists and geographers have approached this question since the 1950s by focusing on the measures and the intensity of the unequal distribution of populations in cities. Some pioneering French geographers worked during the 1950s on intra-urban inequalities: for example, George (1950) in the Paris center, Roncayolo (1952) in Marseille, and a group of sociologists around Chombart de Lauwe (1952). In the 1970s and 1980s, the field of research on urban segregation was structured in a context of relative reduction in regional inequalities and the emergence of questions about urban settlement (Korsu 2002). The notion of urban segregation was discussed in tandem with that of the social division of space and Marxist approaches to understanding urban spaces (Brun and Chauviré 1983;

---

10 Thus, in British cities, the Bengali population experience more segregation than the Black population.

Brun and Rhein 1994). In the 1990s, scientific debates around the notion of segregation focused on measurement issues to which we will return later. The 2000s were marked by discussions on social diversity (Lehman-Frisch 2009) (the notion of a ghetto used to describe French "*quartiers*" (neighborhoods) (Fitoussi et al. 2004; Maurin 2004)), and new orientations of urban renewal policies (Gilbert 2011). Urban segregation was mainly used to understand working-class neighborhoods (in terms of income or socioprofessional categories), whereas this relational notion precisely makes it possible to consider inequalities at the scale of the center, including the most favored in the analysis.

In France, few studies compare the intra-urban segregations of different centers. Madoré (2015) identifies around 10 such studies before the mid-2000s, then notes a renewal with the work of Schwabe (2007), Rivière (2008), Dasre (2012) and Dabet and Floch (2014). This work shows that urban segregation is more or less extreme depending on the center. Segregation is higher in large urban areas and in regions marked by deindustrialization, with the notable exception of cities in the mining areas of northern France, which are relatively less segregated (Madoré 2015). A recent study by *France Stratégie* (2020) analyzed the evolution of residential segregation in the 55 urban units of more than 500,000 inhabitants between 1990 and 2015, according to socioprofessional category, migratory status and origin, and housing occupancy status[11]. The authors show that executives and business leaders are much more segregated than workers and employees and that the level of segregation of non-European immigrants is very high, especially that of young people. While the segregation indices (see later in this chapter for the methodological debates on the construction of these measures) of the different studied categories are on the whole stable or decreasing, they are increasing for these two groups. The study also reveals significant differences between cities: the urban unit of Paris shows the highest levels of segregation, while the old industrial cities of northern France are characterized, as in previous studies, by particularly low indices of segregation of workers and employees.

In general, the results of these analyses depend on the variables as well as the indicators used: for instance, Dabet and Floch (2014) studied 118 urban areas of more than 150,000 inhabitants, considering household tax incomes, and concluded that it is important to consider several indicators and to extend the analyses to the national level through localized studies, which make it possible to grasp historical

---

11 This is an institution under the prime minister, which produces expertise (evaluation of public policies in particular), reports and prospective analyses on social, economic and environmental subjects. Created in 2013, *France Stratégie* succeeded the *Commissariat général du plan* (1946–2006) and the *Centre d'analyse stratégique* (2006–2013).

particularities. The latter have been particularly studied in the Paris region. Much of the work on urban segregation in France has focused on the Paris urban area (Pinçon-Charlot et al. 1986; Tabard 1987; Rhein 1994a; Préteceille 1995, 2003, 2006; François et al. 2003; Fleury et al. 2012; Clerval and Delage 2014; Ribardière 2019). Census databases allow for detailed analyses, at the neighborhood level IRIS[12], of the distribution of populations by occupational or income groups. Rhein (1994) has shown that the between 1954 and 1975, the segregation of the Parisian space seems to have diminished for the most affluent groups, but appears to have remained strong vis-à-vis the opposition between the working class and upper classes, the working-class municipalities in the north and east contrasted with a central area (the "*beaux quartiers*" and middle-class neighborhoods) and with the suburbs, which were not very urbanized at the time, in the south and west of Paris.

For Préteceille (1995), changes between 1968 and 1982 in Île-de-France correspond to an increase in social segregation in the majority of the most polarized areas, which however only account for 40% of the population studied. The other areas, which are more mixed, experienced diverse changes: "While social segregation is, in the Paris region, an indisputable and striking phenomenon, it is also a complex one, which cannot be reduced to the binary opposition of certain spaces and certain social categories, and which, for the majority of the population, rather takes the form of social mixtures of variable proportions" (ibid., p. 54). The 1982–1990 period was marked by an increase in the gaps between the opposing types of spaces, which resulted from a reinforcement of the exclusive character of higher types of spaces (the most favored), but also from the popular character of a number of workers' spaces (Préteceille 2003). The reinforcement of the homogeneity of large upper class spaces does not, however, allow us to speak of spatial "dualization", because this phenomenon only concerns a minority of neighborhoods in Île-de-France. Préteceille (2006) therefore calls into question the models of generalized separatism (Maurin 2004) and the secession of the middle classes (Donzelot 2009), which we will discuss later. The increase, between 1990 and 1999, in the divide between upper class neighborhoods and working class ones in the Parisian center has also been observed by François et al. (2003), who based their analysis on household income instead of socioprofessional category. A study updating these results (Fleury et al. 2012) shows that two trends have been at work since 1990: a process of gentrification of certain Île-de-France areas and an increase in social

---

12 This acronym stands for *îlots regroupés pour l'information statistique* (meaning clusters grouped together for statistical information). Insee created this division at the neighborhood level for the 1999 census. It is the basic building block for the dissemination of sub-municipal data in France. An IRIS corresponds to approximately 2,000 inhabitants. France has more than 16,000 IRISs.

polarization around two geographical sectors (the west and north of Paris) which are relatively close geographically, but increasingly socially opposed. Based on detailed census data, Clerval and Delage (2014) also highlight the gentrification of the Île-de-France region between 1990 and 2008. They note that this gentrification is selective and that it explains the greater differences between the different profiles of municipalities and the maintenance of segregation. The social divisions of space are also manifested in an accentuated way at the infra-municipal level. Finally, based on household income tax, Ribardière (2019) has shown that segregation is on the rise. The social specialization of the poorest municipalities increased between 1999 and 2015 and almost reached that of the wealthiest municipalities. Some municipalities are experiencing a real decline and impoverishment, while other spaces are transforming due to gentrification. Thus, work on the Île-de-France region has highlighted the increasing inequalities between poor and rich municipalities over several decades, even if most areas remain relatively diverse.

Since the mid-2000s in France, sociological and geographical analyses have been characterized by the emergence of concepts such as gentrification (i.e. the replacement of inhabitants of working-class neighborhoods by more high-income households, in terms of education, income, socioprofessional category and so on) or suburbanization (i.e. the extension of built-up urban areas, thereby transforming rural areas). These concepts describe the organization of urban spaces but focus less on residential inequalities. Yet, recent work is renewing approaches to urban segregation, in particular by integrating the temporal dimension. While most studies focus on the differentiation of urban spaces at one point in time, or consider the changes in these differentiations, few analyses focus on the geographical mobility of populations and the transformations that this entails for urban spaces. Le Roux et al. (2018) thus propose a "historical and generational approach that relies on the analysis of geographical and social trajectories understood as a succession of socioresidential positions" (ibid., p. 3). The trajectories of the generations born between 1911 and 1950 in the Île-de-France region must be put in context (i.e. changes in transport accessibility, the housing crisis, transformation of the production system and the job market). By combining quantitative and qualitative data, they highlight the low populations of the working classes in the central areas where the upper classes reside, and the link between upward mobility and the social mobility (for the middle and working classes) and the dynamics of suburbanization. Some working classes remain relegated to the fringes of the Île-de-France region, with little access to transport.

Another perspective that allows us to go beyond the mere comparison of the residential spaces of populations consists of working from the electoral angle. To this end, Rivière (2017, p. 1041) utilized data from the 2017 French presidential election to present an "electoral socio-geography that emphasizes the spatial dimension of the electoral effects of social inequalities". The results showed a strong correlation between social classes and voting (with, for example, a correlation coefficient of 0.81 between the presence of senior professionals and voting for Emmanuel Macron, or of 0.76 between the presence of non-graduates and abstention). Thus, "within urban worlds traversed by strong inequalities, the notion of class voting is far from obsolete [...] because of the social embedding of electoral choices in local spaces where votes take place and take on meaning" (ibid., p. 1063). In other words, votes, which are linked in local contexts, make it possible to approach residential segregations from another angle. A more recent work (Barrault-Stella et al. 2020) at the local level of the 18th arrondissement in Paris compares two polling stations located in very distinct neighborhoods, one of which is described as "segregated". In addition to the political dispersion of the working class, this chapter highlights the influence of ethno-racial markers between groups in the neighborhood and the politicization processes through the experience of discrimination in these environments.

Unlike in the United States, the racial dimension of urban segregation is late to appear and remains little dealt with, notably because of the absence of "ethnic" statistics in France. Administrative data nevertheless allows us to work on migration trajectories and to observe the distribution of immigrant populations (i.e. those who are foreign-born, whatever their nationality may be at the time of the study)[13]. By examining, at the municipal level, eight urban areas between 1968 and 1999, Safi (2009) showed that there was a decline in the segregation of immigrant groups over the period, but that non-European immigrants experienced a continually high level of segregation. Préteceille (2009) focused his work on the Paris urban area between 1982 and 1999. He showed that immigrants of North African, sub-Saharan and Turkish origin experienced the highest levels of segregation. This unequal distribution of immigrant populations in the Paris metropolitan area is growing moderately and greater than segregation according to income or socioprofessional categories, but much lower than the racial segregation in the metropolises of the United States. On this point, Préteceille notes that the vast majority of immigrants lived in mixed neighborhoods. Pan Ké Shon (2009) points out that, although not insignificant, residential mobility is lower for immigrants from Africa, who are more likely to remain in disadvantaged neighborhoods. Verdugo (2011) showed that the share of immigrant populations living in social housing increased sharply in the

---

13 One limitation of these studies is that they do not consider the descendants of immigrants, which could restrict the measures. However, Pan Ké Shon and Verdugo (2014) estimate, based on surveys centered on the Paris region (Préteceille 2009) or "problem neighborhoods" (Pan Ké Shon 2009), that the descendants of immigrants generally occupy less disadvantaged residential positions (and are therefore probably less segregated) than their parents.

1970s, and that "between 1968 and 1999, segregation between the different districts of urban units changed from segregation according to national origin to segregation according to regional origin (by continent or sub-continent) for people living in social housing, especially for immigrants of non-European origin" (ibid., p. 192). Extending the analysis to 2007 data, Pan Ké Shon and Verdugo (2014) showed that the intensity of urban segregation has decreased for each immigrant group by country of birth, but has increased when considering immigrant populations together: "French segregation does not operate in the mode of a single national origin. It is neither Arab, nor Black African, nor Asian. It is more the segregation of immigrants that makes sense in France. In reality, the majority of migrants have spread across the entire sociospatial spectrum of the neighborhoods and only a small but very real fringe of migrants experience situations of strong segregation" (ibid., p. 248)[14].

Moreover, this segregation "is less about *race* and more about *class* [...]. The grouping would be more on modest social characteristics, frequent among migrants and obviously also observed among natives" (ibid., p. 271). Studies that aim to articulate the racial and social class dimensions therefore need to better understand the construction mechanisms of complex residential trajectories in today's French urban areas.

This question of the link between the social and racial characteristics of populations in the processes of urban segregation has crystallized an important debate in France, around the perception of the ghetto. The use of racial characteristics would be inappropriate to describe the segregated neighborhoods of French metropolises according to certain authors, following the example of Wacquant (2006) who proposes instead to include these spaces in the processes of urban marginality (mechanisms of distancing linked to social inequalities, objectified through discrimination, the place of menial jobs, access to cultural resources, etc.) and to leave the term "ghetto" to be the description of American situations of strong racial segregation. Contrarily, Lapeyronnie (2008) proposes to work on the social organization and the logics that mark these neighborhoods from the point of view of their inhabitants (injustice, contempt). But "the differences in approach should not hide the empirical points of convergence" (Kokoreff 2009, p. 555) between these two perspectives, the gap between the two fields being partly due to the survey period. Based on Lapeyronnie's analyses, Kokoreff highlights "a strong gender segregation in these working-class neighborhoods, which is reflected

---

14 In 2007, North African immigrants, who are the most concentrated along with Asians, live in neighborhoods where they present between 0% and 18% of the population (ibid., p. 268).

in the rumors and reputations spread by boys about girls, the territorialization of sexual taboos, but also the role of families, who contribute to withdrawal into oneself while watching over the matrimonial market. This segregation has obviously been reinforced in recent years in the estates" (ibid., p. 564). Beyond the elements related to the evolution of distancing in working-class neighborhoods at the turn of the 2000s, the sociological positions around working-class neighborhoods have been the subject, since the 1990s, of intense theoretical and empirical debates, as demonstrated by the analyses of the "exile quarters" (Dubet and Lapeyronnie 1992) and "exile neighborhoods" (Dubet 2008), for example. The latter can indeed participate in building "a model for describing social housing districts" which "unifies diverse territories under a common and strong experience, that of the struggling [...] and is the theoretical basis of the idea of an erasure of conflicting social relations and the disappearance of organized mobilizations" (Tissot 2005, p. 63).

This historical detour on the emergence and use of the notion of segregation in the United States, Europe and France allows us to show that urban segregation is part of a broad theme of research on sociospatial inequalities, urban fragmentation, urban differentiation and the social division of space. These stakes are embodied in concepts, notably that of the ghetto, that center the perception of the working class. Recent approaches treat the issue in terms of diversity or "superdiversity", yet this erases the social selectivity of certain spaces and the distancing of the working classes which are essential when analyzing urban segregation. Thus, "if one can sometimes reproach research on segregation for not being sufficiently situated in intersectional perspectives, for limiting itself to a reductionist vision of the individual (identified only according to his socio-professional positions or origins) and to omit the multiple interactions and relationships of daily life, we can simultaneously regret that the perspective of diversity understates the mechanisms and the underlying social devices" (Adisson et al. 2020, p. 38).

The relational perspective opened up by the notion of segregation makes it possible to understand the urban distribution of social groups as interdependent and linked to the functioning of labor markets and housing and transport policies. Thus, urban segregation is a notion that makes it possible to grasp the processes of relegation, discrimination and exclusion, and questions not only the *forms*, but above all the *causes* of these unequal distributions of populations in urban areas[15].

---

15 As Verdugo (2011) explains, the relative lack of segregation in terms of immigrant populations in France compared to the United States can be linked to distinct mechanisms.

7.3. Analyzing the causes of segregation

In the literature, segregation is attributed to three main sets of causes, depending on the authors and schools of thought. It is explained by the choices and preferences of individuals, by the structural logics involving economic and social mechanisms, or by institutional and political logics (Oberti and Préteceille 2016).

7.3.1. *Segregation as the result of individual preferences*

A first series of works analyzed segregation as the result of individuals' preferences and choices. In these approaches, based on classical and neo-classical economic theory, decisions regarding choosing a location for activities and households, as well as determining land prices, are based on a process of aggregating the preferences and decisions of urban agents competing for the best locations (Grafmeyer and Joseph 1990). In other, rather similar types of modeling, segregation is said to result from a combination of individual behaviors that tend to keep out those considered undesirable. This type of approach was notably developed by Schelling in *The Tyranny of Small Decisions* (1980), which showed that segregation can be the collective result of a combination of individual discriminatory behaviors. These behaviors do not necessarily aim at deliberately producing segregated situations: they are the result of individuals defining minimal requirements in terms of neighborhood, referring to desirable or tolerable cohabitation situations. The combination of these individual choices nevertheless results in segregated situations, which have been modeled by Schelling.

This approach – centered around individual preferences and the rational decisions of urban agents – has remained prevalent in the work of spatial economists (Thisse et al. 2003). It also permeates the work of Maurin (2004), who presents segregation as a process of social separatism that has become one of the "structuring principles of social coexistence" (ibid., p. 6). As such, the mechanisms of segregation run through the whole of society, with all individuals implementing "avoidance strategies". Maurin describes a "society of interiors" (ibid., p. 11) in which "each one of us discovers himself to be a more or less active accomplice in the segregation process" (ibid., p. 6). Segregation is "a widespread, fractal tension, giving its face to the whole country, but whose principle is entirely contained in the social organization of the smallest district of the smallest suburban municipality", including the understanding of the "deep spring" which requires "descending into the intimacy of the residents, their fears and their aspirations" (ibid., p. 21).

Sociologists have also taken up the idea that segregation is the spatial translation of the sum of individual strategies. Donzelot (2009) defends the image of "the three-speed city", "that of the relegation of social housing estates, that of the suburbanization of the middle classes who fear proximity to the 'excluded' from the estates, but feel 'forgotten' by the elite of 'winners' inclined to invest in the process of gentrification of old centers" (ibid., p. 17). This logic of separation and "tripartition of the contemporary city" (ibid., p. 37) is regarded as the result of generalized avoidance strategies and different forms of self-segregation (i.e. selective self-segregation and elective, forced self and protective self).

The Chicago school's early work on segregation could in some ways be interpreted as belonging to the neoclassical model of individual preferences, insofar as it emphasizes competition between land uses and competition between agents for the appropriation of a space governed by the laws of the market. Thus, the processes of invasion – a succession that explains the distribution of populations in the city – are linked to the unequal possibilities of the different agents to occupy the most coveted spaces. However, as Grafmeyer and Joseph (1990) point out, the explanatory model of the Chicago school is not based solely on the aggregation of individual behaviors: "The analysis of the mechanisms of filtering, selection, and grouping of populations involves something other than scattered individuals" (ibid., p. 30). The processes that are being analyzed involve social or professional groups, as well as collective representations that determine behavior.

7.3.2. Segregation as a consequence of structural mechanisms

A second series of works, which used structural mechanisms with an economic and social basis to explain segregation, was developed in France in the 1970s by Marxist sociologists (Oberti 2007). In this strand of research, segregation is viewed as the result of the structure of class relations and social relations of production. The social divisions of space are interpreted as a reflection of the unequal structure of social relations in capitalist society. In *The Urban Question*, Castells (1972, p. 169) defines urban segregation as "the tendency to organize space into zones with a high internal social homogeneity and strong social disparity between one another, this disparity being understood not only in terms of difference, but also hierarchy". Urban segregation results from the distribution of the places of residence, which "brings about regroupings according to the social capacity of the subjects, that is to say, in the capitalist system, according to their income, their professional status, educational level, ethnic group, age group, etc." (idem). Similarly, in their book *Monopolville*, Castells and Godard (1974) highlight the segregative logics that are a result of the development of state monopoly capitalism. In this work, as Oberti (2007a) points out, segregation is the spatial expression of the logics of the capitalist system.

In the same Marxist-inspired vein, the work of Henri Lefebvre, in particular *Le Droit à la ville* (1968), shows how the organization of the city resulting from a centralizing power of the city dispossesses the working class of its labor force and exacerbates segregation. Lefebvre's approach conceptualizes the city and urban space as products, or even "projections" of the social relations of production. But his analysis is distinct from that of state monopoly capitalism by being less focused on the economic mechanisms linked to the circulation of capital and more on the social processes (Costes 2010).

Subsequent work analyzed the effects of the restructuring of the capitalist system in the post-Fordist period and showed how the deindustrialization and spatial recompositions of economic activities resulted in a strengthening of segregation and the concentration of certain social groups in devalued spaces. In the United States, the previously mentioned work of Wilson (1987) emphasized the structural effects of deindustrialization and job loss in inner cities, which led to the formation of an underclass – that is, a group of individuals (which mainly consisted of the Black population) that faced high structural unemployment and impoverishment which made them increasingly dependent on social welfare benefits. In addition, the departure of the Black middle classes from these neighborhoods has created a situation of growing social isolation for these populations. Wilson's (1987) book, *The Truly Disadvantaged*, offers a different understanding of poverty than as an effect of the welfare state (dependency on welfare being the subject of conservative criticism, as mentioned above), explaining it in conjunction with macro-sociological elements, such as the absence or remoteness of jobs, including low-skilled ones, and role models (Théry and Bonnet 2016). The work of Wacquant (2006) is both a continuation of that of Wilson, with his emphasis on the structural processes that led to the formation of ghettos, and a break with Wilson's conceptualization of the underclass, which, according to Wacquant, tends to paint the poor and Black population in a degrading image of cultural traits and deviant behaviors.

The links between economic recompositions and the accentuation of social divisions of space have also been put forward in the works on globalization. For instance, Mollenkopf and Castells (1992) describe New York as a "dual city" in connection with the transformations of global capitalism. Similarly, Sassen (1991), in *The Global City*, shows that the concentration of certain functions in large metropolises leads to a polarization of the social structure, with an upper class involved in high-level tertiary activities, on the one hand, and a class of low-skilled employees working in service of this upper class, on the other hand. This polarization of the social space manifests in the urban space through increased segregation. These analyses of the polarization of social and spatial structures have been discussed by other authors, who have shown that this is not true in the cases of

London and Paris, where the middle classes remain very present in both the social and the urban space, and contribute to maintaining a significant social diversity (Hamnett 1995; Préteceille 1995).

Other works have examined the processes at play within a specific part of the social space. In their research on the "*beaux quartiers*" or upper-class neighborhoods, Pinçon and Pinçon-Charlot (1989) are interested in the social logics of the extreme spatial concentration of the aristocratic families and the great bourgeoisie. Understanding the city to be "one of the parameters of the complete definition of the social position" (Pinçon and Pinçon-Charlot 1994, p. 52), they analyze the residential choices and the modes of appropriation of the space of these social classes and identify logics of aggregation, referring to voluntary, chosen groupings of agents sharing the same social affiliation and, beyond that, numerous characteristics specific to their "milieu".

Recently, research has examined the relationship between sociospatial structures and the land and real estate markets. Without placing the question of segregation at the heart of their questioning, this work sheds interesting light on the interactions between the values of places, and in particular real estate prices, and the social values attributed to spaces. In his thesis on the residential real estate market in Marseille, Boulay (2011) showed the links between the structure of social divisions in Marseille and the structure of the land and real estate markets. Looking at the social construction of spatial values, he showed that real estate prices are the product of social and historical conditions that determine the social qualifications of spaces. Conversely, the structure of the real estate market conditions the distribution of social classes in space. Similarly, Cusin (2016) (whose interests lie in explaining the differentiation of real estate price structures between cities through the sociogenesis of social divisions of space) shows, on the basis of a comparative analysis of the 100 main urban areas of France, that spatial values are constructed in the interaction between settlement dynamics, socioeconomic changes and urban policies.

The analysis of real estate markets emphasizes the role played by the supply of housing in segregation in segregation processes: the respective shares of the different segments of the housing stock (home ownership, private rental housing and social housing) partly determine the settlement of an area. As such, public policies – which can influence the level of housing production, the distribution between the different types of housing stock and the choice of actors involved (in particular, private developers and social landlords) – play an essential role in the evolution of segregation. To this end, studies have shown the contribution of public policies to the creation, maintenance and reinforcement of segregation processes.

7.3.3. Segregation resulting from public policies

The Jewish ghetto in Europe, apartheid in South Africa and racial segregation in the United States (as mentioned earlier) as a result of the Jim Crow laws from the end of the 1870s until the passing of the Civil Rights Act of 1964, are all emblematic of situations of extreme segregation that have been orchestrated by public authorities[16].

Even where the legal provisions for segregation have been removed, some segregation mechanisms and institutional arrangements may remain. In the United States, this is the case for "redlining" strategies, which were implemented after the 1929 Wall Street Crash and have persisted long after their being ruled unlawful in 1968[17]. Redlining was practiced by the Federal Housing Administration and the banks; it consisted of evaluating the financial risks of housing loans granted to households on the basis of a typology of neighborhoods based on race (Massey and Denton 1993). Similarly, "benign neglect" or "planned abandonment" strategies have targeted the poorest neighborhoods with Black populations in declining American cities, exacerbating the degradation of these neighborhoods and the segregation processes (Metzger 2000; Béal et al. 2016). Wacquant, whose work has been mentioned above, has shown that it is the "collapse of public institutions resulting from the policies of urban abandonment and punitive restraint of the Black sub-proletariat that emerges as the most powerful and distinctive cause of the entrenchment of marginality in the American metropolis" (Wacquant 2006, p. 8).

In France, research has focused on the role of urban policies in the construction of segregation processes. In the Marxist approaches mentioned above, the State fulfills the essential function of organizing the space in the service of capitalism and the dominant classes (Castells and Godard 1974). Similarly, Harvey (2003), in *Paris, Capital of Modernity*, showed that the development of modern capitalism was actively supported by the State, including through a policy of major works that promoted new urban forms that allowed for both the control of urban space and social reproduction (Huriot 2013). As such, the work carried out by Haussmann

---

16 After the abolition of slavery in the United States, Jim Crow laws were put in place in the Southern States to prevent African Americans from enjoying all human rights. They introduced segregation in public services, including schools and transportation, and imposed separation in public places, distinguishing citizens on the basis of their race. These laws were abolished by the Civil Rights Act of 1964.

17 Redlining was a discriminatory practice that resulted in banks refusing to make home loans in neighborhoods designated as "risky" from a loan repayment perspective. These neighborhoods (outlined in red on the maps) were those inhabited primarily by Black populations. This effectively limited homeownership for African Americans until the Fair Housing Act of 1968, which theoretically ended these practices.

(between 1853 and 1870) was at the origin of a process of segregation that marked the beginning of an opposition between the Parisian center and its outskirts.

Increased segregation can also be the unplanned and unintended result of policies focused on specific issues and objectives. In France, for example, policies promoting home ownership, particularly from the 1960s onwards, have contributed to the abandonment of large low-income housing estates by the middle class as well as by the most established French citizens from the working classes who lived there. These exits out of social housing neighborhoods, combined with settlement policies (e.g. social housing allocation policies), which sometimes tend to favor the grouping of immigrant populations in the same neighborhoods (Lelévrier 2004), have led to very strong segregation in certain areas.

Paradoxically, the policies of social diversity implemented in these neighborhoods, in particular within the framework of urban renewal, have, in the name of the fight against segregation and the concentration of poverty, frequently resulted in a reinforcement of the sociospatial fragmentation. Indeed, the policies of rehousing poor populations after demolition of part of the social housing often result in a reconcentration of these populations rather than the desired dispersion (Lelévrier 2010). Thus, social diversification strategies, by attempting to curb residential dynamics perceived as negative, often produce segregative effects on a finer scale and can bring about new forms of social division of space.

7.3.4. Segregation as the result of a combination of several processes

Beyond the diversity of approaches, which is reflective of the many, often irreconcilable theoretical positions, segregation can be understood as the result of the combination of several processes, which varies according to spatial and temporal contexts (Oberti and Préteceille 2016). Segregation can appear to be the result of a combination of structural mechanisms, strategies linked to the social positions that individuals seek to defend or strengthen, and public policies or institutional mechanisms that are more or less intentional.

To illustrate this, let us take as an example the growing concentration of the working classes in areas in decline. In regions that have been affected for a long time by deindustrialization, research describes the precarity at work in former industrial cities (Miot 2012), medium-sized cities (Guéraut 2018) and in rural areas (Coquard 2019). In these territorial contexts, too succinctly grouped under the homogenizing expression of "peripheral France" (Guilluy 2014), the economic recompositions of neoliberal capitalism have caused a large portion of the jobs to disappear. The most educated and qualified populations have left these spaces, while the inhabitants with the least educational capital are very often unable to leave. As Coquard (2019, p. 9) points out, "in this logic of school sorting, those who stay are those who do not have the necessary resources to be mobile". This process of social selectivity of residential mobility is at work in all shrinking territories (Rudolph 2017). At the national level, studies have also shown that residential mobility tends to reinforce the social marking of spaces and segregation (Observatoire des Territoires 2018). The process of precariousness, which manifests itself in territories in decline, linked both to the social effects of post-Fordist economic restructuring and to socially selective residential mobility, is moreover accentuated by public austerity policies which, far from compensating the territorial inequalities created by these recompositions, result in a territorial withdrawal of the State (Artioli 2017; Béal et al. 2019). The residential spaces of the precariat working classes described in the works of Coquard (2019) and Vincent Jarousseau (2019) are particularly affected by the shrinking of public services and the reduction of the presence of the State. This example therefore illustrates the way in which mechanisms of very distinct origins (such as residential mobility, State withdrawal, economic restructuring, etc.) can combine to produce and exacerbate segregation (or a process thereof).

Urban segregation can thus be explained through a combination of these three types of mechanisms – individual strategies, structural causes and urban policies – without focusing on one of these elements mechanically prejudging the authors' theoretical framework. Indeed, each segregation mechanism can be understood from a more or less individual or holistic perspective. For example, it is possible to consider individual residential strategies as intrinsically linked to the social position of the agents in a social space, in a Bourdieusian approach (movements in residential space being linked to the position of agents, which goes hand in hand with a certain space of residential possibilities), in a reading that is both structural and constructivist, or as a result of individual preferences in an individualist reading (we then consider the choices or strategies of households). Another example is that real estate markets can be understood in an individualist approach as the result of the aggregation of the behavior of actors (buyers, sellers, tenants, lessors, real estate agents, etc.), or in a bourgeois approach as a field structured by capital, ranking struggles and reproduction strategies. The same applies to the analysis of public policies which can be made in a structuralist perspective (i.e. field, social classes, capitals), for example, in a Marxist one (as we have seen) or an individualist one (e.g. actors' games). These choices of theoretical framework can be objectively assessed from the concepts, vocabulary and bibliographical references, but also from the *methods* chosen by the authors.

7.4. Methodological debates concerning the measurement of segregation

Research on urban segregation highlights the importance of methodological debates to measure the unequal distribution of populations in an urban space and how this changes over time (Rhein 1994). According to Préteceille (2003), there are three crucial elements to methodological choices: the statistical methods themselves (i.e. the choice of indices); the scale of the spatial division of the zones whose population profiles are being compared (e.g. districts, blocks, municipalities and so on); and the descriptive variables of the social structure (how social groups whose urban distribution is being compared are defined, i.e. not only their division – the fineness of the categories – but also the point of view chosen – one group in relation to the others, comparison of two groups, or multi-group observation).

There are many complementary ways to measure the unequal distribution of groups in a population, which often takes the form of an index calculation (Apparicio 2000). The different indices for measuring segregation do not have the same mathematical properties (i.e. robustness and decomposition) (Givord et al. 2016a). Moreover, they are not all easily interpreted by field actors: "There is no ideal index, and the choice to favor one or the other is the result of a compromise that balances the different properties considered 'indispensable' according to the problem being studied" (ibid., p. 24). These indices allow comparisons in time and space between territories with differing average social compositions (as opposed to a simple dispersion index such as the coefficient of variation). The most traditional indices are segregation (understanding the unequal distribution of a group in a space) and dissimilarity (comparing the distributions of two groups in a space), which were developed in the 1950s (Duncan and Duncan 1955a, 1955b).

Apparicio (2000) distinguishes five dimensions of these indices following Massey and Denton (1988):

– equality measures the over- or under-representation of a group in spatial units or its unequal distribution relative to the overall population or to another population (e.g. segregation indices, dissimilarity, entropy and Gini coefficient);

– exposure which is the potential contact, that is, the probability that a member of a group will encounter another member of the group or a member of another group within their spatial unit;

– concentration refers to the share of territory occupied by a group within a space;

– grouping describes the shape of the spatial units occupied by a group (e.g. contiguity and dissemination);

– centralization takes into account the more or less central location of the spaces occupied by a group.

Givord et al. (2016a) identify several important properties for these segregation indices:

– Monotony according to the groupings: if we consider a finer scale (e.g. neighborhoods), the index will be equal to or higher than the one corresponding to the previous scale (e.g. the municipality).

– Scale invariance: whatever the variation of the global population, the index remains the same if the distribution of groups is similar.

– Composition invariance: the value of the index does not depend on the size of the groups in the overall population, allowing for the comparison of values of units where the overall distribution of groups is different.

– Decomposition: according to the groups and the observation units, in order to simplify the interpretation of the index.

For example, the segregation and dissimilarity indices are invariant, which allows for comparisons between groups, but are not decomposable. Their invariance property implies an interpretation that takes into account the size of the groups: small numbers can go hand in hand with very high segregation or dissimilarity indices. Pan Ké Shon and Verdugo (2014) emphasize the interest of taking into account both the intensity of segregation (the value of the index) and its magnitude (the size of the groups considered). The entropy index can be decomposed, which makes it an index often used in research, for example, to identify the division of segregation between classes and in different schools. Most indices can be calculated for one group (relative to the distribution of the overall population) by comparing the distributions of two groups (often workers or very high/low-income earners), or in a multi-group version that takes into account all groups. There are several applications that can be used to quickly calculate the most common indices. This requires a database that is constructed at a scale and with variables that play a crucial role in the analysis. The finer the mesh size for a space, the less heterogeneous the meshes will be, which favors high segregation indices: we observe "a mechanical increase in segregation indices as the size of the units decreases" (Givord et al. 2016a, p. 25). This principle is relatively intuitive (working at the stairwell level is likely to reveal a certain social homogeneity[18], whereas a

---

18 This is, in fact, the criticism leveled at Maurin's work by Oberti and Préteceille (2016). By working on the scale of complexes of about fifty dwellings, it is not surprising that Maurin's analysis brings about situations of very strong social homogeneity.

study at the borough level will reveal more diversity in the settlement). This approach is based on the use of a "staircase" model (e.g. a staircase model may reveal some social homogeneity, whereas a borough-level study will reveal more diversity in the settlement of this larger grid) but has recently been discussed using multilevel indices (Manley et al. 2019). The multilevel indices allow us to measure segregation by considering each scale as independent, making it possible to show that certain groups are less concentrated at the neighborhood level than at the level of the center, where neighborhoods are clustered together. Whatever the indices, it is necessary to identify empirically *the* relevant scales of analysis for understanding the settlement of an urban area. The latter's perimeter is also a source of methodological difficulties – for example, do we stop at the inner suburbs of Paris or do we consider the urban area? Moreover, comparisons over time can be hampered by changes in the perimeters of the grids considered (take for example the creation of IRIS districts by Insee for the 1999 census)[19]. Finally, not all data that describes populations is available for all scales. On this, Dabet and Floch (2014) point out the approach by income, which is localized at the address.

The increasing geolocalization of urban data can renew methodological approaches to segregation, for example, by considering population flows and not just locations (which are usually residential or school locations). The recent work of Le Roux et al. (2017) on data from the 2010 global transport survey in the Paris urban area shows that segregation decreases during the day, with commuting, but that the most segregated social group, namely the upper classes, is not only segregated on the basis of the number of commuters, but also on the basis of the number of jobs. However, the most segregated social group, the upper classes, is segregated not only in terms of residence (at night), but also in terms of daily activity. Geolocalization can allow a step aside from the methodological debates on the definition of the analysis grids: it is thus possible to consider individual neighborhoods ("egohood") by observing a certain number of geolocated neighbors closest to each individual (Malmberg et al. 2018). Geolocalized data are often used to describe urban differentiation and are often reduced to residential (census) data. It is possible to base analyses of school segregation on increasingly detailed data (at the scale of the classroom and not only at the school level), and even on the geolocation of students' homes. Election data at the polling station can be linked to neighborhood data, with methodological difficulties also allowing for a return to ecological approaches and scales of analysis (Rivière 2017). The ordinal indices proposed by Reardon (2009) make it possible to measure the unequal distribution of ordered groups (by salary level, academic level) in unordered categories

---

19 More information available at: www.insee.fr/fr/information/2434332.

(neighborhoods, racial or gendered groups, institutions), which constitutes another avenue of research to account for complex situations.

> **A participatory research study on youth in Île-de-France working-class neighborhoods**
>
> Between 2017 and 2020, an ANR study entitled POP-PART, coordinated by Marie-Hélène Bacqué and Jeanne Demoulin, aimed to uncover the social and urban reconfigurations in working-class neighborhoods of the Paris region, through the prism of children's practices. The experiences of the children, both girls and boys, revealed territorial anchors, trajectories and social representations linked to the past and present history of working-class neighborhoods. The methodological basis of this research is to build it with the participants: the development of audiovisual tools and the workshops allowed us to conduct research with the young people of 10 working-class neighborhoods on their practices. This original material is combined with interviews with the young people participating in the workshops.
>
> The first results of this research make it possible to deconstruct the dominant representations of young people in working-class neighborhoods and their practices, by highlighting their great heterogeneity. This opens up critical perspectives for studies on urban segregation, considering the prism of age, gender (e.g. the differentiation of girls' mobility practices) and "race" as determinants in the urban experience, which is sometimes felt to be ostracizing. This research also showed the importance of inequalities in the Paris region. Some neighborhoods are poorly connected by public transportation, which means that they have to develop tactics for getting around and accessing places of study or employment (carpooling, for example). The material difficulties of the parents were not often mentioned by the young people, but they are significant (unemployment, disability), as are certain experiences of discrimination (particularly for certain Muslim girls who wear the veil).

Box 7.1. *POP-PART, understanding working-class areas in the Paris region based on the practices of young people (source: ANR – Agence nationale de la recherche)*[20]

Finally, while methodological debates have focused on measurement issues (and thus on the availability of data, the construction of indices and scales of analysis), the methods of research on segregation go beyond strictly quantitative approaches. In the perspective of the founding work of the Chicago school, analyses based on qualitative data (such as observation, interviews, life stories, analysis of public policies or media debates and so on) make it possible to grasp the forms and mechanisms of urban segregation, whether in the form of synthetic theoretical

---

20 The ANR is the French funding agency for project-based research.

contributions (Wacquant 2006) or individual research projects constructed on more local scales, including those at the neighborhood level (Authier et al. 2007). Box 7.1 looks back at an ongoing research project in the Paris region, which uses a wealth of qualitative material to shed light on the dynamics associated with urban segregation.

Whatever the scales, mobilities or measurement methods used, the construction of the population groups whose distribution is compared is a central issue. We have seen, for example, that researchers in France used country and nationality of origin to research ethnic and racial segregation, and that the results diverged depending on whether the groups by nationality were considered or all immigrants as a whole group. The structuring of databases is therefore essential, as is the construction of modalities by researchers (constituting income groups, grouping socioprofessional categories, grouping minorities by country or region of birth, etc.).

Beyond measurement issues, the most heated academic debates concern the problem of the effects of segregation.

7.5. The effects of segregation

Segregation is obviously not without impacts on populations. As Bourdieu (1993, p. 167) has shown, "the gathering in the same place of a homogenous population in dispossession also has the effect of redoubling the dispossession". These "place effects" manifest themselves in various ways.

They result first and foremost in inequalities of access to resources and above all to the "socially rarest goods" (ibid., p. 165), for example museums, the most reputable educational establishments, the most more qualified, etc. The question of inequalities in accessing urban resources as a result of social divisions of space has been little analyzed. Nevertheless, in the 1980s, the work of Pinçon-Charlot et al. (1986) underlined the links between the sociospatial structure and the location of collective facilities in Île-de-France. They showed that segregation was accompanied by unequal access to material and symbolic goods offered by the city. They noted high inequality between the center and the periphery, according to a radio-concentric model, as well as between the working-class municipalities and the bourgeois districts: the best equipped towns and neighborhoods were those where the bourgeoisie and the upper and middle intellectual strata dominated, while the working class was for the most part in areas least endowed with collective amenities. This research approach, which received little attention in the years that followed, was the subject of new work in the 2000s, highlighting the inequalities in accessing urban resources between rich and poor municipalities in the Lyon region (Caubel 2006) and the outer suburban areas of the Île-de-France region (Motte-Baumvol 2007). However, these approaches remain few in number, both in France and in the international literature.

Conversely, work that analyzes the links between residential and school segregation has undergone significant development. While school segregation, understood as the unequal distribution of students in schools, was the subject of early research in the United States, this theme was developed in France in the 1980s, at the intersection of the sociology of education, urban science and social geography. This work in France since the 1980s has shown that school segregation partly reflects the residential segregation of large metropolises (Barthon 1998; Oberti 2007) but that it is also the result of families' school choices and avoidance strategies, as evidenced by enrolment in private or public schools outside the "catchment area" defined by the school map (Van Zanten and Obin 2010). More broadly, the context in which schools are located – the popularity of the neighborhood, competition with neighboring schools, as well as the residential position of students – are crucial variables in understanding school choices (François and Poupeau 2008), especially since the easing of the school map in France in 2007, which went hand in hand with the promotion of the "free choice" of schools (Oberti 2007). While school segregation only imperfectly reflects residential segregation, their relationship is complex and bilateral: choosing to live in the area with highly reputed public schools, for example, in Paris (Fack and Grenet 2009), is an educational strategy that implies one has economic capital. Recent reports highlight the importance of the unequal distribution of students between classes (in terms of level, options, etc.) but also, and more importantly, between schools, especially in metropolitan areas and at the middle-school level (Ly and Riegert 2015; Givord et al. 2016b). The term "segregation" implies that this unequal distribution is partly the result of institutional mechanisms (i.e. the result of the functioning of the private sector, differentiation of the training offer, orientation and assignment mechanisms) and results in inequalities of trajectories for students (Van Zanten 1996).

Segregation can also result in processes of territorial discrimination, whether they are carried out to the detriment of certain areas by public policies or to the detriment of individuals. The work compiled by Hancock et al. (2016) highlights, on the one hand, the ways in which chronic under-equipment and a deficit of public services exist in the residential areas of the working class, such as Seine-Saint-Denis (a Parisian suburb), which echoes the work of Pinçon et al. (1986). On the other hand, they also identify the "address effects" by which residents of disadvantaged neighborhoods are discriminated against in hiring because of their place of residence (L'Horty and Petit 2016).

The links between segregation and access to employment have also been the subject of much literature, focusing on the notion of "spatial mismatch"[21]. Researchers have tried to demonstrate the effects of segregation on the chance of access to employment for the most disadvantaged groups in the North American context. The large amount of research on this topic has fueled lively debates on the respective roles of space (and therefore segregation) and other factors (such as lack of qualifications and racial discrimination) in the inequalities in accessing employment for poor individuals and minorities (Taylor and Ong 1995; Ong and Blumenberg 1998; Blumenberg and Manville 2004). In France, the work of Wenglenski (2005) has highlighted inequalities in access to employment between socioprofessional categories, linked in part to differences in residential location between social groups.

In relation to the work on spatial mismatch, the question of "neighborhood effects" has been the subject of intense debate for several decades in the English-language literature, particularly in the United States (Bacqué and Fol 2007). Segregation, by confining groups dominated by their social background or origin to certain neighborhoods that are poorly served, poorly equipped and more exposed to threats, clearly deprives these groups of access to the most valued urban resources. This observation refers to Bourdieu's (1993) analysis of the effects of place mentioned above: "Those who lack capital are kept at a distance, either physically or symbolically, from the socially rarest goods, and are condemned to rub shoulders with the most undesirable and least rare people or goods. The lack of capital intensifies the experience of finitude; it shackles one to a place." The literature on neighborhood effects attempts to measure the impacts of the concentration of poor populations on the social destiny of individuals by seeking to determine whether living in a poor neighborhood doubles the effects of poverty and reduces the possibilities of integration. The so-called neighborhood effects thesis was based in part on Wilson's (1987) work on the underclass, mentioned above, which highlights the link between poverty, structural unemployment, the increasing social isolation of individuals in segregated neighborhoods and the development of behavioral traits, such as weakened work ties, increased single-parent families, marriage difficulties, school dropout, etc. Massey and Denton (1993) also point to the devastating effects of racial segregation, which exposes Black populations to a much harsher economic and social environment than that experienced by any other ethnic group.

---

21 Spatial mismatch has been defined by Kain (1968) as the difference spatially between the residential locations of poor and ethnic minority populations and the location of the jobs that these populations are likely to hold.

While these studies are able to highlight the structural social effects of segregation, they often start from the postulate of a social dysfunction in poor neighborhoods and attempt to identify "deviant" behavior there by adopting a normative point of view on the behavior of inhabitants of poor neighborhoods (Wacquant 1993; Marpsat 1999; Bauder 2002), which often comes close to the analyses in terms of the "culture of poverty" mentioned above. The poor neighborhood is thus locked into an all-encompassing negative vision that ignores its essential role as a resource for its inhabitants. However, poor neighborhoods are not a "social desert" (Bauder 2002). On the contrary, many studies, although very few have been taken up by the literature on neighborhood effects, show that social networks play an essential role in the daily lives of inhabitants of poor neighborhoods (Barnes 2003). These networks are a resource, including in the search for employment (Chapple 2000).

While this debate has given rise to an abundancy of literature in North America (Ellen and Turner 1997) and, to a lesser extent, in Europe (Musterd et al. 2012), French sociology has contributed little to it (Authier 2007). While place effects have been put forward, empirical work that measures them has remained rare (Bidou-Zachariasen 1997; Marpsat and Laurent 1997). French economists have examined this question (Fitoussi et al. 2004) but have yet to provide convincing answers[22]. Instead, French studies suggest that poor neighborhoods should be seen as places of resources for their inhabitants, highlighting the importance of social networks (Vignal 2005; Fol 2010) and the autochtony capital (Retière 1994). In these approaches, the working-class neighborhood is understood to be a place where material and symbolic resources are available to its inhabitants (Collectif Rosa Bonheur 2019).

In France, but especially in the United States, research on neighborhood effects is a key component of public policies aimed at combating segregation.

7.6. Anti-segregation policies

Policies that aim to combat segregation are relatively recent (Bacqué and Fol 2007). In the United States, they are partly the result of legal actions by associations linked to the civil rights movement, which obtained several Supreme Court rulings imposing the implementation of desegregation measures starting in the 1960s. This is the case of the Gautreaux experiment in Chicago, named after a civil rights

---

22 For these authors, urban segregation gives rise to a process of "spatial hysteresis" that results in the spatial inscription of mass unemployment, leading not only to a de-skilling of the unemployed, but also to their lasting distance from employment by loss of capacity, mobility and information.

activist who initiated a complaint against the Chicago Housing Authority (CHA). The program aimed to encourage the residential mobility of Black families living in poor neighborhoods by granting personalized assistance (both technical and financial) to relocate voluntary families (Black families who volunteered for the program) in one of the affluent neighborhoods of the center. This experiment, which involved 7,100 families between 1988 and 1992, served as a model for a federal program launched in 1992, Moving to Opportunity (MTO), funded by the federal Department of Housing and Urban Development (HUD). Conducted in five cities (Baltimore, Boston, Chicago, New York and Los Angeles), the MTO program rehoused 4,600 families that lived in social housing in neighborhoods where at least 40% of the individuals were considered to be living under the poverty line. This individual residential mobility assistance was also developed to accompany the demolition of social housing neighborhoods in the context of the HOPE VI programs set up in 1994 by the Clinton administration.

Evaluations of these programs, conducted by experts and academics, are very mixed (Bacqué and Fol 2007). While moving to affluent neighborhoods has enabled some households to escape insecurity, improve their state of health and have their children benefit from better schooling conditions, the results of the programs in terms of the stated objectives of professional and social integration remain very disappointing (Galster and Santiago 2006). For some households, the move resulted in increased social isolation and new difficulties that sometimes led them to return to their old neighborhoods (Comey et al. 2008). In general, the evaluations give extremely nuanced conclusions, showing that the results of desegregation policies are more due to individual and family characteristics than those of the host neighborhood (Berube 2005). If the experiences of residential desegregation have not produced the expected results, the school desegregation policies implemented through busing have also given rise to mixed evaluations. In particular, they are accused of having increased the flight of the White middle classes to the suburbs, as well as a strong educational escape from public schools to private schools.

There have also been desegregation policies in Europe, in particular in the Netherlands, the United Kingdom, Germany, Sweden, Finland and France (Musterd and Andersson 2005). In France, they have taken shape notably through urban policy, for example, which aims to respond to the growing concentration of poverty in large social housing complexes built between the 1950s and 1970s. In 1973, the Guichard circular put an end to the construction of these buildings, which were considered to be poorly integrated with the city and as promoting social segregation. In the early 1980s, a policy for the "social development of neighborhoods" called for "renewed intervention aimed at populations considered to be relegated to specific territories" (Tissot 2005). Based on the diagnosis of the precariat nature of the population of certain districts and on the criticism of the urban form embodied by the whole, this policy is accompanied by a territorialization of public action and the implementation forms of positive territorial discrimination, as evidenced by the creation of priority education zones in 1982, and various measures centered on "districts" (local security contracts, local missions for the professional integration of young people, etc.). Piling up many devices over the years (major city projects, large urban projects, free urban zones, etc.), city policy has been the subject of multiple evaluations which have generally shown its limited effectiveness on segregation processes. However, it is necessary to take into account the relative lack of resources that have been devoted to city policies, and above all, the contradiction inherent in territorialized policies, which aim to find spatialized answers to problems whose origins are structural. Tissot and Poupeau (2005) have highlighted the contradictions of this "spatialization of social problems", which separates the "problem of neighborhoods" from the structural causes of the deterioration of living conditions among the working classes, by instead attributing them to the individual characteristics of their inhabitants (Masclet 2005).

In 2003, the fight against segregation in France was renewed with the implementation of the urban renewal policy, established by the Borloo law, which aimed "to reduce social inequalities and development gaps between the territories" (according to Article 1 of the Law). Urban renewal marks a break with the previous measures by the scale of the financial resources mobilized and by the establishment of a centralized procedure under the control of the National Agency for Urban Renewal (ANRU). For Gilbert (2011), "the choice of words used, i.e. the 'ghetto', to refer to these neighborhoods not only has a descriptive effect: it produces real effects on these territories, contributing to the orientation of public policies concerning them." This representation of the ghetto "offers a spatial explanation of poverty and social integration", with urban renewal reflecting "a radical reorientation of city policies". Demolition is a major tool, since it makes it possible to remove an offer deemed obsolete in terms of buildings and problematic in terms of its social occupation. It goes hand in hand with two main modes of action: on the one hand, the reconstitution of a better-quality offer opening the possibility of a social diversification of the population of the district under renovation and, on the other hand, the rehousing and possible displacement of the former inhabitants. The objective of reducing development gaps in the development of territories is therefore linked to two types of complementary action: the diversification of the supply of housing and the population within the perimeter of urban renewal operations, and the triggering of residential mobility processes that should allow poor households to be deconcentrated by relocating them to other, more favorable neighborhoods. The fight against segregation, through the implementation of a social diversity objective, is therefore at the heart of the urban renewal policy.

Since the 1990s, this theme of social diversity has appeared recurrently among the objectives of urban policies implemented in France. In a context of increasing and increasingly different forms of urban poverty, the notion of social diversity is strongly linked to that of exclusion. Faced with the development of precariat processes, the success of the objective of diversity is based on the ideal of a "balanced" society, harmoniously mixing social classes, ethnic groups and generations to combat the effects of the concentration of poverty (Bacqué 2003). The matter of social diversity is not new: it is present, more or less explicitly, in the debates that accompanied the first public interventions in housing. Throughout the 20th century, it was the subject of debates and criticisms which culminated with the famous article by Jean-Claude Chamboredon and Madeleine Lemaire (1970), which undermined the evidence of the link between spatial proximity and social proximity.

In France, from the 1980s, diversity was held up as a political objective and the subject of several laws. The Besson law (of May 31, 1990), which aimed to implement the right to housing, links the reception of disadvantaged households to diversity and solidarity. The Orientation City Law (*Loi d'orientation pour la ville*), known as the anti-ghetto law (of July 13, 1991), affirmed the "right to the city for all". It stated that municipalities with more than 200,000 inhabitants with less than 20% social housing have to build social housing or pay a tax[23]. In 1998, the law on the fight against exclusion reaffirmed the importance of social diversity. Its housing section initiated a reform of social housing allocation and redefined the missions of social housing "intended for low-income or disadvantaged households […], but with respect for social diversity". However, it was in December 2000 that the law on solidarity and urban renewal (*solidarité et le renouvellement urbain* – SRU) truly implemented the principle of social diversity. The SRU law reaffirmed the principles of the Orientation City Law of 1991 by imposing on urban municipalities of a certain size a minimum rate of 20% social housing. If the target of 20% social housing was not achieved, then a deduction from fiscal resources was made. The implementation of the SRU law has been the subject of various studies, particularly before the implementation of the Duflot law which, in January 2014, increased the minimum rate of social housing to 25% for urban municipalities. These assessments show that if the SRU law was accompanied by an increase in the production of social housing and a strengthening of their presence in the municipalities that did not reach the minimum rate set by law, then it was far from fundamentally reversing the processes of segregation. Indeed, the municipalities whose elected officials are the most opposed to the construction of social housing continue to resist the pressure of the State services, whereas other municipalities act as "the good students" by

---

23 As it was not applied, this did not enter into force. The objective of social diversity has remained a dead letter.

primarily increasing their supply of intermediate housing, which is intended for the middle classes, rather than that of "truly social" housing.

Likewise, in terms of social diversity policy, research shows that the issue is less about the supply of social housing and more about the strategies for allocating social housing and settlement policies (Desage 2012; Desage et al. 2014). Discrimination, whether it be more or less intentional, remains very present in the allocation of social housing (Sala Pala 2008; Bourgeois 2019). The most recent provisions (e.g. Equality and Citizenship Act, the ÉLAN Act, etc.) aim to prevent allocation policies from maintaining or even reinforcing the concentration of poor populations in poor neighborhoods. Once again, it is the areas that are most affected by segregation that are being targeted, but without the mechanisms that lead to these structural inequalities regarding access to housing being called into question.

Finally, since the end of the 1970s and increasingly over the last few decades, anti-segregation policies have become territorialized. However, by targeting the territories that are struggling the most, these policies ultimately aim less to reduce segregation in a structural way than to correct the most glaring manifestations, because they are spatialized, of social inequalities. The response by an increasing number of measures aimed at restoring "equal opportunities", for example, in educational matters (e.g. priority education agreements in the Grandes écoles[24], social openness measures in the Grandes écoles, boarding schools of excellence, scholarship quotas, cordées de la réussite[25], etc.) does not seem likely to resolve the structural causes of educational inequalities. The assessment of positive discrimination policies, whether in the field of education (priority education zones), in the field of employment (free urban zones) or urban and social policies (sensitive urban zones), is not very conclusive: not only is the reduction of inequalities far from proven but, moreover, the assessments show that the increased resources that were to be devoted to the targeted territories have generally not compensated for the lack of resources, or even the withdrawal of certain sections of public action from these territories.

Moreover, the territorialization of policies is today difficult to separate from the context of neoliberalization in which these policies are implemented. The evolution of city policy or that of social housing is marked by the rise of market logic, while new forms of governance giving a large place to negotiation and cooperation between public and private actors are growing. The place given to private promoters in the implementation of the social diversification of neighborhoods undergoing urban renewal testifies to this evolution. Public service standardization policies are part of the same trend and produce comparable effects by exacerbating territorial

---

24 Specialized institutions of higher education in France.
25 Networking programs for institutions to support orientation projects.

inequalities to the detriment of the areas with the most disadvantaged populations. The neoliberalization of anti-segregation policies can result in a paradoxical territorialization: based on territorial categories ("problem neighborhoods" and "priority establishments") and participating in the increase in territorialized inequalities, they nevertheless value more and more individualization of pathways (of pupils or households). As such, Rochex (2011) speaks of a third generation of priority education policies, marked by a decline in territorial targeting, a multiplication of systems (and target audiences) with the objective no longer of compensating teaching conditions (equity), but of maximizing each student's chances of success (equal opportunity): "The central reference is no longer the objective of combating the inequalities in schooling and learning of which the dominated classes or social categories are victims, but of maximizing the chances of each individual" (ibid., p. 8). The policy of boarding schools of excellence (created in 2008, then becoming boarding schools for success in 2013) is a good illustration of this individualizing shift in policy aimed at combatting the effects of residential and school segregation, and which are centered around the "promotion of students […] of 'deserving' working-class suburbs with a 'potential' that they could not express or realize in the environment and schooling conditions that are theirs" (ibid., p. 9).

7.7. Conclusion

Segregation is contiguous to other geographical and sociological notions, such as gentrification (Clerval 2016), suburbanization (Cartier et al. 2008; Lambert 2012) and the clubbization of suburban spaces (Charmes 2007), which describe forms of social marking of neighborhoods and the construction of socially and spatially differentiated residential trajectories. In a fairly broad sense, segregation describes a type of social differentiation of urban spaces and is close to the notion of inequality. What is interesting about this notion is that it consists in part of opening up a broad perspective on urban inequalities, ranging from the distribution of social groups, to public policies or residential strategies. Nevertheless, its origins, its association with urban phenomena (such as the ghetto), its use in critical approaches to urban processes (institutional logics and territorialization of social problems) show the interest of politicizing the notion of segregation, avoiding reduce to a methodological debate on the measurement of spatialized deviations, to discuss the mechanisms producing such deviations. Questioning spatial justice, namely what is or is not socially accepted in terms of inequalities with causes and effects that can be objectified in their spatial dimension, constitutes another way of politicizing the notion of segregation. For example, this allows us to consider segregation in the light of social movements, by adopting an intersectional perspective to account for the intertwining of social relations (such as age, gender, class and race) in residential trajectories, in schools as well as in the mobility that structures urban spaces. The intrinsically relational character of segregation also makes it possible to deconstruct essentializing approaches centered on working-class neighborhoods, by always considering the relevance of scale and divisions in the analysis of urban inequalities. This relational approach defended by Wacquant can also be found in North American research on the construction of indices and the debates on measurements: to this end, Massey (2012) emphasizes that the notion of segregation shows all the interest of comparative studies between groups, over the long term and on the scale of entire centers, to grasp the evolutions and the mechanisms of social stratification.

7.8. References

Adisson, F., Bellanger, E., Frouillou, L., Vermeersch, S. (2020). Des ségrégations aux diversités urbaines ? Une question sociale, un enjeu de recherche. In *Pour la recherche urbaine*, Adisson, F., Barles, S., Blanc, N., Coutard, O., Frouillou, L., Rassat, F. (eds). CNRS, Paris.

Albouy, V. and Legleye, S. (2020). Conditions de vie pendant le confinement : des écarts selon le niveau de vie et la catégorie socio-professionnelle. *INSEE Focus*, 1997.

Amdaoud, M., Arcuri, G., Levratto, N. (2020). Covid-19 : analyse spatiale de l'influence des facteurs socio-économiques sur la prévalence et les conséquences de l'épidémie dans les départements français. *Economix* [Online]. Available at: https://economix.fr/pdf/dt/2020/WP_EcoX_2020-4.pdf.

Apparicio, P. (2000). Les indices de ségrégation résidentielle : un outil intégré dans un système d'information géographique. *Cybergeo European Journal of Geography* [Online]. Available at: https://journals.openedition.org/cybergeo/12063.

Artioli, F. (2017). Les politiques du retrait territorial de l'État : réformes de la carte militaire et gestion des mobilisations locales (1989–2012). *Gouvernement et action publique*, 1(1), 81–106.

Authier, J.Y. and Bidou-Zachariasen, C. (2008). Éditorial. *Espaces et sociétés*, 132(133), 13–21.

Authier, J.Y., Bacqué, M.H., Guérin-Pace, F. (eds) (2007). *Le quartier : enjeux scientifiques, actions politiques et pratiques sociales*. La Découverte, Paris.

Bacqué, M.H. (2003). *Mixité sociale. Dictionnaire critique de l'habitat et du logement, sous le regard des sciences sociales*. Armand Colin, Paris.

Bacqué, M.H. and Fol, S. (2007). Effets de quartier : enjeux scientifiques et politiques de l'importation d'une controverse. In *Le quartier : enjeux scientifiques, actions politiques et pratiques sociales*, Authier, J.Y., Bacqué, M.H., Guérin-Pace, F. (eds). La Découverte, Paris.

Barnes, S. (2003). Determinants of individual neighborhood ties and social resources in poor urban neighborhoods. *Sociological Spectrum*, 23, 463–497.

Barrault-Stella, L., Baloge, M., Berjaud, C., Dahani, S., Taiclet, A.F. (2020). Voter entre soi et contre les autres. *Actes de la recherche en sciences sociales*, 232(233), 30–49.

Barthon, C. (1998). La ségrégation comme processus dans l'école et dans la ville. *Revue européenne de migrations internationales*, 14(1), 93–103.

Bauder, H. (2002). Neighbourhood effects and cultural exclusion. *Urban Studies*, 39(1), 85–93.

Béal, V., Fol, S., Rousseau, M. (2016). De quoi le "smart shrinkage" est-il le nom ? Les ambiguïtés des politiques de décroissance planifiée dans les villes américaines. *Géographie, économie, société*, 18, 211–234.

Béal, V., Cary, P., Fol, S., Rousseau, M. (2019). Les villes en décroissance à la croisée des chemins. *Géographie, économie et société*, 21, 5–22.

Berube, A. (2005). *Overcoming Barriers to Mobility: The Role of Place in the United States and UK*. The Brookings Institution, Washington.

Bidou-Zachariasen, C. (1997). La prise en compte de "l'effet de territoire" dans l'analyse des quartiers urbains. *Revue française de sociologie*, 38(1), 97–117.

Blumenberg, E. and Manville, P. (2004). Beyond spatial mismatch: Welfare recipients and transportation policy. *Journal of Planning Literature*, 19(2), 182–205.

Botton, H., Cusset, P.Y., Dherbécourt, C., Geaorge, A. (2020). L'évolution de la ségrégation résidentielle en France : 1990–2015. Working document, France Stratégie, Paris.

Boulay, G. (2011). Le prix de la ville. Le marché immobilier à usage résidentiel dans l'aire urbaine de Marseille-Aix-en-Provence (1990–2010). PhD Thesis, Université Paris 1 Panthéon-Sorbonne.

Bourdieu, P. (1993). Effets de lieu. In *La misère du monde*, Bourdieu, P. (ed.). Le Seuil, Paris.

Bourgeois, M. (2019). La managérialisation des HLM : vers davantage de discriminations ? *Métropolitiques* [Online]. Available at: https://www.metropolitiques.eu/La-managerialisation-des-HLM-vers-davantage-de-discriminations.html [Accessed 18 March 2019].

Brandily, P., Brébion, C., Briole, S., Khoury, L. (2020). A poorly understood disease? The unequal distribution of excess mortality due to Covid-19 across French municipalities. Working Paper, Paris School of Economics [Online]. Available at: https://hal.science/halshs-02895908v1.

Brun, J. (1994). Essai critique sur la notion de ségrégation et son usage en géographie urbaine. In *La ségrégation dans la ville*, Brun, J. and Rhein, C. (eds). L'Harmattan, Paris.

Brun, J. and Chauviré, Y. (1983). La ségrégation sociale : questions de terminologie et de méthode. *Espace populations sociétés*, 1, 75–85.

Brun, J. and Rhein, C. (1994). *La ségrégation dans la ville*. L'Harmattan, Paris.

Bugeja-Bloch, F. and Lambert, A. (2020). Le logement, vecteur des inégalités. *La vie des idées* [Online]. Available at: https://laviedesidees.fr/IMG/pdf/20200427_logement.pdf.

Camilotto, N. (2020). Un virus de pauvre : en Seine-Saint-Denis les vies valent moins qu'ailleurs. *Mediapart* [Online]. Available at: https://blogs.mediapart.fr/nicolas-camilotto/blog/280420/un-virus-de-pauvre-en-seine-saint-denis-les-vies-valent-moins-qu-ailleurs.

Cartier, M., Coutant, I., Masclet, O., Siblot, Y. (2008). *La France des petits-moyens*. La Découverte, Paris.

Cary, P. and Fol, S. (2012). Les métropoles face aux dynamiques de ségrégation et de fragmentation. Introduction au numéro spécial. *Géographie, économie, société*, 14(2), 113–126.

Castells, M. (1972). *La question urbaine*. Maspéro, Paris.

Castells, M. and Godard, F. (1974). *Monopolville. Analyse des rapports entre l'entreprise, l'Etat et l'urbain à partir d'une enquête sur la croissance industrielle et urbaine de la région de Dunkerque*. Mouton, Paris.

Caubel, D. (2006). Politique de transports et accès à la ville pour tous ? Une méthode d'évaluation appliquée à l'agglomération lyonnaise. PhD Thesis, Université Lumière Lyon 2.

Cefaï, D. (2008). Le ghetto. *Sociologie du travail*, 50(3), 442–444.

Chamboredon, J.C. and Lemaire, M. (1970). Proximité spatiale et distance sociale. Les grands ensembles et leur peuplement. *Revue française de sociologie*, 11(1), 3–33.

Chapoulie, J.M. (2000). Le travail de terrain. L'observation des actions et des interactions, et la sociologie. *Sociétés contemporaines*, 40, 5–27.

Chapple, K. (2000). Paths to employment: The role of social networks in the job search for women on welfare in San Francisco. PhD Thesis, University of California, Berkeley.

Charmes, É. (2007). Carte scolaire et "clubbisation" des petites communes périurbaines. *Sociétés contemporaines*, 67(3), 67–94.

Chombart de Lauwe, P.H. (1952). *Paris et l'agglomération parisienne*. PUF, Paris.

Clark, K.B. (1989). *Dark Ghetto. Dilemmas of Social Power*. Wesleyan University Press, Middletown.

Clerval, A. (2016). *Paris sans le peuple : la gentrification de la capitale*. La Découverte, Paris.

Clerval, A. and Delage, M. (2014). La métropole parisienne : une mosaïque sociale de plus en plus différenciée. *Métropolitiques* [Online]. Available at: https://metropolitiques.eu/La-metropole-parisienne-une-mosaique-sociale-de-plus-en-plus-differenciee.html.

Collectif Rosa Bonheur (2019). *La ville vue d'en bas. Travail et production de l'espace populaire*. Editions Amsterdam, Paris.

Comey, J., Briggs, X., Weismann, G. (2008). Struggling to stay out of high-poverty neighborhoods: Lessons from the moving to opportunity experiment. *Urban Institute*, 6, 1–12.

Coquard, B. (2019). *Ceux qui restent*. La Découverte, Paris.

Costes, L. (2010). Le droit à la ville de Henri Lefebvre : quel héritage politique et scientifique ? *Espaces et sociétés*, 140(141), 177–191.

Cusin, F. (2016). Y a-t-il un modèle de la ville française ? Structures urbaines et marchés immobiliers. *Revue française de sociologie*, 57(1), 97–129.

Dabet, G. and Floch, J.M. (2014). *La ségrégation spatiale dans les grandes unités urbaines de France métropolitaine : une approche par les revenus*. Insee, Paris.

Dasré, A. (2012). Les mesures du regroupement spatial des populations : aspects méthodologiques et applications aux grandes aires urbaines françaises. Thesis, Université Montesquieu, Bordeaux.

Desage, F. (2012). La ségrégation par omission ? Incapacités politiques métropolitaines et spécialisation sociale des territoires. *Géographie, économie, société*, 14(2), 197–226.

Desage, F., Morel Journel, C., Sala Pala, V. (2014). *Le peuplement comme politiques*. Presses universitaires de Rennes.

Donzelot, J. (2009). *La ville à trois vitesses et autres essais*. La Villette, Paris.

Dubet, F. (2008). *La galère. Jeunes en survie*. Le Seuil, Paris.

Dubet, F. and Lapeyronnie, D. (1992). *Les quartiers d'exil*. Le Seuil, Paris.

Duncan, O.D. and Duncan, B. (1955a). A methodological analysis of segregation indexes. *American Sociological Review*, 20(2), 210–217.

Duncan, O.D. and Duncan, B. (1955b). Residential distribution and occupational stratification. *American Journal of Sociology*, 60, 493–503.

Ellen, I.G. and Turner, M.A. (1997). Does neighborhood matter? Assessing recent evidence. *Housing Policy Debate*, 8(4), 833–866.

Fack, G. and Grenet, J. (2009). Sectorisation des collèges et prix des logements à Paris. *Actes de la recherche en sciences sociales*, 180, 44–62.

Fitoussi, J.P., Laurent, E., Maurice, L. (2004). Ségrégation urbaine et intégration sociale. Report for the Conseil d'Analyse Économique, La Documentation française, Paris.

Fleury, A., François, J.C., Mathian, H., Ribardière, A., Saint-Julien, T. (2012). Les inégalités socio-spatiales progressent-elles en Ile-de-France ? *Métropolitiques* [Online]. Available at: https://metropolitiques.eu/Les-inegalites-socio-spatiales.html.

Fol, S. (2010). Mobilité et ancrage dans les quartiers pauvres : les ressources de la proximité. *Regards sociologiques*, 40, 27–43.

Fol, S. (2013). La politique de la ville, un outil pour lutter contre la ségrégation ? *L'Information géographique*, 3, 6–28.

François, J.C. and Poupeau, F. (2008). *Le sens du placement : ségrégation résidentielle et ségrégation scolaire*. Raisons d'agir, Paris.

François, J.C., Mathian, H., Ribardière, A., Saint-Julien, T. (2003). Les disparités des revenus des ménages franciliens en 1999 : approches intercommunales et infracommunales et évolution des différenciations intercommunales 1990–1999. Report, Direction régionale de l'Equipement d'Île-de-France, Paris.

Frouillou, L. (2015). Les mécanismes d'une ségrégation universitaire francilienne : carte universitaire et sens du placement étudiant. PhD Thesis, Université Paris 1 Panthéon-Sorbonne.

Galster, G.C. (2006). What's the hood got to do with it? Parental perceptions about how neighborhood mechanisms affect their children. *Journal of Urban Affairs*, 38(3), 201–226.

George, P. (1950). *Études sur la banlieue de Paris. Essais méthodologiques*. Armand Colin, Paris.

Gilbert, P. (2011). "Ghetto", "relégation", "effets de quartier". Critique d'une représentation des cités. *Métropolitiques* [Online]. Available at: https://metropolitiques.eu/Ghetto-relegation-effets-de-quartier-Critique-d-une-representation-des-cites.html.

Givord, P., Guillerm, M., Monso, O., Murat, F. (2016a). Comment mesurer la ségrégation dans le système éducatif ? Une étude de la composition sociale des collèges français. *Éducation et formations*, 91, 21–51.

Givord, P., Guillerm, M., Monso, O., Murat, F. (2016b). La ségrégation sociale entre les collèges. Quelles différences entre public et privé, aux niveaux national, académique et local ? *Éducation et formations*, 91, 53–76.

Grafmeyer, Y. (1994). Regards sociologiques sur la ségrégation. In *La ségrégation dans la ville*, Brun, J. and Rhein, C. (eds). L'Harmattan, Paris.

Grafmeyer, Y. and Joseph, I. (2004). *L'école de Chicago : naissance de l'écologie urbaine*. Flammarion, Paris.

Guéraut, E. (2018). Ascension et fragilisation d'une petite bourgeoisie culturelle : une enquête ethnographique dans une ville moyenne en déclin. PhD Thesis, Université de la Sorbonne, Paris.

Guilluy, C. (2014). *La France périphérique : comment on a sacrifié les classes populaires*. Flammarion, Paris.

Hamnett, C. (1994). Social polarisation in global cities: Theory and evidence. *Urban Studies*, 31(3), 401–424.

Hancock, C., Lelévrier, C., Ripoll, F., Weber, S. (eds) (2016). *Discriminations territoriales. Entre interpellation politique et sentiment d'injustice des habitants*. L'œil d'or, Paris.

Harvey, D. (1973). *Social Justice and the City*. University of Georgia Press, Athens.

Harvey, D. (2003). *Paris: Capital of Modernity*. Routledge, London.

Herzberg, N. (2020). En France, le Covid-19 a beaucoup tué dans les villes pauvres. *Le Monde*, July 20th [Online]. Available at: https://www.lemonde.fr/planete/article/2020/07/20/le-covid-19-frappe-plus-durement-les-pauvres_6046774_3244.html.

Huriot, J.M. (2013). Haussmann, de la modernité à la révolution. *Métropolitiques* [Online]. Available at: https://www.metropolitiques.eu/Haussmann-de-la-modernite-a-la.html [Accessed 15 February 2013].

Jarousseau, V. (2019). *Les racines de la colère*. Les Arènes, Paris.

Kain, J. (1968). Housing segregation, negro employment and metropolitan decentralization. *Quarterly Journal of Economics*, 82, 175–197.

Kokoreff, M. (2009). Ghettos et marginalité urbaine. *Revue française de sociologie*, 50(3), 553–572.

L'Horty, Y. and Petit, P. (2016). Le lieu de résidence, vingtième critère de discrimination. In *Discriminations territoriales. Entre interpellation politique et sentiment d'injustice des habitants*, Hancock, C., Lelévrier, C., Ripoll, F., Weber, S. (eds). L'œil d'or, Paris.

Lambert, A. (2012). Des "pionniers" prisonniers : immobilité résidentielle et déclassement social des pavillonnaires en ville nouvelle. *Espaces et sociétés*, 148(149), 53–72.

Lapeyronnie, D. (2008). *Ghetto urbain : ségrégation, violence, pauvreté en France aujourd'hui*. Laffont, Paris.

Le Roux, G., Vallée, J., Commenges, A. (2017). Social segregation around the clock in the Paris region (France). *Journal of Transport Geography*, 59, 134–145.

Le Roux, G., Imbert, C., Bringé, A., Bonvalet, C. (2018). *Transformation sociale de Paris et de ses banlieues au cours du XXe siècle : une approche longitudinale et générationnelle de la ségrégation urbaine*. Ined, Paris.

Lehman-Frisch, S. (2009). La ségrégation : une injustice spatiale ? Questions de recherche. *Annales de géographie*, 665(666), 94–115.

Lefebvre, H. (1968). *Le droit à la ville*. Anthropos, Paris.

Lelévrier, C. (2004). Politique de la ville et regroupements d'immigrés. *Raison présente*, 151, 41–54.

Lelévrier, C. (2010). La mixité dans la rénovation urbaine : dispersion ou re-concentration ? *Espaces et sociétés*, 140(141), 59–74.

Lewis, O. (1959). *Five Families. Mexican Case Studies in the Culture of Poverty*. Basic Books, New York.

Ly, S.T. and Riegert, A. (2015). Mixité sociale et scolaire, ségrégation inter et intra établissement dans les collèges et lycées français. Report, CNESCO, Paris.

Madoré, F. (2015). Approche comparative de la ségrégation socio-spatiale dans les aires urbaines françaises. *Annales de géographie*, 706(6), 653–680.

Malmberg, B., Andersson, E.K., Nielsen, M.M., Haandrikman, K. (2018). Residential segregation of European and non-European migrants in Sweden: 1990–2012. *European Journal of Population*, 34(2), 169–193.

Manley, D., Johnston, R., Jones, K. (2019). Decomposing multi-level ethnic segregation in Auckland, New Zealand, 2001–2013: Segregation intensity for multiple groups at multiple scales. *Tijdschrift Voor Economische En Sociale Geografie*, 110(3), 319–338.

Marchal, H. and Stébé, J.M. (2018). *La France périurbaine*. Éditions Que sais-je ?, Paris.

Marpsat, M. (1999). La modélisation des effets de quartier aux États-Unis, une revue des travaux récents. *Population*, 54(2), 303–330.

Marpsat, M. and Laurent, R. (1997). Le chômage des jeunes est-il aggravé par l'appartenance à un quartier en difficulté ? In *Ces quartiers dont on parle*, Collectif (ed.). Éditions de l'Aube, La Tour d'Aigues.

Masclet, O. (2005). Du bastion au ghetto. Le communisme municipal en butte à l'immigration. *Actes de la recherche en sciences sociales*, 159, 10–25.

Massey, D.S. (2012). Reflections on the dimensions of segregation. *Social Forces*, 91(1), 39–43.

Massey, D.S. and Denton, N.A. (1988). The dimensions of residential segregation. *Social Forces*, 67(2), 281–315.

Massey, D.S. and Denton, N.A. (1993). *American Apartheid. Segregation and the Making of the American Underclass*. Harvard University Press, Cambridge.

Maurin, E. (2004). *Le ghetto français : enquête sur le séparatisme social*. Le Seuil, Paris.

Mead, L. (1989). *Beyond Entitlement: The Social Obligations of Citizenship*. Free Press, New York.

Metzger, J.T. (2000). Planned abandonment: The neighborhood life-cycle theory and national urban policy. *Housing Policy Debate*, 11(1), 7–40.

Motte-Baumvol, B. (2007). La dépendance automobile pour l'accès des ménages aux services : le cas de la grande couronne francilienne. *Revue d'économie régionale et urbaine*, 5, 897–920.

Murray, C. (1984). *Losing Ground: American Social Policy, 1950–1980*. Basic Books, New York.

Musterd, S. (2005). Social and ethnic segregation in Europe: Levels, causes and effects. *Journal of Urban Affairs*, 27(3), 331–348.

Musterd, S. and Andersson, R. (2005). Housing mix, social mix and social opportunities. *Urban Affairs Review*, 40(6), 761–790.

Musterd, S., Galster, G., Andersson, R. (2012). Temporal dimensions and measurement of neighborhood effects. *Environment and Planning A: Economy and Space*, 44, 605–627.

Oberti, M. (2007a). *L'école dans la ville : ségrégation, mixité, carte scolaire*. Presses de Science Po, Paris.

Oberti, M. (2007b). Le piège du libre choix scolaire. *Mouvements*, 52, 145–152.

Oberti, M. and Préteceille, E. (2016). *La ségrégation urbaine*. La Découverte, Paris.

Observatoire des territoires (2018). Les mobilités résidentielles en France. Tendances et impacts territoriaux. Report, CGET, Paris.

Ong, P. and Blumenber, E. (1998). Job access, commute and travel burden among welfare recipients. *Urban Studies*, 35(1), 77–93.

Pan Ké Shon, J.L. (2009). Ségrégation ethnique et ségrégation sociale en quartiers sensibles. L'apport des mobilités résidentielles. *Revue française de sociologie*, 50(3), 451–487.

Pan Ké Shon, J.L. and Verdugo, G. (2014). Ségrégation et incorporation des immigrés en France. *Revue française de sociologie*, 55(2), 245–283.

Park, R.E. and Burgess, E.W (1921). *Introduction to the Science of Sociology*. The University of Chicago Press.

Paugam, S. (ed.) (1996). *L'exclusion : l'état des saviors*. La Découverte, Paris.

Philpott Thomas, L. (1978). *The Slum and the Ghetto: Neighborhood Deterioration and Middle-Class Reform, Chicago, 1880–1930*. Oxford University Press, New York.

Piketty, T. (2013). *Le capital au 21e siècle*. Le Seuil, Paris.

Pinçon, M. and Pinçon-Charlot, M. (1989). *Dans les beaux quartiers*. Le Seuil, Paris.

Pinçon, M. and Pinçon-Charlot, M. (1994). De l'espace social à l'espace urbain. Utilité d'une métaphore. *Annales de la recherche urbaine*, 64, 50–53.

Pinçon, M. and Pinçon-Charlot, M. (2007). *Les Ghettos du Gotha : comment la bourgeoisie défend ses espaces*. Payot, Paris.

Pinçon-Charlot, M., Préteceille, E., Rendu, P. (1986). *Ségrégation urbaine. Classes sociales et équipements collectifs en région parisienne*. Anthropos, Paris.

Préteceille, E. (1995). Division sociale de l'espace et globalisation. Le cas de la métropole parisienne. *Sociétés contemporaines*, 22(1), 33–67.

Préteceille, E. (2003). La division sociale de l'espace francilien. Observatoire sociologique du changement. Report, CNRS, Science Po, Paris.

Préteceille, E. (2006). La ségrégation sociale a-t-elle augmenté ? La métropole parisienne entre polarisation et mixité. *Sociétés contemporaines*, 62, 69–93.

Préteceille, E. (2009). La ségrégation ethno-raciale a-t-elle augmenté dans la métropole parisienne ? *Revue française de sociologie*, 50(3), 489–519.

Reardon, S.F. (2009). Measures of ordinal segregation. In *Occupational and Residential Segregation*, Flückiger, Y., Reardon, S.F., Silber, J. (eds). Emerald Group Publishing Limited, Bradford.

Retière, J.N. (1994). *Identités ouvrières. Histoire sociale d'un fief ouvrier en Bretagne 1909–1990*. L'Harmattan, Paris.

Rhein, C. (1994a). La division sociale de l'espace parisien et son évolution (1954–1975). In *La ségrégation dans la ville*, Brun, J. and Rhein, C. (eds). L'Harmattan, Paris.

Rhein, C. (1994b). La ségrégation et ses mesures. In *La ségrégation dans la ville*, Brun, J. and Rhein, C. (eds). L'Harmattan, Paris.

Ribardière, A. (2019). Les territoires populaires du Grand Paris : entre paupérisation, gentrification et moyennisation. *Métropolitiques* [Online]. Available at: https://www.metropolitiques.eu/Les-territoires-populaires-du-Grand-Paris-entre-pauperisation-gentrification-et.html [Accessed 18 February 2019].

Rivière, J. (2008). De l'étalement urbain à la fragmentation sociale ? Typologie des trajectoires d'évolution des aires urbaines françaises de 1968 à 1999. In *Étalement urbain et ville fragmentée à travers le monde*, Zaninetti, J.M. and Maret, I. (eds). Presses Universitaires d'Orléans.

Rivière, J. (2017). L'espace électoral des grandes villes françaises. *Revue francaise de science politique*, 67(6), 1041–1065.

Rochex, J.Y. (2011). Les trois "âges" des politiques d'éducation prioritaire : une convergence européenne ? *Propuesta Educativa*, 35, 75–84.

Roncayolo, M. (1952). Évolution de la banlieue marseillaise dans la basse vallée de l'Huveaune. *Annales de géographie*, 327, 342–356.

Rudolph, M. (2017). Ceux qui partent, ceux qui restent. Les mobilités résidentielles dans les villes en décroissance. *Métropolitiques* [Online]. Available at: http://www.metropolitiques.eu/Ceux-qui-partent-ceux-qui-restent.html [Accessed 24 May 2017].

Safi, M. (2009). La dimension spatiale de l'intégration : évolution de la ségrégation des populations immigrées en France entre 1968 et 1999. *Revue française de sociologie*, 50(3), 521–552.

Safi, M. (2013). *Les inégalités ethnoraciales*. La Découverte, Paris.

Sala Pala, V. (2008). Les discriminations ethniques dans l'accès au logement social. Le modèle français universaliste au travers du miroir britannique. In *Crises et politiques du logement en France et au Royaume-Uni*, Fée, D. and Natives, C. (eds). Presses Sorbonne Nouvelle, Paris.

Sassen, S. (1991). *The Global City: New York, London, Tokyo*. Princeton University Press.

Schelling, T. (1980). *La tyrannie des petites décisions*. PUF, Paris.

Schwabe, M. (2007). La ségrégation résidentielle dans les plus grandes villes françaises (1968–1999) : quel modèle urbain ? *Cybergeo: European Journal of Geography* [Online]. Available at: https://journals.openedition.org/cybergeo/10182.

Shevky, E. and Williams, M. (1949). *The Social Areas of Los Angeles. Analysis and Typology*. University of California Press, Los Angeles.

Tabard, N. (1987). Espace et classes sociales. In *Données sociales*, Fouquet, A. and Marpsat, M. (eds). Insee, Paris.

Taylor, B.D. (1995). Spatial mismatch or automobile mismatch? An examination of race, residence and commuting in US metropolitan areas. *Urban Studies*, 32(9), 1463–1494.

Théry, C. (2016). La sociologie américaine de la pauvreté, du ghetto wilsonien à la ville globale. *Sociologie*, 7(1), 77–94.

Thisse, J.F., Wasmer, E., Zenou, Y. (2003). Ségrégation urbaine, logement et marchés du travail. *Revue française d'économie*, 17(4), 85–129.

Tissot, S. (2005). Une discrimination informelle ? Usages du concept de mixité sociale dans la gestion des attributions de logements HLM. *Actes de la recherche en sciences sociales*, 4(159), 54–69.

Tissot, S. and Poupeau, F. (2005). La spatialisation des problèmes sociaux. *Actes de la recherche en sciences sociales*, 4, 4–9.

Verdugo, G. (2011). Logement social et ségrégation résidentielle des immigrés en France, 1968–1999. *Population*, 66(1), 171–196.

Vignal, C. (2005). Logiques professionnelles et logiques familiales : une articulation contrainte par la délocalisation de l'emploi. *Sociologie du travail*, 47, 153–169.

Wacquant, L. (1993). Urban outcasts: Stigma and division in the Black American ghetto and the French urban periphery. *International Journal of Urban and Regional Research*, 17(3), 366–383.

Wacquant, L. (2005). Les deux visages du ghetto. Construire un concept sociologique. *Actes de la recherche en sciences sociales*, 160, 4–21.

Wacquant, L. (2006). *Parias urbains. Ghetto – Banlieues – État*. La Découverte, Paris.

Wenglenski, S. (2004). Une mesure des disparités sociales d'accessibilité au marché de l'emploi en Île-de-France. *Revue d'économie régionale et urbaine*, 4, 539–550.

Wilson, W.J. (1987). *The Truly Disadvantaged. The Inner City, the Underclass and Public Policy*. University of Chicago Press.

Wirth, L. (1956). The ghetto. *American Journal of Sociology*, 33(1), 57–71 [Online]. Available at: https://www.journals.uchicago.edu/doi/epdf/10.1086/214333.

Zanten, A. (1996). Fabrication et effets de la ségrégation scolaire. In *L'exclusion. L'état des savoirs*, Paugam, S. (ed.). La Découverte, Paris.

Zanten, A. (2001). *L'école de la périphérie : scolarité et ségrégation en banlieue*. PUF, Paris.

Zanten, A. and Obin, J.P. (2010). *La carte scolaire*. PUF, Paris.

List of Authors

Éric CHARMES
EVS
ENTPE
Vaulx-en-Velin
France

Laurent DAVEZIES
CNAM
Paris
France

Xavier DESJARDINS
Médiations
Sorbonne Université
Paris
France

Philippe ESTÈBE
Acadie
Paris
France

Sylvie FOL
Géographie-Cités
Université Paris 1 Panthéon-Sorbonne
France

Leïla FROUILLOU
CRESPPA
Université Paris Nanterre
France

Thomas PIKETTY
EHESS
Paris
France

Frédéric SANTAMARIA
Pacte
Université Grenoble Alpes
France

Magali TALANDIER
Pacte
Université Grenoble Alpes
France

Josselin TALLEC
Pacte
Université Grenoble Alpes
France

Index

A, B

access to services, 125, 185
accessibility, 185, 207, 224, 244
areas, 1, 2, 4, 5, 8–21, 23, 24, 26–31, 44, 51, 53, 55, 57, 58, 64, 85, 89, 92, 95–97, 99, 101, 107–115, 117, 119, 120, 124, 127, 132–136, 144, 145, 150, 151, 157, 168, 170, 173, 174, 180–182, 186, 194, 195, 199, 201, 205, 207, 211–220, 222, 227, 237, 238, 240, 242–247, 251, 253, 258–260, 266
authorities, 30, 44, 66, 68, 80, 85, 178, 181, 203–205, 208, 221, 227, 252
balance (*see also* imbalances *and* migrations), 3, 59, 60, 62, 69, 92, 93, 98, 122, 134, 135, 148, 179, 198, 199, 203, 222, 223
base, 3, 10, 22–24, 92, 130, 165, 166, 168, 173, 209, 217, 228, 257
benchmarks, 196, 198, 200
beneficiaries, 59, 65, 74, 155, 178, 188
bonuses, 100, 202, 224
boundary object, 195, 196
Brexit, 72, 155, 171
budgets, 43, 59–63, 65, 66, 68–71, 73, 100

C

call for projects, 204, 206, 228
capacities, 83, 91, 97, 116, 169, 179–181, 196, 206, 208, 226
capitalism, 249, 250, 252, 253
catch-up, 179
centers, 2, 10–15, 17, 19, 21, 27, 28, 30, 31, 75, 93, 100, 107, 110, 111, 124, 126, 129, 131, 179, 193, 196, 201, 203, 206, 207, 210, 212, 214, 216, 221–227, 229, 238, 242, 249, 268
change, 10, 19, 23, 31, 33, 34, 37, 52, 53, 55, 74, 88, 97, 98, 116, 119, 120, 122, 130, 151, 161, 182, 212, 214, 218, 223, 224
charges, 120, 227

city (*see also* inner city), 2, 5, 11, 13, 19, 21–23, 28, 31, 54, 69, 88, 91, 98, 102, 108–115, 117, 122, 123, 125, 128, 129, 131, 134, 135, 193, 195, 198, 199, 208, 210–213, 218, 221–224, 226, 227, 229, 236–239, 241, 249–251, 259, 263–266
classes, 115, 122, 123, 127, 129, 209–211, 235, 239, 240, 243–245, 247, 249–254, 256, 257, 260, 263–267
clubbisation, 118, 130, 136, 267
clusters, 26, 206
commercial vacancy, 207
community (*see also* gated communities), 46, 64, 92, 149, 181, 187, 202
commutes, 108, 125
commuting, 27, 59, 108, 110, 195, 214, 257
compensation, 63, 188, 199, 202
competition, 74, 76, 83, 119–121, 135, 148, 173, 177, 179, 181, 183, 205, 206, 239, 249, 260
competitiveness, 31, 103, 145, 146, 151, 152, 177–179, 181, 185, 188, 196, 199, 204–206, 225
complementarities, 208, 227
concentration, 1, 2, 4–8, 12, 19, 21, 23, 31, 50, 51, 62, 89, 90, 95, 100, 108, 148, 199–202, 204, 206, 209, 212, 224, 238–240, 250, 251, 253, 255, 261, 263, 265, 266
conditions, 79, 82–84, 93, 102, 108, 144, 147, 148, 179, 180, 193, 197–199, 207, 210, 211, 216, 222, 226, 235, 239, 251, 263, 264, 267
connectivity, 91, 95, 208
consumption, 3, 23, 55, 100, 124, 211
contracts, 30, 135, 203, 221, 224, 264
contributors, 63, 73, 74, 155

convergence, 20, 21, 101, 151, 152, 168–170, 177, 205, 246
conversion, 203, 224
cooperation, 45, 75, 119, 130, 135, 143–145, 149, 151, 152, 154, 156, 157, 178–180, 183, 187, 225, 266
coordination, 30, 177, 186, 201, 203, 205
correction, 198–200
countryside, 2, 5, 8, 29–31, 88–91, 94–96, 102, 103, 107–109, 111, 112, 114–116, 120, 123, 125, 128–130, 132, 134, 135, 235
county towns, 90

D

DATAR, 93, 99, 100, 148, 198, 203, 205, 206, 218, 222, 226
decentralization, 44, 48, 93, 97, 99–101, 198, 200, 201, 203, 205, 221–223, 225
decline, 3–5, 31, 53, 57, 58, 127, 133, 178, 180, 193, 217, 227, 244, 245, 253, 254, 267
deconcentration, 5, 21, 198, 203, 222, 223
deindustrialization, 121, 238, 242, 250, 253
densification, 133
density, 5, 20, 21, 80, 87, 95, 101, 109, 110, 117, 131, 180, 236
development, 1, 3, 4, 8–11, 22, 24, 29–31, 38, 43–50, 64, 65, 70, 74, 80–84, 90, 92, 94, 95, 97–100, 102, 103, 108, 115, 117, 124, 128, 129, 133, 143–152, 156, 157, 168, 174, 176, 178–188, 193, 195, 196, 198–212, 217, 218, 221–229, 249, 252, 258, 260, 261, 263–265
diagnosis, 102, 198, 263

diagonal of the void, 86
differentiation, 196, 204, 208, 209, 218, 227–229, 240, 244, 247, 251, 257, 258, 260, 267
discontinuities, 168
divergence, 170
diversity, 17, 24, 28, 185, 186, 204, 210, 212, 216, 218, 220, 242, 247, 251, 253, 257, 264–266
division, 1, 83, 101, 103, 201, 202, 223, 229, 239, 241, 243, 247, 253, 255

E, F

economic
 crises, 218, 223
 externalities, 212
 lock-in, 212
economies, 2, 24, 28, 31, 74, 120, 144, 149, 170, 177, 208, 212, 225
education, 48, 81, 83–87, 90, 129, 148, 175, 186, 193, 201, 226, 240, 244, 260, 264, 266, 267
employment areas, 24, 51, 57, 58, 227
engineering, 1, 179, 227
enhancement, 118, 129, 205
enlargement, 151, 154, 173
environments, 204, 207, 227, 245
equality, 54, 80, 83, 84, 91, 93, 98, 147, 177, 197, 199, 205, 207, 210, 226, 255, 266
Europe, 22, 30, 44, 46, 47, 62–66, 68, 70–72, 74, 80, 89, 115, 143, 144, 146, 147, 149, 151, 152, 154, 155, 157, 160–162, 165, 168–170, 172, 178, 186–188, 205, 237, 241, 247, 252, 262, 263

European
 Commission, 45, 62, 73, 147, 150, 151, 156, 161, 174, 178, 181–184
 construction, 143–145, 147–149, 184
 Union, 64, 143, 169, 201, 202, 205
exclusion, 181, 237, 247, 265
exclusionary zoning, 118
exodus, 3–5, 8, 89, 94, 109, 114, 115, 218
expenditure, 24, 58–60, 62, 66, 86, 120, 171, 172
externalities, 212, 225
exurbs, 111
fiscal dumping, 176, 177
flows, 1, 2, 5, 21–24, 26–31, 54, 197, 208, 257
forward-looking, 81, 189
fragmentation, 21, 44, 66, 71–73, 89, 91, 93, 227, 247, 253
French General Planning Commission, 198
fringes, 127, 133, 244
functions, 31, 64, 66, 68, 90, 101, 102, 108, 195, 196, 208, 218, 221–223, 226–229, 250
funds, 46, 58, 59, 63, 64, 145, 150–152, 154–156, 174, 178, 181, 182, 188, 203

G, H

gated communities, 117, 240
GDP, 45–50, 57–60, 63–68, 70, 73, 74, 151, 152, 157, 161–166, 168, 169, 171–173, 175, 186, 198

gentrification, 51, 53, 129, 131, 243, 244, 249, 267
geography, 2, 3, 21, 23, 26, 46, 49, 81, 83, 86, 90, 96, 135, 198, 199, 244, 260
ghetto, 236–242, 246, 247, 252, 264, 265, 267
gilets jaunes, 102, 108, 125–127, 132, 133, 135, 235
globalization, 1, 74, 75, 101, 107, 144, 151, 202, 204, 208, 218, 223, 226, 228, 229, 250
governance, 30, 117, 179, 202, 225, 266
growth, 1–5, 8, 19–21, 23, 31, 49, 50, 55–57, 90, 97–100, 102, 109, 114, 122, 130, 151, 152, 177–179, 199–202, 204, 206, 207, 210, 211, 214, 216–223, 225, 226, 229
harmonization, 68, 177
hinterland, 9, 28–30, 123, 222
housing, 48, 53, 108, 117, 121, 124, 126, 131–133, 182, 198, 222, 225, 227, 235, 241, 242, 244, 245–247, 249, 251–253, 263–266
hybridization, 134

I

imbalances, 70, 200
impoverishment, 14, 244, 250
incomes, 3, 10, 13, 14, 18–20, 23, 24, 31, 49, 51, 55, 58, 61, 73, 123, 125, 127, 161, 229, 242
indices, 46, 73, 242, 255–258, 268
industrial districts, 226

inequalities, 1–4, 8, 10, 14–22, 24, 26, 28, 30, 31, 43, 44, 50–55, 57, 58, 63, 64, 66, 73, 79, 80, 83, 87, 88, 93, 95, 96, 103, 118, 125, 127, 130, 143–149, 151, 152, 156, 157, 161, 163, 168, 169, 171, 173, 177, 179, 180, 183–188, 193–200, 202, 207–211, 218, 220, 221, 224–229, 235, 236, 240–242, 244–247, 254, 258–261, 264, 266–268
inertia, 168, 195, 199, 207, 209, 212
inner city, 238
insecurity, 148, 263
institutionalization, 222
institutions, 45, 50, 64, 86, 92, 93, 143, 147, 150, 161, 179, 180, 198, 206, 212, 226, 240, 252, 258
instruments, 156
integration, 70, 74, 94, 119, 143, 146, 147, 149, 157, 176, 198, 218, 238, 239, 261, 263, 264
interdependence, 115, 202
intergovernmentalism, 146, 179
intermediation, 222, 226
intermunicipality, 119–122, 135
internationalization, 205, 225
intersection, 206, 224, 227, 238, 260
interterritoriality, 208
interventionism, 197, 200

L, M, N

levels, 10, 14, 20, 23, 30, 44, 65, 67, 91, 92, 130, 152, 157, 161, 163, 164, 166, 168, 173, 177, 185–188, 195, 202, 228, 241, 242, 245
liberal model, 148
liberalization, 173

living environment, 116–118, 123, 124, 128, 129, 134, 201
location, 2, 100, 124, 178, 235, 248, 256, 259, 261
loosening, 218
mass, 84, 89, 100, 131, 195, 206, 225, 262
metropolization, 1, 2, 8–10, 12, 19, 21, 23, 31, 101, 108, 111, 115, 195, 204, 207, 208, 210, 211, 214, 228
migrations, 70
  balances, 218
mobility (*see also* upward social mobility), 5, 9, 22, 23, 26, 27, 29, 31, 51–54, 59, 64, 70, 87, 115, 125, 126, 128, 132, 148, 182, 199, 204, 208, 210, 214, 238, 244, 245, 254, 258, 262–264, 267
modernization, 94, 208, 211
municipalities, 2–5, 7, 10–16, 20, 21, 26–28, 51, 53, 55–57, 66, 75, 85, 91–94, 101, 109–111, 113, 114, 117–122, 124, 125, 130, 133, 135, 195, 203, 212, 213, 221, 222, 236, 243, 244, 255, 259, 265
neighborhoods, 53, 54, 118, 129, 131, 181, 237–240, 242–247, 250–253, 256–264, 266, 267
neo-rural, 115
network(s), 2, 21, 64, 90, 91, 93–96, 102, 103, 157, 174, 195, 198, 207, 208, 239, 221, 225, 226, 229, 262
networking, 156, 197, 208, 225

O, P

outsourcing, 218
peripheral
  France, 2, 14, 102, 107, 108, 120, 134, 135, 195, 253
  positions, 229

peripheries, 2, 5, 10, 14, 29
periurbanization, 4, 108, 109, 114, 118, 123, 129, 132, 133–135
planning, 22, 30, 51, 92, 93, 95, 97–100, 103, 108, 117–119, 123, 128, 156, 180, 183, 184, 193, 196–200, 202–211, 216, 221, 222, 224, 225, 227–229
plans, 92, 187, 189, 205, 226
polarizations, 168
policies, 2, 4, 30, 31, 53, 54, 62, 63, 66, 68, 75, 80, 84, 85, 88, 92, 93, 100, 103, 120, 124, 125, 128, 133, 143–147, 149, 155–157, 161, 171–174, 177, 180–183, 185–188, 193–207, 209–211, 222, 223, 227–229, 236, 239, 241, 242, 247, 251–254, 258, 260, 262–267
polycentrism, 111, 148, 184, 187, 223
pooling, 224, 225
poverty, 43, 48, 54, 55, 57, 102, 126, 181, 182, 238–240, 250, 253, 261–265
precarity, 253
prefectures, 90, 93, 115, 221
  sub-, 90, 93
production, 3, 12, 15, 17, 18, 23, 24, 28, 46, 59, 70, 74, 75, 89, 94, 95, 97, 99–101, 134, 184, 186, 194, 196, 200–202, 206, 210, 217, 218, 223, 224, 228, 229, 244, 249–251, 265
productivity, 99, 120, 218
programming, 150, 152, 180, 181, 198
prosperity, 144, 148, 200
purchasing power standards, 162

R

reciprocities, 208
recompositions, 212, 217, 223, 228, 229, 250, 253, 254

reconstruction, 97, 197, 200
redistribution, 22–24, 28, 29, 31, 51, 57–59, 62, 64, 66, 68–70, 73, 95, 100, 102, 155, 179, 199, 200, 202, 206, 211, 226, 228
reduction, 2, 4, 5, 52, 57, 62, 63, 73, 79, 98, 101, 145, 147–149, 151, 156, 174, 177, 179, 184, 186, 187, 202, 211, 228, 238, 241, 254, 266
regional aid, 45, 150, 174
regulation, 118, 148, 174, 221, 237
relationships, 2, 28, 135, 210, 211, 225–227, 247
relegation, 108, 236, 247, 249
renewal, 5, 115, 132, 242, 253, 264–266
residential
  desegregation, 263
  trajectories, 133, 246, 253, 267
resilience, 169
resources, 58, 60–62, 66, 84, 114–116, 119–121, 125, 128, 134, 148, 150, 168, 171–173, 175, 177, 179, 184, 185, 197, 199, 203, 210, 229, 246, 254, 259, 261, 262, 264–266
revenues, 100
revitalization, 114, 115, 125, 132, 134, 206, 227, 228
  of the countryside, 114, 125, 132
runoff, 199
rural, 3–5, 8, 9, 14, 15, 19–21, 24, 26, 28, 31, 44, 80, 85, 87–89, 91–97, 103, 107, 109, 111, 114–116, 118–120, 124, 125, 127, 129, 132–135, 145, 157, 174, 180, 186, 195, 198, 207, 218, 221, 223, 244, 253
  territories, 85, 125, 195, 223
rurality, 93, 111, 115, 133

S

secession, 74, 118, 243
sectors, 1, 9, 22, 53, 75, 201, 203, 206, 224, 226, 227, 229, 243
segregation, 66, 118, 235–268
  processes, 251, 252, 264
separatism, 243, 248
settlement, 3, 53, 85, 132, 134, 241, 251, 253, 257, 266
social
  benefits, 20, 46, 126, 161, 200
  distance, 238
  welfare, 59–61, 100, 148, 238, 250
soft spaces, 183
solidarity, 43, 44, 47, 64, 66, 71, 73–76, 93, 94, 96, 143, 145, 147, 148, 150, 155, 171, 179, 188, 239, 265
spatial
  distribution, 3, 5, 23, 150, 194, 207, 209
  mismatch, 239, 261
specialization, 51–54, 66, 95, 101, 102, 178, 201, 212, 218, 227, 244
specificities, 179, 185, 208, 209
spillover, 196, 207
sprawl, 27, 109, 124, 131–133, 135, 193, 214, 227
stagnation, 89, 133, 216
standardization, 3, 84, 144, 147, 168, 266
stocks, 208
subsidiarity, 66, 175
suburban, 11, 13, 14, 16, 19, 20, 29–31, 127, 195, 214, 227, 248, 259, 267
superdiversity, 247

T

tax relief, 202
taxation, 120, 177
taxes, 10, 11, 23, 33, 46, 51, 59, 62, 64, 66, 68, 84, 108, 116, 126, 127, 161, 173
territorial
    approach, 180, 181, 183, 188
    injustices, 207
    project, 181, 197, 203, 204, 209
territorialization, 180, 181, 246, 264, 266, 267
territories, 1, 2, 10, 12, 18–21, 24, 26–31, 43–46, 48–55, 57–59, 66, 70, 72–75, 79, 80, 82–87, 91–93, 97, 98, 101, 102, 107, 108, 117–119, 121, 124, 125, 130, 131, 134, 135, 144, 145, 148, 150, 152, 154, 156, 157, 173, 174, 177, 178, 180, 181, 183, 186, 188, 193, 195–209, 211, 212, 216, 221, 223–229, 247, 254, 255, 263, 264, 266
theory, 2, 22, 23, 49, 59, 70, 131, 248
tourism, 20, 24, 26, 27, 30, 59, 222, 225
towns, 3, 5, 14, 19, 23, 24, 90, 92–95, 98, 102, 108, 114, 115, 120, 123, 125, 127, 134, 195, 201, 227, 259
trajectories, 1, 133, 177, 178, 195, 196, 207, 209–211, 217, 219, 220, 223, 226, 227, 229, 244–246, 253, 258, 260, 267

transition, 8, 31, 89, 132, 134, 147, 152, 154, 182, 198, 202, 204, 210, 227, 240
transnational, 98, 143–145, 147, 152, 157, 183
transport, 70, 102, 108, 125, 126, 128, 131, 132, 146, 147, 173, 174, 182, 183, 185, 198, 202, 208, 225, 244, 247, 257

U, V, W, Z

underclass, 238, 239, 250, 261
upward social mobility, 238
urban (*see also* suburban)
    dimension, 125, 181, 182
    framework, 201, 221, 222, 224, 225
    unit, 4, 195, 212, 214, 242, 246
urbanity, 131
urbanization (*see also* periurbanization), 4, 5, 114, 118, 212, 214, 224
value, 1, 23, 45–47, 58, 81, 131, 172, 196, 199, 208, 256, 267
villages, 8, 93, 98, 108, 109, 114–118, 121–124, 132, 134, 135
white flight, 122
zoning, 11, 110, 111, 113, 114, 117, 118, 150, 151, 173, 195, 199, 202, 203, 212–214, 221, 223, 224, 227